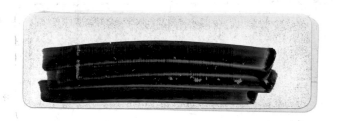

D0821051

Behavior and the
Natural Environment

Human Behavior and Environment

ADVANCES IN THEORY AND RESEARCH

Behavior and the Natural Environment

EDITED BY

IRWIN ALTMAN

University of Utah
Salt Lake City, Utah

AND

JOACHIM F. WOHLWILL

Pennsylvania State University
University Park, Pennsylvania

PLENUM PRESS · NEW YORK AND LONDON

Library of Congress Cataloging in Publication Data

Main entry under title:

Behavior and the natural environment.

  (Human behavior and environment; v. 6)
  Bibliogrpahy: p.
  Includes index.
  1. Environmental psychology. 2. Nature—Psychological aspects. I. Altman, Irwin. II. Wohlwill, Joachim F. III. Series.
BF353.H85 vol. 6   155.9s [155.9'1]   83-7285
ISBN 0-306-41099-0

© 1983 Plenum Press, New York
A Division of Plenum Publishing Corporation
233 Spring Street, New York, N.Y. 10013

Printed in the United States of America

Contributors

PERRY J. BROWN • Department of Resource Recreation Management, School of Forestry, Oregon State University, Corvallis, Oregon

WILLIAM R. CATTON, JR. • Department of Sociology, Washington State University, Pullman, Washington

TERRY C. DANIEL • Department of Psychology, University of Arizona, Tucson, Arizona

BEVERLY DRIVER • Rocky Mountain Forest and Range Experiment Station, USDA Forest Service, Fort Collins, Colorado

JANET FREY TALBOT • School of Natural Resources, University of Michigan, Ann Arbor, Michigan

RACHEL KAPLAN • School of Natural Resources, University of Michigan, Ann Arbor, Michigan

STEPHEN KAPLAN • Department of Psychology, University of Michigan, Ann Arbor, Michigan

STEPHEN R. KELLERT • School of Forestry and Environmental Studies, Yale University, New Haven, Connecticut

RICHARD C. KNOPF • North Central Forest Experimental Station, USDA Forest Service, Saint Paul, Minnesota

ROGER S. ULRICH • Department of Geography, University of Delaware, Newark, Delaware

JOANNE VINING • Department of Psychology, University of Arizona, Tucson, Arizona

JOACHIM F. WOHLWILL • College of Human Development, Pennsylvania State University, University Park, Pennsylvania

Preface

The theme of the present volume concerns people's response to the natural environment, considered at scales varying from that of a household plant to that of vast wilderness areas. Our decision to focus on this particular segment of the physical environment was prompted in part by the intrinsic interest in this subject on the part of a diverse group of social scientists and professionals—and of laypersons, for that matter—and in part by the relative neglect of this topic in standard treatments of the environment–behavior field. It also serves to bring out once again the interdisciplinary nature of that field, and we are pleased to have been able to include representatives from geography, sociology, social ecology, and natural recreation among our contributors. We believe that this volume will serve a useful purpose in helping to integrate the findings and concepts in this presently somewhat fragmented field, scattered as they are over a very diverse array of publications representing a similarly varied group of specialties. It is hoped that the result will be to stimulate future development of this area and to add a measure of increased coherence to it.

Volume 7 of our series will be devoted to the theme of elderly people and the environment, with M. Powell Lawton joining us as guest co-editor. The titles of the papers comprising Volume 7 are shown on page v.

Irwin Altman
Joachim F. Wohlwill

Contents

Chapter 2

Methodological Issues in the Assessment of Landscape Quality

TERRY C. DANIEL
JOANNE VINING

Chapter 3

Aesthetic and Affective Response to Natural Environment

ROGER S. ULRICH

CHAPTER 4

THE ROLE OF NATURE IN THE URBAN CONTEXT

RACHEL KAPLAN

CHAPTER 5

PSYCHOLOGICAL BENEFITS OF A WILDERNESS EXPERIENCE

STEPHEN KAPLAN
JANET FREY TALBOT

CHAPTER 6

RECREATIONAL NEEDS AND BEHAVIOR IN NATURAL SETTINGS

RICHARD C. KNOPF

CHAPTER 7

AFFECTIVE, COGNITIVE, AND EVALUATIVE PERCEPTIONS OF
ANIMALS

STEPHEN R. KELLERT

CHAPTER 8

SOCIAL AND BEHAVIORAL ASPECTS OF THE CARRYING
CAPACITY OF NATURAL ENVIRONMENTS

WILLIAM R. CATTON, JR.

CHAPTER 9

CONTRIBUTIONS OF BEHAVIORAL SCIENTISTS TO RECREATION
RESOURCE MANAGEMENT

BEVERLY DRIVER
PERRY J. BROWN

Introduction

The present volume concerns a topic that is, one might say, as old as the hills—or at least as old as the emergence on earth of a species able to perceive and respond affectively, attitudinally, and behaviorally to the hills, valleys, forests, seashores, oceans, and other parts of the natural environment. Nature has always loomed large in the minds of human beings, eliciting affection and even idolatry, as well as feelings of concern, anxiety, and fear.

As this volume documents, the study of relationships between natural environments and behavior is rich in problems, issues, and theories, and a substantial body of knowledge concerning the subject has accumulated. Surprisingly, with but a few individual exceptions, environmental psychologists as a group have contributed less than their share to the study of people's thinking, imagination, feelings, and behavior with respect to natural environments. (The topic is hardly mentioned in most of the standard texts and anthologies in environmental psychology.) Most of the work in this area has been undertaken primarily by investigators in such academic disciplines as geography and sociology and by representatives of such professional fields as landscape architecture, recreation, forestry, and natural-resource management. This field has thus become a truly multidisciplinary one, and this diversity of disciplines is reflected in the list of contributors to this volume, which, as has been true of prior volumes in our series, includes representatives from many fields.

The initial chapter in this volume is an analysis of the concept of nature from the perspective of a psychologist (Wohlwill). This chapter makes no pretense of providing an exhaustive treatment of the diverse conceptions of this highly elusive concept or of the varied psychological perspectives from which it can be viewed. Rather, it adopts an approach that emphasizes the properties of environmental stimuli denoted by the concept of nature and the perceptual and cognitive consequences of variations in stimulus qualities.

The second chapter (by Daniel, also a psychologist) examines meth-odological issues in the assessment of natural scenery and landscape. Perhaps even more than is the case for the built environment, the study of the perception and evaluation of natural environments involves diffi-cult problems of measurement and definition of relevant environmental dimensions. Daniel compares a number of current approaches to these problems emanating from theoretical and applied issues, and he as-sesses their respective merits and limitations. Of particular interest, at least from a psychological perspective, is his comparison between a psychophysical model in which variables defined in stimulus terms are systematically related to given perceptual or judgmental responses and a psychological model that is focused on dimensions of the individual's experience.

Chapter 3 (contributed by Ulrich, a geographer) presents an analy-sis of responses to the natural environment in terms of concepts drawn from theories of emotion and motivation, with arousal being one central concept. Ulrich proposes a framework that emphasizes intrinsic, general determinants of affective and evaluative responses to nature, based on specific stimulus properties of the environment.

The following cluster of chapters examines more specific aspects of our topic. In Chapter 4, Knopf (an outdoor-recreation specialist with the United States Forest Service) considers both the motivational bases of people's choices of natural areas for recreational purposes and the psy-chological functions served by outdoor-recreation settings. In view of the popularity of this form of recreation, the practical and theoretical significance of these issues is apparent. In Chapter 5, two psychologists (S. Kaplan and Talbot) describe the psychological impact of wilderness experiences. Their chapter summarizes research on wilderness-training programs, which are designed to enhance feelings of self-sufficiency and self-reliance of participants, to provide survival skills, and to devel-op one's sensitivity to and awareness of nature. The results of one such program are cited as evidence for the psychological benefits of wilder-ness training.

R. Kaplan, a psychologist, brings us closer to home in Chapter 6, as she addresses the role of nature in everyday environments as reflected in parks, trees, gardens, plants, and the like. Her analysis illustrates the psychological value of nature in the midst of built environments and the sense of deprivation that is experienced in their absence. Kaplan reviews the small amount of research on this topic and proposes a theoretical framework to account for the attachment of people to samples of nature in and around the home.

Up to this point, nature has been treated almost exclusively in its inanimate manifestations (although including, of course, the realm of plant life). In Chapter 7 (by Kellert, a social ecologist) the treatment is extended to the animate realm. The chapter describes the diverse value systems, attitudes, and cognitive and affective orientations to animals held by different populations.

The two concluding chapters address broad ecological social system and policy-related issues. Chapter 8 (by Catton, a sociologist) examines the concept of carrying capacity, which has been used to study the ability of localized areas to absorb and withstand human use, particularly for recreational purposes. In his analysis, Catton extends this concept to refer much more broadly to the impact of population growth on the depletion and potential renewal of resources and to the capacity of large-scale environments to support life.

In the final chapter, Driver and Brown (specialists in recreation and natural-resource management) address problems of public policy and management of natural recreation areas that are faced by professionals in forestry, natural-resource management, and outdoor recreation. The authors provide a framework for analyzing environmental management problems, and they describe the role of behavioral science research in relation to the solution of a variety of such problems.

This volume reviews a range of existing theory and research concerning the relationship between human behavior and the natural environment. Its goal is to identify areas of established findings, gaps in our knowledge, and promising directions of research and theory. In so doing, we hope that the volume will contribute to our understanding of the role of the natural environment in the minds and lives of those who interact with it.

The Concept of Nature

A PSYCHOLOGIST'S VIEW

JOACHIM F. WOHLWILL

INTRODUCTION

For all the debate and philosophizing and frequently polemical argument concerning nature and its relationship to man,[1] the concept of nature does not seem to have proved a very natural one for psychologists. As noted in the introduction to this volume, the individual's response to the natural environment has not been at the forefront of problems chosen for psychological investigation—not even among environmental psychologists. A perusal of the index of *Psychological Abstracts* reveals that *Nature* serves as an indexing term only in its adjectival form, and then only in reference to two very limited topics: *Natural Childbirth* (i.e., a process unaided by external intervention) and *Natural Disasters*. The prominent place of the latter as a subject of behavioral science research (though better represented within geography than psychology) may hark back to the historical fear of nature as a dangerous and potentially evil force in the affairs of man. But it is apparent from

---

[1]It goes without saying that the term *man* and its derivatives (e.g., *man-made*) refer not to individuals of the male sex, but to the human race, *Homo sapiens*. Unlike German, the English language happens to use the same term to designate the male of the species and the species as a whole. Since the context makes apparent which of the two meanings is intended, there is no issue here of sexist language. This use corresponds, furthermore, to generally accepted practice in scientific writing, notably in anthropology and biology.

JOACHIM F. WOHLWILL • College of Human Development, Pennsylvania State University, University Park, Pennsylvania 16802.

any discussion of environmental problems and treatments of the relationship between human activity and the physical environment that nature is a much more salient concept, for the lay person and the scientist alike, than one would suppose from the classification schemes of psychologists or from the subject matter of their research.

Indeed, nature appears to qualify as one of those "natural" categories that are important in terms of the way in which individuals organize their world and that have recently become the focus of systematic investigation by cognitive psychologists (see Rosch & Lloyd, 1978). This suggestion is reinforced by findings from studies of spontaneous organization of environmental stimuli via similarity judgments—analyzed by multidimensional scaling—which consistently uncover a dimension of naturalness (or natural vs. developed) as one of the primary dimensions that appear to underly such judgments (Ullrich & Ullrich, 1976; Ward, 1977). There can be little doubt of the importance of the concept of nature in our perception and thinking, our attitudes, and our affective lives. This is, in fact, the assumption underlying the present volume; thus, a chapter in which an attempt is made to externalize some of the alternative meanings of the concept of relevance for psychology should serve a useful function in introducing the reader, and the psychologist in particular, to the subject matter that follows.

This chapter starts with a discussion of the definitional problems encountered in attempting to differentiate between two domains, one called "nature," the other "man-made," in terms that are useful for a psychological analysis of an individual's response to the realm of nature—a difficult undertaking to be sure, but one that is unavoidable if any semblance of conceptual clarity is to be attained in the following treatment of the problem. We then proceed to outline an attempt at an analysis of nature in stimulus terms, following a Gibsonian view of the nature of the perceptual world. Certain aspects of the problem that seem to provide difficulties for such an analysis are considered, along with several alternative conceptions that have been or might be suggested in its stead. Finally, buttressed by results from an exploratory study, a research program on the structure and the developmental history of the concept of nature is outlined, based both on the Gibsonian view of perception emphasizing the specification of a set of stimulus properties, and on a model of concept formation suited to deal with such a multidimensional, fuzzily defined concept.

SOME DEFINITIONAL PROBLEMS

The term *nature* is among the more elusive and vaguely defined concepts in our vocabulary. At one extreme, it appears to include the domain of both the life sciences and the physical sciences—that is, the broad range of phenomena that conform to the laws of matter and energy (as contrasted on the one hand with the domain of social and behavioral science and on the other with the realm of the *super*natural, the mystical, and the *meta*physical).

This definition of nature is obviously far too broad to suit our purposes in dealing with the natural environment. A second sense comes closer, but still falls short. This is the term *natural,* as employed in reference to organic processes operating in the biological world and as shown in the expression: "He died of natural causes," or in the previously cited term, "natural childbirth." Natural is contrasted here not with the realm of the supernatural, but rather with such events as accidents or murders which violate the ongoing life processes of the individual, or to more benign forces intervening in such processes from the outside. In this sense, natural refers to the organic processes that permeate the world of nature and have come to be known as the *ecosystem.* This definition of what is natural is thus relevant to us; but it is still unsatisfactory, since it is unlikely that there are specific human responses directed at the natural domain in this sense of organic life.

We come, finally, to the term *natural environment,* which is most relevant to the theme of this volume. This is the vast domain of organic and inorganic matter that is not a product of human activity or intervention. It is, in other words, defined largely by exclusion. It deals with the landscape rather than with the built environment. It includes the world of rock and sand, of shoreline, desert, woods, mountains, etc., and the diverse manifestations of plant and animal life that are encountered there. It excludes the man-made world: our cities and towns, our houses and factories, along with the diverse implements devised by mankind, for transport, recreation, commerce, and other human needs.

Whether such a distinction is a legitimate one is clearly open to debate. The real question is: How fruitful is it? How valuable will it prove to be in actual application, in explaining phenomena or relationships that refer specifically to the natural environment, as opposed to the built (and by extension, the social and cultural) environment, or in disclosing important differential responses between the two?

Boundary-Line Problems

While the last-mentioned definition permits us to differentiate in an intuitive way between natural and nonnatural environments, like most distinctions it is far from ironclad. The two categories represent, in fact, a good example of "fuzzy sets," that is, concepts that lack a completely determinate definition or discrete identity and are thus not unequivocally differentiable from other neighboring sets or concepts. Concepts of this type have in recent years become the subject of concern for cognitive psychologists (Kochen, 1975; Oden, 1977; Rosch, 1973) and information specialists (Zadeh *et al.*, 1975). Let us consider three particular problems raised by this definition of nature. First, what shall we do with the boundary cases represented by environments that are "natural" (in the sense that they do not include any artifacts) but nevertheless show strongly the imprint of human activity? Here we would include stretches of cultivated farmland, abandoned strip mines, partially logged forests, stands of planted forest, reservoirs and other artificial lakes, etc.

Such boundary cases, vexing though they may be in some instances, may at the same time help us to formulate a sharper differentiation between our two "pure" cases than the above definition afforded us. Let us start with the last of our examples: the artificial lake. If we leave aside for the moment those created by dams, or perhaps just the portions of those lakes in which the dam or similar artifacts are visible, their "artificial" origin ceases to be discriminable by the average individual. It thus appears implausible to expect them to elicit in a person a different response from that which a purely natural lake evokes. The point is brought home by the illustrations in Figure 1. It seems unlikely that even visitors to the actual scenes shown in these photographs would be able to detect the artificiality of the man-made lake. Obviously, this does not mean that the two lakes are not distinguishable—a limnologist, ecologist, or geologist could undoubtedly point to certain differences between them. But apart from such specialists, the typical individual would necessarily respond to both in virtually identical fashion, unless of course the actual artificial character of one were pointed out. Such knowledge, particularly if reinforced by explanations or illustrations of the impact of the artificial inundation of the original plain or riverbed, would be expected to alter the individual's response to the area. This is illustrated by the case of Lake Powell, which transformed the rugged Glen Canyon of the Colorado River into an expansive recreation area for speedboats and the like (cf. Porter, 1963).

Let us turn to a very different example, that of cultivated farmland. This lies, in a sense, at the opposite pole from the artificially created lake, for here the alteration of the natural environment is typically quite obvious. There is thus little likelihood of anyone confusing a cornfield or apple orchard with an equivalent hillside or stretch of plains landscape that had been left in its natural (i.e., uncultivated) state. The cornfield or orchard may yet retain a large element of the natural, as in the case of apple trees in bloom. Yet, if only because of the regular spacing of the rows of trees or furrows of corn, the imprint of human activity is so

Figure 1. Illustrations of a natural lake and an artificial one. Which is which?

noticeable in such areas (even in the absence of any concrete artifacts such as houses, barns, silos, fences, and machinery), that in either a functional or a psychological sense it ceases to form a part of what we choose to call "the world of nature." The criterion for dealing with such borderline cases, in other words, is whether the evidence of the effects of past human activity in such areas is discriminable. This criterion appears all the more reasonable given the fact that few land areas remain on our globe that have not at one time or another witnessed some kind of human activity; thus, even the concept of "wilderness" is fundamentally a relative one.

A second problem in delimiting a set of environments that we may identify with the "world of nature" derives from the ubiquity of human artifacts in all but the most remote wilderness areas: roads, power lines,

fire towers, bridges, oil derricks, buildings of varying degrees of perma-
nence, and such signs of human presence as beer cans and abandoned
automobiles left to rust. Clearly, this is a question of the degree of
intrusiveness of the artifacts. Few people would consider a lake in the
wilderness to be outside the natural realm simply because of the sight of
a canoe plying its waters. At the other extreme, little appears to be left of
the sense of a natural environment at some sites in heavily developed
natural recreation areas, such as the "Old Faithful" area of Yellowstone.
On the whole, however, a lenient criterion is apt to serve us best, that is,
one that allows us to include in our discussion of response to the domain
of nature settings that may in fact have experienced considerable intru-
sions through buildings, roads, and artifacts of different kinds—provided that the natural aspects remain predominant over the built ones
and that the area remains identified as a "natural" or "scenic" one, in
terms of the use made of it. Thus, an area containing a military post such
as Camp Pendleton, located on a beautiful stretch of California coastline,
would not qualify by this criterion, while Yosemite Valley would, in
spite of its highly obtrusive built-up character. As already noted, there is
inevitably an arbitrary element in such a decision. Fortunately, a logically airtight definition or delimitation of the world of nature is not
essential for our purposes.

The third problem arises in situations in which bits of nature have
been imported into the built environment—ranging all the way from a
modest flower bed on the balcony of an apartment house to a far-flung
park running the length of a city, such as Fairmount Park in Philadelphia. Nor are such importations limited to the field of botany—what
about our zoological "gardens"? The importance attached to such signs
of the natural world in our man-made environment itself testifies to the
value ascribed to the domain of nature, possibly as a counterforce to the
domination of artifacts felt by the residents of our cities. But here, by a
criterion similar to that of the preceding issue, we are led to exclude
most if not all such importations from our definitions of the natural
domain. People do not equate a zoo with the natural setting in which the
animals they have come to see roam and they do not expect to obtain an
experience of nature from visiting the zoo (excepting possibly such inno-
vations as those of the San Diego Zoo, which attempts to recreate a more
nearly natural environment for its animals). Similarly, a visit to an urban
park is not intended as a truly natural experience, by and large. Again
there are exceptions in the form of certain very large parks such as the
aforementioned Fairmount, where it is in fact possible to hike or ride on
horseback for extended distances while remaining within strictly natural
surroundings and encountering a minimum of human artifacts—much

as in a state or national park. But these are clearly exceptions; furthermore, they have generally been brought about by *preserving* stretches of nature within an urban or urbanized area, as opposed to *creating* a park through the planting of trees, grass, and flowerbeds, or the construction of a small artificial lake.

There thus appears a valid basis for differentiating between the small park or garden and larger, unadorned and unplanned natural environments as environmental settings for behavior or as objects of attraction to the individual. Indeed the concept of the garden, both in its limited literal sense of a small patch of land utilized to cultivate flowers or vegetables and in its broader metaphorical sense as embodied in the (utterly unnatural!) "Garden of Eve," both denotes and connotes an environment created by people (cf. Shepard's discussion of the "Image of the Garden," 1967). Yet there is no denying the strong element of nature contained in such environments, in the sense of organic, and more particularly, plant life. The subject thus deserves to be included in our consideration of human response to the world of nature (see Chapter 4).

A final comment is in order concerning attempts to carve out a domain of nature set apart from that of human activity and influence. Such an attempt may seem to fly in the face of the historical and cross-cultural evidence (e.g., Lowenthal & Prince, 1976; Shepard, 1967) typically interpreted to mean that the conception of nature and landscape—and by implication the differentiation between the natural and the artificial—is itself a product of our own culture. Indeed, the proposed dichotomy appears altogether incompatible with the view of nature of such diverse peoples as the Navaho, with their sense of oneness with nature, and the Japanese, who through their gardens and their art appear to infuse their experience of nature with a distinctly human character. Admittedly, the view being taken here is of limited use in studying those cultural orientations toward nature that emphasize the intimate link between nature and mankind to the point of fusing the two into an inseparable whole. We will return to this issue later in this chapter. At this point I should only like to argue that, perhaps as the result of the domination of our lives by the artifacts of technology, our own society has, on the contrary, widened the gap between the natural and the man-made. Within the context of our society, the stance taken in this paper thus appears defensible. It can, in fact, be suggested that without postulating such a sharp distinction it is impossible to do justice to the differences in the ways in which people respond to the natural environment, as opposed to the built or artificial environments that are so commonly encountered in our society (e.g., Kaplan, Kaplan, & Wendt, 1972;

Ullrich & Ullrich, 1976; Ward, 1977; Wohlwill, 1976, 1977). Here, then, we confront a question of relevance to the psychologist: What is the basis for people's differential response to these two types of environments? This is the question that will concern us for the balance of this chapter.

TOWARD A PERCEPTUALLY BASED ECOLOGY OF NATURAL ENVIRONMENTS

To start, I should like to propose that it is possible to identify a set of stimulus attributes in terms of which natural environments may be differentiated from man-made ones. This proposition, although as yet untested, gains plausibility when viewed from the perspective of James Gibson's (1950, 1966, 1979) analysis of the information contained in the visual array, which this writer considers eminently relevant to the study of the perception of the physical enviornment. Gibson, both in his earlier work on space perception (1950) and in his subsequent concern for "ecological optics," which led him to a more broadly conceived ecological approach to visual perception, was always interested in the environment writ large, as opposed to the highly restricted, artificial environments in which much of perceptual research in the laboratory has taken place. In fact, it was his concern for the richness of the environment as a source of stimulation that led him to argue for a process of perceptual learning based on differentiating an information-laden perceptual input, in contrast to enriching an input supposedly devoid of sufficient information to yield a determinate percept (cf. J. Gibson & E. Gibson, 1955).

Unfortunately, although illustrations taken from outdoor settings occur in his books (notably the 1950 one), Gibson never concerned himself with the natural environment as a source of stimulation of a particular kind, whose stimulus attributes might be differentiated from those characterizing man-made environments. Indeed, his last book states explicitly that "it is a mistake to separate the natural from the artificial as if there were two environments" (J. Gibson, 1979, p. 130), on the grounds that artifacts have to be manufactured from natural substances. Here we see a retreat, to a degree, from Gibson's earlier stress on the qualities of the visual array as the prime determinant of our perceptions and a concomitant greater stress on a quasi-functional view embodied in his concept of "affordances." These are the properties of an object, or an environment, that account for what the individual does with it, or in it, or what happens to an individual in it. Thus some terrains afford locomotion, while others (e.g., a cliff) afford injury or danger. This analysis represents a marked shift from the earlier concern for the qualities of the stimulus array *per se*, though it should be noted that affordances too are based on certain perceptual and perceived attributes of the environment (e.g., the sharp visual gradient that marks a visual edge such as a cliff). But the theory as a whole appears more relevant to the designed and artifactual world—the world of chairs and saddles, of paved versus cobblestone roads, of carpets and wood-paneled floors. As Gibson notes, it is to change what the environment affords that man has changed the shape and substances of the environment (cf. p. 130). For our present purposes, on the other hand, and specifically for our attempts to establish an ecologically valid differentiation between the natural and the man-made realms, it is the earlier Gibson, notably that of the "visual world" (J. Gibson, 1950), that appears the most relevant.

Gibson's emphasis on the information-laden character of the everyday world that the individual normally perceives (at least here on earth) and the demonstration by him and his associates that the perceiver is indeed sensitive to such information—or can be made so through focused experience—provide a potential underpinning for a stimulus-based analysis of the differentiation between the natural and the nonnatural domains. It needs to be supplemented, however, by a full-scale ecological study of these domains, in order to determine the extent to which they are indeed composed of different kinds of information—Gibson's own assertions to the contrary notwithstanding. Pending such a survey, we are left with some unproven, though plausible-sounding arguments, along with the insights of artists and aestheticians and others (such as naturalists, photographers, geographers, and landscape architects) who have commented on the natural realm on the one hand, and the urban scene on the other.

The most immediately compelling point in this regard is that, although the artifactual world may be composed of "natural" substances and materials (particularly in the man-made structures encountered in our outdoor world), its form is generally very different from the forms that characterize the natural domain. It would be surprising if it were otherwise, for the processes that have shaped the natural world over eons of time, both in its animate and inanimate forms, are of an entirely different kind from the technological and cultural processes that have produced the buildings, highways, vehicles, and other structures that make up the domain of the artifactual.

What are some of these perceptual differences? The most obvious ones are illustrated in Figure 2, where exemplars of the natural environment characterized by irregular lines and curvilinear lines and edges, continuous gradations of shape and color, and irregular, rough textures

Figure 2. Examples of natural and man-made environments, illustrating the role of curvilinear versus rectilinear patterns (A, B), gradual versus abrupt transitions (C, D), and rough, irregular versus smooth, regular textures (E, F) as stimulus variables differentiating the two kinds of environments. (Figure 2B from *Man-Made Philadelphia* by R. S. Wurman. Copyright 1972 by MIT Press. Reprinted by permission. Figure 2E from *Rocks, Time, and Landforms* by Jerome Wyckoff. Published 1965 by Harper and Row. Copyright by the Union Pacific Railroad. Reprinted by permission. Figure 2F from *Techniques of Landscape Architecture* by A. E. Weddle (Ed.). Published 1968 by American Elsevier. Copyright by William Heinemann Ltd. Reprinted by permission.)

are contrasted with exemplars of the man-made environment, consisting of regular lines and rectilinear edges, sharp discontinuities and abrupt transitions, and highly regular, smooth textures.

The question immediately arises, of course, of how representative the two sets of scenes actually are as exemplars of the two domains. Certainly, exceptions could be found for each of the attributes cited, in the form of scenes from the natural environment containing regular lines (though rarely if ever perfectly rectilinear contours), sharp contrasts or discontinuities, and smooth textures. Conversely, man-made structures may contain irregular lines and curvilinear edges; they may also lack sharp discontinuities and contain rough textures. Examples of such exceptional cases—assuming for the moment that they are indeed exceptional—are given in Figure 3.

Do these latter examples represent the proverbial exception that prove the rule? That would be an all too facile answer. The real question is whether we may be entitled to speak of a rule at all, at least in a statistical sense. That is, would an ecological analysis confirm a probabilistic association between the above-cited attributes and the natural–man-made distinction? If so, that would be ample reason to suspect that these attributes are implicated in perceptual as well as affective differentiation between the two domains, since the role of probabilistic cues in learning and evaluative judgment has been amply demonstrated (Bruner, Goodnow, & Austin, 1956; Brunswik, 1956). Admittedly, no attempt at such a systematic analysis has been made thus far. But let us grant, if only for the sake of the argument, that the answer to this question would be positive, and agree on the potential validity of differentiating the man-made from the natural environment in terms of the stimulus attributes characteristic of each. The question that remains is: How relevant is such a distinction to the actually observed differential responses to the two kinds of environments? While here again clear-cut evidence is lacking, it appears possible to relate at least some of the perceptual attributes differentiating the two domains to such differential responses, notably in the affective and evaluative realm.

This subject is treated more extensively in Chapter 3 (cf. also Wohlwill, 1976), but it may be observed that a number of the stimulus characteristics cited above appear to implicate the diversity or complexity dimension (e.g., regularity of lines and of textures). There is abundant evidence that diversity and complexity are strongly related to affective arousal and pleasure, or preference judgments, according to an inverted U-shaped relationship, such that an intermediate level of diversity is most conducive to pleasure. Of the three dimensions cited above and illustrated in Figure 1, two (regularity of lines and of textures) appear to

Figure 3. Instances of natural environments that feature straight lines (A) and smooth textures (B) and of man-made environments characterized by curvilinear shapes (C) and rough textures (D) representing presumed exceptions to the differentiating variables illustrated in Figure 2. (Figure 3A from *Analysis of Landforms: Introduction to Geomorphology* by C. R. Twidale. Copyright 1976 by Wiley Interscience. Reprinted by permission. Figure 3B from *Man-Made Philadelphia* by R. S. Wurman. Copyright 1972 by MIT Press. Reprinted by permission. Figure 3C from *Shifting Sands: The Story of Sand Dunes* by R. Maher. Published 1968 by John Day. Copyright by Arabian American Oil Company. Reprinted by permission.)

operate in ways that make natural environments *more* complex than man-made ones; it may be suggested, however, that when combined with the third (continuity) the net effect is one of stimulus fields that tend to converge in the intermediate range with regard to overall complexity, as opposed to man-made scenes that may be either highly complex or virtually lacking in diversity to the point of monotony. This possibility receives some partial support from the writer's experience in trying to construct sets of slides representing the two types of environments matched for diversity (based on independent judges' ratings of specific aspects of the scenes); it proved impossible to locate slides of the natural environment that were as high in diversity as the highest of the man-made ones (cf. Wohlwill, 1976, for a brief account of this research). At the same time, it seems likely that what is being formulated here as a unidimensional variable of complexity, based on diversity, should rather be considered as involving a combination of factors, which together create a sense of order or unity (Wohlwill, 1980). Perhaps it is this aspect that represents the effective basis on which the two domains should be differentiated.[2]

Going beyond the aforementioned visual characteristics of texture and form, there remain at least two further aspects that need to be considered in any comprehensive attempt to differentiate, in stimulus terms, the natural domain from the artificial. One refers to the dynamic side of the two types of environments and the other concerns the role of information in modalities other than visual—notably the auditory mode.

If we consider patterns of motion in the two realms, there appear some immediately obvious differences between them. First, natural environments in general (and again we are dealing with statistically rather than absolutely valid distinctions) are characterized by a relative absence of gross movement, or by motion of a less intense, less strongly kinetic sort—as in the rustling of leaves, the propagation of waves over the water, and the flight of insects and birds. When we compare this type of motion with that which is in an ecological sense the most prevalent form in the man-made environment (at least outdoors), namely that of vehicular traffic, the difference in intensity becomes clear. To be sure, a stam-

---

[2]The determination of the degree of complexity represented in any given scene is considerably complicated by the dependence of the perceived complexity on the degree of resolution afforded by the stimulus field, which is of course a function of the viewer's distance from it. Thus, the true diversity and intricacy of patterning actually contained in an array of plants (e.g., in a desert landscape such as that of the Saguaro National Monument in Arizona) will not become obvious until viewed at close range. Similarly, textures (of water, sand, stone) that may appear to be smooth and regular from a distance will be revealed as much rougher and irregular when seen in a closer view.

pede of elephants can exceed in vigor and kinetic impact anything we are likely to encounter on streets or freeways, but natural phenomena of this sort are rarely encountered by most of us, and even they could probably be duplicated by the impact of a passing freight train or the ponderous movement of a jumbo jet at takeoff or landing.

Suppose we accept for the moment the plausibility of the assumption that the prevalent instances of movement observed in the two environments differ in their intensity. If we add to that differences in regularity or predictability of such movement (which may be assumed to be greater for the natural as opposed to the man-made realm, again considering primarily the outdoor environment), we may have already part of the answer to the supposedly greater relaxation and restoration that people experience or look for in natural environments.

A complete account of the differences in the quality and quantity of motion encountered in the two types of settings is complicated by the role played by human beings, since people are typically in motion outdoors and thus contribute to the sense of movement and indeed of life conveyed by an environment. But since *Homo sapiens* is found in motion in both types of settings, the difference between them should be attenuated as far as this kinetic aspect is concerned. On the other hand, both quantitatively and qualitatively there undoubtedly remain major differences in human motion (e.g., on a street or plaza vs. the natural environment) in terms of pace, uniformity of direction, and, above all, in terms of sheer amount. Admittedly, on summer weekends some of our parks become beehives of activity, and to that extent tend to resemble the hustle and bustle associated with a busy urban area. For that very reason, however, natural settings under these conditions lose some of their intrinsic value *qua* natural environments.

Finally, what about differences in the smell and sounds of natural and man-made environments? Here we are clearly reduced to vague intuitions and to differences of a predominantly qualitative sort. We can all differentiate between the smell of the woods, or of the ocean air, and the air along a major traffic artery, but we would find it difficult to abstract any clearly definable properties from the differential stimulation characterizing them that could be generalized to other settings. In the case of the sonic environment, it might seem that the man-made environment offers a greater diversity and complexity of sounds than we find in most natural settings; in actual fact however, the soundscape of the outdoor environment is in most places dominated by the ubiquitous sound of traffic, which again differs from most typical natural sounds (most obviously in intensity). There are probably other, less easily specified qualitative differences as well (cf. Cermak & Cormillon, 1976), but these remain poorly described, let alone systematically analyzed.

The preceding attempt at establishing some clear differentiation between the man-made and the natural domains on the basis of the stimulus attributes of these environments is admittedly a largely speculative effort. Since the postulated differences are valid, if at all, only in a statistical sense, a thorough ecological inventory of the major types of environmental settings encountered on earth with respect to the previously mentioned qualities of stimulation will be required to verify their validity. Yet such an undertaking would run into some fairly formidable problems of sampling and measurement. For the moment, it will suffice to argue for the plausibility of demonstrating such a differentiation along the kinds of dimensions cited above.

THE SIMULATION OF THE NATURAL REALM

A good way of reformulating the question of the relevant differences between the natural and the man-made is to ask ourselves what it would take to *simulate* a natural environment, one that would in fact be accepted as a satisfactory surrogate by us. Some aficionados of nature would probably shrink in horror at the very suggestion that anyone might try to undertake such a simulation, or would dismiss it out of hand as a pointless undertaking, foredoomed to failure. Such a reaction is exemplified in the sense of outrage with which Iltis (1973), a biologist, responded to Krieger's (1973) provocative article, "What's wrong with plastic trees?"

Krieger was actually less concerned with the feasibility or desirability of simulating nature or substituting artificial equivalents for it as with the broader question of the economic and social value to be placed on nature and on tracts of nature to be preserved in an untrammeled, undeveloped condition. He did, however, maintain that our conception of nature was of purely cultural origin and that it was thus legitimate to consider possibilities for altering or intervening in natural environments, through technological means as well as through suitably devised policies for managing such areas, in order to enhance access to and enjoyment of them by larger segments of the population. Iltis, more concerned with the preservation of ecological values and of meeting a need that he, as a biologist, imputed to man for an experience of nature in its pure, unaltered state, took sharp exception to this proposal for basing the use of natural environments on such "technological fixes," as he saw it.

This issue patently transcends the limitations of a behavioral science perspective. For a psychologist, however, the question remains: To what extent do people in fact accept artificial substitutes for the real thing when it comes to the natural environment? Few of us have not, at some time or other, mistaken artificial flowers for real ones; indeed, their ready availability commercially indicates that many people obtain satisfaction from such a surrogate for some purposes.[3]

It is a long way, obviously, from a display of artificial flowers in a dentist's office to the recreation of a total natural environment through artificial simulation. Even as seemingly simple and innocuous a "natural" object as a lawn (which is of course far from representing nature in a pure form) can be replicated through artificial means only rather imperfectly, as the reception accorded to synthetic turf, even on baseball fields, demonstrates. Thus, one major-league ballpark (San Francisco's Candlestick Park) has recently seen its artificial surface replaced with natural grass. Even if that change resulted in part from practical considerations (e.g., injuries to players), it demonstrates the functional nonequivalence between the two types of surfaces. In a purely perceptual sense it is apparent that it is far easier to create an illusion of a natural environment by recording its actual sights and sounds on film and audio tape and reproducing them in a theatre, for instance, than it would be to construct via artificial simulation a three-dimensional pseudonatural world of even remotely comparable fidelity.

The reasons presumably have to do with the character of a natural environment as an organic milieu. Although bits and pieces from such a milieu (the leaf of a plant, a piece of moss, the fruits of a tree) could be simulated to a reasonable degree of verisimilitude through appropriately chosen materials, it is doubtful that on a larger scale the attempt to recreate a forest, a mountain slope, or a beach would stand up under closer scrutiny, as shown in occasional attempts of this sort in museums and similar displays. In the aggregate, it appears virtually impossible to recreate artificially the intricate interpatterning of inanimate and organic matter in terms of its visual, aural, and olfactory qualities, and of the

---

[3]In regard to people's willingness to accept surrogate forms of nature, it may be significant that sales of artificial flowers seem to be declining, at least in the United States. While no actual figures on such sales appear to be available, the volume of imports of artificial flowers—which, according to an official from the Artificial Flowers Board of Trade in New York City accounts for virtually all the artificial flowers sold for private use—has declined from $43 million in 1964 to $33 million in 1979. When one considers that these figures are not adjusted for inflation, the actual decrease in purchases of such instances of plastic nature reflected in these figures is clearly very substantial. (*U.S. General Imports, Schedule A: Commodity by Country*. U.S. Bureau of the Census, Publication FT 135.)

subtle dynamics of motion created by water and wind, not to mention the diverse forms of animal life.[4]

Simulation remains nevertheless a useful approach if we wish to determine precisely what it is that people look for, discriminate, and respond to in the natural environment. This use of simulation can be taken both in a strict sense (what does it take to create a simulated natural environment artificially that will not be detected as different from "the real thing"?) and more plausibly in a looser sense (what kinds of simulated environments will be acceptable substitutes for "the real thing," for limited purposes: indoor decorations, picture-window views, playgrounds?). This kind of simulation has scarcely been undertaken as yet on any systematic basis, however. (For a study relevant to this point, though limited in scope, see Young & Berry, 1979.)

However speculative, the preceding foray into the problems of simulating the realm of nature should prove valuable in loosening and perhaps challenging our staunchly held convictions concerning the inviolate character of nature and its ironclad separation from the man-made domain. Ultimately, however, one suspects that our intuitive sense of real separation between them will survive such a challenge.

ALTERNATIVE VIEWS OF NATURE IN PSYCHOLOGICAL TERMS

The preceding treatment of nature in terms of the properties of the stimulus environment characterizing that realm as distinct from the man-made world is clearly only one among a number of different views of this problem. Let us consider three alternative views in particular. They involve, (1) the notion of nature as a manifestation of processes of growth and change, (2) nature as a refuge, and (3) nature as a symbol. It should be noted that, with the possible exception of the last, these alternative views are to be taken not as contradicting an account of the natural environment in stimulus terms, but rather as potentially com-

---

[4]Admittedly a fair amount can be accomplished through methods of environmental simulation (e.g., through the use of landscape models), particularly as employed in the Berkeley Environmental Simulator (McKechnie, 1978), which generates actual visual trips through such a simulated environment, projected by closed-circuit television or on film, that convey a high degree of fidelity to the original scene. Although this technique, combining the skills of the landscape architect and the engineer, commands one's respect and admiration and succeeds in conveying a sense of the actual environment in regard to its perceptual character, it does so only at a relatively coarse-grained level (i.e., one that does not depend on response to fine detail in the environment); it is even less adequate in eliciting overt behavioral responses to natural-environmental settings.

patible with such an account, though formulated in different, largely functional terms.

NATURE AS A REALM OF CONTINUOUS CHANGE AND GROWTH

Accounts of nature and its impact on the individual are frequently one-sided, due to a tendency to equate nature with wilderness. Only a small fraction of our population has in fact had any direct experience with wilderness, but we find manifestations of the world of nature, both inanimate and animate, scattered throughout our environment, frequently imported into our man-made world at considerable expense, and maintained at the cost of much time and effort. This is the subject of Chapter 4, so there is no need to delve at length into the motivations behind the diverse activities—keeping plants indoors, gardening, visiting a local park—that we have devised to keep us in touch with nature. But it is worth calling attention to these phenomena, since neither the analysis of natural environments in terms of the properties of the stimulation they afford nor the conception of nature as a refuge can go very far in accounting for the attraction of natural elements on a small scale, from that of a flower pot to that of a garden or a vest-pocket park.

Is it some intrinsic power of the coloration provided by chlorophyll that moves us to "Keep America"—and our own apartments, yards, and parks—green, as Kaplan (1978) appears to imply? Is it perhaps a more general desire for color in our environment, possibly borne of the need for contrast? Undoubtedly these aspects play a part, but they are quite readily satisfied through purely artificial means, including specifically the artificial flowers discussed previously. If the realm of the artificial does not succeed in satisfying people's desire for flowers, grass, and trees in their immediate surroundings, it must be because of what it lacks in comparison with the "real article," *viz.*, the capacity for growth and for spontaneous change. The opening, unfolding, and eventual wilting and death of a flower bud, the seasonal changes in our trees, perhaps even the rapid growth of the grass on our lawns in summer—though we may curse it if we are responsible for keeping it mowed—all these phenomena of organic life surely contribute to our appreciation of the natural domain and cause us to feel discontented if we are deprived of them for any length of time. (Consider the search for an apartment in a city and the dissatisfaction experienced at the sight of nothing but houses, streets, and vehicles from the living-room window.)

To the extent that this emphasis on processes of change and growth as a major factor in people's desire for elements of nature in their environment is valid, it would require not so much an abandonment of the preceding framework focusing on stimulus features as it would an extension of our approach to perception, so that it encompasses the dimension of time and of change occurring over extended periods of time.

NATURE AS A REFUGE

One of the values frequently mentioned as representing the basis for people's desire to seek out the natural in all of its forms, from a major urban park to a distant wilderness area, is the sense of refuge from the everyday world and from human activity and interaction that it provides. The realm of nature, in other words, affords a change of pace from the high intensity levels, the tensions, and the fast-paced character of life in Western (particularly urban) society. This view receives support from studies of the motivation for the visitation of natural recreational areas, which typically list this kind of benefit near or at the top of the list (cf. Rossman & Ulehla, 1977), as well as from the general finding that residents of urban areas are overrepresented among the visitors to such areas (cf. Hendee, 1969).[5]

Because of its presumed importance in natural recreation behavior, this aspect of the concept of nature in psychological terms will receive more detailed consideration in other chapters in this volume, particularly Chapters 5 and 6. Suffice it here to note that this capacity of the natural environment to serve as a refuge or to provide a context within which the recreative powers of the individual may be exhibited (the "recharging of the batteries," as it is sometimes put metaphorically) is in part, but only in part, traceable to some of the properties of the stimulus environment considered above—properties such as a relative absence of complexity, of sharp contrast, of intense levels of stimulation, and of the frenetic movement to be found in our man-made environments. But this is only part of the story. If nature can afford refuge, it is surely in considerable measure because of the opportunity it presents for individuals to escape temporarily from the pressures and tensions of their interpersonal and social lives, at work, at home, in school, etc.

This may appear as a rather negative way of looking at nature and

---

[5]Mercer (1976), in reviewing this research, suggests that the evidence in favor of the hypothesis of a desire for change in the recreation literature is not nearly as clear-cut as is sometimes implied, and he points to some important complicating and qualifying factors affecting the behavior of a particular person in search of a particular kind of environment or recreational activity.

its restorative powers. But it is possible to reformulate it in more positive terms by suggesting that one of the critical features of a natural environment, and of a wilderness area in particular, is that it is nonresponsive; it is this characteristic that permits nature to serve as a refuge, providing relief from our normal interactions and interchanges with other persons. As thus stated, this may sound implausible—after all, the human being is a gregarious animal who in general welcomes, if not demands, the presence of others for most of its active life. Yet social interaction accounts for a large share of the stresses and tensions that arise in our lives. Quite apart from interpersonal conflicts, clashes of personality, and the like, it can be argued that it is the pervasive role of feedback characterizing our interpersonal, and increasingly our man–machine, interactions that exacts a toll; this may be the reason for our experiencing the need for the change of scenery and the change of pace that a purely natural area affords.

But why should feedback have such a negative impact on us? At first, this suggestion may appear counterintuitive, since feedback is generally something we value, and even demand. Yet, though we may agree to the evident positive value of feedback in our lives, the possibility should be considered that in certain forms it may constitute a source of stress. This may be true particularly in situations in which response feedback operates without being animated by a communality of purpose. In certain cases such communality is simply absent, and our actions are functionally independent of those of others—as in the case of shoppers dodging each other in a crowded department store or drivers weaving in and out of lanes on a congested highway. In other cases, where we are in an adversarial relationship with others—whether in a friendly game of tennis, in a spirited argument at the family dinner table, or, in a more extreme form, in a barroom slugfest—the strain entailed by such continuous feedback experiences is undoubtedly more severe.

What all these cases have in common is that they force us continually to monitor the behavior of others, in order to adapt our responses to their previous responses, while at the same time remaining sensitive to the effects that our responses have produced. In this respect our interactions with the natural environment, especially in a wilderness setting, provide a marked contrast. For that environment rarely responds back to us; in fact, it generally remains blissfully unaffected by our presence or our actions in it. Limited exceptions to this rule may be cited, as in the case of the stone dislodged in climbing that may hit us in the shinbone, but these tend to be relatively minor events and do not contradict the general principle that feedback from the environment is at a minimum in a wilderness setting.[6]

It does not seem too farfetched to suggest that, along with the overall change in levels of intensity of stimulation, attenuation of sharp contrasts, and reduction of discontinuous temporal change, it is the virtual absence of the extended feedback loops characterizing our interactions with other people (and with machines as well) that serves to differentiate our contacts with the world of nature from the conditions of our everyday lives. This failure of the wilderness to be in any way moved by the person entering it may indeed be at the heart of the restorative powers claimed for it. More particularly, it could readily account for the feeling of freedom and oneness with nature engendered by the wilderness—where the individual experiences so little reaction to or acknowledgement of his or her own presence that the boundaries between the self and the environment become muted and lose definition. At the same time one would expect this feature of a wilderness area to provoke discomfort and anxiety for some people, namely those who are highly dependent upon signs of responsiveness from their environment.

Let us reiterate a point noted previously: the unresponsiveness that has been claimed as a significant aspect of a large-scale natural environment can at best represent a necessary, but clearly not a sufficient, condition for the impact of such an environment on a person. It would be easy to recreate this characteristic in a purely man-made setting, such as downtown Manhattan on a Sunday morning, virtually deserted and quiet, or, for that matter, a nondescript tract of farm land in the Midwest. The fact is that we do not find persons flocking to such areas to get their "batteries recharged," or to feel a sense of communion with their environment. Undoubtedly we have to look at this absence or sharp reduction in feedback as operating in a particular context compatible with it, that is, an environment characterized by the relative quiet, stillness, and stability, and those as yet only dimly understood features that account for the aesthetic appeal of most natural settings.

Conversely, it is important to recognize that most so-called natural

---

[6]One case that represents possibly a more substantial exception to this rule is that of river running, where the fluidity of the medium being traversed and the continual alteration of that medium through the river-runner's own actions provides for considerable feedback, notably while negotiating stretches of white water rapids and similar precarious spots. This element, which of course accounts for the thrill experienced by the sport's practitioners, renders this an experience that is fundamentally different from that of the hiker, or the canoeist on a tranquil lake.

recreation does not take place in wilderness areas, but rather in areas that may be relatively heavily traveled, feature high densities of people, and be subject to many of the same phenomena that characterize our everyday lives and that the typical vacationer wants to escape—at least according to the refuge theory. As any frequenter of Yosemite Valley on a summer weekend well knows, levels of pollution and noise, tensions arising from traffic jams, altercations with frequently overtaxed park personnel, and squabbles with family members and neighbors (e.g., among the house trailer set) are more apt to recreate the character of the environment that the visitors are supposedly fleeing than to provide a true recreational experience for them. (Indeed, even the incidence of crime in such areas has started to approach that of our major urban areas.) In these cases it is apparent that, whatever the individuals' reason for seeking out such "natural" areas, they act rather to maintain the kinds of stimuli, and the levels of stimulation associated with them, to which they have become accustomed—right down to the blare of a television set or radio. Yet it must be the search for a natural setting, in some sense of that word, that has brought the visitors there; if not, why should they travel frequently considerable distances to reach these settings?

Nature as a Symbol

Both of the preceding views of the basis for our response to the natural environment either refer to or imply some property or feature of such an environment. In contrast, according to the conception to be considered presently, nature represents a construct, that is, a product of our intellect and imagination, determining the characteristics, as well as the powers, that we attribute to it. Such a view is at least implicit, and often made explicit, in discussions of the human view of and relationship with nature to be found in the writings of humanists, historians, and essayists (e.g., Glacken, 1967; Jackson, 1951; Lowenthal & Prince, 1976; Shepard, 1967). It is consonant, furthermore, with experiential conceptions of the environment such as that of Wapner, Kaplan, and Cohen (1973).

No reasonable person would want to deny that the concept of nature has through history been invested with a rich layer of meanings, symbolic elaborations, and transformations, as well as significant affective and attitudinal responses. This phenomenon itself testifies to the centrality and salience of the concept for the human animal. In and of itself, however, it does not preclude the existence of an objective base for the symbols and meanings attached to nature, no more than the varied symbols and myths that relate to the sun, for instance, can be considered as totally divorced from the physical properties of the visual and thermal stimulation emanating from this celestial object. This is not to say that this penumbra of symbol and meaning that is part and parcel of an individual's conception of nature can be accounted for wholly in terms of such physical properties. The point is, rather, that the two are interrelated; thus, a focus on the stimulus attributes of natural environments should be considered as complementary to, rather than incompatible with, a focus on meanings.

There remains, however, the issue of the *differential* meanings attached to the natural environment by people at different historical times, or in different cultures today. These differences have been effectively captured in the contrasting orientations toward nature that characterize different historical periods and ethical systems described by Dubos (1972), among others, as well as in the analyses of differences in the value systems of various cultural groups in a single geographic area (Kluckhohn & Strodtbeck, 1961). How shall one account for these differential ways of responding to nature, except through recourse to such concepts as symbols, values and value systems, and others that refer to processes of transformation or even distortion of some external world of reality? This is clearly a complex topic, and one that could not possibly be dealt with effectively here. Yet there are several points to be noted that suggest ways of handling such differences without necessarily abandoning the framework for analysis of the nature concept that has been developed in this chapter. Let us consider three aspects of the problem.

First, there are surely enormous differences in the character of the natural environments experienced by different cultures and at different times. Quite apart from any differences in value systems, culturally based beliefs, and other variations, one would hardly expect a group of Eskimos to evolve a concept of nature similar to that of the Watusi of equatorial Africa, or of the Indians of the American plains. Indeed, a major branch of anthropology is concerned with relationships between tribal belief systems and practices and the ecological conditions in which these peoples live and obtain their sustenance.

Furthermore, a culture's response to nature must be viewed in the context of that culture's total environmental experience at a given time. Consider the first white settlers in the United States, who emphasized the hostile, threatening, inhospitable side of nature and regarded it as something to be tamed, in contrast to contemporary environmentalists who sing its praises and rise to protect it. This difference in orientation is attributable only in part to actual changes that have occurred in people's experience of nature—the sharp reduction in forms of animal life dangerous to man, the vast increase in accessibility, the invention of equipment to protect those venturing into natural areas from the elements, and other developments. We need to take into account also the tremendous concomitant changes in the built environment that have taken place over this period, from the small villages that were the predominant human habitat in the seventeenth century in the United States (and which afforded not only shelter, but intimate and satisfying forms of community life), to the conditions of urban decay, suburban sprawl, and other such characteristics of our contemporary habitat. The everyday environment in which we live and work thus affords a very different context for the evaluation of the natural environment today.

At the same time it must be recognized that symbolic elaborations of the world of reality do not unfold in isolation, but can be presumed to be intimately related to the values and belief systems that a particular cultural group has evolved. The Pilgrims who landed in Massachusetts undoubtedly formed a concept of nature different from that of the native people that greeted them, just as marked variations among different cultural groups residing in the same geographic area have been traced in our contemporary world (Kluckhohn & Strodtbeck, 1961). Does that mean, then, that these divergent concepts of nature develop divorced from the features of the environment encountered by these groups?

Not necessarily. It would seem more reasonable to interpret variations in the responses of different groups to a single environment as reflecting differences in the particular features and characteristics selected by each. Since the physical environment is, after all, a highly diversified, complex entity, it is quite possible, and indeed to be expected, that different sets of characteristics will be attended to by different individuals. We need only to postulate some filtering process, as yet only imperfectly understood, that would be affected by other aspects of a person's experience, including his or her value and belief systems and past experience. Indeed, such a selection process is intrinsic to the differentiation view of perceptual learning proposed by the Gibsons (J. Gibson & E. Gibson, 1955) as noted above. Recall that James Gibson in particular emphasized the richness of the information available to the perceiver; similarly, Eleanor Gibson's (1969) theory of perceptual learning goes at some length into the processes of information extraction and selective attention characterizing the perceptual process. Selectivity is indeed of the essence in perception generally, and environmental perception in particular (just as it is in social perception). There is thus ample room for differing conceptions of nature to emerge, based on differences in the particular features of the natural environment that are attended to by a given individual or a given culture, and it is plausible that such differences would bear some relationship to other aspects of personality and experience.

Finally, the dependence of the conception of nature developed by a given individual living at a particular moment in time and in a particular location on that individual's prior experience needs to be considered in a very specific sense, that is, in terms of the role of the familiarity, novelty, or strangeness of an environment for that person. Thus, much has been made of the change in our view of mountains and wilderness, from a forbidding, dangerous kind of world filled with evil spirits—an environment to be avoided—to one that for some of the more devoted and enthusiastic members of the backpacking set appears to have displaced the canine species as man's best friend. What seems to have been ignored in much of the discussion of this topic is the role of unfamiliarity and strangeness as both a potential stimulus for exploration and a source of fear and consequent avoidance. This conflict is resolved differently by different persons. A traveler in the 14th century, Adam of Usk, apparently found the prospect of crossing the St. Gotthard Pass in the Alps so frightening that he had himself carried across it blindfolded (Shepard, 1967, p. 131). Yet the same prospect must have appeared rather less terrifying to Hannibal many centuries earlier, as he decided to traverse this foreign, hostile realm with his large army of men and elephants. (In fact, it appears to have been the elephants rather than the human contingent participating in this prodigious enterprise that proved unable to cope, for most of them perished during the course of the traversal.) Conversely, one suspects that there were many American soldiers who found the horrors of warfare enhanced, rather than attenuated, by the unfamiliar, hostile-appearing environment in which they had to fight (e.g., the jungles of Guadalcanal and the Philippines).

But in recent years an increasing number of persons, especially in the United States, have had the opportunity to develop a very intimate familiarity with the wilderness, due to facilitation of access, increased knowledge about it (much of it transmitted through the media), and more effective protection against its dangers and discomforts, from rainproof tents to anti-snakebite kits. Thus, it is not surprising that a very different view of wilderness, and of nature in general, should have evolved in contemporary society, while at the same time there remain many individuals (such as inner-city youths) for whom even a seemingly innocuous forest constitutes an alien and consequently threatening environment.

Nor is this role of familiarity or lack of it limited to our response to wilderness. This writer well remembers the case of a young man transposed from the plains of Nebraska to the wooded, hilly terrain of New England, and daily having to negotiate that terrain as a traveling salesman. It apparently was a most frustrating experience for him, at least at the outset. "Why don't they cut down all those goddamn trees" he expostulated in an exasperated tone "so a guy can see where the hell he's going!" Are the Easterner's reactions on first encounter with the wide-open spaces and flatness of the Midwest any more attuned to the beauties of that novel environment?

CONCLUSION: NATURE AS A "NATURAL" CATEGORY

THE DEVELOPMENTAL ORIGINS OF THE NATURAL/ARTIFICIAL DIFFERENTIATION

Central to the interpretation of the nature concept developed in this chapter is the premise that nature represents a "natural" category par excellence, in Rosch's (1973, 1978) sense, precisely because of the existence of a varied set of stimulus properties that serve to identify this category and to differentiate it from its complement, that of the man-made. Some evidence in support of this contention was cited in the Introduction. The developmental origins and history of the formation of this category and of the establishment of its differentiation from the man-made remain, however, largely unknown. A very limited pilot study carried out by Holcomb (1977) with nursery school children suggests that the differentiation in question is alien to the spontaneous categorization of everyday objects exhibited by children at this age level. Apart from being limited to four-year-old children, however, the study is at best a pilot effort based on a small number of subjects and fairly unsystematic procedures. In view of the evident interest of the question, a more comprehensive developmental attack on this issue is surely warranted.

In this connection, a preliminary study carried out by the writer to investigate this question is of interest. It entailed presenting a diversified set of environmental scenes of the natural and the man-made environment to children between the ages of 6 and 14. Some of the scenes represented common exemplars of each domain (such as a meadow, or a bus) while the other involved less typical exemplars (e.g., a geyser or a prehistoric village).[7] The study focused on the children's mode of categorizing this material by means of several sorting tasks varying from completely spontaneous (the children were simply asked to arrange the set of pictures into as many piles as they wanted) to partially constrained (the children were asked to divide the set into just two piles) and finally to externally imposed (the experimenter reinforced sortings according to the Nature/Man-made differentiation through appropriate feedback of "right" and "wrong").

The results of the study showed conclusively that from the age of six or seven, children respond quite readily in terms of the Nature versus Man-made categories even at a spontaneous level; indeed, the age differences between 6 and 14 years in this regard were relatively slight. Thus, at all ages the spontaneous sortings into n groups made by the children tended very predominantly to respect the Nature/Man-made differentiation (i.e., whatever and however many groups the child constructed, very few involved a mixture of man-made and natural stimuli). Similarly, the spontaneous dichotomous sortings reflected the Nature/Man-made distinction to a very high (and frequently perfect) degree, especially for the "typical" set. By the same token, most children had little difficulty learning the experimenter-imposed differentiation between Nature versus Man-made. What changed with age primarily were the explanations given by the children for their responses. While those of the young children were inconsistent, exemplar specific, and concrete, the older children's categories generally were not only more consistent, group encompassing, and abstract, but they made specific references to the terms "nature" and "man-made" (or its equivalent). At the same time, spontaneous use of evaluative and attitudinal terms also became increasingly frequent at the older age levels. There was thus an indication that cognitive coding of objects or scenes in the everyday world in terms of the Natural/Man-made differentiation became overlayed with affective and evaluative components that presumably presaged the establishment of differential attitudes to the two domains.

These results thus reinforce the view that the domain of nature does

---

[7]In principle, this differentiation between Typical and Non-Typical, rather than being based on familiarity versus novelty, as was the case here, should have proceeded according to Rosch's (1978) criterion of the number of modal attributes shared by each instance. That would, however, have presupposed agreement on what those attributes are and on the selection of scenes containing differing combinations of them. There was no opportunity to carry out the extensive spade work required for this purpose, which might well form one aspect of the first component of the research program to be proposed in the following section.

indeed represent a very "natural" category, and that its differentiation from the man-made domain becomes established at a fairly early age. Clearly, cultural and, more specifically, educational influences need to be taken into account in interpreting these findings. (The children in this study were attending a school in a lower-middle-class section of West Berlin.) Replication on different population of children is thus needed, especially to determine whether the predominantly negative evaluation attached to the built environment by many of the older children represents an idiosyncracy of this particular sociocultural group, or perhaps of the instruction they were receiving in their classrooms. The outcome of this study nevertheless appears promising with respect to the general approach being suggested for the study of this problem, and for its extension and expansion in a more programmatic fashion (to be outlined in the next section).

A PROGRAM OF RESEARCH ON THE PERCEPTUAL, COGNITIVE, AND AFFECTIVE COMPONENTS OF THE NATURE CONCEPT

Let us consider a possible comprehensive research program designed to reveal the origins and stimulus determinants of the concept of nature formed by an individual, along with the establishment of a superstructure of attitudes, values, and affective responses to nature. Such a program can be described as a two-pronged one.

The first component would investigate the concept in the adult person by examining the role of the various attributes of stimuli taken from the natural environment (referred to in the first part of this paper as essential ingredients of the concept.) Among the techniques available for this purpose are sorting techniques, such as Anglin (1977) has employed to advantage in similar work on the "animal" concept. This approach might start from clearly differentiated instances of the natural and the man-made domains to establish a nature versus man-made set, and then gradually move to abstracted stimuli of less clear referent or meaning (e.g., through line drawings) that exhibit the various features and dimensions postulated to pertain to the natural domain, singly and in combination, to determine their respective weight for the individual. To discover the character of the individual's cognitive representation of the concept, investigators could employ techniques such as that used by Carey (1978) in her work on the development of the concept of animal—focusing on the properties considered to be characteristic of diverse instances of the concept in question, and the narrowness or breadth displayed by the individual in allocating a given property to these instances. These approaches, along with that employed by Bruner, Goodnow, and Austin (1956) in their work on probabilistic concepts, would help to reveal the role played by specific stimulus properties of the environment in the concept of nature that individuals—both mature adults and developing children—exhibit. It would further elucidate the manner in which the individual deals with the "fuzzy set" character of this concept mentioned previously, as well as the handling of boundary cases of different kinds.

The vertical aspect of the problem (i.e., the status of nature as a concept unifying the animal, plant, and inorganic realms) would demand somewhat different approaches, based either on procedures devised to study abstract hierarchical concept formation (cf. Kofsky, 1966; Welch & Long, 1940) or, in a less formal sense, on techniques of clustering in recall (Worden, 1976) that reveal the degree to which horizontal and vertical organization among a domain of verbally designated objects affects the order of their recall in memory. The point of this phase of the research would be to determine the extent to which nature does in fact function as a concept binding together the three different realms mentioned above, and whether these three subordinate levels operate as coequals or have different weights attached to them.

A second component would address the connotative and affective aspects of the concept by comparing the location of the concept of nature in semantic-differential space to that of other concepts concerning the man-made realm of comparable generality (e.g., technology, culture, and architecture). Specific instances of the natural and man-made domains might further be presented pictorially, and similarly placed in semantic-differential space, in order to indicate the extent to which the nature concept represents an averaging process from the denotatively defined exemplars as opposed to a selective emphasis on certain types of environments. This same method lends itself to systematic comparisons among individuals and groups and thus to correlating differences in the meaning attached to the concept with differences in geographic experience, as well as other attributes of the individual and his or her culture.

Similar comparisons among different individuals could, of course, be undertaken in the first part of the program and should undoubtedly be carried out. It is this writer's hunch, however, that individual differences in the perceptual-cognitive area will turn out to be much less systematic and consistent than those in the attitude-value area.

This leads us, finally, to two interrelated points by way of conclusion. First, it is important to recognize that nature represents a very high-level abstraction, one that is made on the basis of quite diverse instances, and which undoubtedly occurs by means of a series of abstractions at lower levels. The nature concept, in other words, stands at the apex of a pyramid established on an intricate and rich substructure. This feature does not in the least militate against the potential value or plausibility of an approach to this problem that focuses on the stimulus ecology of the natural environment. It only serves to indicate that the role of particular stimulus properties is filtered through the layers of cognitive organization that constitute an individual's cognitive representation of the environment, both natural and man-made.

The second point is that the concept's cognitive, structural intricacy and level of abstraction probably serve to enhance the likelihood that a rich context of connotative associations will be connected with it, through which affective and evaluative responses to natural environments may be mediated or strengthened. It is undoubtedly that context that has provided the basis for the temptation to interpret response to the natural environment in terms of individual personality traits, cultural values, and the like. Yet, a stimulus-property focus need not be inappropriate or irrelevant to an analysis of individual or cultural differences in response to the natural environment. These should prove interpretable by recourse to such processes as selection and filtering. Furthermore, consistent relationships across individuals and groups between stimulus properties and affective or evaluative responses have been demonstrated repeatedly in the literature, as well as in this volume (see Chapter 3). But this affective component of man's response to the natural environment clearly deserves not only study in its own right, alongside a perceptual/cognitive focus, but it should be brought into direct relationship with such a focus. Here, if anywhere, an Aristotelian separation of cognition from emotion is surely amiss. Indeed, it may well be in the study of the interrelationships between the two that we can look for some of the most exciting developments in future research on this problem.

A FINAL COMMENT

It is well to remind ourselves that the analysis offered in this chapter of the concept of nature is written from the perspective of a psychologist who sees nature as one side of the environment to which people respond at all levels—from perception, to affect, to overt behavior. It is this perspective, coupled with this writer's particular preference towards an analysis of the environment in stimulus terms, that underlies the sharp differentiation between nature and the self made throughout this chapter.

In a larger sense, there is assuredly more to nature than something existing on the outside, for the person to contemplate and to respond to.

For a biologist, or even an ethologically or sociobiologically minded behavioral scientist, the human being is an integral part of nature, whose behavior is in principle subject to and analyzable as a natural process. This has led some (e.g., Iltis, 1973) to propose that *Homo sapiens* has through purely evolutionary forces become optimally adapted to a natural environment that conforms most nearly to the conditions under which the species evolved.

The argument is clearly subject to debate—not only do human beings seem to be able to thrive in highly artificial surroundings such as those of the space shuttle, but the success that psychologists have had in altering the fundamental nature of cognitive development in an animal species such as the chimpanzee by radical modification of its environmental experience should be sufficient to caution one against too blithe assumptions about the essentiality of a "natural" environment for survival. Yet, as Ulrich argues persuasively in Chapter 3, the evolutionary heritage of the individual may well underlie man's consistent preference for stimuli taken from the natural environment. *A fortiori* it may help to explain the "naturalness" of nature as a cognitive category, and the consistency with which it is differentiated from the domain of the nonnatural. However paradoxical it may seem, therefore, the insistence in the present analysis on a sharply articulated, externally based dichotomy between the natural and the man-made may derive added plausibility from the consideration that all of us, ultimately, form a functional part of the first, a part which perhaps will never be fully supplanted by the second.

REFERENCES

Anglin, J. M. *Word, object and conceptual development.* New York: Norton, 1977.

Bruner, J. S., Goodnow, J. J., & Austin, G. A. *A study of thinking.* New York: Wiley, 1956.

Brunswik, E. *Perception and the representative design of psychological experiments.* Berkeley: University of California Press, 1956.

Carey, S. *The child's concept of animal.* Paper presented at the meetings of the Psychonomic Society, San Antonio, 1978.

Cermak, G. W., & Cormillon, P. C. Multimensional analyses of judgments about traffic noise. *Journal of the Acoustical Society of America*, 1976, *59*, 1412–1420.

Dubos, R. *The God within.* New York: Scribners, 1972.

Gibson, E. J. *Principles of perceptual learning and development.* New York: Appleton-Century Crofts, 1969.

Gibson, J. J. *The perception of the visual world.* Boston: Houghton-Mifflin, 1950.

Gibson, J. J. *The senses considered as perceptual systems.* Boston: Houghton-Mifflin, 1966.

Gibson, J. J. *The ecological approach to visual perception.* Boston: Houghton-Mifflin, 1979.

Gibson, J. J., & Gibson, E. J. Perceptual learning: Differentiation or enrichment? *Psychological Review*, 1955, *62*, 32–41.

Glacken, C. H. *Traces on the Rhodian shore: Nature and culture in western thought from ancient times to the end of the eighteenth century.* Berkeley: University of California Press, 1967.

Hendee, J. C. Rural-urban differences reflected in outdoor recreation participation. *Journal of Leisure Research,* 1969, *1,* 333–341.

Holcomb, B. The perception of natural vs. built environments by young children. In *Children, nature, and the urban environment: Proceedings of a Symposium-Fair* (General Tech. Rep. NE-30). Upper Darby, Pa.: U.S. Forest Service Northeastern Experiment Station, 1977, pp. 33–38.

Iltis, H. Can one love a plastic tree? *Bulletin of the Ecological Society of America,* 1973, *54* (4), 5–7; 19.

Jackson, J. B. Ghosts at the door. *Landscape,* 1951, *1* (1), 3–9.

Kaplan, R. The green experience. In S. Kaplan & R. Kaplan (Eds.), *Humanscape.* North Scituate, Mass.: Duxbury Press, 1978, pp. 186–193.

Kaplan, S., Kaplan, R., & Wendt, J. S. Rated preference and complexity for natural and urban visual material. *Perception and Psychophysics,* 1972, *12,* 334–356.

Kluckhohn, F. R., & Strodtbeck, F. L. *Variations in value orientations.* Evanston, Ill.: Row-Peterson, 1961.

Kochen, M. Applications of fuzzy sets to psychology. In L. A. Zadeh *et al.* (Eds.), *Fuzzy sets and their applications to cognitive and decision processes.* New York: Academic Press, 1975, pp. 395–408.

Kofsky, E. A scalogram study of classificatory development. *Child Development,* 1966, *37,* 191–204.

Krieger, M. What's wrong with plastic trees? *Science,* 1973, *179,* 446–455.

Lowenthal, D., & Prince, H. C. Transcendental experience. In S. Wapner, B. Kaplan, & S. Cohen (Eds.), *Experiencing the environment.* New York: Plenum Press, 1976, pp. 117–132.

McKechnie, G. E. Simulation techniques in environmental psychology. In D. Stokols (Ed.), *Perspectives on environment and behavior.* New York: Plenum Press, 1978, pp. 169–190.

Mercer, D. C. Motivational and social aspects of recreational behavior. In I. Altman & J. F. Wohlwill (Eds.), *Human behavior and environment* (Vol. 1). New York: Plenum Press, 1976, pp. 123–162.

Oden, G. C. Integration of fuzzy logical information. *Journal of Experimental Psychology: Human Perception and Performance,* 1977, *3,* 565–575.

Porter, E. *The place no one knew: Glen Canyon on the Colorado.* San Francisco: Sierra Club, 1963.

Rosch, E. Natural categories. *Cognitive Psychology,* 1973, *4,* 328–350.

Rosch, E. Principles of categorization. In E. Rosch & B. B. Lloyd (Eds.), *Cognition and categorization.* Hillsdale, N.J.: Lawrence Erlbaum, 1978, pp. 28–48.

Rosch, E., & Lloyd, B. B. (Eds.). *Cognition and categorization.* Hillsdale, N.J.: Lawrence Erlbaum, 1978.

Rossman, B. B., & Ulehla, Z. J. Psychological reward values associated with wilderness use: A functional reinforcement approach. *Environment and Behavior,* 1977, *9,* 41–66.

Shepard, P. *Man in the landscape.* New York: Knopf, 1967.

Ullrich, J. R., & Ullrich, M. F. A multidimensional scaling analysis of perceived similarities of rivers in western Montana. *Perceptual and Motor Skills,* 1976, *43,* 575–584.

Wapner, S., Kaplan, B., & Cohen, S. An organismic-developmental perspective for understanding transactions of men in environments. *Environment and Behavior,* 1973, *5,* 255–289.

Ward, L. M. Multidimensional scaling of the molar physical environment. *Multivariate Behavioral Research*, 1977, *12*, 23–42.

Welch, L., & Long, L. The higher structural phases of concept formation in children. *Journal of Psychology*, 1940, *9*, 59–95.

Wohlwill, J. F. Environmental aesthetics: The environment as a source of affect. In I. Altman & J. F. Wohlwill (Eds.), *Human behavior and environment* (Vol. 1). New York: Plenum Press, 1976, pp. 37–86.

Wohlwill, J. F. *Visual assessment of an urban riverfront.* Unpublished manuscript, 1977.

Wohlwill, J. F. The place of order and uncertainty in art and environmental aesthetics. *Motivation and Emotion*, 1980, *4*, 133–142.

Worden, P. E. The effects of classification structure on organizational free recall in children. *Journal of Experimental Child Psychology*, 1976, *22*, 519–529.

Young, H. H., & Berry, G. L. The impact of environment on the productivity attitudes of intellectually challenged office workers. *Human Factors*, 1979, *21*, 399–407.

Zadeh, L. A., *et al.* (Eds.). *Fuzzy sets and their applications to cognitive and decision processes.* New York: Academic Press, 1975.

2

Methodological Issues in the Assessment of Landscape Quality

TERRY C. DANIEL and JOANNE VINING

INTRODUCTION

The purpose of this chapter is to provide an overview of contemporary landscape–quality assessment methods. Several reviews of the pertinent literature are available (Arthur, Daniel, & Boster, 1977; Brush, 1976; Fabos, 1971; Feimer, 1983; Palmer, 1981; Redding, 1973; Wohlwill, 1976). However, research and application in landscape assessment is a very active field and new issues and methods appear frequently. Furthermore, the field has matured to a point where several different underlying conceptual models can be identified as a means for organizing and evaluating the growing number of specific methods and techniques.

The approach taken in this chapter is to define several landscape assessment "models" or conceptual approaches that interrelate specific methods. No individual method is discussed in detail, but several methods are cited and described to exemplify features of the various assessment models. Because the underlying conceptual model is rarely made explicit, assignment to the different conceptual categories frequently must be inferred from explicit characteristics of the individual methods

---

TERRY C. DANIEL and JOANNE VINING • Department of Psychology, University of Arizona, Tucson, Arizona 85721.

and their applications. As with any classification scheme, not all methods can be neatly categorized and no method completely adheres to any one model. Still, classification is useful in providing an overview of the options in landscape–assessment methods and in identifying common and distinguishing features of the various techniques.

Within a classification, models tend to share basic assumptions and goals, even though they may differ somewhat in the specific techniques that they employ. Criticism of assessment methods must consider these underlying conceptual frameworks; different goals and assumptions must be taken into account.

Evaluation of approaches can be based on general criteria that have traditionally been applied to measurement systems of all kinds (Craik & Feimer, 1979; Daniel, 1976; Feimer, Smarden, & Craik, 1981). A primary requirement is *reliability*, usually gauged in terms of the agreement or consistency in measures obtained from one application of a method to another. Balancing the reliability criterion is the requirement that a measurement method also be *sensitive* to changes in the relevant properties of that which is being measured. A good landscape–quality assessment method is one that achieves a balance between reliability and sensitivity. Given this balance, the next consideration is *validity*. A method must not only provide reliable and sensitive measures, but the measures must reflect changes in the property that the system purports to measure. This criterion has high intuitive appeal—a landscape–quality assessment method should measure landscape quality—but it is often very difficult to test the validity of a measurement method, especially when the property being measured is not clearly defined. In such situations, validation is usually approached by comparing different measures provided by independent applications of different methods to the same objects. If two or more independent assessments agree, each gains some support for its validity. Validation of a landscape–quality assessment method is a continuous process, and no single "test" can confirm or disprove a method's validity. Perhaps the best that a method could achieve is the consensus of researchers and practitioners that the method measures "landscape quality."

In addition to meeting the reliability, sensitivity, and validity criteria, landscape–quality assessments should provide measures that are useful. *Utility* of a method is usually gauged in terms of efficiency and generality. Efficient methods provide precise, reliable measures with relatively low costs in time, materials and equipment, and personnel. Generality refers to the extent to which a method can be applied successfully, with minor modifications, to a wide range of landscape–quality assessment problems. Utility is of obvious importance for methods that have been developed in a practical, applied context. However, even methods claiming a basic theoretical motivation must meet utility criteria; the ultimate goal of all scientific research and theory construction is to meet human/social needs. Another important utility factor is the extent to which landscape–quality measures can be integrated with other relevant environmental quality measures. Measures of landscape quality should be systematically related to physical/biological and social features of the environment so that accurate predictions of the implications of environmental change can be made (Arthur *et al.*, 1977; Wohlwill, 1976). These relationships are essential to guiding the management of landscape resources.

Measures of landscape quality should also be systematically related to other human social values. Landscape assessments cannot be taken as direct or absolute measures of social value, but must be amenable to some separate *valuation process* that allows combinations, comparisons, and trade-offs with other social values (Daniel & Zube, 1979). In the case of commodity resources, the valuation mechanism is typically some market system, often accompanied by sociopolitical perturbations. No similar valuing system exists for aesthetic (amenity or noncommodity) resources. For commodities and for landscape–quality identification, location, amount, and grade must be assessed before value or worth can be determined. These prerequisites to valuation are the proper focus of landscape–quality assessment methods.

LANDSCAPE QUALITY

Before discussing models of landscape–quality assessment, it is useful to further define the goals of these assessment systems. There is a tendency to ask too much of landscape–quality measurements. Often *landscape quality* is defined as including a wide array of environmental/ecological, sociocultural, and psychological factors. The term *landscape* clearly focuses upon the *visual* properties of the environment[1]— thus biological functions, cultural/historical values, wildlife and endangered species, wilderness values, opportunities for recreation activities, and a large array of tastes, smells, and feelings are not included. This is not to say that these factors are not important to the quality of the human environment, but they must be assessed and considered separately from landscape quality. Interrelationships or interactions among

---

[1]Landscape: "an expanse of natural scenery seen by the eye in one view." (*Webster's New World Dictionary*, 2nd College Edition).

these factors and landscape quality can be investigated and used to determine the larger array of human values associated with a given land area.

Having stated what landscape quality is not, there is still considerable ambiguity regarding what landscape quality is. As mentioned above, it is clear that visual properties of the land are relevant, but concern is with the quality of the landscape. In dictionary definitions and in landscape–assessment practice there are two distinct meanings for the term *quality:*

1. Any of the features that make something (a landscape) what it is; characteristic elements; attributes
2. The degree of excellence which a thing (a landscape) possesses

Some assessments focus on the first definition, seeking to determine the *character* of the landscape. In many respects, this amounts only to a taxonomic procedure—labeling landscape types and identifying elements or properties that define each type. Landscape taxonomies may be necessary and worthwhile, as when the preservation of unique cultural or biological resources is at issue, but character typing does not provide distinctions among landscapes with regard to excellence. The second definition of quality seems closer to the intent of legislation such as the National Environmental Policy Act of 1969, which seeks in part to "assure for all Americans esthetically pleasing surroundings." The concern is to protect and enhance the aesthetic value, or *beauty,* of the landscape, that aspect which gives "pleasure to the senses." The implication for landscape assessment is that landscapes should be located along a quality dimension, with some landscapes being more beautiful (or providing more pleasure to the senses) than others. Landscape–quality assessment, then, involves systematic assignment of numbers to landscape instances so that at least ordinal excellence relationships are indicated.

The landscape–quality dimension has been variously labeled as "scenic quality" (Daniel, Wheeler, Boster, & Best, 1973; Zube, 1974), "visual attractiveness" (Brush, 1979), "visual quality" (USDA, 1974), "aesthetic quality" (Feimer *et al.*, 1981), and "landscape preference" (Buhyoff & Wellman, 1978). Daniel and Boster (1976) considered these alternatives and concluded that "scenic beauty" best labeled the landscape–quality dimension that motivates environmental policy and public-land management. Brush (1976) cited the importance of a conceptual distinction between "preferential judgments" and "comparative appraisals" of landscape quality. The former emphasize personal likes and dislikes regarding landscapes while the latter emphasize social conventions and consensus. Craik and Zube (1976) make the same distinction but emphasize that comparative appraisals require comparisons of landscapes relative to some standard of excellence. While the distinction between personal preferences and comparative appraisals may be conceptually clear, empirical studies have not found significant differences in landscape assessments based on these two approaches (Buhyoff, Arndt, & Probst, 1981; Daniel & Boster, 1976; Zube, Pitt, & Anderson, 1975). In part, the failure to find differences may be attributed to the characteristically high consensus among observers, regardless of which orientation is given, when evaluations of reasonably restricted sets of natural landscapes are required. Moreover, as long as a quality distinction (by the second definition) is to be made, neither approach can avoid basing landscape assessments on human, subjective value judgments (Daniel, 1976).

Landscape–quality assessment thus seeks to determine the relative location of different landscapes along a dimension of scenic beauty. Some landscapes will "give pleasure to the eye" more than others. Because human subjective judgment is unavoidable in assessments of landscape quality, a relevant question is whose judgments are to be followed. Historical standards, expert standards, contemporary public standards, or estimates of the standards of future populations are all options. When there is high consensus across different populations, choices among standards are of little importance. When opinions diverge, some negotiation, compromise, or trade-off would seem to be required. Whatever referent population is chosen, landscape–quality assessment requires that human aesthetic standards be applied to evaluate the visual impression made by a landscape.

LANDSCAPE–ASSESSMENT MODELS

There are dozens of landscape–assessment techniques and methods currently in use or available for use. Some are suited only to very particular applications, others are much more general. These methods can be classified in many ways. They vary in *scope* from site-specific models to regional scale assessments. They are based on expert judgment and user-based models. The classification scheme adopted in this chapter organizes methods according to features of underlying conceptual models—models that represent different assumptions about the relevant properties of the landscape and different choices regarding relevant aesthetic standards.

For purposes of this chapter, five conceptual models have been identified: (1) Ecological, (2) Formal Aesthetic, (3) Psychophysical, (4) Psychological, and (5) Phenomenological.

A very similar classification of landscape–quality assessment methods has been developed independently by Zube and his associates (Zube, Sell, & Taylor, 1982). In their system, ecological and formal aesthetic methods are combined into an expert judgment category, and psychological methods are labeled as cognitive approaches. Otherwise, methods are categorized as in this chapter, indicating some degree of validity for both classification schemes.

Each model is described in general terms, and several specific methods are briefly described to illustrate features of each conceptual approach. The methods based on each model are generally evaluated by reference to the criteria for assessment systems: reliability and sensitivity, validity, and utility. The implications of each approach for the separate process of valuation are also discussed.

ECOLOGICAL MODEL

Much of the concern for scenic beauty and other aesthetic or amenity resources grew out of a more general concern for the protection and preservation of the natural environment. The environmental movement was motivated in part by alarm over degradation of the physical/biological environment. Human-caused pollution of the air and water, and careless development of the land were seen as threatening the integrity of the natural ecosystem. Often pleas for environmental safeguards were justified in terms of human welfare; an environment that endangers the survival of wildlife species may ultimately be unfit to support human life as well. Frequently, however, environmental protection efforts were motivated by a belief in the intrinsic value of the natural ecosystem, an ecosystem defined so that humans their developments are viewed as external, disruptive elements.

Many contemporary landscape–assessment methods preserve the heritage of the environmental movement. "Natural" amenities are most often the object of landscape assessments and "naturalness" is very frequently an important evaluative dimension. Methods based on the ecological model (e.g., Leopold, 1969b; McHarg, 1967) place primary emphasis on naturalness. As a group, these methods tend to define the aesthetic quality of the landscape in biological terms, and they generally treat any evidence of human influence as a negative aesthetic factor.

Assessments are usually carried out by an expert who is typically trained in ecology or some other branch of the biological sciences. Emphasis is on the classification and mapping of land areas in terms of their ecological classes or functions (e.g., riparian zones, edges, grasslands). Premiums are frequently assigned for areas that are classed as "critical environments" (such as bird-nesting areas and estuaries) or as being high in "ecological diversity." Human elements, ranging from litter to bridges and homes are typically assigned negative values. The impact of management or development on aesthetic values are assessed in terms of the degree of disturbance of, or conflict with, natural elements. By the ecological approach, landscape quality is anchored at the high end by pure ecosystems, undisturbed by humans. The low end of the scale is defined by landscapes evidencing disruptive, incompatible human developments. Distinctions between natural environments at the high end of the scale may be based upon ecological constructs such as diversity, biomass production, habitat classification, or successional stage. Within human-influenced environments, distinctions are based on the amount and visibility of human impact; the closer a development approximates an undisturbed natural environment, the more aesthetically acceptable it becomes. Some distinctions are based upon qualitative judgments regarding the appropriateness of a development; despite equivalent physical impacts, a hiking trail may be evaluated as having less negative aesthetic effect than a pipeline.

EXAMPLE

Leopold's (1969b) "uniqueness ratio" illustrates a landscape–assessment methodology based primarily on ecological measures of the landscape. Leopold begins with the explicit philosophical assumption that a unique landscape is of more significance to society than a common one. Whether this assumption is based on intuitions about human value systems or on some biological notion about gene pools is not clear. In any case, the uniqueness of a given landscape is defined by multiple physical, biological, and human-use dimensions that reflect the implicit assumption that aesthetic value is primarily a function of ecological criteria.

Using river landscapes in several western states, Leopold and Marchand (1968; Leopold, 1969a, 1969b) developed a uniqueness index of landscape quality. This index is constructed from individual uniqueness ratio values on 46 component dimensions. These dimensions are classified into three larger summary headings. The physical category includes factors such as water depth and velocity and riverbank erosion. Biological factors include water turbidity and algal or faunal content. The human-use and interest category is the most diverse, including ecological measures such as environmental degradation and recovery rates, and perceptual measures such as extent or diversity of view. Each of the 46 component factors is measured or estimated with a five-point rating scale. Some factors have continuous rating scales and some are categorical. While Leopold maintains that these measures and estimates are free of personal preference or bias, some reflect a substantial degree of subjective judgment. For example, extent of trash is measured by type and frequency per 100 feet of river, while the water condition measurement scale ranges from "none" to "overused."

Uniqueness ratios are calculated by comparing the individual scale value for a site with the frequency of values in that category for all sites under consideration. For example, if a factor for a particular site falls into the third category on the rating scale and the overall frequency for that category is 10, then the uniqueness ratio for that factor and site is 1/10 or .10. High uniqueness does not necessarily indicate high aesthetic value. In a comparison of several Idaho rivers, Leopold (1969a) found a high uniqueness index for the Little Salmon River, which he described as sluggish, shallow, and algae infested. Because the uniqueness index may reflect extremes of pollution or degradation as well as more positive values, its meaning for a given site must be interpreted in the context of the other sites with which it is compared. Individual uniqueness ratios range from $1/N$, where N is the total number of sites, to 1.0, and reflect the relative frequency of site evaluation on a given factor. Uniqueness ratios on individual factors may be combined to form composite indices for physical, biological, and human-use summary categories or to compute an overall uniqueness index for a specific site. Compared sites are typically rank-ordered in terms of overall uniqueness.

The overall uniqueness index for a specific site is constructed by adding uniqueness ratios for the 46 component factors. Leopold (1969a) noted that this index does not reflect the importance or weight of individual factors. "Unweighted" summing implies equal weights for all factors, however, and represents a weighting or importance scheme that is no less free of subjective judgment than any other scheme. Because 40 of the 46 individual factors are "ecological," while only 6 could be classified as "visual or scenic beauty" factors, overall uniqueness is largely determined by scores on the ecological factors.

A site can be evaluated in terms of a particular criterion, such as scenic attractiveness. Factors judged to be relevant to the selected dimension must be identified and then synthesized using multidimensional translations until a final criterion scale value is obtained. Thus uniqueness indices may be used to evaluate differences across sites on aesthetic or scenic factors or any other factor or combination of factors.

The more typical procedure, however, has been to rely on the overall uniqueness index.

Reliability and Sensitivity

Because the ecological model typically relies on expert judgment, reliability depends on the consistency and accuracy of the individual applying the method. Direct reliability testing could be accomplished by having a number of experts independently assess the same landscape areas, but this has not been done. Perhaps it is expected that biological classifications will be applied consistently by appropriately trained experts, but this may not be a completely safe assumption. Furthermore, the required classification and evaluation of human influences on the landscape would seem to be even more open to idiosyncratic judgment and disagreement among individual experts. To date, there is no direct evidence of the reliability of landscape–assessment methods based on the ecological model.

The sensitivity of these methods is also difficult to determine, in part because the results of the method usually depend upon categorical or ordinal classifications of spatially delineated land areas. Also, applications have generally been tailored to specific areas and projects (e.g., the effects of a dam on a particular river system). It is therefore difficult to ascertain the ability of these methods to distinguish between environments or to differentially assess the relative impacts of alternative developments. Certainly ecological methods are more sensitive in distinguishing between natural and human-influenced environments than in making distinctions within either of those classes.

Validity

A major underlying assumption of the ecological model is that landscape quality is directly related to naturalness, or ecosystem integrity. This assumption has not been subjected to any direct test, and such a test may be difficult or impossible to perform. If public perception and aesthetic judgment are accepted as reasonable criteria for assessing landscape quality, the ecological assumption gains some support from the tendency for natural areas to be preferred over built or developed areas (Brush & Palmer, 1979; R. Kaplan, 1975). On the other hand, Daniel *et al.* (1973) found that forest areas recognized as being managed were judged as more scenically attractive than forests in wilderness areas. The ecological assumption requires very specific relationships, such as a direct correlation between measures of ecological diversity or integrity and landscape quality. Although these relationships have not been investigated, they are crucial to the validity of the ecological model.

Utility

Ecological methods could be very efficient, since biological assessments made for other purposes might be directly incorporated for use in landscape–quality assessments. If biological analysis shows that a development will destroy critical wildlife habitats and reduce species diversity, these same factors can be added as negative components for landscape quality with no further analysis. Of course, this redundancy in assessments could lead to a "double counting" of biological concerns, while visual aesthetic values, to the extent that they are not directly determined by ecological measures, would be undercounted. Assumptions regarding the relationship between landscape quality and ecological values are again critical but untested.

A major factor affecting the utility of ecological methods of landscape assessment is their relative lack of sensitivity in distinguishing among alternative human developments or environmental manipulations. If the alternatives for land management are to manipulate or not manipulate the enviornment, the ecological models will almost invariably indicate against any manipulation. More often, of course, the question for managers is *how* to manipulate, in which case the ecological models will favor doing as little as possible to alter the environment.

Valuation

Ecological assessments of the landscape have several implications for human values. Natural ecosystems could be viewed as having intrinsic value, that is, they are valued separately from any reference to other social values or human welfare. The validity of this approach is not subject to empirical or scientific analysis; rather, it would have to be approached from a moral philosophical perspective. Alternatively, the value of natural (critical or diverse) environments may be based on the long-range health and welfare of the human race. Confirmation or disconfirmation of this basis for natural landscape values could be approached scientifically, as by longitudinal studies of persons living in different environments that vary in terms of their ecologically relevant characteristics. Even if their health values were confirmed, however, they might not provide an appropriate basis for the value of landscape quality or scenic beauty. Health benefits of natural environments might be derived from many factors other than scenic quality.

As a third approach, it might be argued that people find natural places and undisturbed ecosystems to be scenically attractive and that scenic value can be gauged in the context of other human desires. This interpretation, however, would be more consistent with psychophysical or psychological models that would apply perceptual assessment methods to determine how strongly and extensively these values are held in the human population. By this approach, natural landscape values would be placed in the relative context of other human values (security, comfort, entertainment, etc.) allowing trade-offs and cost–benefit considerations. An important implication is that, in principle, it may be possible for human-designed and built environments to equal or exceed the value of natural environments. That is, there is no assumption of an inherent superiority of natural landscapes; thus, managed or built environments might be able to duplicate or improve upon the positive features of natural environments.

FORMAL AESTHETIC MODEL

The most widely used methods for landscape–quality assessment have been developed within the design traditions of architects and landscape architects. A basic tenet of the formal aesthetic model is that aesthetic value is inherent in the abstract features of the landscape. More specifically, aesthetic quality resides in the *formal* properties of the landscape. These properties are defined as basic forms, lines, colors and textures and their interrelationships. Expert judgments of the variety, harmony, unity and contrast among the basic landscape elements are the principal determinants of aesthetic value. These abstract aesthetic determinants are assumed to transcend different landscapes and landscape types and to transcend individual and cultural differences among landscape observers. This analysis is assumed equally applicable to natural and human-influenced landscapes, individual landscape scenes and regional landscape types, forests, deserts, jungles, and oceans. The abstract elements are taken to be aesthetic universals.

The formal aesthetic model approaches all landscape–assessment problems in essentially the same way. Landscapes are first analyzed into their formal abstract properties, such as forms, lines, textures, and colors. The relationships among these elements are then inspected to classify each landscape area or scene. The emphasis is upon classifying each area in terms of variety, unity, integrity, or other complex formal characteristics. This analysis requires formal training, so the method is almost always applied by an expert, typically a landscape architect. The landscape architect may use photography, maps of topography, vegetation and water features, or direct visual inspection, but it is left to his or her trained judgment to ascertain the relevant formal features and interrelationships represented by the landscape. Other factors, such as visual access to the area, number of viewers, and "intent" of viewers (e.g., recreators and sightseers vs. commuters) may all modify the final classifications, but the formal classifications determine landscape quality. A roughly ordinal classification results with monotonous landscapes in the lowest category and landscapes exhibiting greater contrast and variety of features in the highest category. The positive effects of variety and contrast may be tempered by the requirement of some level of integrity, unity, or harmony.

The effects of human influences are assessed in the same formal terms, with the emphasis on the contrast or harmony of the formal elements of a human effect with those of the natural surroundings. Again, the relative contrast or harmony must be judged by an expert trained to analyze the landscape's basic forms, lines, textures, and colors. Contrasting structures may increase the scenic quality of a monotonous landscape. On the other hand, landscapes already exhibiting higher levels of variety and contrast may be damaged scenically by the introduction of a strongly contrasting feature.

Example

The Visual Management System (VMS) is a methodology that has been developed with the expressed purpose of evaluating scenic resources within a land–management framework (USDA, 1974). Based on a system developed by Litton (1968), VMS assumes that scenic quality is directly related to landscape diversity or variety. The VMS method assesses and maps landscape quality through a categorical classification system. Landscape classification schemes are based on land character, distance from the viewer, and visual variety. VMS is typically employed by a landscape architect who evaluates and maps a particular area as an aid to land managers.

Scenic-quality assessment involves the classification and mapping of variety class and sensitivity level within a character type. Character type denotes the broad distinguishing visual characteristics of the land. The four major character subtypes are gorge lands, steep mountain lands, foothill lands, and rolling plateaus. Thus, character type focuses upon the general distinguishing properties or "qualities" (by definition one) of the landscape.

A more important classification, and the heart of VMS, is the variety classification. The three variety classes are based on visual assessment of the landscape with respect to diversity of form, line, color, and texture. Variety class A is the "distinctive" category into which areas with the greatest diversity of visual features would be classified. Class B areas have features which are common or not unusual within the character type. An area classified in the C category would have minimal diversity of form, line, color, or texture. Variety classification is possible for water as well as land forms.

Sensitivity level, the third major VMS category system, refers to the relative importance of the landscape as a visual or recreational resource. Sensitivity level incorporates the distance from and context in which the landscape will most often be viewed, providing a sort of weighting system for visual importance. Sensitivity level 1 includes any area that can be seen from a primary travel route (water, land, or air) for which scenic quality is a major concern for at least one quarter of all viewers. Level 2 areas are those along primary routes where less than one quarter of all viewers would have major concern for visual quality, or secondary routes of major visual importance. Level 3 incorporates secondary routes where scenic quality is of minor importance.

The landscape architect employing VMS to assess landscape quality prepares a composite map of variety classes and sensitivity levels to determine management recommendations, which, like the other phases of the system, are stated categorically. Each land area is classified for *preservation, retention, partial retention, modification,* or *maximum modification.* "Visual Quality Objectives" are directly defined by the composite of sensitivity level and variety class. For example, an area that is classified in variety class A and is in the foreground, midground, or background of a sensitivity level 1 view will be assigned the retention objective. The visual quality objectives imply an ordering from high (preservation, retention) to low (modification, maximum modification) landscape quality.

EVALUATION

Reliability and Sensitivity

As for any expert judgment method, reliability of the formal aesthetic methods must be gauged in terms of agreement between independent experts or between different applications by the same expert. A straightforward approach would have several landscape architects independently assess the same landscape and then compare their resulting classifications. The literature reveals no instance in which such a test has been applied in moderate or large-scale studies. There have been several studies of agreement between landscape architects in the assessment of individual scenes, usually represented by color slide or photographs, with mixed results.

Arthur (1977) presented slides of ponderosa pine forest scenes to professional and student landscape architects. Each independently rated the scenes on a series of scales that included contrast, unity, variety, and other formal landscape elements. Comparison of ratings among landscape architects showed reasonably good agreement with a few exceptions. These data are only partially supportive of the formal aesthetic model, since Arthur's study was somewhat artificially constrained. All observers saw the same slides and were required to express their judgments in a precise quantitative format (a five-point rating scale). These factors may have led to greater agreement than could be achieved in the much less constrained "field" situation, where individual experts assess relatively large heterogeneous land areas. Also, reliability was expressed in terms of overall (average) panel agreement, not in terms of rater-to-rater agreement on an individual basis.

A more recent assessment of agreement between independent applications of formal aesthetic methods has been reported by Feimer et al. (1981). University students were given a two-hour training session to familiarize them with landscape-rating procedures following the Bureau of Land Management's Visual Resource and Impact Assessment Systems. They then rated a number of landscape scenes on dimensions that included color, form, line, and texture, as well as complexity, intactness, unity and vividness. A global rating of scenic beauty was also obtained. Pairs of scenes depicted various landscapes before and after human modification. Rater reliability coefficients varied depending upon the rating dimension, but all coefficients were low (ranging from .05 for line/postimpact to .49 for complexity/preimpact). "Contrast ratings," where observers judged the extent to which landscape modifications changed the values represented by the unmodified scenes, had lower reliability than "direct ratings" of the separate scenes. Feimer and his colleagues point out that these are individual rater reliabilities and that aggregating the ratings of 10 independent judges greatly improves the reliability of all scales. Of course, formal aesthetic methods typically employ only a single expert for any assessment.

It might be argued that the poor reliability levels found by Feimer et al. were due to the use of inadequately trained college students, rather than experienced professionals. Their study did, however, include BLM professional staff members and a sample of 41 United States Forest Service landscape architects. Intra-rater reliability was not significantly better for the professional panels. As with the Arthur (1977) study, Feimer and his associates imposed a number of constraints not found in actual applications of these landscape–assessment methods. Direct field applications at an operational scale would very likely yield even less argeement in results between individual experts.

The sensitivity of the formal aesthetic methods is necessarily limited by the categorical nature of the assessment. Landscapes are generally classed into one of three (or sometimes four) general categories depending upon their formal characteristics. These categories are roughly ordinal, yielding a high, medium, and low type of scenic quality classification, with most areas falling into the medium category (such as variety class B or partial retention in VMS). As a result, these methods do not make very fine distinctions between different landscape modifications.

In light of the rater reliability problems discussed above, it is clear that sensitivity and reliability should be assessed both in terms of agreement from one landscape architect to another and in terms of the consistency of assignment of landscape areas to different quality classes. Neither of these evaluation bases have been explored to any significant extent.

Validity

Unless an assessment method is sensitive and reliable, it can not achieve an acceptable level of validity. Even if the formal aesthetic methods were found to be reliable and sensitive, however, there are several questions that must be addressed regarding their validity as landscape–quality assessment methods. One question concerns whether the analysis of the landscape into a set of abstract formal elements captures all of the aesthetically relevant aspects of the landscape. That is, do form, line, color, and texture and their interrelationships, harmony, variety, contrast, unity, etc., exhaust the set of scenically relevant characteristics of the landscape? A related question focuses upon the nature of the relationship between expert assessments of formal properties and landscape scenic quality. The model assumes, and the methods imply, that the relationship is direct—the formal properties, especially variety, determine the landscape quality. But variety, in the form of contrasting lines, textures, forms, and colors can be added to a landscape in a way that is clearly not aesthetic. Unity can be achieved by a consistency of features that produces monotony. Perhaps more complex qualifications are needed, such as *harmonious variety*, or *unity with variety*. In any event, the relationship of these formal elements to aesthetic value or scenic quality must be more precisely specified and tested.

Several studies provide evidence of the validity of formal aesthetic landscape assessments. All these studies have compared expert (landscape architects) judgments of variety (or related dimensions such as unity or complexity) or global judgments of scenic quality with general public panels' judgments of scenic beauty. Color-slide representations of landscape scenes were used in all of these studies. Correspondence between landscape architects' judgments and public judgments have ranged from moderate (Arthur, 1977; Craik, 1972; Daniel & Boster, 1976; Zube, 1973, 1974; Zube *et al.*, 1975) to very low (Buhyoff, Wellman, Harvey, & Fraser, 1978). Even these low levels of agreement were achieved only by comparing the combined (averaged) judgments of a number of experts with the judgments of groups of public observers. Feimer *et al.* (1981) correlated the change in a panel of Forest Service landscape architect's ratings of formal properties of landscape scenes before and after modification with changes in the same panel's global judgments of scenic beauty before and after modification. Changes in rated compatibility, congruity, form, and intactness all showed substantial positive correlations with changes in scenic beauty for Forest Service panels, but not for BLM panels. Other rating dimensions (e.g., color, line, texture, unity, complexity, vividness) did not show significant correlations with scenic beauty judgments. The significant correlations were between a panel of landscape architect ratings of the formal elements and the same panel's ratings of scenic beauty made at the same time. Thus, as a group, landscape architects' ratings of some formal elements do correspond somewhat with *their own* ratings of scenic beauty for an identical set of color-slide simulated landscapes. Some features do not correlate for any panel, and none correlate for every panel.

The validity of formal aesthetic landscape assessments is still open to question. At least, the assumed direct relationship between expert judgments of formal landscape properties and some independent measure of landscape scenic quality has not been proven.

Utility

The principal evidence of the utility of the formal aesthetic methods is that they are so widely in use. The Forest Service, the Bureau of Land Management, and a large number of private and semipublic agencies routinely assess landscape quality by means of formal aesthetic methods. Although the reliability, sensitivity, and validity of these methods has not been demonstrated, they do offer the potential advantage of economy. Rather large-scale landscape assessments can be accomplished by one or two qualified landscape architects. Much of the data needed for these assessments (e.g., topographic maps, aerial photos, and vegetation maps) are collected in the context of other studies associated with the same project. Because the landscape architect is generally a regular staff member, the assessment can be done in-house, avoiding the costs of consultants and outside contracts. Perhaps another factor is that over the past 10 years agencies and managers have become familiar and somewhat comfortable with these methods.

Though widely used, the formal aesthetic methods do have some important disadvantages. A major shortcoming is the lack of sensitivity in the assessment; outcomes are typically restricted to only three or four roughly ordered categories of landscape quality. Furthermore, the greatest majority of any landscape area will almost always be classified as being moderate in quality, and the method provides no formal means for distinguishing among landscapes within that broad category. When combined with assessments of visual sensitivity (or importance), still only general categories or "management objectives" result. These categories offer only very general guidelines for management actions. This lack of specification may be viewed as either a disadvantage or an asset, depending upon the motives of the manager/decisionmaker who must respond to the assessment. In any event, the implications for management actions are often stated in terms of formal elements (e.g., "basic lines and textures must be retained"), requiring that the landscape architect serve as an interpreter of the aesthetic assessment throughout the management process.

Perhaps the most serious question regarding the utility of formal aesthetic methods concerns their validity. How well do these landscape assessments reflect "true" aesthetic/scenic values of the landscape? There is some question whether landscape architects agree with each other in their assessments and even more question regarding the relationship between these assessments and public preference and appreciation. Public preference may not be the sole criterion for landscape–quality assessment, but continued use of formal aesthetic methods for assessing and managing the public landscape without some resolution of the reliability and validity issues is difficult to justify.

Valuation

The Formal Aesthetic Model takes no particular position on the question of valuing scenic resources. There is some indication, if the visual quality objectives of VMS, for example, are assumed to be fixed constraints on management, that aesthetic properties of the landscape are intrinsically valuable; that is, changes between quality categories are not permitted regardless of other social costs or benefits. Although there may be considerable room for management variations within a visual quality category (e.g., partial retention), there seems to be no specified way to negotiate between categories.

Because the landscape–quality assessment results in ordered categories, and not in cardinal or interval measures, it is difficult to relate these assessments to economic or trade-off types of valuation processes. Actions that result in landscape changes within a category must be assumed to have equal aesthetic benefits or costs, even if they differ in economic or other costs and benefits. Changes that result in a different landscape–quality classification produce stepwise changes in aesthetic benefits, but these steps are of unspecified magnitude. Thus, valuing landscape quality relative to other social values is rather restricted.

PSYCHOPHYSICAL MODEL

Classical psychophysics (e.g., Fechner, 1860/1966) sought to establish precise quantitative relationships between physical features of environmental stimuli and human perceptual responses. The emphasis was upon simple stimuli such as lights, sounds, or objects that were varied on a single dimension such as brightness, loudness, or weight. The response of the observer/judge was also constrained to a simple choice, yes–no judgment, rating, or numerical estimate based upon perception of the relevant properties of stimuli presented. Contemporary psychophysical methods have focused upon articulating functional relationships for a broader range of physical stimuli and psychological responses.

Psychophysical methods of landscape assessment seek to determine mathematical relationships between the physical characteristics of the landscape and the perceptual judgments of human observers. Landscape assessments are based on the reactions of persons representative of visitors to and viewers of the landscape. The relationships of interest are those between physical features of the environment (e.g., topography, vegetation, water, etc.) and psychological responses (typically judgments of preference, aesthetic value, or scenic beauty). Efforts may focus on a single dimension of landscape variation, such as area of insect damage to a forest (Buhyoff & Leuschner, 1978), or may encompass any landscape variations that contribute to explaining or predicting human perceptual responses (e.g., Arthur, 1977). Relevant landscape variables may be defined in photographic terms, such as areas of a picture covered by sky, trees, and water (Shafer, Hamilton, & Schmidt, 1969), or in terms of "manageable features," such as trees per acre less than 20 inches in diameter, pounds per acre of grass, and cubic feet of downed wood (Daniel & Schroder, 1979). Observer perceptions may be expressed in any of several ways; paired-comparison choices (Buhyoff & Wellman, 1978), rating scales of various kinds (Brush, 1979; Daniel & Boster, 1976), Q-sorts (Pitt & Zube, 1979), rank orders (Shafer & Brush, 1977) or magnitude estimates (Buhyoff et al., 1981). Applying appropriate scaling models in each case, measures of perception should not change as a function of the method of expressing judgments. Data from several studies confirm this theoretical expectation (Daniel & Boster, 1976; Pitt & Zube, 1979; Hull & Buhyoff, 1981).

Psychophysical methods have been applied with increasing frequency in recent years, both as a research tool and in practical settings. The majority of applications do not carry the analysis to the point of specifying a psychophysical function. In many cases landscape settings are simply scaled in terms of percent choice or average rating and their physical characteristics are described in general terms. More complete applications include formal transformations of choice or rating responses to standardized interval scale values and specification of a unidimensional or multidimensional relationship between the perceptual scale and specified physical features of the landscape. Relationships are typically derived by an empirical process, although the candidate landscape features may reflect a priori theoretical or practical objectives. The analysis of the landscape can be very molar (landscape type, land use, general topography) or very molecular (number per acre of ponderosa pines between 5 and 9 inches in diameter). The choice of analytic methods and landscape descriptor variables will determine the components of any resulting psychophysical model.

The psychological (perceptual) response is usually limited to a single dimension, with scenic quality, scenic beauty, or landscape preference the most often employed. Other dimensions can and have been used, including perceived naturalness or, conversely, evidence of human disturbance (Daniel et al., 1973) or the fittingness of a development to its surroundings (Wohlwill, 1979).

Multiple observers are generally employed with the assessed value for any given landscape being determined by some form of average response for the observer panel. The number of landscape scenes evaluated by each observer depends upon the response-indicator method used; paired-comparison and ranking methods allow relatively few scenes to be assessed (usually no more than 10 or 15), while rating scales and magnitude estimation allow for considerably more (100 to 150 per observer). Observer samples are generally taken from the "general public" or students, but the selection is usually by convenience rather than by a formal random-sampling procedure. Frequently "special interest" or particular user groups are employed as a means of determining cross-group consistency in assessed landscape quality (e.g., Daniel & Boster, 1976; Zube, 1974).

The goal of the psychophysical methods is to develop models that provide accurate and reliable predictions of persons' perceptions of landscape quality based on objective measures of the physical features of the landscape. When this goal is achieved, the need for direct assessments of landscapes by observer panels will decrease. The development of sufficiently precise and reliable psychophysical models would allow estimation (prediction) of human landscape perceptions based only on a direct measurement of the relevant physical features of the landscape in question.

EXAMPLE

Daniel and his associates (Anderson, 1981; Arthur, 1977; Daniel & Boster, 1976; Daniel et al., 1973; Daniel, Anderson, Schroeder, & Wheeler, 1977; Schroeder & Daniel, 1980, 1981) have developed and tested a psychophysical method for assessing the scenic beauty of forest landscapes. This method has been applied to measure differences in the scenic consequences of alternative forest watershed treatments, harvest prescriptions, and downed-wood disposal methods (including prescribed fire), and to evaluate alternative forest road alignments. The Scenic Beauty Estimation (SBE) Method (Daniel & Boster, 1976) requires that landscapes be observed and judged by panels of persons representative of targeted populations. Assessed forest areas are typically represented by a set of randomly sampled color slides. Observers view the color slides and independently rate the scenic beauty of the area represented. Slides are used as surrogates (not simulations, Daniel & Ittelson, 1981), in that observers are instructed to ignore photographic features (exposure, focus, framing, etc.), to use the slide as an indication of what the depicted *area* is like, and to rate the scenic beauty of the area (not the slide). A variation of Thurstone's Law of Categorical Judgment (Torgerson, 1958) and signal-detection theory (Green & Swetts, 1966) scaling models is used to transform individual ratings of slides into a standardized interval scale measure of the perceived beauty of each landscape.

To develop psychophysical models using the SBE method, a number of different landscapes must be assessed and the relevant physical characteristics of each determined. Early modeling efforts (Arthur, 1977; Daniel & Boster, 1976) attempted to measure physical features from the color slides used for the scenic-beauty ratings. More recent models (Daniel & Schoeder, 1979; Schroeder & Daniel, 1981) have employed physical measurements made at the actual landscape sites.

Daniel & Schroeder (1979) used 90 ponderosa pine forested sites in northern Arizona to develop a near-view model of scenic beauty. Each one-acre site was represented by eight (stratified) randomly oriented color slides. Slides were used to obtain SBEs for each site. A battery of physical/biological measurements were also taken at each site. Physical features were selected on the basis of United States Forest Service management needs and capabilities (i.e., features that are routinely inventoried, monitored, and managed) and forest service sampling and measurement techniques were used. Measured features included: numbers of different species and sizes of trees, volumes of grasses, forbs, and shrubs, and volumes of downed wood and slash. All measures were expressed as per-acre averages.

A number of statistical procedures, including factor and cluster analyses, were used to determine interrelationships among physical variables and correlations of each variable or groups of variables with perceived scenic beauty, SBE. Multiple regression analyses yielded a number of linear models for predicting SBE values as a function of combinations of the physical features of the forest sites; one model, restricted to the 64 sample sites having ponderosa pines (PP) totaling at least 90% of the total trees at the site, was able to explain 52% of the variation in SBEs with a linear combination of 7 physical features. Specifically, the model showed that

$$SBE = \ .20(\text{lbs./acre forbs}) + .60(\text{PP/acre} > 16'' \text{ DBH})$$
$$-.01(\text{ft.}^3/\text{acre slash}) + .26(\text{lbs./acre shrubs})$$
$$+.04(\text{lbs./acre grass}) - .001(\text{PP/acre} < 5'' \text{ DBH})$$
$$-.02(\text{PP/acre } 5''-16'' \text{ DBH}) - 3.87$$
$$(r^2 = .52, p < .001)$$

(DBH is diameter at breast height, a forestry convention for gauging the size of a tree.) The scenic-beauty model meets a number of statistical criteria and is intuitively reasonable. Large pines and lush ground cover (grass, forbs, shrubs) enhance forest beauty; large numbers of small trees and large volumes of slash detract from scenic beauty. With minor adjustments, this model was also extended to predict perceived scenic beauty of new sites sampled from insect-damaged pine forests in the Colorado Front Range (Schroeder & Daniel, 1981).

Another major effort to develop psychophysical models of landscape quality is represented by the work of Buhyoff and his associates (e.g., Buhyoff & Leuschner, 1978; Buhyoff & Riesenman, 1979; Buhyoff

& Wellman, 1980; Buhyoff, Wellman, & Daniel, 1982). These investigators have typically employed color slides of forest "vistas" or pan-
oramic views and presented these to observers in a paired-comparison
format. Observers are presented with all possible pairs of selected
scenes and each observer indicates which member of a pair is preferred.
Thurstone's (1927) Law of Comparative Judgment scaling procedures
are employed to obtain interval scale measures of landscape preference.

Psychophysical models for landscape vistas have been developed
by relating measured characteristics of the vista (taken from the photographic representation) to scaled landscape preference. Buhyoff and
Wellman (1980) measured variables such as percent of scene covered by
snow, insect-damaged trees, foreground vegetation, and sharp mountains in the foreground, midground, and background of landscape
scenes sampled from the Colorado Front Range. Measures were obtained by a grid-overlay method suggested by the early work of Shafer *et
al.* (1969). Multiple regression of these and other landscape features on
landscape–preference values yielded the following psychophysical
model:

$$
\begin{aligned}
\text{LS preference} = \quad & 10.83 \ (\text{area in sharp mountains}) \\
& - 0.59 \ (\text{area in sharp mountains})^2 \\
& + 1.57 \ (\text{area in distant forest}) \\
& - 8.6 \ (\text{middle ground area of insect-damaged} \\
& \qquad \text{trees}) \\
& - 64.59 \ (\text{proportion of forested area}) \\
& + 0.97 \ (\text{area in flat topography}) \\
& + 131.09
\end{aligned}
$$

This model accounted for 57% of the variance in landscape preferences, and also appears intuitively reasonable. Sharp mountains make
positive contributions to preference, while insect damage has negative
effects. The presence of the negative sharp-mountains-squared term in
the model indicates a nonlinear effect on preference; sharp mountains
improve the quality of a scene up to a point, but having too much of the
scene covered by sharp mountains makes it less preferable. Vista–preference models of this type have been successfully extended to include a
larger set of landscape scenes (Buhyoff *et al.*, 1982).

Recent collaborative research efforts have demonstrated that
paired-comparison judgements of landscape preference and rating scale
judgments of scenic beauty give virtually identical assessments of landscape quality after appropriate (comparative or categorical judgment)
scaling transformations. Near-view and vista landscape–quality models
have been combined to provide a comprehensive assessment of scenic

impacts of insect infestations in the Colorado Front Range (Daniel, Buhyoff, & Wellman, 1981). These psychophysical models make it possible for forest managers to obtain relatively precise quantitative estimates of the scenic implications of alternative management options in southwestern ponderosa pine forests.

EVALUATION

Reliability and Sensitivity

Of all landscape assessments, psychophysical methods have been subjected to the most rigorous and extensive evaluation. Test-retest reliabilities within and between observers, consistency between response indicator methods, precision (error) of measurement, and context stability have all been empirically verified on several occasions (e.g., Buhyoff et al., 1981; Daniel & Boster, 1976; Daniel et al., 1977; Pitt & Zube, 1979; Zube, 1974). The methods have been shown to be very sensitive to subtle landscape variations and psychophysical functions have proven very robust to changes in landscapes and in observers. These and other tests of the properties of landscape quality indices follow the pattern of tests that have traditionally been applied in psychophysical research and psychological measurement.

In some application of psychophysical methods only average ratings (or percent choice) values are computed for each landscape (e.g., Brush, 1979; Schomaker, 1979). Formally, ratings (or choices) provide only an ordinal scaling or ranking of landscapes. This does not take advantage of the full precision and generality of psychophysical measurement, but for many purposes, averages based on reasonably large numbers (20 or more) of homogeneous observers can provide adequate precision and do not seriously violate assumptions of standard statistical tests and procedures. Where more precision is required and where general psychophysical relationships are desired, formal scaling procedures have been applied (Buhyoff & Wellman, 1980; Daniel et al., 1977; Schroeder & Daniel, 1981). Another advantage of using complete interval scaling is that resulting landscape assessments are directly comparable regardless of the response indicator method used. With proper transformations, rating scales having various numbers of points, paired comparisons or other forced-choice procedures, rankings, Q-sorts, or magnitude-estimation methods will all yield comparable scalings of landscapes. (Buhyoff et al., 1982; Daniel & Boster, 1976; Pitt & Zube, 1979).

Reliability of psychophysical methods can be gauged in terms of agreement between observers, either individually or in groups. Most direct tests have compared averaged judgments of observer panels and have found very high levels of agreement; reliability coefficients exceeding .90 have been reported (e.g., Buhyoff *et al.*, 1982; Daniel *et al.*, 1977; Malm, Kelley, Molenar, & Daniel, 1981). Good reliabilities are typically obtained even when panels are selected from rather diverse observer populations, though very specialized observer groups may differ in their judgments. Individual rater reliabilities would be lower, perhaps in the range of the intra-rater reliabilities reported by Feimer *et al.* (1981). Unlike the expert-based methods, however, psychophysical methods generally rely on averaged judgment from groups of public observers, so group measures are appropriate.

Psychophysical prediction models, such as those developed by Buhyoff and Daniel and their associates have been tested for replicability. Each has been independently applied to landscapes that were not included in the development of the models and each was found to make accurate predictions of preference or scenic beauty. Similarly, models developed for one observer group have been quite effective in predicting scenic judgments of other observers sampled from similar populations. There is the recognition that models would be different for specific special interest groups or for specially trained or instructed observers (Anderson, 1981; Buhyoff *et al.*, 1982).

The pattern of high consistency or reliability of measures is coupled with substantial levels of sensitivity. Relying on ordinal or interval scales of measurement, Psychophysical methods have consistently been able to provide different landscape–quality assessments for landscapes that vary only subtly. Scenic effects of different levels of insect damage, changes in the size or density distributions of trees, or variations in land-use management patterns all have been successfully assessed. Recent studies have shown that the scenic effect of very subtle changes in lighting and atmospheric conditions (e.g., air pollution) can be measured for a constant landscape scene. Further, atmospheric effects on landscape scenic beauty have been represented in precise psychophysical models that relate lighting and atmospheric conditions to perceived scenic beauty and to perceived visual air quality (Latimer, Daniel, & Hogo, 1980; Latimer, Hogo, & Daniel, 1981; Malm *et al.*, 1981).

The reliability and sensitivity of psychophysical assessments and prediction models have consistently been confirmed. This type of internal consistency is important to any measuring system, especially where comparisons and interrelationships with other environmental and social variables are important.

Validity

The most frequently cited validity tests for psychophysical methods have addressed the representation of landscapes by color slides. The usual result has been very close correspondence between perceptual judgments based on color slide representations and judgments made at the actual sites where those photographs were taken (Daniel & Boster, 1976; Jackson, Hudman, & England, 1978; Malm *et al.*, 1981; Shafer & Richards, 1974; Zube *et al.*, 1975). Although this is an important test, it is only one aspect of measurement validity and should not be over-emphasized. Other tests are necessary to determine whether psychophysical methods measure landscape quality.

A central assumption of the psychophysical model is that the aesthetic judgments of public panels provide an appropriate measure of landscape quality. Some would argue that more sensitive, more educated, expert judgments are more valid indicators of aesthetic merit (Carlson, 1977). While there is frequently agreement between expert and lay observers (Schomaker, 1979), there are some differences (Buhyoff *et al.*, 1978), so the question of which provides the more valid measure is important. The question cannot be answered by empirical tests and remains an unresolved philosophical issue. Given the high consistency that generally obtains among diverse public groups in their assessments of the scenic quality of the natural landscape, there are compelling arguments for using public judgment as a basis for assessing publicly owned landscapes. Also, where psychophysical models have been derived, public judgments do seem to distinguish landscapes on the basis of features that are intuitively appropriate. For example, rushing water, large trees, grassy meadows and jagged mountain peaks have all been found to be positive aesthetic features by the criterion of public judgments. Downed wood and slash, dense stands of small trees, and recently killed trees have been found to be negative aesthetic features. The "consumer evaluation" approach, then, has a number of features to its credit.

A somewhat more troublesome validity issue for psychophysical methods concerns the sufficiency of unidimensional perceptual judgments as a basis for landscape appraisals. If *scenic beauty* is accepted as the appropriate basis for assessment, as the wording of much of the landscape–protection legislation suggests, psychophysical methods would seem to be sufficient. If, however, the intent of landscape assessments is to predict behaviors, such as frequency or duration of visits, or psychological outcomes such as mental health, stress reduction, or happiness, then perceived scenic beauty may not be an adequate basis for measurement. Because most of the psychophysical methods either explicitly state or strongly imply that they measure perceived scenic quality (not other actions or outcomes), these methods do seem to "measure what they purport to measure." In that sense, then, they are valid landscape–assessment methods. From some perspectives, however, they may not be completely sufficient assessments of landscape quality.

Tests of conjoint validity have been reported and have shown good agreement between different methods (e.g., Buhyoff et al., 1981, 1982; Daniel & Boster, 1976; Hull & Buhyoff, 1981; Pitt & Zube, 1979). Of course, all of these comparisons are between sets of observer-based scenic-quality assessments. In a different type of study, Schomaker (1979) found that observer panels consistently rated sketches exemplifying "high quality landscapes" (in the judgment of professional landscape architects) as being higher in scenic beauty than "low quality landscapes." This study could be taken as evidence for the validity of assessments based on both public judgment and landscape architects' (at least one) design intuitions about landscape quality.

Utility

In the short term, psychophysical assessments are not highly efficient. If every landscape or landscape modification must be represented (photographically or otherwise) and subjected to the inspection and judgment of panels of public observers, considerable time and expense is required. In the long run, however, with reliable psychophysical models, these methods could prove very efficient. If accurate predictions of public scenic perceptions can be based on physical features that are routinely measured (inventoried) for other management and planning purposes, psychophysical landscape assessments could be obtained at essentially no additional cost.

Other features that make psychophysical assessments useful in many management contexts are quantitative precision, objectivity, and a basis in public perception and judgment. When scenic quality is expressed in terms of an interval scale index, differences between landscapes and the implications of management actions can be measured with considerable precision. Evaluation of trade-offs or costs and benefits between different management plans is facilitated and landscape quality can be better integrated with biological and other concerns that are typically expressed in quantitative terms. Psychophysical assessments are not based on one expert's opinion, but reflect a measured consensus among observers representative of the public that views landscapes and is affected by management actions. This basis for landscape values is easily rationalized for public lands, and is also very consistent with the current emphasis on public involvement in land-use planning.

Valuation

Psychophysical methods can provide precise assessments of public perception of the *relative* scenic beauty of landscapes. These assessments do not, however, provide any *absolute* measure of scenic quality and do not indicate the value of sampled landscapes relative to other (unassessed) landscapes or to other social values (such as water, timber, jobs, recreation, etc.). As with other assessment methods, valuation requires an additional set of economic or sociopolitical trade-off processes (Schroeder, 1981). These valuation processes are facilitated by the quantitative precision of psychophysical assessments and by the explicit relationship of scenic quality indices to physical features of the environment. For example, the cost of achieving specific levels of scenic beauty in the forest can be measured in terms of timber left unharvested and/or the costs of slash and downed-wood disposal for aesthetic purposes. Having these costs and the aesthetic benefits quantitatively and explicitly stated could facilitate sociopolitical determination of whether the scenic benefits of a certain management plan are worth the costs; at the least, the costs and scenic benefits can be displayed as a guide to management.

PSYCHOLOGICAL MODEL

Rather than defining landscape quality in terms of environmental features, the psychological model refers to the feelings and perceptions of people who inhabit, visit, or view the landscape. The emphasis is upon the cognitive and affective reactions evoked by various landscapes. A high-quality landscape is one that evokes positive feelings, such as security, relaxation, warmth, freedom, cheerfulness, or happiness. Low-quality landscapes are associated with stress, fear, insecurity, constraint, gloom, or other negative feelings. The behavioral consequences of various landscape settings, such as exploration, abandonment, or modification are also important, but are less often directly observed and measured. The aesthetic or scenic quality of the landscape is generally viewed as but one of several dimensions of human response to views of the natural environment. Frequently the aesthetic dimension is found to be closely related to other psychological dimensions; a landscape that is judged as scenically beautiful also tends to elicit positive feelings of tranquility, freedom, etc.

The conceptual and methodological base for this approach to landscape assessment is in the psychological models associated with personality theory, attitude measurement, and, to a lesser extent, clinical and humanistic psychology. Characteristically, reactions to various landscapes are assessed by having observers rate each setting on a battery of perceptual, cognitive, and affective scales. For example, landscape scenes represented by color slides might be rated on the dimensions of size, openness, colorfulness, complexity, information, value, orderliness, fearfulness, beauty and stress. Alternatively, subjects may be given adjective checklists that include terms such as large, open, colorful, etc. The number of observers checking each trait is an index of how strongly a landscape evokes that feeling or reaction. Sometimes openended interview responses are scored for references to these same psychological dimensions.

The assessment of each landscape may be presented in terms of its location in a multidimensional space (e.g., Dearinger, 1979) or as a "profile" of values along each dimension (e.g., Lowenthal & Riel, 1972). *Beauty* might be one of the several dimensions along which landscapes can be systematically ordered. Interrelationships among these various dimensions may be investigated to define higher order dimensions, especially potency, evaluation, and activity, and to articulate interdimensional dependencies; for example, landscapes that are judged to be beautiful are also more relaxing, less fearful, and moderately complex (or vice versa).

Occasionally, landscapes that have been scaled on these dimensions or on the higher order dimensions are independently subjected to a preference scaling. Following procedures such as those employed in the psychophysical methods, observers are asked to rate or choose the landscape settings that they prefer. In some cases particular uses or activities are specified (e.g., as places to live, visit, or recreate in some fashion). Relationships between the perceptual, cognitive, and affective scales and the preference scale are used as a basis for inferences and hypotheses regarding the psychological features of the landscape that determine human landscape preferences. The motivation for these studies is sometimes practical, as when alternative sites or landscape modifications are being considered. More often, however, the goals are theoretical; the investigator seeks to discover and describe the psychological basis for landscape preferences.

A series of studies by R. Kaplan, S. Kaplan, and associates (e.g., R. Kaplan, 1975; S. Kaplan, 1975; S. Kaplan, R. Kaplan, & Wendt, 1972) illustrate the psychological model of landscape assessment. A basic method in these studies is to identify relevant psychological variables in photographs of landscapes. Preference ratings and ratings on the *a priori* dimensions are then obtained from naive observers. Factor of cluster analysis of ratings is used to reorganize the stimuli with regard to higher order composite factors. The object of this process is not only to identify and correlate salient psychological dimensions of the environment, but also to predict landscape preferences with respect to these dimensions.

In an early study, Kaplan *et al.* (1972) examined the relationship between ratings of preference and complexity, and the nature of rated scenes. Photographs of various scenes were sorted on an *a priori* basis into four content categories: pristine natural scenes, urban views, rural scenes, and natural scenes with minimal human artifacts. Subjects rated these scenes with regard to preference for the scene and for the level of complexity they perceived in the scene. A factor analysis of these ratings produced two environmental categories identified as "urban" and "natural." Preference and complexity ratings were then compared across these two new environmental categories. Natural scenes were vastly preferred over urban scenes, but were perceived as less complex. The researchers concluded that complexity did not account for or predict differences in preference for urban or natural scenes.

In an extension of the preceding study, two new variables, *mystery* and *coherence*, were identified intuitively from inspection of photographs and were evaluated empirically (R. Kaplan, 1975; S. Kaplan, 1975). Independent groups of subjects were asked to rate the photographic scenes with regard to mystery, defined as the promise of further information, and coherence, defined as the extent to which a scene "hung together." While coherence was not found to be a predictor of preference, mystery was a strong positive predictor. In addition, natural scenes were judged as significantly more mysterious than urban scenes.

Ulrich's (1977) study of roadside scenes provides an example of mixing elements of the psychological and psychophysical methods. A series of photographs of rural roadsides were evaluated and rated by a panel of subjects on the dimensions of complexity, coherence, and depth, and by an independent panel on the dimensions of focality, ground texture, and mystery. The same series of slides was then shown to groups of American and Swedish students who were asked to rate them with respect to preference. Ulrich predicted that preference would be positively related to complexity, focality, homogeneous ground texture, depth, and mystery. Subject ratings in fact correlated well with focality, even ground texture, depth and mystery, but not with complexity. Factor analysis of preference ratings produced five factors, three of which were related to the properties of ground texture, depth, and complexity. Ulrich concluded that these three dimensions were components of the legibility of a scene, which, combined with complexity and mystery, forms a complex of salient psychological variables that may have adaptive significance for humans.

The preceding studies have in common the methodological attempt to relate subjective preference for a landscape with various psychoenvironmental variables. Some of these variables presumably have objective physical referents in the landscape, especially complexity, depth, and ground texture (Ulrich, 1977). The landscape variables in the Kaplans' model are necessarily assessed by subjective judgment, a procedure that is unavoidable for variables such as mystery, coherence, and legibility.

EVALUATION

Reliability and Sensitivity

In a typical application of psychological methods, panels of observers view and rate landscape scenes or settings on a number of different psychological scales. Landscapes may be verbally described, represented by color slides, prints, or sketches, or visited directly. Each observer provides a scale value (i.e., a rating) for each landscape on each dimension specified. Reliability then can be assessed in terms of the consistency with which a given landscape is assigned the same or similar scale values from one observer (or observer panel) to the next. While there is variability from scale to scale (e.g., judgments of size may be more reliable than judgments of cheerfulness), the level of observer agreement in the scaling of landscapes has generally been moderate to high. When substantial disagreement is encountered, efforts are often made to subdivide the observer sample into like-responding groups. Then observer characteristics (e.g., familiarity with the landscape, introvert–extrovert, urban-rural orientation) are investigated to find the source of rating differences. An important advantage of these methods, then, is that reliability can be determined and has generally been found to be relatively high.

Psychological methods may be viewed as highly sensitive in that they reveal differences among landscapes along many different dimensions of human reaction. On the other hand, many of these dimensions are highly redundant and perhaps are not different at all. Typically only two or three higher order dimensions are required to account for all the systematic variation in reactions. Also, in many application of psychological methods only a small number of very diverse landscapes are used; within a single study, scenes may vary from urban slums to national parks (e.g., Ward & Russell, 1981). Under these conditions, rating differences and observer reliability coefficients can be expected to be high. When multidimensional ratings are assigned to different landscapes that are all of the same basic type, sensitivity and reliability may be considerably lower.

Because psychological methods use multiple observers and yield one or more quantitative scale values for each assessed landscape, their reliability and sensitivity can be precisely determined. That is, in any given application it is usually possible to calculate a standard error of estimate for scale values and to determine the scaled differences between landscapes relative to that error. This is an important advantage, since users of these assessments can know the degree of precision and confidence in the landscape values produced. Thus, if the methods were to prove insensitive for differentiating a particular set of landscape settings, at least this could be discovered.

Validity

Psychological methods, like the psychophysical methods, base landscape assessments on the reactions and judgments of the people who experience and/or use the landscapes. In this regard there is an important element of validity inherent in the methods. Although, some will argue that the reactions of common landscape-users (who may not be high in environmental or aesthetic sensitivity) should not be the basis for landscape–quality appraisals (e.g., Carlson, 1977), few would argue that user preferences are not an important consideration. When landscape assessments are intended to guide or evaluate management decisions and actions for public lands, users or even more general public samples provide a particularly appropriate basis for measurement.

Another source of support for the validity of psychological methods is provided by studies of the consistency in assessments despite variations in the particular method used. For example, Ward and Russell (1981) found that landscape assessments are very similar whether rating scales, adjective checklists, or simple pairwise similarity judgments are used to express observer reactions. Such consensus across nominally different methods suggests that each method is measuring the same underlying psychological properties. However, this convergent validity may be an artifact of the scaling methodology. Daniel and Ittelson (1981) have shown that the consistent scaling reported by Ward and Russell using color slides of landscape settings is duplicated when only short verbal labels (e.g., "sweeping view of the Grand Canyon," "grocery store aisle") are substituted for the color slides. The question raised is whether the consistency of scaling is in any clear way related to observers' perceptions of the environment. Consistent patterns in landscape scaling may reflect semantic relationships inherent in the common language used to label those dimensions; for example, "things" that are cheerful also tend to be warm, colorful, exciting, and liked (Lowenthal & Riel, 1972). The typical procedure of having observers simultaneously rate diverse landscapes on many interrelated scales would seem to encourage these consistent language-determined relationships.

Another important validity question for the psychological model is how closely the multidimensional ratings resemble natural human reactions to the landscape (Seamon, 1979). Given the experimental setting and an instruction to rate landscapes on twenty or so "dimensions," subjects will undoubtedly comply. This does not mean, however, that people normally react to the environment in terms of its cheerfulness, mystery, warmth, or legibility. At least, these dimensions should be shown to be capable of predicting human reactions to landscapes under more natural conditions.

Utility

If valid, the dimensions scaled by psychological methods could serve to characterize human environmental reactions in a way that transcends the particular features of any specific landscape. That is, if mystery in a landscape leads to a particular pattern of response, then this pattern would be expected for any landscape exhibiting this characteristic, whether the landscape is natural or man-made, rural or urban, desert or jungle. Such generality would be very useful to a method of landscape assessment.

To take advantage of this potential generality, however, it is necessary that psychological dimensions such as mystery, cheerfulness, or potency, be related to identifiable, independently measurable, and perhaps even manipulatable features of the physical environment. Of course, this would result in essentially a psychophysical model, with the added feature of psychological cognitions and affects intervening between physical features and perceived landscape quality. Unless this step is accomplished, however, psychological landscape assessment would always be after-the-fact; each setting and landscape modification would have to be subjected to a psychological scaling in order to determine its relevant characteristics. Further, alternative landscape modifications or selections would have to be designed with little or no guidance as to the relevant physical features affecting the psychological outcome. The utility of psychological assessments, then, will depend upon how well the principal psychological dimensions can be tied to physical features of the landscape on one hand (Wohlwill, 1976) and to relevant aspects of realistic human responses to the landscape on the other (Seamon, 1979).

Valuation

In one sense, psychological assessments have direct relevance for valuation; measures of the happiness, worth, or relaxation associated with various landscapes could provide rather direct measures of human/social value. Still, it would be necessary to have comparable measures for other social benefits and costs that might be associated with each landscape. Suppose, for example, that the landscape eliciting the highest happiness ratings could be obtained only by expending more dollars than would be required to obtain the environmental conditions represented by the second-ranking landscape. To decide which of these two conditions represents the greatest net value (to society) either the extra dollars spent (or saved) would have to be related to happiness, or *happiness* would have to be assigned some dollar value. This is not a trivial problem in either case.

Another approach to valuation that is particularly compatible with psychological assessments is the relation of landscape quality to human health and productivity. In general, landscapes that are perceived as relaxing (not stressful), exciting (not dull), cheerful (not depressing), and *happy* (not sad) should be more healthful environments for people and should lead to greater productivity, less sickness, and less strife. All these states have value to society, and some of this value can be expressed in conventional economic terms. Thus, the value of high landscape quality might be related to health (including mental health), which in turn is related to economic measures of productivity. These latter measures are commensurate with many other social values that are expressed in dollars, so benefits of landscape quality could be directly compared to benefits of resource utilization or to costs of achieving and maintaining the indicated landscape–quality levels. Of course, several important links in this valuation process have not yet been established; the link between psychological assessment dimensions and health and productivity, and the link between psychological assessments of land-scape quality and the costs of obtaining or maintaining these quality levels are the most obvious. Even if this process has not been completed, the general outline of the procedure seems clear and the needed links can be identified. Thus, future work could be directed toward determining the needed relationships between psychological assessments and measures of human welfare and of relevant environmental characteristics.

PHENOMENOLOGICAL MODEL

Both psychophysical and psychological models place considerable emphasis on the role of the observer in interaction with the landscape. The phenomenological model places even greater emphasis on individual subjective feelings, expectations, and interpretations. Landscape perception is conceptualized as an intimate encounter between a person and the environment. The person brings many things to this encounter, including an environmental history, a particular personal context for the encounter, a special sensitivity and openness to the environment, and a particular set of intentions and motivations for being in that place at that time. All these, the phenomenologists argue, must be taken into account in landscape–quality assessment.

The principal method of phenomenological assessment is the detailed personal interview or verbal questionnaire. Often the individual experiences and impressions of the investigator are the source for assessments. Assessments may be conducted on-site, but are more often conducted by asking the respondent to recall or think about a place or a type of place. Responses are generally verbal, though sketches or cognitive maps may also be used. Analysis is very particular and detailed, focusing on person–landscape–context complexes rather than on comparative assessments of different landscapes. Emphasis is upon determining the meaning and significance of various aspects of the environment to the particular person. Individual impressions may be inspected and their content analyzed in an effort to discover common features of landscape experience. Unlike the psychological methods, impressions are rarely averaged or subjected to reliability tests.

In many respects, phenomenological methods are not land-scape–assessment methods at all. They are not often used to provide measures or relative rankings of the excellence of various landscapes, and the results of a phenomenological analysis would be very difficult to use in deciding upon a particular land-management plan. On the other hand, this method has been used extensively in comparisons of various regions of the world, cities, and particular built environments. (Lowenthal & Riel, 1972; Lynch, 1960; Saarinen & Cooke, 1971). Furthermore, in the context of the natural landscape, many of the public's efforts to express the values they seek to preserve in the landscape have the personal, experiential flavor of the phenomenological analysis. Writings in this vein, as those of Thoreau, Muir, and A. Leopold, have been very influential in shaping Western standards of landscape quality. Thus, this approach should be considered in order to leave open as many options as possible at what is still a very early stage in the development of landscape–quality assessment methods.

EXAMPLE

The most extensive literature on applications of the phenomenological methods is devoted to studies of developed landscapes (e.g., Lowenthal, 1972; Lynch, 1960; Saarinen & Cooke, 1971), or to perception of environmental hazards (Burton & Kates, 1974; Saarinen, 1966). There is some discussion addressing perception and experience in natural landscape settings (e.g., Tuan, 1974), but there are few specific studies seeking to assess natural landscapes. Some aspects of the work reported by Seamon (1979) are at least suggestive of a phenomenological approach to landscape assessment.

Seamon used "environmental interest groups" to study examples of everyday environmental encounters. Members of the group met twice a week to discuss their personal experiences. Discussions were directed by selected topics, such as "movement in space," "centering," "off-centering," "emotions related to space," "destinations," and "disorientation," among others. The contents of these discussions were analyzed to determine different levels of environmental experience. Distinctions were drawn between "insideness" and "outsideness." Insideness includes experiences classed as vicarious, behavioral, empathetic, and existential. Behavioral experience is characterized by attention to details of the place (especially visual details), while empathetic experience emphasizes emotional involvement and "mergeance" with the environment. Under outsideness experiences are classed as existential, objective, and incidental. Objective experiences focus upon dispassionate orientation to a place; the place is viewed simply as a location. Existential experience in the insideness mode is characterized by feelings of belonging and personal identity. In the outsideness mode, existential experience is characterized by "meaningless identification" and by "alienation from the environment."

Seamon criticizes other landscape–assessment methods, such as the psychological and psychophysical methods, for failing to take into account all the relevant personal, experiential factors of landscape experience. He and other phenomenologists argue that the emotional and intentional state of the landscape observer/experiencer are critical to understanding landscape quality. "Studies in landscape preference reduce the multifaceted modes of encounter to the artificial situation of person actively evaluating a real or simulated landscape" (Seamon, 1979, p. 123). He suggests that studies must place the observer in his "natural attitude" with respect to the landscape and that landscape assessment must be approached with a "delicate empiricism."

EVALUATION

Reliability and Sensitivity

Phenomenological approaches have largely sacrificed reliability in favor of achieving high levels of sensitivity. In effect, every landscape encounter is viewed as being so multifaceted and so influenced by personal, experiential, emotional, and intentional factors that each encounter is unique. Consistency of experience is neither expected nor sought by the methods. Instead, every person–landscape–context situation produces a distinct multidimensional representation that seeks to capture all of the personal qualitative features of the individual's landscape experience.

Generalizations are derived by analysis of the contents of detailed introspective accounts of landscape experiences. These accounts may be collected by interviews and questionnaires with inhabitants or visitors to an area or by introspections of the investigator. Categories of landscape experience tend to be very abstract, such as Seamon's "Insideness- Outsideness" concepts and notions such as "mergence" and "barriers" between the environment and the experiencer. The analytic procedures and the conceptual categories derived tend to be highly idiosyncratic to the specific investigator, making it is difficult or impossible to determine consistencies across different assessments.

Validity

As a system of measuring landscape quality, phenomenological methods may err by including too much. By emphasizing very particular personal, experiential, and emotional factors, the visual properties of the landscape become only very tenuously associated with landscape experience. It follows from this analysis that landscape features, and any efforts to manipulate or manage those features, will not be influential in affecting perceived landscape quality. Instead, educational programs designed to increase observers' "environmental sensitivities" and to modify their expectations and intentions regarding the landscape experience will be more effective.

Perhaps the phenomenological model provides a more valid conceptualization for landscape–quality assessment than the models that place more emphasis on the role of objective landscape features. There is no direct way to decide this issue, and it is certainly not amenable to empirical investigation. If the phenomenologists are correct, however, assessment and management of the visual aesthetic benefits of the landscape are immensely more complex tasks than has been envisioned by the other assessment models. Assessments must be sensitive to very fine details of the environment and must also take into account a very large array of individual psychological factors as well. Indeed, landscape assessment may require much more psychological analysis of the observer and much less measurement and description of the landscape.

Utility

Phenomenological assessment may be too sensitive to be useful. In many respects these methods are analogous to an undampened scale that fluctuates so continuously that no reading or recording is possible. When comparative evaluations of different landscape settings or different management options are sought, phenomenological methods may yield as many different assessments for each alternative as there are combinations of contexts and observers of each landscape. Thus, alternatives would be distinguished only by complex patterns of observer reactions. Furthermore, only a relatively small share of the variance in assessments would be due to landscape differences, with the majority of variance contributed by differences in observers and contexts. Implications for landscape management would be very difficult to determine.

The efficiency of phenomenological methods is low in comparison to other methods, but low efficiency may be necessary if detailed personalized assessments are taken to be the proper objective for landscape assessments. Also, assessments may have to change as observers change their experience with the landscape or with related landscapes; in effect, no single assessment could be taken as final. Philosophical or theoretical justification for such an approach might be mustered, but the practical implications for a public-land management agency exclude this type of assessment on any large scale. Perhaps such assessments, in a research context, could serve to cross-check other more restricted, but more efficient, assessments by helping to identify potentially important landscape, observer, and contextual factors that might otherwise be overlooked.

Valuation

Similar to the psychological methods, phenemonological assessments may enter the valuing process by way of human health and productivity. Still, this does not cover the values that are ascribed to landscape experience by this approach. Concern with matters of identity, existential experience, and emotional (almost spiritual) aspects of person–landscape encounters suggests that higher value systems are involved. The highly personalized nature of assessments would hamper any efforts to derive general social utility functions or other links to conventional economic valuing models.

Perhaps the conceptualization of landscape–quality assessment as a means for ordering landscapes on a continuum of beauty or excellence is incompatible with the phenomenological model. Instead, each landscape seems to be taken in its own right, with emphasis upon the experiences, feelings, and understandings that the landscape may convey to a particular observer at a particular time. Thus, there may be no greater or lesser value for any given landscape, but there could be value in preserving a wide array of different kinds of landscapes to encourage a breadth of experience and understanding for the people who encounter them.

CONCLUSION

Many different landscape–assessment techniques have been developed in the past 10 to 15 years. Some have been applied only once, while others have been practiced extensively. Some have apparently been accepted without being subjected to traditional tests of reliability, sensitivity, and validity. Others have been intensively tested to document their precision and consistency. Methods differ substantially in their details, but many of them can be related by common underlying conceptual frameworks. In this chapter, methods have been classified under five general models: Ecological, Formal Aesthetic, Psychophysical, Psychological, and Phenomenological. These models are distinguished by their approaches to several central issues in landscape assessment: the definition of landscape quality; the determination of aesthetically relevant attributes of the landscape; the involvement of the landscape observer and the importance of observer perceptions, feelings, and interpretations; and the relationship between landscape quality and other human/social needs and values.

All models acknowledge that the environment (the "actual landscape") plays some role in determining landscape quality, but each model characterizes the environment somewhat differently. All models assign some role to humans, but there are substantial differences in the nature and importance of the human contribution to determining landscape quality. Ecological and formal aesthetic models both place humans in a peripheral position, with landscape quality determined entirely by features of the environment.

Within the ecological model, the environmental features that are relevant to landscape quality are primarily biological or ecological. The landscape is characterized in terms of species of plants and animals present, ecological zones, successional stage or other indicators of ecological processes. Humans are placed in a peripheral position in this model. Characterized as *users* of the landscape, their contribution is in the form of negative environmental impacts; the emphasis is on pollution, litter, and other forms of "disturbance" of natural features and processes. Human factors enter the model as modifications of the relevant environment/landscape features that rather directly determine landscape quality.

The formal aesthetic model characterizes the landscape in terms of formal properties, form, line, unity, variety, etc. While some judgment by an individual expert such as a landscape architect is required, the formal properties are assumed to be inherent in the landscape. For an appropriately trained individual, the identification of formal features is viewed as no more subjective than an inventory of plant and animal species by a trained biologist. If there is a role in the formal aesthetic model for human judgment, it is a historical one—presumably the classic aesthetic features were originally based on some form of human judgment. Aside from that historical influence, however, landscape quality is determined directly by the formal aesthetic features of the environment with no direct human influence.

Psychophysical, psychological, and phenomenological models all place humans in a central position; landscape quality is determined by the effects of the landscape on people. Each of these models does, however, characterize the environment and the human's role somewhat differently. For the psychophysical model the relevant features of the environment are characterized in objective physical or biological terms. These features may be measured from photographs or by direct inventory procedures, and vary from relatively abstract features, such as "perimeter squared of dense brush," to more concrete features, such as "number of trees greater than 16 inches in diameter." In any case, relevant landscape features are objectively measured or are in principle objectively measurable. The person, characterized as an observer/judge, perceives the landscape and expresses preferences or relative appraisals that directly determine landscape quality.

Psychological models characterize the landscape in more subjective terms by usually relying on human judgments of complexity, mystery, legibility, etc., to determine relevant features. The judgment of humans, characterized as experiencers of the landscape, is also central in determining the nature of landscape effects expressed in terms of an array of cognitions and feelings. Landscape–quality assessments may be left in multidimensional terms, or the multiple dimensions may be related to a single preference or landscape–quality dimension.

The phenomenological model represents the extreme of subjective determination of relevant landscape features, with each individual serving as an interpreter of unique environmental encounters. The effects of any environmental encounter are viewed as highly complex and subjective, depending as much on the state of the human as on the features of the environment. Each encounter produces a unique outcome for the individual interpreter and is valued in its own right. There is rarely any effort to order landscapes on a quality (excellence) dimension.

When traditional criteria for measurement systems are applied, each landscape–quality assessment approach is found to have both advantages and limitations. From the perspectives of this chapter, the ideal landscape–assessment method would provide sensitive and reliable measures of the scenic quality (excellence) of a wide range of landscapes. These measures would be systematically related to objectively measurable, practically manipulatable properties of the physical environment and to commensurable measures of other human/social values. Against this standard for comparison, some of the landscape-–assessment models fare better than others.

Ecological assessment methods might achieve considerable sensitivity and reliability, though actual tests of these characteristics have not been reported. The validity of these methods, however, depends upon the assumption that "natural" areas undisturbed by humans are highest in landscape quality. Even if this assumption were found generally to hold, finer distinctions would require a rather precise relationship between landscape quality and naturalness. Such a relationship remains to be proven, and present data seem not to be supportive. Furthermore, this approach makes landscape–quality assessment superfluous, since it would be redundant with other environmental quality assessments.

Formal aesthetic methods have been found seriously deficient with regard to the fundamental criteria of sensitivity and reliability. Because these methods rely so heavily upon the judgments of individual experts, there seems to be little hope of improving on this situation. Unless the approach is changed substantially, low levels of precision and high degrees of inconsistency will continue to limit formal aesthetic methods. In many respects these faults arise because the formal model is poorly suited to assessment or measurement—it is essentially and most appropriately a model for landscape design. Opportunities for individual expression may be assets for a design system, but they lead to unacceptable inconsistency in a measurement system. The continued wholesale use of formal aesthetic methods to meet landscape–quality assessment requirements can not be justified.

Unlike the formal aesthetic model, the psychophysical model was explicitly developed as a measurement model. It is not surprising, then, that landscape–quality assessment methods based on this model have emphasized traditional measurement goals of sensitivity and reliability. High levels of precision and consistency have been achieved, but to some extent this has been at the expense of generality; psychophysical models are typically very specific and are restricted to a particular landscape type and to a specified viewer population and perspective. Still, for those landscape–quality assessment contexts where psychophysical models have been developed, no other approach has come so close to meeting the criteria of the ideal assessment system. Certainly no other perceptual approach relates landscape quality so systematically to the objective properties of the environment. The psychophysical methods may be weakest on the psychological side—human response is typically restricted to a single quality dimension.

The psychological model emphasizes the multidimensional analysis of human landscape experience. A complex array of cognitive, affective, and evaluative psychological dimensions may be required to fully characterize the landscape experience of humans. To be practically or theoretically useful, however, this array must be systematically related to indices of landscape quality or preference on the one hand, and to objectively specified measures of landscape features on the other. It is the latter connection that has been least well developed in the methods based on the psychological model. Without clear relationships to objectively determined environmental features, the psychological methods leave landscape assessment in a correlational feedback loop; psychological reactions to the landscape are explained only in terms of other psychological reactions. From a practical perspective, this leaves the landscape manager with both feet firmly planted in midair.

Phenomenological methods also fail to establish systematic relationships between psychological responses (interpretations) and landscape features. In that respect these methods are more "psychological" than the psychological methods. There is also no effort to relate the complex array of psychological reactions to a dimension of landscape quality or preference. For this reason it is probably inappropriate to treat these methods as assessment techniques; they provide no consistent means for ordering landscape instances along a dimension of quality-/excellence. Still, methods based on the phenomenological model have been used and are frequently discussed in the context of landscape–quality assessment. Also, by emphasizing the unique role of individual experiences, intentions, and expectations, the phenomenological model serves to point out the importance of the human context in which landscapes are encountered.

At the present time, none of the models described completely meets all of the goals of landscape– quality assessment. By the criteria outlined in this chapter, it is unlikely that either the ecological or the formal aesthetic models can serve as a basis for an adequate landscape– assessment system. For very different reasons, the phenomenological model is inadequate. While neither the psychophysical nor the psychological models are sufficient alone, a careful merger of these two approaches might well provide the basis for a reliable, valid, and useful system of landscape–quality assessment.

REFERENCES

Anderson, L. M. Land use designations affect perception of scenic beauty in forest land-
    scapes. *Forest Science*, 1981, *27*, 392–400.
Arthur, L. M. Predicting scenic beauty of forest environment: Some empirical tests. *Forest
    Science*, 1977, *23*, 151–160.
Arthur, L. M., Daniel, T. C., & Boster, R. S. Scenic assessment: An overview. *Landscape
    Planning*, 1977, *4*, 109–129.
Brush, R. O. Perceived quality of scenic and recreational environments: Some meth-
    odological issues. In E. Zube & K. Craik (Eds.), *Perceived environmental quality indices*.
    New York: Plenum Press, 1976, pp. 47–97.
Brush, R. O. The attractiveness of woodlands: Perceptions of forest landowners in Mas-
    sachusetts. *Forest Science*, 1979, *25*, 495–506.
Brush, R. O., & Palmer, J. F. Measuring the impact of urbanization on scenic quality: Land
    use change in the northeast. In *Our national landscape* (USDA Forest Service Tech. Rep.
    PSW-35). Berkeley, Calif.: Pacific Southwest Forest and Range Experiment Station,
    1979.
Buhyoff, G. J., & Leuschner, W. A. Estimating psychological disutility from damaged
    forest stands. *Forest Science*, 1978, *24*, 424–432.

Buhyoff, G. J., & Riesenman, M. F. Experimental manipulation of dimensionality in landscape preference judgments: A quantitative validation. *Leisure Sciences*, 1979, *2*,
221–238.

Buhyoff, G. J., & Wellman, J. D. Landscape architect's interpretation of people's landscape
preferences. *Journal of Environmental Management*, 1978, *6*, 255–262.

Buhyoff, G., & Wellman, J. D. The specification of a non-linear psychophysical function
for visual landscape dimensions. *Journal of Leisure Research*, 1980, *12*, 257–272.

Buhyoff, G. J., Wellman, J. D., Harvey, H., & Fraser, R. A. Landscape architects' interpretations of people's landscape preferences. *Journal of Environmental Management*,
1978, *6*, 255–262.

Buhyoff, G. J., Arndt, L. K., & Probst, D. B. Interval scaling of landscape preference by
direct and indirect measurement methods. *Landscape Planning*, 1981, *8*, 257–267.

Buhyoff, G. J., Wellman, J. D., & Daniel, T. C. Predicting scenic quality for mountain pine
beetle and western spruce budworm damaged vistas. *Forest Science*, 1982, *28*, 827–838.

Burton, I., & Kates, R. W. The perception of natural hazards in resource management.
Natural Resources Journal, 1964, *3*, 412–441.

Carlson, A. A. On the possibility of quantifying scenic beauty. *Landscape Planning*, 1977, *4*,
131–172.

Craik, K. H. Psychological factors in landscape appraisal. *Environment and Behavior*, 1972,
1, 255–266.

Craik, K. H., & Feimer, N. R. Setting technical standards for visual impact assessment
procedures. In *Our national landscape* (USDA Forest Service Tech. Rep. PSW-35).
Berkeley, Calif.. Pacific Southwest Forest and Range Experiment Station, 1979, pp.
93–100.

Craik, K., & Zube, E. (Eds.). *Perceived environmental quality indices*. New York: Plenum
Press, 1976.

Daniel, T. C. Criteria for development and application of perceived environmental quality
indices. In E. Zube & K. Craik (Eds.), *Perceived environmental quality indices*. New York:
Plenum Press, 1976, pp. 27–45.

Daniel, T. C., & Boster, R. S. *Measuring landscape aesthetics: The scenic beauty estimation
method* (USDA Forest Service Research Paper RM-167). Fort Collins, Colo.: Rocky
Mountain Forest and Range Experiment Station, 1976.

Daniel, T. C., & Ittelson, W. H. Conditions for environmental perception research: Comment on "The psychological representation of molar physical environments" by Ward
and Russell. *Journal of Experimental Psychology: General*, 1981, *110*, 153–157.

Daniel, T. C., & Schroeder, H. W. Scenic beauty estimation model: Predicting perceived
beauty of forest landscapes. In *Our national landscape* (USDA Forest Service Tech. Rep.
PSW-35). Berkeley, Calif.: Pacific Southwest Forest and Range Experiment Station,
1979, pp. 514–523.

Daniel, T. C., & Zube, E. H. Assessment of esthetic resources. In T. C. Daniel, E. H. Zube,
& B. L. Driver (Eds.), *Assessing amenity resource values* (USDA Forest Service Tech. Rep.
RM-68). Fort Collins, Colo.: Rocky Mountain Forest and Range Experiment Station,
1979, pp. 2–3.

Daniel, T. C., Wheeler, L., Boster, R. S., & Best, P. Quantitative evaluation of landscapes:
An application of signal detection analysis to forest management alterations.
Man–Environment Systems, 1973, *3*, 330–344.

Daniel, T. C., Anderson, L. M., Schroeder, H. W., & Wheeler, L. W., III. Mapping the
scenic beauty of forest landscapes. *Leisure Sciences*, 1977, *1*, 35–53.

Daniel, T. C., Buhyoff, G. J., & Wellman, J. D. *Assessment of public perceptions and values
regarding mountain pine beetle and western spruce budworm impact in the Colorado Front*

Range (Final Report, Cooperative Agreement No. 16-930-Gr). Fort Collins, Colo.: Rocky Mountain Forest and Range Experiment Station, 1981.

Dearinger, J. A. Measuring preferences for natural landscapes. *Journal of the Urban Planning and Development Division*, 1979, *105*, 63–81.

Fabos, J. G. An analysis of enviornmental quality ranking systems in recreation. In USDA Forest Service, *Recreation symposium proceedings*. Upper Darby, Pa.: Northeastern Forest Experiment Station, 1971, pp. 40–55.

Fechner, G. *Elements of psychophysics*, 1860. (H. E. Adler, trans.) New York: Holt, Rinehart & Winston, 1966.

Feimer, N. R. Environmental perception and cognition in rural contexts. In A. W. Childs & G. B. Melton (Eds.), *Rural psychology*. New York: Plenum Press, 1983, pp. 113–149.

Feimer, N. R., Smardon, R. C., & Craik, K. H. Evaluating the effectiveness of observer-based visual resource and impact assessment methods. *Landscape Research*, 1981, *6*, 12–16.

Green, D. M., & Swetts, V. A. *Signal detection theory and psychophysics*. New York: Wiley, 1966.

Hull, R. B., & Buhyoff, G. J. On the law of comparative judgment: Scaling with intransitive observers and multidimensional stimuli. *Educational and Psychological Measurement*, 1981, *41*, 1083–1089.

Jackson, R. H., Hudman, L. E., & England, J. L. Assessment of the environmental impact of high voltage power transmission lines. *Journal of Environmental Management*, 1978, *6*, 153–170.

Kaplan, R. Some methods and strategies in the prediction of preference. In E. H. Zube, R. O. Brush, & J. A. Fabos (Eds.), *Landscape assessment: Values, perceptions, and resources*. Stroudsburg, Pa.: Dowden, Hutchinson & Ross, 1975, pp. 118–119.

Kaplan, S. An informal model for the prediction of preference. In E. H. Zube, R. O. Brush, & J. A. Fabos (Eds.), *Landscape assessment: Values, perceptions, and resources*. Stroudsburg, Pa.: Dowden, Hutchinson & Ross, 1975, pp. 92–101.

Kaplan, S., Kaplan, R., & Wendt, J. S. Rated preference and complexity for natural and urban visual material. *Perception and Psychophysics*, 1972, *12*, 354–356.

Latimer, D. A., Daniel, T. C., & Hogo, H. *Relationship between air quality and human perception of scenic areas*. San Rafael, Calif.: Systems Application, 1980.

Latimer, D. A., Hogo, H., & Daniel, T. C. The effects of atmospheric optical conditions on perceived scenic beauty. *Atmospheric Environment*, 1981, *15*, 1865–1874.

Leopold, L. B. Landscape esthetics. *Natural History*, 1969, *78*, 36–45. (a)

Leopold, L. B. *Quantitative comparison of some aesthetic factors among rivers* (U. S. Geological Survey Circular 620). Washington, D.C.: U. S. Department of the Interior, 1969. (b)

Leopold, L. B., & Marchand, M. O. On the quantitative inventory of the riverscape. *Water Resources Research*, 1968, *4*, 709–717.

Litton, R. B., Jr. *Forest landscape description and inventories: A basis for land planning and design* (USDA Forest Service Research Paper DSW-49). Berkeley, Calif.: Pacific Southwest Forest and Range Experiment Station, 1968.

Lowenthal, D. Research in environmental perception and behavior: Perspectives on current problems. *Environment and Behavior*, 1972, *4*, 333–342.

Lowenthal, D., & Riel, M. The nature of perceived and imagined environments. *Environment and Behavior*, 1972, *4*, 189–207.

Lynch, K. *The image of the city*. Cambridge, Mass.: MIT Press, 1960.

Malm, W., Kelley, K., Molenar, J., & Daniel, T. Human perception of visual air quality (uniform haze). *Atmospheric Environment*, 1981, *15*, 1875–1890.

McHarg, I. L. *Design with nature*. Garden City, N.Y.: Doubleday, 1967.

Palmer, J. Approaches for assessing visual quality and visual impacts. In K. Finsterbusch & C. P. Wolf (Eds.), *Methodology of social impact assessment.* Stroudsburg, Pa.: Dowden, Hutchinson & Ross, 1981, pp. 284–301.

Pitt, D. G., & Zube, E. H. The Q-sort method: Use in landscape assessment research and landscape planning. In *Our national landscape* (USDA Forest Service Tech. Rep. PSW-35). Berkeley, Calif.: Pacific Southwest Forest and Range Experiment Station, 1979.

Redding, M. J. *Aesthetics in environmental planning.* Washington, D.C.: U. S. Environmental Protection Agency, 1973.

Saarinen, T. F. *Perception of drought hazard on the Great Plains* (Research paper 106). Chicago: · University of Chicago, Department of Geography, 1966.

Saarinen, T. F., & Cooke, R. V. Public perception of environmental quality in Tucson, Arizona. *Journal of the Arizona Academy of Science,* 1971, *6,* 260–274.

Schomaker, J. H. Measurement of preferences for proposed landscape modifications. In T. C. Daniel, E. H. Zube, & B. L. Driver (Eds.), *Assessing amenity resource values* (USDA Forest Service Tech. Rep. RM-68). Fort Collins, Colo.: Rocky Mountain Forest and Range Experiment Station, 1979, pp. 67–70.

Schroeder, H. W. The effect of perceived conflict on evaluations of natural resource management goals. *Journal of Environmental Psychology,* 1981, *1,* 61–72.

Schroeder, H. W., & Daniel, T. C. Predicting the scenic quality of forest road corridors. *Environment and Behavior,* 1980, *12,* 349–366.

Schroeder, H. W., & Daniel, T. C. Progress in predicting the perceived scenic beauty of forest landscapes. *Forest Science,* 1981, *27,* 71–80.

Seamon, D. *A geography of the lifeworld.* New York: St. Martin's Press, 1979.

Shafer, E. L., & Brush, R. O. How to measure preferences for photographs of natural landscapes. *Landscape Planning,* 1977, *4,* 237–256.

Shafer, E. L., & Richards, T. A. *A comparison of viewer reactions to outdoor scenes and photographs of those scenes* (USDA Forest Service Research Paper NE-302). Upper Darby, Pa.: Northeastern Forest Experiment Station, 1974.

Shafer, E. L., Hamilton, J. F., & Schmidt, E. A. Natural landscape preferences: A predictive model. *Journal of Leisure Research,* 1969, *1,* 1–19.

Thurstone, L. L. A law of comparative judgment. *Psychological Review,* 1927, *34,* 278–286.

Torgerson, W. S. *Theory and methods of scaling.* New York: Wiley, 1958.

Tuan, Y. *Topophilia: A study of environmental perception, attitudes, and values.* Englewood Cliffs, N.J.: Prentice Hall, 1974.

Ulrich, R. S. Visual landscape preference: A model and application. *Man–Environment Systems,* 1977, *7,* 279–293.

USDA Forest Service. *National forest landscape management, Volume 2* (Agriculture Handbook No. 462). Washington, D. C.: U. S. Government Printing Office, 1974.

Ward, L. M., & Russell, J. A. The psychological representation of molar physical environments. *Journal of Experimental Psychology: General,* 1981, *110,* 121–152.

Wohlwill, J. F. Environmental aesthetics: The environment as a source of affect. In I. Altman & J. F. Wohlwill (Eds.), *Human behavior and environment* (Vol. 1). New York: Plenum Press, 1976, pp. 37–86.

Wohlwill, J. F. What belongs where: Research on fittingness of man-made structures in natural settings. In T. C. Daniel, E. H. Zube, & B. L. Driver (Eds.), *Assessing amenity resource values* (USDA Forest Service Tech. Rep. RM-68). Fort Collins, Colo.: Rocky Mountain Forest and Range Experiment Station, 1979, pp. 48–57.

Zube, E. H. Rating everyday rural landscapes of the northeastern U.S. *Landscape Architecture,* 1973, *63,* 370–375.

Zube, E. H. Cross-disciplinary and intermode agreement on the description and evaluation of landscape resources. *Environment and Behavior*, 1974, *6*, 69–89.

Zube, E. H., Pitt, D. D., & Anderson, T. W. *Perception and measurement of scenic resources in the Southern Connecticut River Valley* (Institute of Man and His Environment Publication R-74-1). Amherst: University of Massachusetts, 1975.

Zube, E. H., Sell, J. L., & Taylor, J. G. Landscape perception: Research, application and theory. *Landscape Planning*, 1982, *9*, 1–33.

3

Aesthetic and Affective Response to Natural Environment

ROGER S. ULRICH

INTRODUCTION

Affect is central to conscious experience and behavior in any environment, whether natural or built, crowded or unpopulated. Because virtually no meaningful thoughts, actions, or environmental encounters occur without affect (Ittelson, 1973, p. 16; Izard, 1977; Zajonc, 1980), an affective state is an important indicator of the nature and significance of a person's ongoing interaction with an environment (Lazarus, Kanner, & Folkman, 1980, p. 190). Research concerning affective and aesthetic response, therefore, may have a central role in advancing our understanding of human interactions with the natural environment and could prove pivotal in the development of comprehensive theories. Further, this area of research relates to important questions in environmental planning and design, including, for instance, visual landscape assessment, the provision of vegetation and parks in cities, and issues of wilderness management and recreation. Concerning the latter, it appears that aesthetic and emotional experiences are the most important benefits realized by many recreationists in the natural environment (Rossman & Ulehla, 1977; Shafer & Mietz, 1969).

ROGER S. ULRICH • Department of Geography, University of Delaware, Newark, Delaware 19711.

This chapter is restricted to aesthetic and affective reactions associated with visual perception of natural environments. This is somewhat artificial because environmental perception is obviously multimodal and is not restricted to vision. Although vision is by far our most important sense, many sounds and smells in natural settings surely also influence our feelings. Unfortunately, empirical studies of affective and aesthetic response to auditory and olfactory components of natural environments are virtually nonexistent. Despite the restriction to the visual environment, the topic remains broad and relevant work is found in numerous disciplines, reflecting approaches as diverse as phenomenology and psychophysiology. There can be no attempt here to achieve a comprehensive review of all related studies, and the intuitive literature is largely omitted. One principal purpose is to summarize selectively studies that derive conclusions from empirical observation structured by a research design. A second major objective is to advance a theoretical framework that provides an organized perspective for interpreting and integrating findings. This framework, which is set out in some detail in the initial sections of the chapter, draws heavily on recent emotions theory and research. It proposes an explanation of how affects arise in the natural environment, postulates their functions, and explicitly links them to cognition, activity in physiological systems, and behavior. To ignore associations between affects, actions, and other systems would be to imply that humans are creatures who, despite a very long period of evolution in the natural environment, are saturated with feelings somehow having neither adaptive value nor links with thought or behavior. The position of this chapter is that aesthetic and affective responses cannot be understood in any depth as isolated phenomena.

DEFINING AFFECTIVE AND AESTHETIC RESPONSE

Most of the theory advanced in environmental aesthetics has consisted of quite general statements lacking in-depth development and unaccompanied by definitions of key concepts. To preclude confusion, certain terms central to this chapter should be defined at the outset. *Affect* is used here synonymously with emotion, although in a strict sense the concepts are different. Many psychologists construe affect as a broader term that encompasses not only emotions, but also feelings in terms of drive states such as thirst and hunger (Izard, 1977). Affect is used here in the narrower sense of emotion, and drives are not discussed. Consistent with many contemporary theories of emotion, no sharp distinction is made between emotions and moods. A mood can be considered an emotional state that, compared to an episode of strong feeling, is less intense and often more diffuse. *Aesthetic response* is defined as preference or like–dislike affect (Zajonc, 1980) in association with pleasurable feelings and neurophysiological activity (Berlyne, 1971) elicited by visual encounter with a natural setting. These variables can be measured separately, although investigations using factor analysis indicate that aesthetic preference and pleasurable feelings, or liking and semantic pleasantness evaluations having a strong affective character (Osgood, 1962), typically load on the same dimension (e.g., Calvin, Dearinger, & Curtin, 1972; Küller, 1972; Zube, 1974). This supports an interpretation of aesthetic preference as affect within the broad pleasantness dimension of emotion that has been prominent in theory and research since Wundt's work in the last century.

Affects or emotions are defined as innate, cross-cultural phenomena, each having characteristic experiential, facial, and neurophysiological components (Izard, 1977). One does not learn to feel afraid or to cry any more than one learns to feel pain or to gasp for air (Tomkins, 1962, 1963). Five emotions can be elicited at birth, and the onset of others may occur in association with age-related maturational processes (Izard, 1971; Izard & Buechler, 1980, p. 1973). The innateness of affects is clearly evident from investigations showing, for instance, that congenitally blind children express emotions facially in the same way as children who can see (Eibl-Eibesfeldt, 1972, p. 22). The empirical case for the cross-cultural nature of fundamental or primary emotions is extremely strong. Numerous studies indicate that emotions have the same experiential qualities and facial expressions across widely different cultures, including isolated preliterate groups having had virtually no contact with Western cultures (Ekman, Friesen, & Ellsworth, 1972; Izard, 1971). Whereas affects are universal, the cognitive accompaniments of a given emotion can vary greatly with factors such as age, experience, and culture; therefore, the quality and complexity of conscious experience change throughout an individual's life as affects become associated with cognition, or as affective-cognitive structures are formed (Izard & Buechler, 1980, p. 176). Thus, if a natural scene elicits pleasantness in two observers, one an adult and the other a child, the position here is that the view has similar influences on the quality or type of the persons' affects. However, the conscious experience of the individuals might vary considerably because of differences in cognition. Presumably, the adult's conscious experience would be more complex than the child's because of a greater number of learned associations and possibly a more elaborated cognitive appraisal of the scene.

TOWARD A THEORY OF AFFECTIVE RESPONSE TO NATURAL ENVIRONMENT

During the last two decades, very substantial progress has been made in the area of emotions theory and research, primarily as the result of efforts by clinically trained research psychologists. This work is potentially a rich resource for environment–behavior researchers, and much of it is relevant to an understanding of affective and aesthetic reactions in the natural environment. One clear theoretical trend is toward viewing affects as adaptive. Different authors have construed the adaptive functions of emotions in terms of evolutionary survival requirements, the fostering of well-being defined broadly, or both. An important implication of this extensive literature is that in order to understand why a given natural view elicits certain feelings, it is necessary to consider adaptive functions of preference and other affects in the situation. In the area of landscape aesthetics, Appleton, a geographer, has advanced a rather extreme, ethologically based adaptive position, postulating that aesthetic pleasantness is a response to elements having either real or symbolic significance for survival (1975).

Both the experimental and intuitive schools in landscape aesthetics have failed to incorporate advances from the emotions literature. This may partly explain why theoretical statements in landscape aesthetics have not addressed in any depth fundamental issues such as the link between affects and adaptive behavior, or what internal processes are involved in generating feelings. By venturing briefly into the recent emotions literature, it is possible to shed light on these and other critical issues and to establish a much firmer foundation for a theoretical conception of affective response to the natural environment. These issues must be addressed; as will become evident, they are central to an understanding of why different natural stimuli or configurations can elicit quite different aesthetic reactions.

Generating Affects: Feelings Precede Thoughts

With the rise of cognitive psychology in the 1960s, feelings came to be viewed as products of thought. If applied to explain aesthetic and affective responses to the natural environment, this general perspective would hold that an observer's affects are postcognitive phenomena resulting from a process of cognitive evaluation or appraisal of a scene. This interpretation is also echoed explicitly or implicitly in most intuitive work and in some of the experimental literature on landscape aesthetics. For instance, Tuan asserts that attractive visual landscapes elicit positive affects "because the mind finds repose or excitement in the comeliness of place and setting" (1978, p. 133).

Given the prominence of such cognitive explanations of affect, it is important to emphasize that there is no evidence that feelings are necessarily preceded by a cognitive process (Zajonc, 1980). To the contrary, there is mounting empirical support for the position of Zajonc, Ittelson (1973), Izard (1977), and others that many affects are essentially precognitive and constitute the initial level of response to environment. Drawing on evidence from several studies, Zajonc cogently argues that affective reactions need not depend on cognition and that the first stage of response to stimuli consists of global, generalized affects related to preferences (e.g., liking, fear) and approach–avoidance behavior. The onset of such reactions occurs quickly and is based on very little information. Indeed, there is evidence that like–dislike emotion in relation to a stimulus can be *independent of recognition* (Moreland & Zajonc, 1977; Wilson, 1979). Zajonc asserts that "we can like something or be afraid of it before we know precisely what it is and perhaps even without knowing what it is" (1980, p. 145). This initial affective response then structures and significantly influences the ensuing cognitive process (Zajonc, 1980; Izard, 1977). Zajonc argues convincingly that initial reactions in many instances speed recognition and sharply increase the efficiency of information processing. From the standpoint of survival requirements in evolution, quick-onset responses motivating approach–avoidance behaviors would have had great adaptive value.

Zajonc speculates that affects can occur with little information and without precise recognition because of a class of features and stimulus characteristics he calls "preferenda" (1980). These are gross, often vague, configural aspects that may be insufficient as a basis for cognitive judgments but can be highly effective in eliciting affect. In a similar vein, Ittelson says that initial affect is a general response to the "ambiance" of an environment (1973, p. 16). The quality and intensity of affect reactions elicited by preferenda can be influenced by internal states or conditions of the individual such as previous experience with stimuli of the same general class, immediately preceding exposures that may produce contrast or similarity, and the person's affective state immediately prior to the encounter (Zajonc, 1980).

A Psychoevolutionary Framework

The notion of preferenda, and the position that affect precedes cognition, are important features of the conceptual framework described here, which is intended as a step toward an integrated theory of aesthetic and affective response to the natural environment. It draws on a cross-section of emotions theory and research, including work by Lazarus (1968), Tomkins (1962, 1963), Plutchik (1970), McDougall (1908) and especially Zajonc and Izard. The result is a theoretical synthesis that (1) describes internal processes generating affects, (2) postulates a number of adaptive functions of affects in natural environment, and (3) explicitly relates affects to behavior. Although developed for natural environment, many notions in the framework would apply to urban visual settings as well.

The framework is summarized in Figure 1. For the sake of clarity, many feedback loops have been omitted from the diagram; as a result, the generation of an affective reaction appears more linear than it is in reality. A general feature of the framework is the conceptualization of affect and cognition as occurring in separate though interrelated systems (Izard, 1977; Zajonc, 1980). In this regard it should be noted that feeling and thought are linked with different parts of the brain. The limbic system, which appeared early in evolution, has a central role in emotions, whereas cognition takes place in the neocortex.

As Figure 1 indicates, the first variable of importance in influencing the eventual feeling/behavior outcome is the observer's affective state immediately prior to the visual encounter. This state is derived from a combination of the person's present and past history, including cognitions. The initial affective state directs and sustains attention (Izard, 1977), thereby influencing selection of the feature or scene that is perceived. When perception of natural environment occurs that reaches consciousness, the framework postulates, with Zajonc and Ittelson, that the first level of the reaction is generalized affect (e.g., liking, interest, fear) motivating approach-avoidance impulses or behavior. The initial affect reaction is based on little information, but it is nonetheless elicited quickly by certain general properties or preferenda of the view. In the event the environmental interaction entails risk or pronounced threat (e.g., a hiker suddenly encountering the edge of a precipice), the initial affect reaction (fear, dislike) can very quickly motivate adaptive avoidance behavior on the basis of only a minimum of cognitive activity. Although Figure 1 portrays initial affect in association with visual perception of the natural environment, a feeling response could also be elicited by imagination or a vivid memory of a natural setting (Singer, 1966).

The framework assumes that in natural environments preferenda for the most part are (1) gross configurational or structural aspects of settings, (2) gross depth properties that require little inference, and (3) general classes of environmental content. It argues that various gross

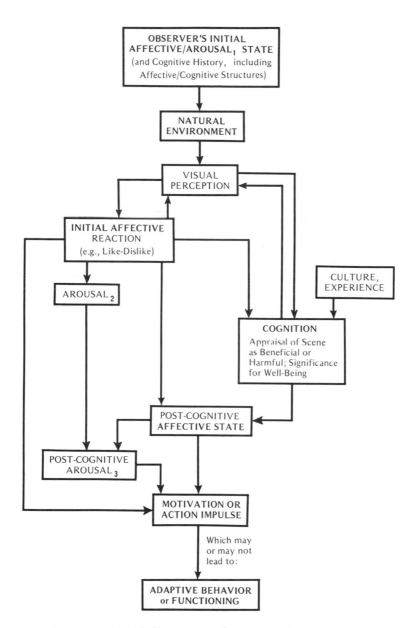

Figure 1. Model of affective/arousal response to a natural scene.

structural properties (e.g., the presence of a focal area and patterning) combine with biases in human perception to convey quickly, and with very little processing, salient general characteristics of a setting that elicit affect. The framework further assumes that certain broad classes of content (e.g., water, vegetation) can produce visual ambiances that quickly elicit affective reactions prior to identification or extensive processing. These assumptions are central in the formulation; later sections discuss them in greater detail and cite some empirical evidence in their support.

The initial affect reaction produces arousal in the electrocortical and autonomic systems, thereby mobilizing the individual for sustaining or undertaking behavior (see Arousal$_2$ in Figure 1). The framework holds that the initial affect reaction then influences an ensuing process of cognitive evaluation of the scene. If the feeling response is strong, it may dominate the cognitive process and be salient in the observer's conscious experience. Further, if the initial affect is strong, the ensuing cognition may be more efficient in the sense that elements will be more quickly recognized and identified, and the view will be remembered better than a comparatively neutral scene (Zajonc, 1980). Thus, remembered views will in most instances be those that elicit reactions such as strong initial liking or dislike. If the initial reaction is weak, it does not significantly influence the subsequent cognition, and, in any case, extensive cognition is quite unlikely if the scene does not elicit the emotion of interest (Izard, 1977).

After onset of the initial affect reaction, the ensuing cognition evaluates the setting in terms of its significance for well-being, broadly defined (Arnold, 1960; Lazarus et al., 1980, p. 193). This process entails recognition, identification, and much more extensive processing of the information. Processing and evaluation will be faster and more efficient when there are present organizational properties and depth cues that facilitate comprehension of the scene in all three dimensions (Ulrich, 1977). In line with traditional cognitive theories of emotion, the framework assumes at this point that the observer's feeling state is affected by the cognitive evaluation of the actual or anticipated outcome of the encounter (e.g., Lazarus et al., 1980, p. 195). The viewer's evaluation, which is influenced by learned associations and expectations, refines and more sharply focuses the comparatively general affect of the initial reaction and may generate other emotions. To the extent that cognition modifies emotion, this will produce changes in physiological arousal as well as in subjective feelings (see Arousal$_3$ and Postcognitive Affect boxes in Figure 1). Evaluation may be accompanied by memories and associations which, along with emerging emotions, add to the complexity of the observer's conscious experience. Emerging affects may in turn influence perceptual activity and cognition, and therefore some encounters will entail a complex, ongoing interplay of feelings and thoughts (Izard, 1977; Lazarus, 1968). As an extreme example, an aesthetically spectacular vista would likely elicit an initial affective reaction of strong preference and interest that could sustain a lengthy and elaborated cognitive process, involving detailed perception and processing of the visual information and thoughts as diverse as memories from a childhood vacation or an idea recalled from a poem. This would be an exception, however, as the vast majority of encounters are with unspectacular natural environments eliciting comparatively weak affective responses that are probably dominated by the initial general affective reaction and involve only elementary cognition.

AFFECTS AND BEHAVIOR IN NATURAL ENVIRONMENTS

To understand more fully why different natural scenes can elicit quite different affective reactions, it is essential to consider the functions and consequences of affects in natural enviornments. This implies the assumption that affective reactions to natural scenes are adaptive in terms of the total behavior of the individual. The framework now converges with some theoretical conceptions in environmental psychology (Ittelson, Franck, & O'Hanlon, 1976, p. 192; Mehrabian and Russell, 1974), as well as many emotion theories, by premising that feelings are inseparably linked to actions. More specifically, it is assumed that an individual's affective reaction motivates, or serves as an action impulse for, adaptive behavior or functioning (Izard, 1977; Tomkins, 1962). The individual is physiologically mobilized to undertake or sustain adaptive actions because affects in relation to the scene have produced appropriate changes in arousal (see Arousal$_3$ in Figure 1). *Adaptive* refers here to a wide array of actions and functioning which are appropriate in terms of fostering well-being. The term *action impulse* reflects the notion that an action motivated internally by affect and expressed in neurophysiological arousal need not be carried out and can be suppressed or denied (Lazarus *et al.*, 1980, p. 198). For instance, a person viewing an attractive natural setting might feel strong preference and interest, and an impulse to explore the area on foot, but could suppress the behavior and simply continue looking from the same vantage point.

Table 1 contains several examples of adaptive behaviors motivated by different affective/arousal reactions to natural scenes. While the list is by no means comprehensive, it does set out what may be some of the most important and frequent behaviors in the natural environment. Common to the different motivating states are feelings of like–dislike

TABLE 1
ADAPTIVE BEHAVIORS MOTIVATED BY AFFECT/AROUSAL REACTIONS TO VISUAL
NATURAL ENVIRONMENT

Motivating state		
Feelings	Arousal[a] change	Behavior or functioning
Interest, anticipation accompanied by preference/pleasantness	Increase	Approach or exploration
Interest and strong preference/pleasantness (elation, exhilaration, joy)	Maintained if initial level is moderately high Increased if initial level is low	Ongoing activity or performance is sustained; challenging activity undertaken
Mild-moderate interest accompanied by preference/pleasantness, including calm, peacefulness	Maintained if initial level is moderate Decreased if initial level is high	Psychophysiological restoration; nonvigilant attention with little scanning
Interest, dislike, accompanied by fear or anxiety	Sharp increase	Deal with threat—e.g., avoidance or flight
Interest and dislike accompanied by one or more of following: fear, caution, uncertainty	Increase	Vigilant attention with scanning

[a]Arousal may be electrocortical, autonomic, or both.

and interest, and most of the states are linked to approach–avoidance behaviors or impulses. Approach behaviors motivated by preference include seeking out, exploring, staying in, and not avoiding a situation (Mehrabian and Russell, 1974, p. 157). Some states motivate overt actions having obvious adaptive functions, such as acquiring environmental information (exploration) or dealing with a survival-related threat (e.g., Appleton, 1975; Berlyne, 1960; Plutchik, 1970, p. 11). It is proposed that an important adaptive function of strongly positive affects can be to sustain ongoing activity (Izard, 1977; Lazarus *et al.*, 1980, p. 209). For instance, a wilderness backpacker who is fatigued might feel exhilaration or elation upon viewing an aesthetically spectacular setting, and these affects would produce physiological arousal and help to sustain his journey. Many aesthetic and affective reactions to natural environments are assumed to motivate behaviors that are not necessarily expressed as observable actions, but which nonetheless qualify as adaptive functioning. For example, if an observer's state prior to a visual encounter is one of stress and excessive arousal, an attractive natural view might elicit feelings of pleasantness, hold interest and block or reduce stressful thoughts, and therefore foster psychophysiological restoration (Ulrich, 1979a). In this instance, adaptive approach behavior might consist simply of staying in and continuing to view the setting, rather than engaging in actions such as exploration. Even the passive intellectual contemplation of a natural setting can be quite adaptive if it provides a breather from stress (Lazarus et al., 1980, p. 208), or gives the observer a sense of competence in terms of mental prowess or efficacy, thereby contributing to a sense of identity (White, 1959). The framework therefore construes adaptive behavior motivated by affects as encompassing a wide range of observable actions and nonmotor (e.g., perceptual) activity.

The following section discusses visual properties that influence affective reactions, and surveys related empirical findings. It will be evident that very few studies have directly addressed behaviors motivated by aesthetic and affective responses to natural scenes. The overwhelming majority of investigations of outdoor environments has been concerned exclusively with aesthetic preference or pleasantness and in some cases with other emotions, such as interest. Some of the literature gives the impression that affects are isolated phenomena having no explicit associations with behavior or even with other systems and processes. In contrast, the framework here stresses that an affective reaction is closely linked to the preceding affective state, to thought, neurophysiological activity, and action. In this light, the following discussion tends to dwell on specific slices of the larger process whereby people interact with natural environment to foster well-being.

VISUAL PROPERTIES INFLUENCING AESTHETIC PREFERENCE AND INTEREST

COMPLEXITY

Complexity refers generally to the number of independently perceived elements in a scene. High complexity is associated with large numbers of elements and with dissimilarity among elements (Berlyne, 1971). Complexity has long been a featured variable in experimental aesthetics, and findings from numerous laboratory studies using randomly generated, unstructured arrays have rather consistently indicated that aesthetic preference or pleasantness are related to complexity in an inverted-U-shaped manner (for a survey of studies, see Berlyne, 1971).

That is, high preference tends to be associated with moderate levels of complexity, whereas low preference is linked with the extremes of either low or high complexity. Additionally, in several investigations using art works and a variety of more artificial stimuli such as random polygons, Berlyne and his colleagues identified generally linear positive relationships between the complexity of an array and judged interestingness, attention (viewing time), and exploratory activity (e.g., Berlyne, 1963; Day, 1967). It can be inferred from these studies that most high-complexity natural scenes should elicit considerable interest/attention, but only low levels of preference. On the other hand, high-preference views will not necessarily elicit strong interest. Consistent with Berlyne's results for nonlandscape stimuli, Wohlwill found that subjects' number of voluntary exposures of landscape slides correlated with judged complexity (1968).

Several investigations have tested complexity as a predictor of preference for natural and urban scenes (e.g., Kaplan, Kaplan, & Wendt, 1972; Ulrich, 1977; Wohlwill, 1968, 1976). Although nearly all studies have found significant associations with preference, in some cases the relationships are inverted-U-shaped, while in others they are linear positive. These conflicting results are probably attributable to the difficulty of assembling samples of natural scenes depicting broad ranges of complexity (Wohlwill, 1976, p. 46). Many studies of natural settings likely sample only low to moderate complexity ranges, and therefore identify a linear positive association between complexity and preference representing the left side of an inverted-U curve.

Complexity is incorporated in an implicit fashion in many scenic-quality assessment procedures. For instance, the successful models developed by Daniel and his colleagues for assessing forest landscapes include variables such as amount of downed wood, slash, and species diversity (Daniel & Schroeder, 1979). It can be argued that these variables are surrogates for complexity, offering in this particular context the considerable advantage of their direct relevance to forest-management practices.

In view of the inverted-U-shaped relation that has emerged in many complexity studies, it should be stressed that the theoretical framework also suggests that high levels of random, unstructured complexity should elicit low aesthetic preference. This position derives from the basic premise that affective reactions are motivators of adaptive behavior. The explanation can be illustrated using the example of a hiker's feelings and actions as he travels through a large-scale natural environment. The individual's journey can be construed as consisting of a large number of approach behaviors of varying durations and distances, punctuated by some avoidance actions and periods of restoration (Table 1). In most instances, an approach or avoidance segment of the trip is motivated by the hiker's affective reaction to the area of landscape immediately in view. If a setting is encountered that is characterized by unstructured high complexity (e.g., a thicket), the individual cannot quickly grasp the salient global aspects of the setting, and has to engage in detailed processing in order to achieve even a modicum of comprehension. Also, this situation warrants a comparatively elaborated process of cognitive appraisal of the anticipated outcome of the encounter. If approach movement continues under these circumstances, important information might be missed, and in some cases the situation could prove dangerous. Therefore, a quick-onset reaction of low preference or dislike is clearly adaptive because such affects generate avoidance impulses, thereby leading to a slowing or cessation of approach movement. Further, the affect reaction should also include interest, because this feeling motivates attention and processing and sustains a process of cognitive appraisal. These affects, dislike and interest, are the major components of the initial level of response, emerging with minimal cognition and before recognition or identification has occurred. This argument implies that disordered high complexity constitutes one type of gross environmental ambiance that very quickly elicits initial affect.

At the other extreme, the theoretical framework suggests that low complexity scenes should elicit low interest and moderately low preference. A flat, featureless open field, for instance, could be processed rather quickly by the hiker, and little additional information would be gained by exploring it. Interest therefore should be low because sustained attention and detailed processing are unnecessary or would yield little in return; weak preference would motivate neither strong approach/exploration nor avoidance impulses. The hiker might move on, avoiding the area, or might walk through it at a faster pace than when traversing a pleasurable, interesting segment (Gustke & Hodgson, 1980). These arguments are in clear accord with findings of the many laboratory studies, and provide a plausible explanation of preference and interest responses in relation to low and high complexity. Preference and interest are largely independent dimensions of emotion, and in some instances can be influenced in different directions by the same combination of visual properties.

STRUCTURAL PROPERTIES

The framework assumes that gross structural or configurational properties are preferenda that elicit initial affective reactions with minimal cognition. If disorder is an environmental ambiance that produces dislike and interest/attention, then gross structure is considered another ambiance that should tend to elicit liking and approach. Considerable research has shown that perception in both humans and animals is characterized by a strong orientation to information that is structured or patterned. Further, it has been demonstrated that affective reactions can occur largely on the basis of the configuration in a visual array, as opposed to individual features. For instance, affective reactions to faces, and facial recognition, appear to be more related to configurations of facial features than to individual features (e.g., Patterson & Baddeley, 1977). A bias towards gross configurations in natural settings would be highly adaptive because large numbers of environmental elements could be grasped as smaller numbers of element groupings or chunks (Ulrich, 1977). This would expedite appropriate affective reactions and would speed up recognition and identification. It follows that even high-complexity natural scenes can be efficiently processed, provided that the complexity is structured. Structuring of natural stimuli can be achieved in a number of ways, such as through the presence of homogeneous textures, redundant elements, groupings of elements, and properties that provide continuity among separated or dissimilar elements. Of particular importance can be patterning that establishes a focal point in the scene.

The rationale for a positive relationship between liking and structure emerges directly from the premise that affective reactions motivate adaptive functioning. If the hiker in the earlier example encountered a setting characterized by moderate complexity and extensive gross structure, he could rapidly grasp global aspects relevant to behavior with very little cognition and perhaps even without identification. The scene should elicit quick-onset liking, since this would expeditiously motivate adaptive approach behavior (exploring, staying in, or not avoiding). The initial reaction would not necessarily include strong interest, however, because lengthy processing motivated by interest would not be required. In some instances, encounters with highly structured scenes should generate both liking and strong interest. An expansive vista of ordered high complexity should elicit comparatively strong interest and liking, because the view would contain a great deal of information about the surrounding area relevant to adaptive functioning. Initial feelings of strong liking/pleasantness would generate approach impulses and would produce physiological arousal to sustain the observer's subsequent actions (see Table 1).

The notion that structural or organizational properties influence aesthetic preference is also prominent in Gestalt theory and in the literature of intuitive design and art where concepts such as "harmony" and "composition" have long been emphasized. In experimental contexts, several authors have proposed structural variables or dimensions. A notable example is Küller's semantic factor—unity—which has been consistently identified in a series of studies, including cross-cultural replications, and emerges for built as well as rural scenes (e.g., Küller, 1972; Kwok, 1979). Concepts such as unity, order, and coherence are extremely general, which suggests they can be broken down into more specific component variables. Wohlwill (1980) has called attention to the neglect by investigators of several related issues, such as pattern perception and unit chunking, that would lead to a deeper understanding of the role of structure.

Focality

The author has identified a "focality" variable that is considerably less general than the above notions, and appears to tap an important gross structural property (Ulrich, 1977). Focality refers to the degree to which a scene contains a focal point, or an area that attracts the observer's attention. It is present when textures, landform contours, and other patterns direct the observer's attention to a part of the scene. Focality is also produced when a prominent feature, or grouping of features, creates a point or subarea of dominance that attracts the viewer's eye. Compared to other structural variables, a major advantage of focality is that it can be unambiguously applied to scenes ranging from very low to very high levels of complexity. Empirical support for a link between focality and preference comes from a study using rural roadside scenes (Ulrich, 1977). The views were scaled for focality using ratings by trained judges and then were shown to two groups (American suburbanites and Swedish university students) who rated the scenes for aesthetic preference. The rank correlation coefficients between focality and preference were .46 for the Americans, and .54 for the Swedes.

It is contended that focality is one type of gross configurational property that is important in eliciting initial affect and which retains a central role in subsequent stages of processing and appraisal. Support for this position is provided by Janssens's pioneering investigation of eye movements in relation to outdoor scenes (1976). Although buildings were prominent in all the views that Janssens analyzed, his major findings may also hold for natural settings. His recordings of eye-fixation sequences strongly suggest that immediately after onset of a view, subjects sought a salient feature or pattern (i.e., a focal area), which nearly all individuals located within about 1.25 seconds. Importantly, Janssens's results support the interpretation that individuals tended to use the focal area as a reference point or "home base" for subsequent perception. For example, a person might follow a major contour out from the focal area for three or four fixations, then return to the focal area and fixate, move away in a new direction for a few fixations, return again, and so on. The critical importance of focality was clearly evident in the finding that a distinct subarea of each scene attracted a disproportionate percentage of all fixations, *especially the earliest fixations*. The Janssens study vividly demonstrates the incompleteness of human visual perception of environments and the central role of structure in grasping a subset of the information in an outdoor scene.

DEPTH

Several investigations have identified significant positive relationships between depth and aesthetic preference for natural or rural scenes (Craik, 1970; Ulrich, 1973, 1977; Wohlwill, 1973). Similarly, studies of forest landscape aesthetics have consistently found that preference levels are higher for tree stands having some visual depth or openness, as opposed to those with restricted depth (e.g., Brush, 1978; Daniel & Boster, 1976). On the basis of data originating in Ulrich's 1973 roadside research, S. Kaplan incorporated depth as a central variable in his evolutionary preference model (1975, p. 97). Küller has identified a spatial semantic factor, "enclosedness," that has emerged in several studies encompassing rural and built visual landscapes (1972).

The framework proposes that depth/spaciousness influences both the initial affective reaction to a scene and the ensuing process of cognitive appraisal. This differs from the usual position that depth is exclusively an inferred property contingent on considerable cognition. It is hypothesized that lack of depth (e.g., a visually impenetrable foreground immediately ahead of the observer) can be a gross ambiance that quickly elicits dislike and uncertainty with minimal cognition. An adaptive perspective suggests that spatial restriction should elicit reaction almost immediately, certainly before a complex, extended inference process that comprehends distances or relationships among elements in three dimensions. The reaction should be based on a very coarse interpretation that depth is absent or highly restricted. A moving, exploring person would be promptly motivated by this initial response to avoid a setting that could contain hidden dangers or constrain opportunities to escape (Appleton, 1975). These arguments are consonant with the finding that scenes having sharply restricted levels of depth are accorded low preference (Brush, 1978; Craik, 1970; Ulrich, 1973, 1977).

Conversely, a gross ambiance of some spaciousness should not elicit dislike and avoidance, because immediate risk or threat would be negligible (Appleton, 1975).

Following the initial affective reaction, specific depth properties will be critical in the process of cognitive appraisal. Evaluation of a setting in terms of its significance for well-being is contingent on accurately inferring distances and relationships among elements in three dimensions (Ulrich, 1977). If depth in the natural environment could not be perceived, features would stand ambiguously in two dimensions and appraisal would be essentially impossible. The observer's cognitive history is of central importance both in the process to infer distances and in appraisal. Settings having numerous depth cues and clear spatial definition facilitate cognitive evaluation, tend to yield more environmental information, and therefore should be liked.[1]

GROUND SURFACE TEXTURE

Textures characterizing ground surfaces in the natural environment are very important in defining depth, and they may strongly influence cognitive appraisal following the initial affective reaction. Gibson's research has clearly shown that ground textural gradients can play a major role in depth perception and that the character of a textural surface profoundly affects the accuracy of depth estimates (1958, p. 420). There is ample basis for concluding that surface textures influence both the inferred depth or space in a setting and the ease of comprehending element relationships in three dimensions (Ulrich, 1977). Importantly, cognitive appraisal following the initial affective reaction to a scene should be facilitated by the presence of uniform, even-length ground textures, as opposed to rough, uneven surfaces. Even textures preserve the sense of a continuous "sheet" or surface between the observer and the environmental elements that Gibson has shown is necessary if distance is to be perceived accurately (1958, p. 421). Therefore, if ground textures tend to be even in a setting, more information can be extracted, and the observer's appraisal should be more definite and positive. Uni-

---

[1]A few individuals may have phobic reactions of extreme dislike, fear, or even panic when they encounter vast expanses (Balint, 1955). However, such agoraphobic disorders much more commonly involve fear of being in spaces that contain people (American Psychiatric Association, 1980) and therefore are strongly tied to social as well as physical aspects of environment. By contrast, claustrophobia (fear of restricted or closed spaces) does not involve the presence of people and is almost exclusively related to spatial conditions (American Psychiatric Association, 1980).

form, relatively smooth textures should also be evaluated positively, generating liking, because an observer knows from previous experience they are conducive to movement or exploration. On the other hand, rough, uneven textures may disrupt the sense of a continuous depth sheet or surface, thereby producing spatial ambiguities, difficulties in grasping a setting, uncertainty, and reduced preference. Further, rough textures are often produced by coarse scrub or brush that are obstacles to movement, and appraisals accordingly should be negative, generating dislike.

In addition to influences on depth perception and appraisals of movement opportunities, ground surface textures affect the complexity and structure of the two-dimensional visual array. Scenes having scruffy, irregular textures present the observer with unordered high complexity that works against preference. Surfaces having even textures, or areas of textural homogeneity, should tend to be preferred because the complexity is ordered. Several arguments, therefore, can be given for a link between uniform ground textures and liking; it is not surprising that the few studies explicitly addressing ground texture have identified strong associations with preference. Rabinowitz and Coughlin (1970) and Ulrich (1973) found consistent patterns of low preference for scenes having rough, scruffy ground surfaces. In the cross-cultural roadside study mentioned earlier, the sample of scenes was rated by trained judges using scales that assessed surface textural unevenness–evenness and coarseness–fineness (Ulrich, 1977). The rank correlation coefficient between ground texture judgments and the American group's aesthetic preference ratings was .66; it was .55 for the Swedish subjects, indicating a clear pattern that groups from both countries prefer settings having even ground textures. Additionally, several studies of forest landscapes have found positive relationships between aesthetic preference and comparatively even-length grass ground covers and negative preference effects of rough ground covers (e.g., Daniel & Boster, 1976; Arthur, 1977).

THREAT/TENSION

An obvious implication of the position that affects motivate adaptive behavior is that natural settings characterized by threat or risk should elicit dislike and often fear, thereby generating adaptive avoidance (Table 1). If dangerous or threatening features are near the observer and are visually salient, they should elicit a reaction almost immediately. The traditional view that emotions result exclusively from a process of cognitive evaluation makes little sense in this context. If an individual is to escape from an immediately dangerous situation, the action must be undertaken long before completion of even a very simple cognitive process (Zajonc, 1980). In this light it is understandable why affective judgments are made faster and with much more confidence than recognition judgments (Kunst-Wilson & Zajonc, 1980; Zajonc, 1980). If a threat is comparatively hidden, fear will not be part of the initial response, but will be generated by the cognitive appraisal process in later stages of the encounter. A threat inference following the initial response obviously results from learned associations and expectations (Zuckerman, 1976).

Surprisingly little empirical work has either addressed the relationship between threat and preference in the case of visual natural landscapes or evaluated different natural phenomena in terms of threat or tension. A recent study explored some of these questions using a collection of 52 slides of natural landscape paintings (Ulrich & Zuckerman, 1981). The collection included works by several European and American artists and depicted a broad range of natural features and geographical settings. The paintings also varied markedly in terms of calm–tension properties, as scored by trained judges using a semantic differential procedure. Nearly all the high-tension paintings contained phenomena that would be extremely dangerous in real encounters, such as stormy seas, an avalanche, the edge of a steep cliff, and a violent thunderstorm and flash flood. Among the landscapes lowest in tension were those containing calm water surfaces. The collection was shown to more than 200 university students, who rated each scene for liking. Results revealed a highly significant inverse relationship between the liking ratings and tension scores. Since the paintings simulated environmental tension or threat, and real danger was absent, it can be expected that real exposures to threat in the natural environment are characterized by an even stronger tension/preference association.

Deflected Vistas

Authors from different fields have pointed out that preference and curiosity are elicited when the line of sight in a natural or urban setting is deflected or curved, signaling that new landscape information is just beyond the visual bounds defined by the observer's position. This property is highly cognitive, and therefore is probably not a major factor in the initial affective reaction. Cullen called attention to this notion in his analysis of townscapes, referring to it as "anticipation" (1961). Using views of curving city streets as his principal examples, he argues that such settings "clearly arouse one's curiosity as to what scene will meet our eyes upon reaching the end of the street" (p. 49). Analogous configurations in the natural environment have been termed "deflected vistas" by Appleton, who lists as examples curving sight lines associated with paths, rivers, and valleys (1975). Essentially the same property has been called "mystery" by S. and R. Kaplan, who define it as a "promise of information" associated with a projected change in vantage point (R. Kaplan, 1973; S. Kaplan, 1975, p. 94). S. Kaplan describes mystery as an inferred property of the three-dimensional array, and he has advanced theoretical arguments for a link between mystery or deflected vista configurations and preference. He asserts that evolution has left its mark on contemporary humans in the form of an innate predilection for exploring and acquiring landscape information. It follows that we should prefer scenes that explicitly convey to the observer a sense that additional information could be gained by moving deeper into the area. The framework in this chapter, however, implies that deflected sight lines or mystery will be positively related to preference only when the observer judges that new information can be gained at low risk—a position consistent with the well-established point that there is a very close and unstable equilibrium between curiosity and fear (McDougall, 1908; Tomkins, 1962).

Importantly, studies using samples of nonthreatening natural scenes have found that views having mystery consistently receive high preference ratings (R. Kaplan, 1973; Ulrich, 1977). This property, by whatever name, may eventually prove to be one of the most efficacious predictors of liking for visual landscapes. Future investigations that also examine interest (curiosity) in relation to this property are needed.

WATER

Water has been described in a large body of intuitive literature as a landscape element that evokes interest, aesthetic pleasantness, and positive feelings, such as tranquility (e.g., Hubbard & Kimball, 1967). Although negative affective reactions can be elicited by some water phenomena (e.g., a stormy sea or a lake dotted with chemical foam pollution), a consistent finding in the experimental literature is that scenes with water features usually are accorded especially high levels of preference or pleasantness (e.g., Brush & Shafer, 1975; Civco, 1979; Palmer, 1978; Penning-Rowsell, 1979; Shafer, Hamilton, & Schmidt, 1969; Ulrich, 1981; Zube, Pitt, & Anderson, 1975). There is considerable evidence to support the conclusion of Zube and his colleagues that water is a dominant visual landscape property that nearly always enhances scenic quality (Zube et al., 1975, p. 152).

The framework assumes that water is a class or dimension of environmental content that produces ambiances that are effective in quickly eliciting affective reactions. This implies that the preference effects of a water feature stem more from content *per se* than from such informational properties as complexity. Perhaps part of the appeal of water is biologically based and largely independent of informational characteristics and learned associations. In terms of the properties discussed above, water may also enhance preference by serving as a focal element and possibly by increasing subjective depth (Hubbard & Kimball, 1967).

SUMMARY OF VISUAL PROPERTIES INFLUENCING PREFERENCE

The earlier theoretical discussion argued that feelings of like–dislike arise very early in visual encounters with natural environment as part of the initial generalized affective reaction and subsequently can be refined or modified by the process of cognitive appraisal. The framework postulated that initial affective reactions to natural scenes are elicited by general ambiances or preferenda that for the most part are (1) the presence or absence of gross structural or configurational aspects, (2) gross depth properties, and (3) general classes of environmental content, such as water. The influences of water on affects are further discussed in a later section addressing the issue of differential responsiveness to natural versus man-made content.

The preceding sections discussed several properties that influence liking for *unspectacular* natural scenes. In terms of these properties, a view should be preferred if:

1. Complexity is moderate to high.
2. The complexity has structural properties that establish a focal point and other order or patterning is also present.
3. There is a moderate to high level of depth that can be perceived unambiguously.
4. The ground surface texture tends to be homogeneous and even and is appraised as conducive to movement.
5. A deflected vista is present.
6. Appraised threat is negligible or absent.

Although the above properties in concert will elicit liking, preference will be even greater if a water feature is present.

By contrast, low preference scenes will be marked by

1. either low complexity, or unstructured high complexity with no focal area;
2. restricted depth;

3. rough, uneven ground surface textures that are obstacles to movement;
4. absence of both a deflected vista and water feature; and
5. high appraised threat. (In contrast to the preceding attributes, which are thought to function in an interdependent, or possibly additive fashion, the presence of moderate to high appraised threat can be expected by itself to produce dislike.)

The efficacy of these properties when used in combination to predict preference can be illustrated with data from the roadside study using American and Swedish subjects (Ulrich, 1977). Since none of the 53 unspectacular rural scenes in the study conveyed a sense of threat or contained water, these properties did not influence the results. The patterns of preference ratings for both the Americans and the Swedes were clearly consistent with this model. Both groups accorded moderately high to high preference to views having at least midrange values for complexity, focality, depth, and ground textural evenness. Also, all scenes in the sample containing a deflected vista received high ratings. For individuals from both countries, the most-liked scenes tended to be parklike in appearance. These typically contained scattered trees or groupings of trees, and all had even ground textures. Complexity in the parklike views consisted primarily of vertical elements, such as trees and bushes, which stood out as depth cues against the unambiguous depth sheet of the even ground surface. Complexity therefore was structured and comprehensible, spaces were well-defined, and the settings could be readily grasped in three dimensions. The finding that parklike scenes were highly preferred is consistent with results from other investigations (Rabinowitz & Coughlin, 1970; Ulrich, 1973).

The results for the American and Swedish groups with respect to the low-preference scenes were also in clear agreement with the model. Several views contained unordered high complexity and rough, uneven ground textures and therefore could not be grasped efficiently or unambiguously. Focality was low or absent, and none of the scenes contained a deflected vista. Scenes that were lowest in preference tended to have restricted levels of depth. Views of flat, featureless fields received below-average ratings, probably because of excessively low complexity. These findings, together with other results surveyed earlier, strongly suggest that the properties featured here are major determinants of preference for visual natural environment.

EXTENT OF AGREEMENT AMONG OBSERVERS FOR PREFERENCE

Several studies have reported high levels of agreement among individuals in their aesthetic preferences for natural environments (e.g.,

Clamp, 1976; Coughlin & Goldstein, 1970; Daniel & Boster, 1976; Penning-Roswell, 1979; Shafer et al., 1969; Zube et al., 1975, p. 157). Although some of these investigations measured preference (like–dislike), and others used affect-saturated scales such as beautiful-ugly, ratings from these different measures are highly intercorrelated (Zube et al., 1975, p. 162). Therefore, despite somewhat different measures, the studies support the same general picture of agreement. There is absolutely nothing in this substantial body of findings to suggest that aesthetic preferences for natural environment are random or idiosyncratic. To the contrary, the strong implication is that aesthetic preference can be analyzed in terms of underlying principles that are quite general from individual to individual. To the extent that some differences exist between groups of individuals, such variations may often be greater between the public and certain professions (Brush, 1976, p. 54) than among groups defined on the basis of such traditional variables as income or rural versus urban background. In this regard a number of studies have found that preferences of professionals such as architects, landscape architects, and range managers can vary significantly from those of the public (e.g., Buhyoff, Wellman, Harvey, & Fraser, 1978; Daniel & Boster, 1976; R. Kaplan, 1973; Küller, 1972).

CULTURAL INFLUENCES ON AESTHETIC PREFERENCE

Culture unquestionably has important influences on innumerable aspects of persons' relations with the physical environment, from constructing homes, to achieving privacy, to developing world views (Altman & Chemers, 1980). In recent decades considerable work on landscape aesthetics, especially in geography, landscape architecture, and, to a lesser extent, psychology, has stressed culture as a preeminent determinant of preference (e.g., Lowenthal, 1968; Tuan, 1973). A writer of this genre might conclude, for instance, that a given natural setting elicits preference and other positive feelings because landscape painters have taught us that it is beautiful, or because our society has conditioned us to revere wilderness and dislike cities. This literature is characterized by a tendency to emphasize the differences, rather than similarities, in the visual landscape preferences of different groups. Indeed, much of the work explicitly or implicitly suggests that the influences of culture and such factors as adaptation to a given landscape are so great as to preclude major similarities in aesthetic preferences across societies.

Unfortunately, relatively few experimental studies have tested this widely held position that aesthetic preferences are determined largely by culture and therefore vary fundamentally between societies. Because many more comparative investigations are needed, especially of non-Western groups, the conclusions of studies to date should be interpreted with caution. Nonetheless, it is noteworthy that findings to date unanimously suggest the possibility of similarity between the preferences of different cultures for visual natural environments. For instance, Shafer and Tooby (1973) showed 100 photographs of diverse rural and wilderness landscapes to 250 campers of several different nationalities in Scotland. The campers' preference ratings correlated very highly (.91) with ratings obtained from American subjects in a previous study using the same scenes (Shafer *et al.*, 1969). Indeed, the *r* value is so high that it indicates that the ranked order of scenes in terms of liking was nearly the same for both groups. In the roadside study previously mentioned, the rank-order correlation between the Swedish and American ratings was .88 (Ulrich, 1977). Agreement across groups was nearly perfect in terms of scenes falling in the extremes of either high or low preference. Even more impressive was the finding that the factor structures of the groups' ratings were nearly the same. Factor analysis identified groupings of interrelated scenes that could be easily categorized in terms of differences in ground surface texture, depth, and complexity, suggesting strongly that individuals from both countries responded sensitively to these properties.

Additionally, broad consistencies across cultures in responsiveness to visual environments are suggested by findings from semantic evaluation procedures. Kwok (1979) used Küller's semantic scales and sample of architectural and landscape slides to obtain data from Chinese students in Singapore and from middle-income British professionals in London. Semantic factors identified for both groups were nearly the same as Küller's factors for Swedish subjects (Küller, 1972), which indicates striking similarity across different cultures in terms of the ways in which the various evaluative judgments were related to one another. Likewise, Berlyne and his colleagues found similar factor structures for broad semantic evaluations of abstract visual arrays by (1) Canadian university students and (2) a diverse sample of 300 Banganda farmers and urban dwellers in Uganda (Berlyne, Robbins, & Thompson, 1974). While noting differences among individuals and ethnic groups, the investigators concluded there were "impressive similarities in the ways in which people with markedly different cultural backgrounds respond to the same visual material" (p. 277). Berlyne subsequently (1975) extended this study to include samples of university students and illiterate villagers in India. He found that the tendency to look longer at high-complexity patterns was somewhat greater for the students. However, the groups' factor structures for semantic evaluations (including pleasantness) were virtually the same, and they closely matched the factors obtained for the Ugandans and Canadians in the earlier study. These similarities are especially striking in view of the fact that some variance must have been introduced by translation of the scales into the Luganda (Ugandan) and Hindu languages, and because the scales were administered by oral interview to the illiterate groups.

Although far from conclusive, these findings nonetheless cast some doubt on the position that preferences vary fundamentally as a function of culture. One interpretation is that learning experiences may be much more ubiquitous than the descriptive cultural literature suggests. Alternatively, as Berlyne has posited (1971, 1975, p. 328), it may be that preference responses are influenced by characteristics of the nervous system that are universal in our species. Likewise, the psychoevolutionary framework outlined earlier gives rise to theoretical arguments for expecting some similarity to characterize the preferences of different cultures for natural scenes. It will be recalled that emotions are universal and have the same qualities across different cultures. A plausible assumption is that, irrespective of culture, liking motivates the approach class of behaviors and dislike motivates avoidance. In this light, scenes characterized by, for instance, disordered high complexity and restricted depth should tend to elicit initial reactions of dislike in different societies because avoidance is initially adaptive regardless of culture. It would be surprising if one culture liked such views, and individuals accordingly engaged in approach actions that would be maladaptive because observers could not have grasped a setting or completed an appraisal process. Therefore, some correspondence in preference should be evident, since the general approach or avoidance behavior appropriate in a given setting should be more or less similar across cultures.

Another major argument for similarity derives from the fact that there is no evidence that fundamental perceptual and cognitive processes vary between cultures (Cole & Scribner, 1974; Kennedy, 1974). The similarities across cultures in terms of perception and cognition are much more impressive than the differences. Thus, it would be quite unexpected if, for instance, one culture liked views having focality and other structural properties, while another culture liked unordered scenes. Such an outcome would imply nothing less than major differences between the groups in terms of information processing, chunking, and other aspects of cognition. This finding would also conflict with a vast body of intuitive literature, produced over centuries by many cultures, that stresses the importance of structure and composition in landscape design and art, and which implies a measure of cross-cultural agreement in aesthetic preferences (Ulrich, 1977).

These arguments, together with the findings surveyed earlier, imply that much previous work on preferences for visual landscapes has perhaps overstated the role of culture. This in no way suggests that culture is unimportant; indeed, an ideal or complete preference theory should include culture as a component. The conceptual framework assumes that culture is especially important as a factor that can in some instances produce wide variations in cognitive appraisals of natural settings subsequent to initial affective reactions (see Figure 1). In this regard the descriptive cultural literature is particularly valuable for shedding light on learned associations and meanings in relation to landscapes (e.g., Lowenthal & Prince, 1965). The view here is that culture can be a significant variable influencing aesthetic and affective reactions, but that it should not be emphasized to the exclusion of other factors that the experimental literature clearly shows have major—often dominant—effects on preference.

AESTHETIC RESPONSE TO NATURAL VERSUS BUILT ENVIRONMENTS

One of the most clear-cut findings in the experimental literature on environmental aesthetics is the consistent tendency for North American and European groups to prefer natural scenes over built views, especially when the latter lack vegetation or water features. Several studies have been unanimous in showing that even unspectacular or subpar natural views elicit higher aesthetic preference or pleasantness than do all but a very small percentage of urban views (e.g., Bernaldez & Parra, 1979; Kaplan et al., 1972; Palmer, 1978; Wohlwill, 1976, p. 72; Zube et al., 1975, p. 155). Preference levels for the natural scenes are usually so much higher than for the urban views that the distributions of scores for the two domains hardly overlap. This pattern emerged even in an investigation comparing aesthetic preferences for everyday rural scenes and picturesque Scandinavian townscapes (Ulrich, 1981). Also, levels of agreement among individuals' preferences or scenic evaluations tend to be greater for natural than for urban scenes (Coughlin & Goldstein, 1970; Zube, Pitt, & Anderson, 1974). Importantly, the gap in liking or pleasantness between natural and urban views cannot be explained by differences in properties such as complexity and the others discussed above. Rather, individuals appear to respond in fundamentally different ways to natural and man-made material, irrespective of levels of complexity and other variables. One result is a strong tendency for settings containing natural content such as vegetation and water to be preferred.

As mentioned earlier, the presence of water tends to elicit especially high levels of preference or pleasantness. It is also noteworthy that when natural elements are added to urban scenes, preference levels usually rise significantly (Brush & Palmer, 1979; Thayer & Atwood, 1978).

Findings from these studies provide insights into properties that influence whether a visual setting is responded to as natural or man-made (see Chapter 1). Investigations employing factor or cluster analysis have consistently identified groupings or factors of interrelated scenes, where individual factors can be unambiguously categorized as natural or built in character (e.g., Kaplan et al., 1972; Palmer, 1978). Interpretation of scenes comprising such factors indicates that the domain of natural visual environment is by no means restricted to wilderness; it also encompasses man-made settings such as wheat fields, wooded parks, and golf courses. These results suggest the inappropriateness of proposing narrow definitions of what constitutes a natural or a man-made visual environment. In general, American groups appear to respond to a scene as natural if (1) it contains extensive vegetation or water, and (2) if buildings, cars, and other built features are absent or not prominent. To the extent that there is a common general quality to views responded to as natural, it might be characterized as a general ambiance of vegetation and/or water content. These findings support the position that water and vegetation can be considered preferenda that are highly effective in eliciting affective reactions. There is ample empirical justification for including these general classes of content in the list of visual properties that influence aesthetic response.

At this point one might argue that, at certain times, some cultures, including our own, have feared and avoided wilderness environments (e.g., Tuan, 1979). There is no solid evidence, however, that negatively toned affects are elicited by water or vegetation content *per se*. A reaction of strong dislike or fear typically occurs when the context or disposition of natural elements comprising a setting is evaluated as threatening. If an individual responds with fear or uncertainty to a dense forest, this reaction is probably attributable to aggregate properties of the setting and to inferences such as the presence of wild animals, rather than to vegetation *per se*. Therefore, the notion that natural settings sometimes engender fear and dislike is consistent with the conceptual framework and with the preference findings concerning water and vegetation content.

Very little research has addressed behavior motivated by preferences for natural versus urban visual environment. In one study, shoppers in Ann Arbor, Michigan, had a choice between driving on an interstate highway or on a parkway to a large shopping center (Ulrich, 1973). The highway was several minutes faster, but its roadside environment was nonscenic, containing several obtrusive man-made structures. In contrast, the longer parkway route provided a continuous sequence of wooded, undeveloped scenes, and at one point motorists could view a riverscape. Despite the longer driving time, slightly more than half the shoppers' trips used the parkway. Results from a questionnaire procedure strongly suggested that the most important reason for choosing the parkway was to experience its natural scenery. This is noteworthy because in applications of cost–benefit analysis to highway planning, dollar benefits are calculated largely on the basis of time savings for motorists. In this manner, benefits that often total millions of dollars annually are attributed to an expressway or other high-speed design that reduces travel time for users. Following the same logic, the visual encounters with natural settings provided by the parkway must be worth a great deal, since drivers consciously gave up substantial amounts of time in order to have these experiences.

MAN-MADE FEATURES IN NATURAL SETTINGS

The findings summarized in the previous section imply that the presence of prominent man-made features in natural settings will usually depress aesthetic preferences. Some studies have in fact identified strong inverse relationships between liking or rated attractiveness and the presence of built features in natural environments. For instance, Evans and Wood (1980) found that the introduction of even compatible or sympathetic development along a scenic highway in California sharply reduced perceived aesthetic quality. An investigation of English rural landscapes by Clamp (1976) revealed a pronounced negative association between attractiveness evaluations and extent of visible road surfaces. Findings by Brush and Palmer (1979) suggest that certain man-made elements, such as utility poles and wires, can have a more negative influence on aesthetic evaluations than other types of built features.

The design of man-made structures that are visually congruent with natural settings is an important concern of architects, landscape architects, and wilderness managers. In a series of experiments, Wohlwill has shed light on variables influencing the degree of fittingness or congruity between man-made elements in scenes and their natural surroundings (e.g., Wohlwill, 1979; Wohlwill & Harris, 1980). He defines fittingness as the sense of harmony or clashing between a man-made feature and its natural background. Several properties appear to influence whether a feature is evaluated as fitting. Low fittingness (obtrusiveness) correlates highly with: high color contrast between the feature and its surroundings, high textural contrast, size of the feature, and low congruity of shape (Wohlwill & Harris, 1980). Working in Scandinavia, Sorte (1971) has shown that fittingness and unity are usually greater when the feature is appraised as permanent rather than temporary. Examples of permanent features are most buildings, whereas elements such as billboards and cars are temporary (Sorte, 1971). Although Wohlwill's findings strongly suggest that fittingness can be quite important in influencing liking, this property does not correlate with the judged interestingness of a setting, or with curiosity as measured by number of voluntary exposures to a scene (Wohlwill & Harris, 1980). These results are consistent with the point made earlier that aesthetic preference and interest (curiosity) are largely independent dimensions of affect and can in some instances be influenced in different directions by the same combination of visual properties. Wohlwill's research clearly shows there is no simple general relationship between aesthetic preference and the presence or extent of man-made features in natural settings. Rather, preference can vary widely as a function of the degree of integration of the feature into its surroundings. Interestingly, it appears that in certain instances preference may be greater when there is some degree of contrast or obtrusiveness, which suggests the hazardousness of applying a contrast-minimizing approach to design problems in natural environments (Wohlwill, 1979). Because of their relevance to the design of harmonious blends of the man-made and the natural, more studies are needed to confirm and extend these findings.

OTHER AFFECTIVE-AROUSAL RESPONSES TO NATURAL VERSUS URBAN VISUAL ENVIRONMENT

Apart from the issue of aesthetic preference, a widely held notion in urbanized countries is that experiences with the natural environment can be psychologically healthful (Driver & Greene, 1977; Ulrich, 1979a). The intuitively based idea that people benefit emotionally in some broad sense from contacts with nature often forms part of the rationale for actions preserving wilderness or establishing city parks and urban landscaping programs (Driver, Rosenthal, & Petersen, 1978). Because of the importance of this assumption for many planning and political decisions, research is necessary to evaluate its validity and to increase understanding of the benefits in terms of positively toned emotional states that exposures to nature may provide.

Two recent studies have compared influences of exposures to large samples of natural and urban scenes using broad measures of affective/arousal states (Ulrich, 1979a, 1981). The first study addressed the restoration hypothesis (see Table 1)—that is, the notion that stressed or anxious individuals tend to feel better after exposure to natural rather than urban views (Ulrich, 1979a). University students who were experiencing anxiety because of a course examination viewed color-slide presentations of either (1) everyday natural scenes dominated by green vegetation, or (2) unblighted urban views lacking vegetation or water. The individuals' feelings were measured both immediately before and after the slide exposures using the Zuckerman Inventory of Personal Reactions (Zuckerman, 1977). Results showed a clear pattern of restoration for the natural scenes, whereas exposure to the urban views actually tended to be detrimental to emotional well-being on some dimensions. The principal differences between the influences of the natural and urban scenes were for factors of Sadness and Positive Affect. Also, exposure to the natural scenes significantly reduced anxiety in terms of a Fear Arousal factor, although the reduction did not differ significantly from a Fear Arousal decline associated with the collection of urban views. The two categories of environment produced quite different changes in emotional states despite the fact that the complexity levels of the slide samples were equivalent. Since complexity has received considerable emphasis as a variable influencing emotional activation, the findings imply that other visual properties, related to natural versus man-made content, were primarily responsible for the differences.

The second experiment, which was performed in Sweden, measured certain physiological as well as emotional responses to natural and urban scenes (Ulrich, 1981). Physiological influences were evaluated in part through recordings of alpha wave amplitude. Alpha is a valid indicator of cortical arousal and is associated with feelings of wakeful relaxation. Unstressed individuals in normal arousal states viewed lengthy color-slide presentations of either (1) nature dominated by vegetation, (2) nature with water, or (3) Scandinavian urban environments without water or vegetation. The three slide samples were equivalent in terms of complexity and information rate. Results revealed a clear-cut pattern for the two categories of natural scenes—especially water—to have more positive influences on affective states. A major finding was that settings with water, and to a lesser extent vegetation views, sustained attention and interest much more effectively than the urban scenes. Importantly, alpha was significantly higher when subjects viewed vegetation as opposed to urban slides and was higher on average during the water than during the urban exposures. Apart from indicating that the scenes had different effects on arousal as a function of environment, the alpha findings strongly suggest that individuals felt more wakefully relaxed while viewing the natural settings. These results, together with those of the first study, clearly suggest that the significance of visual encounters with natural environment is by no means limited to aesthetic response, but can also include important influences on other emotions and arousal. Although this pattern of evidence favoring natural environments is impressive, it was apparent in these studies that exposure to nature did not have a global, or comprehensively, restorative influence relative to the urban views (Ulrich, 1981). Also, it is likely that the differences between the effects of the environmental categories would have been less if the urban settings had contained prominent amounts of natural content such as vegetation.

Explanatory perspectives stressing either cultural conditioning or adaptation are only weakly consistent with the findings from these two studies. The results were similar for individuals who had grown up in either rural or urban environments. Also, despite the fact the studies were performed in different countries, there was considerable accord in terms of the different emotional influences of natural versus urban content. Cultural traditions and attitudes with respect to nature are quite different in America and Sweden—as expressed, for instance, in folklore, holidays, and common law. The possibility remains, however, that people in both countries tended to associate certain positive experiences, such as vacations, to a greater extent with natural settings, and this may have been a factor in the results.

An alternative explanation for these differential reactions to natural and urban material is implied by the work of authors who contend that response to environment is affected by unlearned factors of evolutionary origin. They assume that because humans evolved over a long period in natural environments, we are to some extent biologically adapted to natural as opposed to built content (e.g., Driver & Greene, 1977; Iltis, Loucks, & Andrews, 1970; Stainbrook, 1968). A theme common to this perspective is that individuals are innately predisposed to respond positively to many natural settings. Such evolutionary notions are not new. For instance, William McDougall argued more than 70 years ago that instinctive or unlearned factors are important in the elicitation of emotional responses (1908). McDougall's views should not be lightly dismissed, because he originated a number of other, remarkably prescient ideas about emotions that have been adopted by contemporary theorists, and which in some instances have been empirically substantiated. McDougall defined an instinct as

> an inherited or innate psycho-physical disposition which determines its possessor to perceive, and to pay attention to, objects of a certain class, to experience an emotional excitement of a particular quality upon perceiving such an object, and to act in regard to it . . . or at least to experience an impulse to such action. (1908, p. 29, as quoted in Izard, 1977)

Although behavioral scientists no longer use the term instinct in relation to humans, parts of McDougall's statement are quite consonant with the empirical record concerning aesthetic and affective reactions to natural as opposed to man-made environments. Faced with such findings as the strong attention-holding properties of water relative to urban content— irrespective of complexity—or the pattern for individuals from different countries to prefer scenes with water or vegetation, an evolutionary position such as McDougall's may seem as plausible to many re- searchers as a more traditional explanatory perspective stressing learn- ing or conditioning. McDougall would probably have no quarrel with the concept of preferenda that is a central feature of the psychoevolu- tionary framework in this chapter. However, the framework also stresses that learned as well as unlearned factors play a critical role in aesthetic and affective response to natural environment.

Visual Landscapes and Psychophysiological Restoration: A Tentative Perspective

On the basis of the admittedly limited evidence from two studies (Ulrich, 1979a, 1981), the proposition suggests itself that restorative in- fluences of unspectacular natural scenes, compared to urban views, may be most pronounced when the observer's initial state is one of stress and excessive arousal. For individuals experiencing stress or anxiety, most unthreatening natural views may be more arousal reducing and tend to elicit more positively toned emotional reactions than the vast majority of urban scenes, and hence are more restorative in a psychophysiological sense. For unstressed individuals in normal arousal states, visual ex- posures to everyday nature may be more effective in holding in- terest and maintaining arousal in the comparatively optimal middle ranges. There are as yet no findings comparing natural and urban views for the case of observers experiencing boredom or excessively low arousal. However, it is entirely possible that, for instance, a window view of a lively urban setting would be more stimulating and restorative for a chronically understimulated person (e.g., a nursing home resident or a long-term fracture patient) than the vast majority of unspectacular natural settings.

This general perspective has a number of implications for environ- mental planning and design. Perhaps location and design decisions for some facilities and institutions, such as hospitals and high-stress work- places, should place considerable importance on providing visual con- tacts with nature. Does a preoperative hospital patient experience less anxiety if his window overlooks a wooded park rather than an urban freeway or parking lot? Do most people recuperate more quickly after a stressful workday if, for instance, their homes allow views of a lake or a forest? Findings from future investigations may indicate the need to evaluate alternative design or planning proposals in light of the potential of different visual environments to influence emotional/arousal states in very different ways.

SUMMARY AND DIRECTIONS FOR RESEARCH

Participants in the developing area of environmental aesthetics and landscape assessment have been considerably more active in generating findings than in formulating theory. Consequently, the rapidly expanding empirical record concerning aesthetic and affective response to natural environments has lacked both the structure and explanatory foundation that could be provided by a well-developed theory. In an attempt to address this weakness, this chapter's coverage has been a balance between findings and theoretical discussion; a principal objective has been to advance an integrated conceptual framework. As its starting point, the framework questions the widely held view that feelings result exclusively from a process of cognition. The cognitive primacy perspective is implicit in many experimental articles, and it dominates the intuitive literature on landscape aesthetics. There is simply no evidence that cognition necessarily precedes affect, and in fact recent findings support the notion that the initial level of response to environment is affective. The theoretical position here is that feelings, not thoughts, come first in environmental encounters, and the observer's initial feeling reaction shapes subsequent cognitive events. The relative sequence of feeling and thinking in environmental encounters represents a fundamental issue that should be addressed in future research. Study designs developed by Zajonc and others for affect/cognition experiments might be adapted for this purpose (for a survey, see Zajonc, 1980).

Aesthetic and affective reactions to the natural environment cannot be understood in any depth if they are treated as isolated phenomena. The framework premises that affective responses are adaptive in terms of the total behavior of the individual and are closely linked not only to cognition, but also to the preceding affective state, neurophysiological activity, and behavior. Since the vast majority of studies to date has been concerned exclusively with aesthetic reactions, the conceptual framework clearly implies a research agenda with a broader array of concerns. This emphasizes the need for studies that include systems and behavior which are inseparably linked to affects. If a thorough understanding of affective response to natural environment is ever to be achieved, it will be necessary to investigate influences of antecedent states ranging from boredom through both positively and negatively toned states of excitement. Other research needs include the measurement of neurophysiological concomitants of feeling responses to natural scenes and the recording of behaviors or functioning motivated by affects. By integrating such findings with data on aesthetic and emotional reactions, a much more complete and in-depth picture of responsiveness to visual natural environment would emerge. The list contained in Table 1 of arousal changes and behaviors associated with different feeling reactions to nature can be viewed as a set of hypotheses for future research. It should also be mentioned that if more investigators undertake studies that combine measurements of affective responses with recordings of neurophysiological activity or behavior, the field of environmental aesthetics would begin to move away from its excessive reliance on verbal measures. Although physiological activity (e.g., brain waves, cardiac response) is comparatively difficult and time-consuming to record, physiological procedures provide a means for validating results obtained from more subjective measures and have a number of other important strengths in the context of landscape aesthetics research (Ulrich, 1979b).

In addition to these research needs, a number of other important questions remain unresolved. One issue that has received virtually no attention is responsiveness to natural settings containing prominent ephemeral phenomena. The intuitive literature is replete with accounts of emotional reactions to, for instance, sunsets, cloud formations, and freshly fallen snow. Although such occurrences may be infrequent in a given natural environment, some ephemeral conditions probably elicit strong affective reactions and therefore are important factors in many memorable experiences in the natural environment. This topic has been so neglected that even responses to common ephemeral conditions associated with seasonal changes, such as the absence of foliage on deciduous vegetation in winter, have not been empirically evaluated.

Another topic requiring study is variation between individuals in reactions to visual natural environments. The relative lack of emphasis in environmental aesthetics on individual variability is perhaps understandable in light of the high levels of agreement among observers reported by many investigators. Future studies should systematically evaluate individual differences along environmentally relevant dimensions of personality, rather than exclusively in terms of traditional demographic variables such as age, sex, and occupation (Wohlwill, 1976, p. 76–77). One personality dimension that will very likely prove important is *sensation-seeking*, which can underlie variability in curiosity, risk appraisals, and preferences for complexity and novelty (Ulrich & Zuckerman, 1981; Zuckerman, 1979). From the standpoint of applied concerns such as wilderness preservation and environmental planning, a critical question in need of research is individual or group variability in relation to the perceived importance or utility of natural scenery. Rather paradoxically, there is evidence that despite high agreement in aesthetic preferences, different individuals may vary markedly with respect to the importance or value they place on visual encounters with natural environments (Ulrich, 1973). Perhaps gross differences in this regard will also be found across cultures.

Another important direction of future research concerns the role of environmental adaptation or familiarity in aesthetic preferences for natural scenes. In some instances, high levels of experience or familiarity with a given setting doubtless give rise to attachments or symbolic associations, and possibly adjustment to particular levels of stimulation, which affect the observer's aesthetic and emotional reaction. The question emerges whether most preference variations attributable to adaptation are of wide magnitude, or whether they are more a matter of degree. A further adaptation issue is the extent to which a visual setting can sustain the intensity and quality of an affective response following repeated exposure. Findings from experiments using abstract stimuli suggest the possibility that habituation will tend to occur more rapidly when settings are low in complexity (e.g., Berlyne, 1970). In view of the substantial body of findings showing gross differences in reactions to natural versus urban environments, the question arises: Do observers habituate significantly less or more slowly to natural than to urban content, irrespective of levels of complexity?

Despite these and other research gaps that remain to be filled, considerable progress has already been made in identifying visual properties of natural environments that strongly influence aesthetic response. Investigators have consistently shown it is possible to account for most of the variance in observers' aesthetic judgments. As noted above, an important related finding is the pattern of widespread agreement among individuals and groups in their aesthetic preferences for natural environments. This picture of agreement, coupled with the success in identifying highly efficacious predictors of preference, contradicts strongly the traditional notion that aesthetic response to environment is an inherently subjective phenomenon, impervious to empirical investigation and devoid of underlying principles that hold for different individuals.

One of the most clear-cut and potentially important findings to date is the consistent tendency for North American and European groups to prefer even unspectacular natural scenes over the vast majority of urban views. This pattern of differential responsiveness appears to extend well beyond aesthetic preference to include other emotions such as interest, and it is probably also expressed in differences in neurophysiological activity. The theoretical view here is that both unlearned and learned factors are responsible for these differences. Debate among investigators will probably intensify over these related questions of responsiveness to natural versus urban scenes and the relative importance of learning as opposed to evolutionary/biological factors. For further elucidation of these issues, one obvious need is a greater volume of cross-cultural studies. However, more convincing conclusions might be obtained from experiments using young children or infants. Psychologists have developed a battery of measures (e.g., eye-movement recording, classification of facial expressions, phasic cardiac response) for assessing attention/ interest, and in some cases other responses in children and infants. If very young subjects are shown slides of natural and built settings equivalent in information rate, do the children evidence significantly greater interest in one of the categories of content? If findings from such studies, as well as from additional cross-cultural investigations, were to corroborate the results of studies to date, this would have considerable significance for the environment–behavior field in general. It would imply the need to recognize explicitly the role of natural versus built material in attempts to develop realistic and accurate conceptions of responsiveness to the physical environment.

REFERENCES

Altman, I., & Chemers, M. M. *Culture and environment.* Monterey: Brooks/Cole, 1980.

American Psychiatric Association. *Diagnostic and statistical manual of mental disorders (DSM-III).* Washington, D.C.: American Psychiatric Association, 1980.

Appleton, J. *The experience of landscape.* London: Wiley, 1975.

Arnold, M. B. *Emotion and personality (Vol. 1): Psychological aspects.* New York: Columbia University Press, 1960.

Arthur, L. M. Predicting scenic beauty of forest environments: Some empirical tests. *Forest Science,* 1977, *23,* 151–159.

Balint, M. Friendly expanses—Horrid empty spaces. *International Journal of Psychoanalysis,* 1955, *36,* 225–241.

Berlyne, D. E. *Conflict, arousal, and curiosity.* New York: McGraw-Hill, 1960.

Berlyne, D. E. Complexity and incongruity variables as determinants of exploratory choice and evaluative ratings. *Canadian Journal of Psychology,* 1963, *17,* 274–290.

Berlyne, D. E. Novelty, complexity and hedonic value. *Perception and Psychophysics,* 1970, *8,* 279–286.

Berlyne, D. E. *Aesthetics and psychobiology.* New York: Appleton-Century-Crofts, 1971.

Berlyne, D. E. Extension to Indian subjects of a study of exploratory and verbal responses to visual patterns. *Journal of Cross-Cultural Psychology,* 1975, *6,* 316–330.

Berlyne, D. E., Robbins, M. C., & Thompson, R. A cross-cultural study of exploratory and verbal responses to visual patterns varying in complexity. In D. E. Berlyne (Ed.), *Studies in the new experimental aesthetics: Steps toward an objective psychology of aesthetic appreciation.* New York: Wiley, 1974, pp. 259–278.

Bernaldez, F. G., & Parra, F. Dimensions of landscape preferences from pairwise comparisons. In *Proceedings of Our National Landscape: A conference on applied techniques for analysis and management of the visual resource.* Berkeley, Calif.: Pacific Southwest Forest and Range Experiment Station, USDA Forest Service, 1979, pp. 256–262.

Brush, R. O. Perceived quality of scenic and recreational environments. In K. H. Craik & E. H. Zube (Eds.), *Perceiving environmental quality.* New York: Plenum Press, 1976, pp. 47–58.

Brush, R. O. Forests can be managed for esthetics: A study of forest land owners in Massachusetts. In *Proceedings of the National Urban Forestry Conference.* Syracuse, N.Y.: SUNY College of Environmental Science and Forestry and USDA Forest Service, 1978, pp. 349–360.

Brush, R. O., & Palmer, J. F. Measuring the impact of urbanization on scenic quality: Land use change in the northeast. In *Proceedings of Our National Landscape: A conference on applied techniques for analysis and management of the visual resource.* Berkeley, Calif.: Pacific Southwest Forest and Range Experiment Station, USDA Forest Service, 1979, pp. 358–364.

Brush, R. O., & Shafer, E. L., Jr. Application of a landscape preference model to land management. In E. H. Zube, R. O. Brush, & J. G. Fabos (Eds.), *Landscape assessment: Values, perceptions, and resources.* Stroudsburg, Pa.: Dowden, Hutchinson & Ross, 1975, pp. 168–182.

Buhyoff, G. J., Wellman, J. D., Harvey, H., & Fraser, R. A. Landscape architects' interpretations of people's landscape preferences. *Journal of Environmental Management,* 1978, *6,* 255–262.

Calvin, J. S., Dearinger, J. A., & Curtin, M. E. An attempt at assessing preferences for natural landscapes. *Environment and Behavior,* 1972, *4,* 447–470.

Civco, D. L. Numerical modeling of eastern Connecticut's visual resources. In *Proceedings of Our National Landscape: A conference on applied techniques for analysis and management of the visual resource.* Berkeley, Calif.: Pacific Southwest Forest and Range Experiment Station, USDA Forest Service, 1979, pp. 263–270.

Clamp, P. Evaluating English landscapes—Some recent developments. *Environment and Planning,* 1976, *8,* 79–92.

Cole, M., & Scribner, S. *Culture and thought: A psychological introduction.* New York: Wiley, 1974.

Coughlin, R. E., & Goldstein, K. A. The extent of agreement among observers on environmental attractiveness. Regional Science Research Institute *Discussion Paper Series, No. 37.* Philadelphia: Regional Science Research Institute, 1970.

Craik, K. H. *A system of landscape dimensions: Appraisal of its objectivity and illustration of its scientific application* (Report to Resources of the Future, Inc.). Berkeley: University of California Institute of Personality Assessment and Research, 1970.

Cullen, G. *Townscape.* New York: Reinhold, 1961.

Daniel, T. C., & Boster, R. S. *Measuring landscape esthetics: The scenic beauty estimation method* (USDA Forest Service Research Paper RM-167). Ft. Collins, Colo.: Rocky Mountain Forest and Range Experiment Station, 1976.

Daniel, T. C., & Schroeder, H. Scenic beauty estimation model: Predicting perceived beauty of forest landscapes. In *Proceedings of Our National Landscape: A conference on applied techniques for analysis and management of the visual resource*. Berkeley, Calif.: Pacific Southwest Forest and Range Experiment Station, USDA Forest Service, 1979, pp. 514–523.

Day, H. I. Evaluations of subjective complexity, pleasingness, and interestingness for a series of random polygons varying in complexity. *Perception and Psychophysics*, 1967, *2*, 281–286.

Driver, B. L., & Greene, P. Man's nature: Innate determinants of response to natural environments. In *Children, nature, and the urban environment* (USDA Forest Service Report NE-30). Upper Darby, Pa.: Northeastern Forest Experiment Station, 1977, pp. 63–70.

Driver, B. L., Rosenthal, D., & Peterson, G. Social benefits of urban forests and related green spaces in cities. In *Proceedings of the National Urban Forestry Conference*. Syracuse, N.Y.: SUNY College of Environmental Science and Forestry and USDA Forest Service, 1978, pp. 98–111.

Eibl-Eibesfeldt, I. Similarities and differences between cultures in expressive movements. In R. A. Hinde (Ed.), *Nonverbal communication*. Cambridge, Mass.: Cambridge University Press, 1972, pp. 297–314.

Ekman, P., Friesen, W. V., & Ellsworth, P. C. *Emotion in the human face*. New York: Pergamon, 1972.

Evans, G. W., & Wood, K. W. Assessment of environmental aesthetics in scenic highway corridors. *Environment and Behavior*, 1980, *12*, 255–273.

Gibson, J. J. Perception of distance and space in the open air. In D. Beardslee & M. Wertheimer (Eds.), *Readings in perception*. Princeton: Van Nostrand, 1958, pp. 415–431.

Gustke, L. D., and Hodgson, R. W. Rate of travel along an interpretive trail: The effect of an environmental discontinuity. *Environment and Behavior*, 1980, *12*, 53–63.

Hubbard, H. V., & Kimball, T. *An introduction to the study of landscape design*. Boston: Hubbard Educational Trust, 1967.

Iltis, H., Loucks, O., & Andrews, J. Criteria for an optimum human environment. *Bulletin of the Atomic Scientists*, 1970, *26*(1), 2–6.

Ittelson, W. H. Environment perception and contemporary perceptual theory. In W. H. Ittelson (Ed.), *Environment and cognition*. New York: Seminar, 1973, pp. 1–19.

Ittelson, W. H., Franck, K. A., & O'Hanlon, T. J. The nature of environmental experience. In S. Wapner, S. B. Cohen, & B. Kaplan (Eds.), *Experiencing the environment*. New York: Plenum Press, 1976, pp. 187–206.

Izard, C. E. *The face of emotion*. New York: Appleton-Century-Crofts, 1971.

Izard, C. E. *Human emotions*. New York: Plenum Press, 1977.

Izard, C. E., & Buechler, S. Aspects of consciousness and personality in terms of differential emotions theory. In R. Plutchik & H. Kellerman (Eds.), *Emotion: Theory, research, and experience*. New York: Academic Press, 1980, pp. 165–187.

Janssens, J. Hur man betraktar och identifierar byggnadesexteriorer—methodstudie. LTH, Sektionen för Arkitektur, *Rapport 2*. School of Architecture, Lund Institute of Technology, Sweden, 1976.

Kaplan, R. Predictors of environmental preference: Designers and clients. In W. Preiser (Ed.), *Environmental design research*. Stroudsburg, Pa.: Dowden, Hutchinson & Ross, 1973, pp. 265–274.

Kaplan, S. An informal model for the prediction of preference. In E. H. Zube, J. G. Fabos, & R. O. Brush (Eds.), *Landscape assessment: Values, perceptions and resources*. Stroudsburg, Pa.: Dowden, Hutchinson & Ross, 1975, pp. 92–101.

Kaplan, S., Kaplan, R., & Wendt, J. S. Rated preference and complexity for natural and urban visual material. *Perception and Psychophysics*, 1972, *12*, 354–356.

Kennedy, J. M. *A psychology of picture perception*. San Francisco: Jossey-Bass, 1974.

Küller, R. *A semantic model for describing perceived environment*. Stockholm: National Swedish Institute for Building Research, 1972.

Kunst-Wilson, W. R., & Zajonc, R. B. Affective discrimination of stimuli that cannot be recognized. *Science*, 1980, *207*, 557–558.

Kwok, K. Semantic evaluation of perceived environment: A cross-cultural replication. *Man–Environment Systems*, 1979, *9*, 243–249.

Lazarus, R. S. Emotions and adaptation: Conceptual and empirical relations. In W. J. Arnold (Ed.), *Nebraska symposium on motivation*. Lincoln: University of Nebraska Press, 1968, pp. 175–266.

Lazarus, R. S., Kanner, A. D., & Folkman, S. Emotions: A cognitive-phenomenological analysis. In R. Plutchik & H. Kellerman (Eds.), *Emotion: Theory, research, and experience*. New York: Academic Press, 1980, pp. 189–217.

Lowenthal, D. The American scene. *Geographical Review*, 1968, *58*, 61–88.

Lowenthal, D., & Prince, H. English landscape tastes. *Geographical Review*, 1965, *55*, 186–222.

McDougall, W. *An introduction to social psychology*. London: Methuen, 1908.

Mehrabian, A., & Russell, J. A. *An approach to environmental psychology*. Cambridge, Mass.: MIT Press, 1974.

Moreland, R. L., & Zajonc, R. B. Is stimulus recognition a necessary condition for the occurrence of exposure effects? *Journal of Personality and Social Psychology*, 1977, *35*, 191–199.

Osgood, C. E. Studies on the generality of affective meaning systems. *American Psychologist*, 1962, *17*, 10–28.

Palmer, J. F. An investigation of the conceptual classification of landscapes and its application to landscape planning issues. In S. Weidemann & J. R. Anderson (Eds.), *Priorities for environmental design research, Part I*. Washington, D.C.: Environmental Design Research Association, 1978, pp. 92–103.

Patterson, K. E., & Baddeley, A. D. When face recognition fails. *Journal of Experimental Psychology: Human Learning and Memory*, 1977, *3*, 406–417.

Penning-Roswell, E. C. The social value of English landscapes. In *Proceedings of Our National Landscape: A conference on applied techniques for analysis and management of the visual resource*. Berkeley, Calif.: Pacific Southwest Forest and Range Experiment Station, USDA Forest Service, 1979, pp. 249–255.

Plutchik, R. Emotions, evolution, and adaptive processes. In M. Arnold (Ed.), *Feelings and emotions: The Loyola symposium*. New York: Academic Press, 1970, pp. 3–24.

Rabinowitz, C. B., & Coughlin, R. E. Analysis of landscape characteristics relevant to preference. *Regional Science Research Institute Discussion Paper Series, No. 38*. Philadelphia: Regional Science Research Institute, 1970.

Rossman, B. B., & Ulehla, Z. J. Psychological reward values associated with wilderness use: A functional-reinforcement approach. *Environment and Behavior*, 1977, *9*, 41–66.

Shafer, E. L., Jr., & Mietz, J. Aesthetic and emotional experiences rate high with northeast wilderness hikers. *Environment and Behavior*, 1969, *1*, 187–197.

Shafer, E. L., & Tooby, M. Landscape preferences: An international replication. *Journal of Leisure Research*, 1973, *5*, 60–65.

Shafer, E. L., Hamilton, J. F., & Schmidt, E. A. Natural landscape preferences: A predictive model. *Journal of Leisure Research*, 1969, *1*, 1–19.

Shuttleworth, S. The evaluation of landscape quality. *Landscape Research* (England), 1980, *5*(1), 14–20.

Singer, J. L. *Daydreaming: An introduction to the experimental study of inner experience.* New York: Random House, 1966.

Sorte, G. J. *Perception av landskap.* Licentiates dissertation. Ås, Norway: Landbruksbokhandeln/Universitetsforlaget, 1971.

Stainbrook, E. Human needs and the natural environment. In *Man and nature in the city.* Proceedings of a symposium sponsored by the Bureau of Sport Fisheries and Wildlife, U.S. Dept. of the Interior, Washington, D.C., 1968, pp. 1–6.

Thayer, R. L., Jr., & Atwood, B. G. Plants, complexity, and pleasure in urban and suburban environments. *Environmental Psychology and Nonverbal Behavior,* 1978, *3,* 67–76.

Tomkins, S. S. *Affect, imagery, consciousness. Vol. I: The positive affects.* New York: Springer, 1962.

Tomkins, S. S. *Affect, imagery, consciousness. Vol. II: The negative affects.* New York: Springer, 1963.

Tuan, Y.-F. Visual blight: Exercises in interpretation. In *Visual blight in America* (Commission on College Geography Resource Paper No. 23). Washington, D.C.: Association of American Geographers, 1973.

Tuan, Y.-F. Raw emotion to intellectual delight. *Landscape Architecture,* 1978, *68,* 132–134.

Tuan, Y.-F. *Landscapes of fear.* New York: Pantheon, 1979.

Ulrich, R. S. *Scenery and the shopping trip: The roadside environment as a factor in route choice.* Doctoral dissertation, University of Michigan, Ann Arbor, 1973. (Available as Michigan Geographical Publication No. 12, Department of Geography, 1973.)

Ulrich, R. S. Visual landscape preference: A model and application. *Man–Environment Systems,* 1977, *7,* 279–293.

Ulrich, R. S. Visual landscapes and psychological well-being. *Landscape Research* (England), 1979, *4*(1), 17–23. (a)

Ulrich, R. S. Psychophysiological approaches to visibility. In *Proceedings of the Workshop on Visibility Values* (USDA Forest Service Report WO-18). Fort Collins, Colo.: 1979, pp. 93–99. (b)

Ulrich, R. S. Natural versus urban scenes: Some psychophysiological effects. *Environment and Behavior,* 1981, *13,* 523–556.

Ulrich, R. S., & Zuckerman, M. *Preference for landscape paintings: Differences as a function of sensation-seeking.* Unpublished research, Departments of Geography and Psychology, University of Delaware, 1981.

White, R. W. Motivation reconsidered: The concept of competence. *Psychological Review,* 1959, *66,* 297–333.

Wilson, W. R. Feeling more than we can know: Exposure effects without learning. *Journal of Personality and Social Psychology,* 1979, *37,* 811–821.

Wohlwill, J. F. Amount of stimulus exploration and preference as differential functions of stimulus complexity. *Perception and Psychophysics,* 1968, *4,* 307–312.

Wohlwill, J. F. *Factors in the differential response to the natural and man-made environments.* Paper presented at the Annual Meeting of the American Psychological Association, Montreal, August 1973.

Wohlwill, J. F. Environmental aesthetics: The environment as a source of affect. In I. Altman & J. F. Wohlwill (Eds.), *Human behavior and environment* (Vol. 1). New York: Plenum Press, 1976, pp. 37–86.

Wohlwill, J. F. What belongs where: Research on fittingness of man-made structures in natural settings. In T. C. Daniel, E. H. Zube, & B. L. Driver (Eds.), *Assessing amenity resource values* (USDA General Tech. Rep. RM-68). Fort Collins, Colo.: Rocky Mountain Forest and Range Experimental Station, 1979, pp. 48–57.

Wohlwill, J. F. The place of order and uncertainty in art and environmental aesthetics. *Motivation and Emotion,* 1980, *4,* 133–142.

Wohlwill, J. F., & Harris, G. Response to congruity or contrast for man-made features in natural-recreation settings. *Leisure Sciences*, 1980, *3*, 349–365.

Zajonc, R. B. Feeling and thinking: Preferences need no inferences. *American Psychologist*, 1980, *35*, 151–175.

Zube, E. H. Cross-disciplinary and inter-mode agreement on the description and evaluation of landscape resources. *Environment and Behavior*, 1974, *6*, 69–89.

Zube, E. H., Pitt, D. G., & Anderson, T. W. *Perception and measurements of scenic resources in the Southern Connecticut River Valley*. Amherst: Institute for Man and Environment, University of Massachusetts, 1974.

Zube, E. H., Pitt, D. G., & Anderson, T. W. Perception and prediction of scenic resource values of the Northeast. In E. H. Zube, R. O. Brush, & J. G. Fabos (Eds.), *Landscape assessment: Values, perceptions and resources*. Stroudsburg, Pa.: Dowden, Hutchinson & Ross, 1975, pp. 151–167.

Zuckerman, M. Sensation seeking and anxiety, traits and states, as determinants of behavior in novel situations. In I. Sarason & C. Spielberger (Eds.), *Stress and Anxiety* (Vol. 3). New York: Wiley, 1976, pp. 141–170.

Zuckerman, M. The development of a situation specific trait-state test for the prediction and measurement of affective responses. *Journal of Consulting and Clinical Psychology*, 1977, *45*, 512–523.

Zuckerman, M. *Sensation-seeking: Beyond the optimal level of arousal*. New York: Wiley, 1979.

4

The Role of Nature in the Urban Context

RACHEL KAPLAN

People need contact with trees and plants and water. In some way, which is
hard to express, people are able to be more whole in the presence of nature,
are able to go deeper into themselves, and are somehow able to draw sustaining energy from the life of plants and trees and water. (Alexander, Ishikawa,
& Silverstein, 1977, p. 806)

INTRODUCTION

Urban nature. The juxtaposition may strike some as a contradiction. If
one thinks of *nature* as somewhere else, removed from human influence
and inaccessible to major segments of the population, then it would
make little sense to speak of nature in the urban context. But nature is an
elusive concept. It can and does exist even in the city. In fact, in that
context, nature not only survives human influence, it often depends on
it.

While nature may need humans for its nurture, the opposite seems
at least as characteristic. At many places, throughout history, people
have shown a special interest in the natural environment. While often it

RACHEL KAPLAN • School of Natural Resources, University of Michigan, Ann Arbor,
Michigan 48109. The author greatly appreciates the support of the Urban Forestry Project
through Cooperative Agreement 13-655, U.S. Forest Service, North Central Forest Experiment Station.

was only the nobility or the affluent who could afford the private garden, both the agricultural use of plants and the vistas of the countryside have served as sources of inspiration for many centuries. Jellicoe and Jellicoe (1975) provide numerous illustrations of this relation from many corners of the globe, even dating back thousands of years. The king of Mesopotamia is shown feasting in his garden (p. 27); Chinese landscape painting dates back to before the year 1200 (p. 71), and Japanese gardens were started hundreds of years before then. There are graden scenes in the tombs of Egyptian pharoahs (p. 112). The victors of the earliest Olympic games were "crowned with leaves of olives" (p. 122) at a location overlooking a sacred grove. And Rome, 2000 years ago, was a "city of parks" (p. 129). It was a long time later, three centuries ago, that Philadelphia was designed with open squares influenced by Georgian London; the design of Washington, D.C., some hundred years later, "included planted avenues reminiscent of Versailles" (Laurie, 1979).

That is not to say that nature, even with respect to vegetation, cannot be formidable and frightening, nor that our current view of nature has been constant over centuries and across cultures. But the tamed and "managed" natural environment has persistently played a special role. The purpose of this chapter is to explore some of the ways in which the urban natural environment can contribute to human well-being. In particular, the intent is to draw as much as possible on empirical work in this area and to encourage others to do research on this important and exciting but largely neglected topic. The focus is on the common, everyday aspects of nature, the trees and grass, bushes and flowers, that can be seen from home or on the trip to work. The concern in this country for urban space, greenbelts, and miscellaneous bits of nature has increased substantially in the last decade or two. Research on the role of urban nature is scant at best. Although it would be premature to draw conclusions concerning the cross-cultural importance of the nearby natural world, an understanding of this issue in the contemporary American context has value in its own right and may yield hypotheses that deserve testing in other contexts as well.

GROWING AWARENESS OF URBAN NATURE

In the last decade several federal agencies with a historical nature-related mission have launched urban programs. The National Park Service has developed some large urban projects in San Francisco (Golden Gate) and New York (Gateway East) in addition to the Capitol Park System. Sudia (1975), then director of research for the National Park Service, authored a series of essays on the urban ecosystem on topics such as "Man Nature City," "The City as a Park," and "Ecology of the Walking City." The Urban Park and Recreation Recovery Program, administered by the Heritage Conservation and Recreation Service (HCRS) of the Department of the Interior, is the outcome of congressional action "enacted in recognition of the severe deficiencies in urban recreation in the United States" (HCRS, undated). It was put into operation in 1979; by the end of 1980, $95.6 million had been granted for 461 projects ("Urban Parks," 1980). The United States Forest Service now has an Urban Forestry Program addressing many of the issues long in its jurisdiction, but in the urban setting. (An abstract of research funded through this program has been compiled by Rowntree & Wolfe, 1980.) These and related programs are important not only because of the federal funds that they make available to large population centers. They reflect an increased awareness that the benefits of the natural environment must be available in the everyday setting.

At the same time that federal land agencies have been reaching out to cities, some of the conservation-oriented public interest groups have also added an urban thrust to their efforts. The Sierra Club, long associated with wilderness protection, in 1979 sponsored a major environmental conference on "City care: Toward a coalition for the urban environment." Organizations such as the Conservation Foundation and the National Wildlife Federation are recognizing that the problem of natural environments must be attacked locally and at every other level as well. The American Forestry Association, established in 1875 to "promote the concept of sound forestry conservation," published its first issue of a newsletter, *The National Urban and Community Forestry Forum*, in the fall of 1981. The association has also established a new council in recognition of the role of sound urban forestry management in improving the quality of life.

As urbanization has spread to the surrounding "natural" countryside, there has been an increasing recognition of what it is that development replaces. The call for open space in guiding urban growth has grown louder and clearer. A report on this subject, funded by the Rockefeller Brothers Fund (Reilly, 1973), points to the importance of the preservation of farmland and water quality in planning for controlled growth. Heckscher (1977) discusses the various opportunities for open space in the city, highlighting the historical role of such spatial patterns. The proceedings of a conference on "The urban setting" (Taylor, 1981) lists 19 national citizen's organizations "that work to preserve open areas in cities.

What becomes evident from the analysis of the natural environment in the urban setting is that it is diverse. Serves a large number of purposes, and can be available on many scales (R. Kaplan, 1978a). Nature cannot be considered simply as "amenity" either. Nature includes the overgrown empty lot, the street trees, the growth along the railroad right-of-way, the backyards, schoolyards, planters, and weeds, as well as the cemeteries, parks, botanical gardens, and landscaped places.

What also becomes evident from such analysis is that there is a strong commitment to the importance of open space, parks, and natural elements. The quote opening this chapter is one of many statements affirming the importance of nature to people. Despite the strong sentiments, tangible evidence of the benefits derived from the natural surrounds is difficult to find. Nonetheless, there *are* some indications that nature plays an important role for many people.

INDIRECT EVIDENCE

Strong efforts on the part of urbanites to preserve urban nature have been demonstrated by court proceedings to stop development, by the establishment of local organizations to help purchase open land, by campaign platforms (e.g., Les Amis de la Terre, 1977), and by bringing relevant issues to a vote. Bond issues for parks, bikeways, and other green areas have been passed on numerous occasions. In 1967, the residents of Boulder, Colorado, approved a sales tax to enable a greenbelt program (Caldwell, Hayes, & MacWhirter, 1976). In 1979, the citizens of the city of Houston "passed an unprecedented $40 million parks bond program"—one phase in a multifaceted effort to extend and enhance the parks, open space, and recreation programs of that city (Delaporte, 1980). It would be interesting to determine the circumstances when such actions have been passed and when the voters were unwilling to carry such a burden. It would also be useful to determine the instances of such actions in large urban areas, as opposed to places with closer links to existing open space.

Nadel and Oberlander (1977) report that New York City's tree program involves planting 11,000 new trees every year, while Vancouver adds 4,000 annually. In Iran, they indicate, "anyone caught uprooting a tree of more than 10 centimeters in diameter must go to jail for 3 years" (p. 21). Collins and Munsell (1981) discuss the devotion of a town to the continuation of its arboreal heritage. Though indirect, such items suggest that trees play important roles in the life of cities.

Gold (1977a) mentions a variety of other forms of evidence of the importance of urban nature. These include higher property values for houses adjacent to well-landscaped parks, lower housing turnover in areas that are well landscaped, "foliage" as a dominant theme in child-

hood memories of the city, and greater dissatisfaction with newer sub-
urbs lacking in vegetation.

Rental costs frequently reflect the value placed on a view of water or
woods. People are willing to pay a monthly charge for their nearby
nature. The value of trees is also reflected in the insurance claims and
income-tax deductions that result from accidental losses. In fact, there
are professional tree appraisers qualified to establish the monetary value
of such losses.

Hounsome (1979) discusses the ways in which "birds have a
therapeutic value to the psychological health of urban man" (p. 180). He
cites the "number of naturalists in town," as well as their publications,
organizations, and the attention devoted to ornithology by the media.
Although Hounsome is writing in the British context, the annual Audubon bird census conducted in many cities in this country attests to
similar widespread interest here.

Another kind of evidence for the role that nature plays in people's
lives becomes apparent when one examines the content of coffee-table
books. Here again, it would be an interesting project to determine the
progression in people's willingness to spend money to have a closer tie
to the natural environment. Many beautiful photography books bring
spectacular, remote places closer to home. In many cases, however, the
pictures are not actually place-specific. The light catching the fern
fronds, the large tree on a misty day, the peaceful meadow in bloom—
these are potentially available within a short journey for many people.
Several books have appeared on the "wilds" of the city—the available
animal and plant life that is adapted to the urban setting. Furthermore,
the how-to books include a large array of advice about growing things
even in tight spaces.

Although such indirect evidence provides useful information on the
role of nature, it can only tell us part of the story. To know that people
are spending more dollars on recreation-related equipment and that
user counts show increasing numbers of people at outdoor facilities does
little to explain the roles these activities play in well-being. The next
several sections of this chapter examine some of the empirical approaches to the question of the importance of nature. These studies
focus on both the kinds of nature that make a difference and on the
kinds of difference that nature makes. There are particular configurations or elements in the urban/natural environment that seem to be
preferred. Some of these are not unique to the natural world, just as
shade can be provided by canopies other than trees. Similarly, the kinds
of satisfactions that people derive from contact with the nearby natural
environment are not necessarily unique to such settings. As it turns out,

however, contact with nature seems to afford such satisfactions for people who may not as readily find comparable fulfillment in other daily activities. The chapter concludes with a discussion of implications for design, planning, policy, and research given the importance of nature in the quality of life.

PREFERENCE FOR URBAN NATURE: CONTENT AND PROCESS

In considering the role that environments play in preference and satisfaction, it is useful to distinguish between content and process. *Content* refers to the things, the substantive categories, that seem to be important to people. An underlying hypothesis in the discussion thus far has been the notion that nature *per se* constitutes such a content domain. The indirect and anecdotal evidence suggests that humans respond to the natural world in some distinct fashion. Further, within that content domain are specific objects or elements that seem to be of particular significance. Trees would seem to be an example of such a specific content; water, too, often plays a special role in the landscape. *Process*, on the other hand, refers to patterns that are content-free or applicable across different content domains. Thus, the natural environment might entail particular configurations that people find satisfying but that are not necessarily unique to the nature content.

Based on environmental preference studies we and our students have conducted over the past decade, a theoretical framework has evolved that considers environmental patterns from an informational perspective. In terms of process, we have argued that "environments that are likely to be preferred are those that permit 'involvement' and 'making sense'" (Kaplan & Kaplan, 1978, p. 148). To enhance involvement, environments must have some complexity or richness. They also need to entice one by promising more information—a characteristic we have called "mystery." Making sense, on the other hand, is enhanced by coherence and legibility, characteristics that permit one to interpret readily what is going on and that facilitate seeing where one is headed. While these properties are in a sense ascribed to the environment, they are not purely environmental configurations. They must, at least to some extent, be a function of one's prior experience. In this way, preference and familiarity are interactive, but their relationship is by no means simple.

The distinction between content and process and the role of making sense and involvement are not specific to the urban setting. The studies presented here, however, focus on these issues in the urban context.

THE URBAN ENVIRONMENT: PERCEPTUAL CATEGORIES

To study the question of content in environmental preference, Kaplan, Kaplan, and Wendt (1972) used 56 color slides, selected from a much larger set, to represent a "continuum ranging from nature, to a predominance of man-made aspects, to urban scenes." Each of these four categories was sampled with nonspectacular, nearby environments. The participants were undergraduate students enrolled in introductory psychology courses and were generally not familiar with the specific scenes that they were asked to rate on a five-point preference scale. These ratings were subjected to two forms of dimensional analysis,[1] each of which yielded two clear groupings: one of urban scenes and one of "nature" scenes. The latter cluster included all of the scenes selected to represent the nature end of the continuum. It also included scenes in which nature predominated but where human influence was hardly subtle (e.g., an unpaved road through a natural area, including a parked car at the edge of a road). The urban grouping included all but two of the scenes selected to represent that end of the continuum, as well as one scene that had originally been included in the next category. The scenes that reflected various residential settings did not form a unique grouping, suggesting that the participants did not perceive these as a distinct content domain.

The preference ratings thus provide an empirical basis for identifying content themes. These are derived from the *pattern* of the responses and reflect similarities across the study participants in their perception of the environments sampled by the slides. The preference ratings are also instructive in themselves. That is, by computing *average ratings* for

---

[1]The use of dimensional-analytic procedures is disdained in some circles: factors are known for their instability, the results are always subject to interpretation; in addition, if the results were not predicted, the exercise is considered little more than a fishing expedition. This is not the place to counter these arguments in detail. The studies discussed here used two very different algorithms (nonmetric factor analysis and hierarchical cluster analysis) to underline the importance of viewing such groupings as but one realization of a "truth" (R. Kaplan, 1975, 1977). While these procedures permit discovery (that is, results other than those that were predicted), it is not the case that they are antithetical to theory. The very choice of pictures and the decision of what aspects of the environment to sample are heavily dependent on theory. Furthermore, there are likely to be hypotheses concerning what items will group together—concerning, in other words, what aspects of the content will shape the empirically obtained categories. Such hypotheses can, of course, be directly supported or falsified by the outcome of a dimensional analytic procedure. As with any empirical work, and especially with research in more applied settings, it is the consistency of results that emerge from many studies that furthers our understanding.

Figure 1. Both of these scenes are from the "urban" grouping. While the one at the left is relatively highly rated for these scenes (mean 2.6), the one at the right was off the distribution relative to the other urban scenes (mean 3.2).

the scenes and for the content groupings (i.e., factor scores) of the study participants as a whole, the ratings provide information with respect to preferred places.

The difference in preference between the items comprising the nature theme and those in the urban set was highly significant. The preference ratings of the 23 nature scenes were all higher than the preference for any of the 13 urban scenes, with a single exception: the urban scene that had not originally been included in that category. This was a scene (at right in Figure 1) of a downtown plaza viewed across a wide street with modern buildings in the background and some young trees in planters in the plaza.

The 27 scenes with mean ratings greater than 3.0 included this one plaza scene, all but two of the nature scenes, and five others that were not included in either grouping (scene B in Figure 2 shows one of these). All five of these scenes showed substantial amounts of vegetation. The 29 scenes with mean preference ratings below 3.0 included very few scenes containing natural elements. The two nature scenes with the lowest preference ratings (C and D in Figure 2) consisted of a flat, open, relatively parched field with a forest in the very distant background and a scene dominated by coarse-textured, disordered foliage with a telephone pole surrounded by high weeds at one edge.

Gallagher's (1977) dissertation on "visual preference for alternative natural landscapes" was concerned with identifying the processes that operate in preference for natural settings. The scenes in his photoquestionnaire were all taken on the grounds of the CUNA Mutual Insurance

Figure 2. Scene (B) (mean 3.4) was not included in the "nature" theme, while (A), (C), and (D) were. The (A) scene, with the river visible through the trees, was highly preferred (mean 4.3). The (C) and (D) scenes were the least preferred nature scenes (means 2.8 and 2.7).

Society office in Madison, Wisconsin, and included both natural areas ("prairie/woodland sites characterized by low levels of management") and ornamental areas. Both employees at CUNA and nearby residents were asked to rate the 32 scenes for preference. Gallagher also had each of the scenes rated by a panel of judges for each of six predictor variables stemming from our previous work (cf. S. Kaplan, 1975).

A seventh predictor, which Gallagher called "naturalness," was included because of his interest in prairie vegetation. Scenes highest in this characteristic ("composed of vegetation and elements which appear unmanaged or in their 'natural' association or groups") proved to be the least preferred.[2] It was not only the apparent scruffiness of these set-

[2]"Naturalness" here is in the context of prairie grasses. This is not to say that other habitats that might also "appear unmanaged or in their 'natural' association or groups" would be rated in a similar way. An "unmanaged" climax forest with little understory and well-spaced trees would be highly favored. In other words, the informational properties of the configuration and not the management practices are critical.

tings that seemed to detract from preference; it appeared that the lack of trees also had a bearing on these judgments. Thus, an eighth predictor was added after the results were partially analyzed. The same judges rated each scene in terms of "the number and size of trees and their dominance in the scene." This predictor accounted for 45% of the preference variance. The most preferred content grouping in this study, consisting of landscaped areas, was strong on this added variable as well as both components of involvement, mystery, and complexity (as predicted).

A third study (Herzog, Kaplan, & Kaplan, 1982) serves as a particularly good example of the perceptual categories that are salient in the urban environment. The study involved 140 color slides of a wide variety of urban settings—commercial buildings, factories, apartments and other residential arrangements, alleys, parks, restaurants, civic and government settings—half of which were included in the preference ratings. While the scenes were of relatively characteristic urban setings, the specific places were unfamiliar to the participants (students taking introductory psychology courses at Grand Valley State College.)

The nonmetric factor analysis (Smallest Space Analysis III, Lingoes, 1972) of these preference ratings yielded five groupings. Examples of four of these are shown in Figure 3. The themes reflected by these groupings differ strikingly from a function-based taxonomy of the urban environment. Eighteen scenes comprised the *Contemporary Life* category. These were all built relatively recently for distinctly different purposes. Six relatively large *Older Buildings* formed a separate grouping, suggesting that apparent age is an important aspect of people's experience of the environment. Six other scenes that emerged as a category had in common the *Unusual Architecture* of the structures. The category consisting of *Alleys and Factories* included 11 scenes that communicate a rather desolate feeling, both because of their facelessness and their scale. The remaining category is particularly pertinent to our discussion. These 9 scenes were dominated by trees and grass, and the buildings that were visible through the foliage varied in size and modernity. This grouping was named *Urban Nature.*

The Urban Nature scenes all had mean ratings greater than 3.0. Of the 18 other scenes that shared this distinction, half showed substantial foliage. Among the lower half of preference ratings, 2 of 35 scenes showed vegetation in any notable amount. All the Alley/Factory scenes were devoid of natural elements (and as a group, were by far the least preferred), and of the 18 Contemporary Life scenes, only 4 can be considered to include a noticeable amount of nature. From this study it would appear that nature in the city is highly valued. Not only is the

Figure 3. Examples from four of the groupings in the Herzog *et al.* study: (A): Older building; (B): Urban nature; (C): Alley/Factory; (D): Contemporary life.

urban nature grouping the most preferred, but the presence of vegetation (mostly in the form of foliage) emerges as perhaps the strongest predictor of preference in this study.

CONTENT AND PROCESS AS PREDICTORS

It is always tempting in retrospect to be unsurprised by empirical results. After all, there have been many proclamations of the importance of nature and of trees in particular. Gold (1977a) has asserted that "the tree is the most dominant natural element in the urban landscape." Similarly, Alexander, Ishikawa, and Silverstein (1977) declare that "trees have a very deep and crucial meaning to human beings" (p. 798). Pitt, Soergell, and Zube (1979) mention a lack of "an overwhelming number of studies which address questions of the perceived value of trees" (p.210), but they mention a few that show that grass and trees have important environmental value. A study by Thayer and Atwood (1978) found significantly higher "pleasurable responses" to scenes with plants as opposed to matched ones lacking vegetation, but it is difficult to discern whether just any type of vegetation will suffice.

The strong and repeated empirical support of the importance of nature content had not, however, been anticipated in the three studies described here. In the first study (Kaplan *et al.*, 1972), the nature grouping based on participants' preference ratings included a far broader range of nature content than had been expected. The presence of human influence did not detract from the perceptual categorization, and the preference for the nature scenes was not a function of the presence or absence of human influence. In Gallagher's study, the importance of trees in predicting preference came as hindsight and the low preference of the prairie grass photographs was contrary to his prior expectations.

The scenes in the Herzog *et al.* study (1982) had not been selected with urban nature in mind, and systematic ratings of this aspect had not been included as a predictor variable. The study had been carried out to explore the salient categories of the urban environment, to determine how citizens (as opposed to planners and realtors, for example) perceive such settings. That nature would emerge as a content category in this context came as a distinct surprise.

It would seem then that nature content is important to people. And certain natural elements such as trees and foliage, water, wildlife, and flowers are particularly appreciated. But what about process? The studies discussed here also serve to show that the importance of the natural elements extends beyond the specific kinds of elements. While nature scenes are rated higher in preference than scenes lacking these features, it is not the case that all natural settings are equally preferred. Trees and foliage enhance preference, but the ground texture and the configuration of the setting must also be considered. "Naturalness," in the sense of least human influence, is not necessarily a characteristic of preferred settings. In fact, the smoothness of the ground texture is an important aspect of preference. The least preferred nature scenes shown in Figure 2 as well as the ones in Gallagher's study were characterized by coarse textures and by vegetation that obstructs one's visual access.

In all three studies, "mystery" was a particularly effective predictor of preference. The 140 slides in the Herzog *et al.* study had been rated on this characteristic (as well as three others) by a different group of participants from the ones who had indicated their preferences for half the slides. The Urban Nature category, by far the most preferred of the five groupings, had by far the highest ratings on mystery (rated as "the promise of further information based on a change in vantage point of the observer"). In Gallagher's study the most preferred settings were also strongest in mystery. And the first study discussed here was the one that originally helped us formulate the notion of mystery.

From the point of view of our environmental preference framework,[3] the most preferred scenes accomplish two missions in terms of their informational attributes: predictability is enhanced by facilitating comprehension of the immediately present situation, and involvement is enhanced by enticing one to explore "beyond the bend." Both these processes are necessary for preference to be heightened. Even with the undramatic bits and pieces of nature found in the urban setting, the combination of these two informational factors, together with the nature content, seems to be important in predicting preference.

THE VIEW FROM HOME

The names given to housing developments suggest that natural elements are valued. "Forest" and "green" appear frequently in subdivision names. References to topographic variation ("hill," "ridge," and "vale") are also common. Particular tree names are popular (pine, spruce, and oak). Some wildlife is also cherished (e.g., "Pheasant Run"), but this aspect of nature must be chosen more carefully to evoke the proper balance between wild and tame, fierce and commonplace.

The arrangement of housing projects also suggests that developers recognize people's appreciation of nature. Large mowed areas are not uncommon. Bushes are often planted along walks and near houses. In some localities, it is required that trees be planted. While these natural features can be found, little research has been reported on how people feel about them. The presence and even use of a large commons area is not sufficient proof of preference.

To explore the role of nature in the immediate home environment, we conducted a survey[4] at nine housing projects ranging in size from 10 to 55 acres and from 167 to 600 units. All these apartment and town house projects are located in Ann Arbor, Michigan; three are operated as cooperatives, the rest as rental units. The projects were all built between 1964 and 1975. Within each of the housing projects, dwellings were selected in terms of their location to include those that face other housing units and those that look out onto less built environments (e.g., fields, park, woods). Within these constraints, residents were selected randomly.

---

[3]A much fuller discussion of this preference framework can be found in S. Kaplan (1979a,b).
[4]This study was funded, in part, by the Cooperative Agreement 13-655, from the U.S. Forest Service, North Central Forest Experiment Station. A more extensive discussion of the results can be found in R. Kaplan (1981b).

A central tool in this study was a photoquestionnaire (R. Kaplan, 1979a,b). The photographs serve both as a means of obtaining preference ratings and as a way to communicate what "nearby nature" entails. The questionnaire consisted of five pages of photographs in the beginning and three more photo pages at the end, with five pages of verbal items in between. A cover letter from the Director of Planning for the city informed the respondents that their feelings about open space and natural areas in multiple-family developments would be important in formulating city regulations for future developments. The responses were to be anonymous and returned in the attached business-reply envelope to the School of Natural Resources; the study involved no cost to the city. Where respondents answered the doorbell, they were handed the material with a quick introduction to its purpose. If no one was at home, or where security prevented individual solicitation, the material was left at the door. Given the lack of follow-up, the length of the questionnaire, the high rate of transiency, and the impersonal distribution method, the 33% response rate is not surprising. The data reported here are based on 268 returned questionnaires.

Table 1 presents some of the demographic characteristics of the sample. The participants tended to be young, childless, relatively non-affluent, and in transition concering their living arrangements.

KINDS OF NATURE

The question of the salient categories of nature can be answered in part in terms of the kinds of activities that people engage in near their homes. From this perspective, areas that permit nature walks, relatively large open areas for playing, children's play areas, and protected areas for sitting outside constitute different kinds of natural environments.

But the activity perspective tells only part of the story. The initial pages of the questionnaire consisted of 40 photographs of areas near or within housing projects such as the ones included in the study. Participants were asked to rate each scene in terms of preference (five-point scale) and to indicate whether such a setting was available within close walking range. These preference ratings were the basis for dimensional analyses that helped to identify how different aspects of the nearby natural setting were perceived.

Results from this procedure indicate that the areas that would appear equally appropriate for tossing a ball fall into distinctly different categories. Large mowed areas are particularly characteristic of many multiple-family housing projects included in this study. These are often in relatively interior spaces, surrounded by the housing units, or be-

TABLE 1

BACKGROUND CHARACTERISTICS OF RESPONDENTS (IN PERCENTAGES)

Sex	Age	Ethnic background	Income (in dollars)	Household composition	People per household	Number of children	Work status	Length at address	Plan to stay
Male 35	Under 20 1	White 88	< 8,000 18	Single 26	One 29	None 67	Full-time 56	Under 1 yr. 16	Under 1 yr. 21
Female 60	20–29 53	Black 5	8–16,000 44	Couple 25	Two 40	One 15	Part-time 20	1 yr. 24	1 yr. 18
Both 2	30–39 34	Other 3	16–24,000 22	Family 35	Three 15	Two 12	Homemaker 24	2–3 yrs. 21	2–3 yrs. 12
N/A 3	40–59 7	N/A 4	24–48,000 12	Unrelated 8	Four 9	Three+ 3	Retired 4	4–7 yrs. 20	4–7 yrs. 10
	60+ 3		N/A 4	Other 2	Five+ 6	N/A 3	Student 31	8–9 yrs. 6	8–9 yrs. 3
	N/A 2			N/A 4	N/A 2			10+ yrs. 11	10+ yrs. 11
								N/A 25	N/A 6

tween housing units and the street. Such areas did not form a distinct content grouping. Rather, the categorizations found in this study suggest that the perception of these places depends on the relationship between the natural elements and the housing itself.

The scenes in Figure 4 all include mowed areas that are fairly well maintained. Scenes C and D (mean preference of 2.2 and 1.8, respectively), however, are part of a grouping that received quite low preference ratings. The scenes in this cluster are characterized by buildings dominated by mowed expanses. They lack mystery. They seem to have a barrenness and anonymity reminiscent of the places that Newman (1972) describes as lacking defensible space. Scenes A and B in Figure 4 (means of 3.2 and 2.7), by contrast, are representative of the Open, Residential grouping that reflects a more balanced proportion of building to vegetation. Although the housing units in the photos in this cluster are in relatively large, open areas, there are trees and other plantings in evidence.

Figure 4. (A) and (B) show two views from the open-residential grouping, while (C) and (D) are from the category that was by far least preferred.

Figure 5. The landscaped arrangements depicted in (A) and (B) were by and large less preferred than the "nature" scenes exemplified by (C) and (D).

The scenes in Figure 5 represent two other categories that emerged in this study. The two views at the top are characterized by landscaping; trees and foliage abound and mystery is an important aspect of the more preferred members of this grouping. Manicured lawns and tidy bushes are not sure paths to positive ratings (scene A is much less preferred than scene B, means 3.1 and 3.8, respectively). On the other hand, scruffy vegetation also tends to be a less preferred alternative. Scenes C and D in Figure 5 are taken from the Nature cluster, with scene D rated considerably lower (mean 3.8) than the scene C (mean 4.4). Although scene D is rated relatively low in preference with respect to the "nature" grouping, only five other scenes in the photoquestionnaire were rated as high. In all the scenes in this grouping, the natural environment is relatively independent of the housing, and even though the ground texture is by no means smooth in all cases, the preferences tended to be relatively high.

These findings suggest that the natural environment is not a simple undimensional construct. People differentiate their immediate residential environment in terms of various features of the natural setting.

These seem to be based on a variety of factors, both visual and functional. The view of parked cars easily detracts and the view of other apartments is much more positively rated if screened or at least partially obscured by some large trees. The assumption that large mowed areas and bushes lining the paths are important selling points is not substantiated by these results. Such factors may or may not be deemed amenities, depending on how the entire setting is designed.

DOES THE VIEW MATTER?

In addition to the photographs, the issues related to the nearby natural environment were also explored through the verbal items. Participants were asked to indicate whether certain objects and features were dominant in the view from the residence and to rate their satisfaction with the views. The four most dominant items differed markedly in terms of participant preference. Between 59 and 69 percent of the sample indicated that parking areas, large mowed areas, small trees, and landscaped areas could be seen either "quite a bit" or were a "dominant part" of the view. The view of small trees and of a landscaped area was greatly appreciated (means 4.5 and 4.4). Seeing a large mowed area, however, did not receive as enthusiastic a rating (mean 3.8), and the modal response for the view of parked cars was 1 (mean 1.7). Nor was it more likely that those for whom the large mowed areas or a parking area were more dominant would enjoy such a view; in this case, familiarity and preference are uncorrelated.

For those whose view included them, the most treasured features of their view were "large trees" (mean 4.8) and "woods" (mean 4.7). Only about half the sample had views of fields, woods, a park, or their own garden—all natural elements that are savored by those who can see them from their home.

The data concerning reactions to the dominant elements of the view help answer the question of what people like. There still remains the issue of whether such elements in the landscape have any wider significance. Are the landscape elements pretty but essentially irrelevant decorations, or are they important features of the residential environment? More specifically, does the view make any difference in the feelings that people have about where they live? In order to obtain data on these questions, a number of measures of *neighborhood satisfaction* were employed. There were two single items and four indexes: Satisfaction with *general layout* of the development, with *appearance* of the grounds, with *nature* (e.g., having enough nature nearby, recreation opportunities, and amount of open space), with *physical* aspects (security and safety, general maintenance, and parking arrangement), with *size* (number of people, number of children), and with *community* (how friendly people are, the variety of people, and sense of community). These satisfaction measures were somewhat interrelated (mean correlation among the scales was .51).

Views of parking areas and intrusive elements (power lines, busy streets) did in fact play a substantial role in reducing neighborhood satisfaction in all aspects with the exception of Community.[5] The view of play areas reduced neighborhood satisfaction to some degree, while views of gardens and large mowed areas were generally neutral with respect to these issues (relating significantly only to the community index).

The strongest forces in predicting positive neighborhood satisfaction were the natural aspects of the view. Seeing woods, large trees, small trees, and landscaping each was strongly related to the four physical aspects of neighborhood satisfaction. Woods and landscaping were also related to satisfaction with the community aspect, and the satisfaction with size was strongly related to seeing woods, large trees, and small trees. The simple question, "about how many trees would you say are very near your home," showed the same pattern as these questions relating to the dominant view. The more trees people reported having near their home, the greater their neighborhood satisfaction (once again, except for the community aspect). Similarly, people who reported scenes such as those comprising the Nature category in the photoquestionnaire (e.g., scenes C and D in Figure 5) as relatively available near their home were strikingly more satisfied with all aspects of their neighborhood.

Neighborhood satisfaction was also related to one other set of items measuring the perceived availability of nature in the immediate residential environment. This involved a set of questions regarding the distance to and the adequacy of the natural environment. Five facets of nature were explored. Of these, "a natural area" and "a good place for taking walks" tended to be intercorrelated and were both strongly related to each of the six neighborhood-satisfaction measures. Where such features were not available, satisfaction was dramatically diminished. The adequacy of a "field or open area for playing" and of "a park" (but not the distance to such facilities) were also strong predictors of the neighborhood-satisfaction measures. The item concerning a "place to grow flowers/vegetables" was strongly related to the participants' satisfaction

[5]Throughout this chapter, results reported from studies we have carried out are significant at $p < .01$.

with their community, but not with other aspects of neighborhood satisfaction. It appears that gardening has a social component less central to other kinds of nearby nature.

This is a fascinating pattern of results.[6] While the findings with respect to the size and community components of neighborhood satisfaction follow a somewhat idiosyncratic pattern, the overall story is one of great importance. If the Director of Planning is genuinely interested in citizen's feelings about the role of natural areas and open space, the answer is quite direct. Not only do people prefer to see the natural world, but having such views and facilities nearby strongly affects their satisfaction with their physical and social environment. People find their large, multiple-family housing to be friendlier, more supportive, and much more attractive when there are trees and woods to be seen. Devoting many acres to large mowed areas, however, seems to gain little mandate from these results.

SATISFACTION FROM URBAN NATURE

Seymour (1969) tells of New York City's first public park, adopted in a resolution of the Common Council "for the beauty and ornament of the said street as well as for the recreation and delight of the inhabitants of the city" (p. 1). The date was 1733. Bowling Green is still there, in the heart of New York's financial district, a place for office workers to have their lunch and for "mid-day band concerts."

Liberty Plaza in Ann Arbor is a similarly tiny park, heavily used at lunchtime, in the heart of a much smaller city. Although it was built almost 2½ centuries after Bowling Green, the two parks might well rate similarly in terms of the satisfactions they offer. Such an evaluation has in fact been made for Liberty Plaza (R. Kaplan, 1980, 1981a). Citizens were very much satisfied with the park, its appearance, the seating arrangement, and plantings. Safety and security did not prove to be strong concerns (contrary to fears expressed during predesign citizen participation, R. Kaplan, 1978b). The biggest source of pleasure that the little park provides, however, is the fact that it is there. "Having the park there" received a mean rating of 4.7 (five-point scale) by some 355 respondents, including both people interviewed while in the park and those working or living in the vicinity.[7] Such cognitive satisfaction is

---

[6]Cooper (1975, p. 220) also comments on the importance of the view from the dwelling and mentions some similar concerns of multifamily housing residents.

[7]Although the sample and context are quite different, Ulrich and Addoms (1981) report surprisingly parallel findings.

easily overlooked. Knowledge of its existence provides this reward, even without seeing or actually using the park.

SATISFACTION WITHOUT ACTIVE USE

Nonuse of parks is a phenomenon that has received some attention (e.g., Gold, 1977a). When evaluation of a park is based on user counts, there is no way to determine its merits for those who are not present. There is little doubt that use is highly correlated with distance. Alexander *et al.* (1977) indicate that "if the greens are more than three minutes away, the distance overwhelms the need" (p. 303). An HCRS brochure (undated) cites the high priority urban residents place on "close-to-home facilities" and the inadequacy of such facilities in many communities.

There are several complex issues intertwined here. To some degree the frequent emphasis on parks obscures the large issue of open space in the community. Parks are not the only outdoor places for recreation. Because many other heavily used areas are not designed for such activities, or are perhaps not in the public domain, their role is easily ignored. The street itself, nearby vacant lots, and even parking lots, as well as residential yards (Halkett, 1978), are not only popular spots, but have been shown to play a significant role in people's perceived life quality (Frey, 1981). In many cases these are more accessible than a designated open space. As Little (1974) suggests, perhaps the role assigned to streets and to parks deserves reexamination.

Park use is not a trivial concern, to be sure. Whyte (1980) has shown that it is the underused places that attract "undesirables," and Heckscher (1977) suggests that "emptiness is the curse of open space as boredom is the curse of leisure" (p. 7). A park that only rarely has people in it, or that people fear to use, is unlikely to be a source of perceptual or cognitive satisfaction. On the other hand, the importance of *some* use does not mean that the use must be explicitly recreational in character, nor that use beyond a certain baseline level is related in any way to the visual and conceptual rewards it provides. As Burton (1978) states, it is a

> mix of many characteristics and roles of open space that gives it its peculiar gift of generating satisfaction. Its actual use for recreation activity is often of relatively minor significance. (p. 77)

The reliance on user counts of official recreation areas presents an additional problem. Counting people at a park and categorizing these numbers in terms of activities is a relatively manageable task. But it is a large leap between knowing these statistics and ascertaining the benefits that are derived from green and open places. To some extent one can infer satisfaction from use. Laurie (1979), for instance, cites the widespread use of rural cemeteries in the last century, including counts in Philadelphia and Brooklyn in 1848, as leading to the realization that "urban people yearned for natural settings in which to socialize and relax" (p. 501). But the inference of benefits from use must be approached cautiously. Although measuring the sources of well-being may be more challenging methodologically, it is important to explore this topic, rather than assuming to know the answer.

A 1973 poll cited by Foresta (1980) suggests that people of different income levels and from different residential settings rate the importance of open space quite similarly. On an *a priori* basis one would have probably thought that "watching birds and animals" and to "run and play games" would have been rated as very important uses of open space for the majority of the respondents. They were not; but "breathe fresh air," "view natural scenery," "enjoy a place unchanged by man," and experience a "feeling of freedom" were consistently given the highest rating. If the nearby natural setting is important for socializing, these results would suggest that other aspects are far more central.

In fact, the aspects of open space rated as particularly important in this study are not necessarily associated with a specific recreational activity. Furthermore, they suggest that nature can be fulfilling and absorbing even without visible activity of any kind. Such satisfactions can be gained from a few moments' time or from a prolonged contact with one's natural surrounds. Rather than emphasizing actions, these sources of satisfaction appear to be more dependent on perceptual and conceptual processes.

Similarly, solitude is a source of satisfaction that nature seems to afford. Alexander *et al.* (1977) wrote of nature as a source of stillness and they dwelled on the importance of finding such a place close to home. "And now many of us have come to learn that without such a place life in the city is impossible" (p. 816). The place for such solitude and stillness, for being in touch with nature, they call "the garden seat." The garden provides a contact with the natural environment that is available to many urban dwellers, rich and poor. It is a setting where nature is not incidental but essential—an ideal place and activity for exploring the kinds of differences that nature affords.

PEOPLE–PLANT RELATIONSHIP

At the time I reported on "the psychological benefits of gardening" (R. Kaplan, 1973), I was oblivious to the New York City Housing Authority's Tenant Gardening Competition (begun in 1962) and to Lewis's keen observations of its effects on public housing participants who so actively engaged in it. Lewis (1972, 1977, 1979) has written of the pervasive benefits derived from this people/plant relationship with respect to community cohesiveness, aesthetic pleasure, and self-esteem. In fact, his intuitive grasp of the importance of this activity in the lives of inner-city dwellers for whom many things are not going well in other respects led to our collaboration on subsequent research on this subject. Unfortunately, none of this research has touched directly on the activities of these participants in the various municipally sponsored tenant gardening projects.

In 1975 Lewis gained the cooperation of members of a men's garden club in Illinois and a horticultural group in Seattle to pretest a questionnaire on gardening benefits. The results of this effort (n = 73), led to a questionnaire that the American Horticultural Society (AHS, sponsors of the People/Plant Program) sent to its members in 1976. The two-page survey, requiring 13 cents return postage, yielded 4,297 usable responses. Not only did this far exceed our wildest expectations, it also generated several kinds of frustration: the project had no funds; the interest in the topic generated an outpouring of correspondence and enthusiasm that I had no way of handling; the membership was never informed about the results, since AHS decided not to publish this material.

The results reported here include, in addition to the AHS participants, 240 surveys from readers of *Organic Gardening and Farming* magazine (OGF) who responded to brief mention in the magazine about the study.[8] Our hope had been to have a very different group of gardeners, suspecting that AHS members are more affluent than the average gardener and perhaps more interested in exotic plants. Of course, there is no claim here that either sample is random, as both groups are self-selected. All states are included in the larger sample and all but 12 in the smaller, with the population distribution surprisingly similar on a regional basis to the census figures. Each group consisted of approximately 16% single and 75% married respondents. The OGF sample was younger (66% under 40) than the AHS group (70% over 40) and distinctly less affluent (63% reported incomes under $18,000, while 65% of AHS group was above that level).

A particularly important difference between the two groups involved the focus on vegetable gardening on the part of the OGF group

[8]Without Jerome Goldstein's help and enthusiasm, this portion of the study would not have been possible.

(74% indicated that their gardens contained "mostly vegetables" and 21% contained flowers and vegetables "about equally"). Only 17% of the AHS sample indicated "mostly vegetables," with the remainder about equally divided between "mostly flowers" and the "both" categories. As would be expected, the OGF sample used "mostly organic fertilizer" (76%). The AHS group was more diverse in this respect, with well over 1000 respondents in each of the three categories: 30% reported mostly organic, 27% mostly chemical, and 41% "about the same amount of each."

GARDENING SATISFACTIONS

Vogt (1966) points out that the mammoth study of the Outdoor Recreation Resource Review Commission (ORRRC) "incredibly does not list 'gardening' as an outdoor recreation" (p. 383). Even when the study was carried out, in the early 1960s, over half the American population was apparently engaged in this activity. But perhaps gardening is pursued for its productive rather than recreational aspects.

One would expect, then, a major source of satisfaction from gardening to be related to the *tangible benefits* of growing one's own food, cutting expenses, and harvesting. For the OGF sample, more concerned with vegetables, this was indeed important (mean 4.3 on 5-point scale) but for the AHS group other benefits were far more significant (mean 3.4). The satisfaction with the tangible aspects of gardening declines for both groups with years of gardening experience. If the productive aspects of gardening were in fact the major source of satisfaction, one wonders what the attraction of gardening might be as one becomes more proficient at this activity. But, as it turns out, this is but a small part of the benefits derived from gardening.

An interesting derivative of the productive aspect of gardening involves *sharing the fruits* of one's garden with others (mean 3.7 for each group). It does not matter that the recipient also has an oversupply of zucchini at the moment; it is rewarding to give others the vegetables and flowers one has grown. There is also another form of sharing that many gardeners enjoy. This involves *sharing information* and being able to help others with their gardening problems (mean 3.4 for each group).

The joy of growing *new kinds of plants,* of having odd and unusual specimens, was of far greater importance to the AHS gardeners (means 4.1 and 3.7). But the *sensory* joy derived from the colors and smells and from walking in the garden were equally vital to both groups (mean 4.3).

A theme that receives some mention with respect to gardening and urban nature involves the sense of control that is possible in these activities. Fogel (1980) cites Jimmy Carter, campaigning in 1976, relating about the many people who "feel they have lost control of their lives. Growing a garden is one small way to gain back some of that control" (p. 28). Manning (1979) extends the theme of control to urban nature in general and shows how consistently control is related to tidiness and orderliness—much as Gallagher's unmanaged natural settings were far less appreciated than the closely clipped manicured lawns. But the satisfaction derived from the *neatness and tidiness* that gardens make possible was not a particularly strong source of satisfaction for either AHS or OGF participants (means 3.2 and 3.0). The correlated theme of *control* ("it's up to me how it looks," "something I can do on my own") received mean ratings of 3.5 for each group and quite some variability in response. It does not take much experience to appreciate that one's control can only go so far in the garden. It would seem that aspects of gardening over which one has least direct control are the sources of greatest satisfaction.

For both groups the most important satisfaction seems at first glance to be only distantly related to the activity of gardening. It seems somehow more "psychological," although psychological theories give it little attention. Interestingly enough, it is a satisfaction that is associated with nature in other contexts as well. The most important gardening satisfaction comes from the "feeling of peacefulness" and the *"quiet and tranquility"* it provides (means 4.3 and 4.5 for AHS and OGF, respectively). It is reminiscent of the "garden seat pattern" that Alexander and his colleagues advocate.

A somewhat related theme and one that rated virtually as highly (means 4.2 and 4.4) involved a scale[9] comprised of seven items. These items express a range of activity from a physical ("working in the soil" and "working close to nature") to a less active form ("seeing plants grow" and "checking to see how plants are doing") to a more cognitive level ("like the planning involved," "get completely wrapped up in it," and "never fails to hold my interest"). These items all express a *Nature Fascination,* a sense of being absorbed and involved.

Once again, an analysis in terms of content and process provides a useful perspective. The sources of greatest gardening satisfaction, Tranquility and Nature Fascination, are both strongly tied to the content: the soil, the greenness, the flowers and vegetables, the trees, the setting. It is in the context of these content domains that powerful process factors

---

[9]All the gardening satisfaction scales discussed here are based on the same dimensional procedures discussed in Note 1. A random subsample of the AHS group, stratified by region, and the OGF sample were the basis for these analyses (n = 478).

are operating. In a paper on "Tranquility and Challenge in the Natural Environment," S. Kaplan (1977) discusses the importance of fascination in achieving cognitive clarity. "The process that people find fascinating is, in the largest sense, the process of coping with uncertainty" (p. 183). The garden provides

> knowledge and requires it. It is a setting that allows of order, but that order is deeply embedded in uncertainty and change. Thus [gardening] challenges the human information-processing capability, and to the extent that the challenge is met, both reward and more challenge are forthcoming. (R. Kaplan, 1973, p. 160)

ORGANIC VERSUS CHEMICAL FERTILIZERS

It could be argued that the use of fertilizers is a form of control. While virtually all respondents used some form of fertilizer, there are some important differences in this area. Organic gardening lacks the instant cures promised by the advertisers of garden chemicals and thus might be viwed as a lesser degree of control. It may therefore demand greater vigilance, more perceptive observation, and a deeper sense of participation in the process. Comparison of the AHS gardeners as a function of the kind of fertilizer they used proved to be very interesting. (For the OGF group this comparison could not be made since organic fertilizers were favored by so large a proportion of the sample.)

Those who tended to use chemical fertilizers indicated consistently lower satisfaction ratings on each of the benefit scales in the study. In addition, their rating of a pair of "life satisfaction" items (e.g., "how satisfying would you say your life has been compared to other people you know") was also significantly lower than for the "organic fertilizer" and "both organic and chemical fertilizer" groups. The latter two groups showed no differences in ratings of the life satisfaction items nor for the "control," "nature fascination," "share-tangible," and "sensory satisfaction" scales. Those who use a mix of fertilizers scored higher on satisfaction from novel plants, sharing information, and having a tidy and neat garden. The organic fertilizer group rated higher items related to tangible benefits and to the peace and tranquility of gardening—both scales that OGF gardeners rated significantly higher than AHS as a whole.

The choice of fertilizer likely expresses far more than an individual's desire for control. There are perhaps differences in the gardener's cognitive involvement in the various phases of this activity. One has to be concerned with subtle signs if relying on more natural approaches to correcting problems. There are a number of factors that might be involved. There may be a greater sense of working with nature, of being in partnership rather than opposition. One may also feel "closer to earth," a participant in an enduring and life-giving natural process. Presumably such feelings may eventually culminate in a sense of "oneness." It is just such a feeling that has been a key factor in other natural environment experiences (cf. Chapter 5) and that James (1902) considered to be a central theme in his study of religious experience.

There is of course no way to ascribe a causal relationship between choice of fertilizer and the benefits derived. On the other hand, the pattern of results fits together in a meaningful way, constituting a strong enticement for further research. Are there life-style differences that relate to these patterns? What is the psychological significance of such experiences as tranquility, and "feeling close to earth"? What conditions are necessary for experiences of this kind to occur?

The psychological satisfactions derived from gardening suggest a great range of ways in which contact with nature is important. Being needed, a sense of control, sensory pleasure, serenity, and fascination are all in short supply for many people. It is no wonder that the subject of gardening evokes so much enthusiasm and serves as a common bond for people of widely varying backgrounds.

URBAN NATURE AND QUALITY OF LIFE

The need for research on the role of nature in the urban context is undeniable. It is hard to believe that behavioral scientists have devoted so little of their effort to a topic that is basic to the well-being of so many people. But the need for action is clear. Both documented and anecdotal evidence suggest that natural elements must be given a more vital place in urban planning and design as well as in policy decisions. In fact, much of the research and action would best be coordinated—both would be enhanced by the development of a conceptual understanding of the importance of nature and the multifaceted ways that it affects behavior.

The purpose of this last section is to bring these threads together. It draws on the empirical findings reported earlier and on proposals made by others. Fortunately, there are also some approaches actually in use that can serve as models for other settings. There are numerous research questions embedded here; some of these will be highlighted.

HUMAN NEEDS AND THE NATURAL ENVIRONMENT

The studies on social indicators and quality of life do little to document the role that natural elements play. Yet life is less satisfying for many people deprived of the opportunity to grow things. Public housing residents have no less a desire for a tree outside their window than do more affluent citizens. And the grief for a lost tree—by disease, natural forces, or for the sake of "progress"—is shared regardless of age, sex, income, or ethnic or religious background. Are the joys of recognizing birds, seeing the seasonal changes in the foliage, or planning next year's garden just momentary pleasures, or is their effect more significant? Can the absence of natural elements simply be compensated by floral upholstery fabric and a potholder emblazoned with a mushroom?

Human motives are closely tied to knowledge and to the process of finding out (cf. Kaplan & Kaplan, 1978). The need to comprehend, to make sense, is pervasive. In fact, failure to meet this need readily leads to hostility and anxiety. In the long run, however, having everything under control and clear-cut does not make for a healthy person either. The desire for involvement, for exploration, is at least as pervasive. Thus there is a continuing tension between understanding and finding things yet to be understood, between comfort in certainty and thrill in uncertainty.

Nature fulfills human needs in diverse ways. The settings that are favored consistently are ones in which the ability to make sense and to provide involvement are nurtured. A large, undifferentiated open space, treeless and homogeneous, is considered boring (uninvolving). But a setting that is overgrown and impenetrable lacks security or the ability to make sense, and also is unpreferred. Yet both kinds of settings are easy to find in or near cities. The notion of open space is, in fact, somewhat misleading. The attractiveness of an open space is considerably enhanced by the presence of trees and by a relatively smooth ground texture. But parks and open spaces are not the only kinds of natural settings that are supportive of these needs. Even a small garden can provide these patterns (as Japanese gardens beautifully exemplify). The sense of both enclosure and an enticing place beyond where one is standing is available even on the small scale of the immediate residential environment.

The natural setting also affords many activities that permit these processes to function. Gardening, as we have seen, is one such activity in which making sense and involvement are constantly interposed. As a miniature natural setting that both requires knowledge and provides it, it is hardly surprising that gardens hold so much fascination. For many people, bird watching shares some of these characteristics. It is an activity in which change is continuous, but knowledge makes it far more predictable. Even high-rise apartment dwellers can enjoy this contact with nature.

The salience of the natural environment in fulfilling these needs is also exemplified by the consequences of the failure of making sense and involvement. If parks are such wonderful places, why are they subjected to vandalism and crime? As has already been mentioned, such behavior is greatly reduced through use. A place is much safer when alive with people. Whyte (1980) provides a telling analysis of the relation of use and problems. Where management took steps that, in effect, reduced use (i.e. removed benches), ordinary people stopped coming, thus leaving the park to pot dealers and their customers. Lewis (1979) mentions the low incidence of vandalism in the tenant gardens because of the intense involvement of the activity. In fact, youths with criminal records were proud participants and the neighborhood tough guys were sought out to protect the cherished seedlings. A *New York Times* analysis of London's Hyde Park describes it as "almost free of crime, rowdyism and noise" ("London's Hyde Park," 1977), although certainly not lacking in people and situated in the heart of the city. While cultural factors may in part explain this pattern, evidently "careful maintenance of the parks inspires respect." There too, litter is increased when the grass is not cut, and litter breeds more of the same. Gold (1977b) also discusses the role of maintenance in reducing vandalism. So the sense of order, in addition to the opportunity for involvement, is important in controlling undesirable behavior.

And yet the common ways to fight vandalism are oblivious to the importance of human needs. Striving for indestructibility often creates a yet bigger challenge. Increasing law enforcement has often led to increased alienation. Replacing the defaced objects as soon as the crime is finished can lead to a never-ending repetition of the cycle. The cure for broken glass—windowless schools—seems to be the cause of other problems of possibly greater magnitude. Fortunately, some more enlightened approaches have also been used. Both Magill (1976) and Clark (1976) discuss the importance of increasing comprehension and involvement in dealing with vandalism in outdoor settings.

PARTICIPATION

Nature matters to people. Big trees and small trees, glistening water, chirping birds, budding bushes, and colorful flowers—these are important ingredients in a good life. To have these available only rarely, when and if one can afford to leave the city, deprives people of tranquility and of spiritual sustenance.

Making sense and involvement also matter to people. People struggle to comprehend their lives, their surroundings, their universe. They are distraught when things do not make sense and restless when not striving for what they want. And yet these needs are all too often unmet in the urban environment, depriving people of meaningful challenge and a sense of efficacy.

In light of this analysis, it is hardly surprising that some of the programs that have produced the most exciting results have addressed these basic informational needs in the context of the urban/natural environment. These are programs that involve participation. They give people the opportunity to gain an understanding and to be needed, and the natural environment serves as the vehicle for the transformation.

Hogan (1980) describes a tiny vacant lot in Philadelphia that was bought from the city for one dollar under the Urban Homesteading Program. It was made into a community park, mostly for "older folks" in the area, by intensive local effort. In five years there had been no vandalism. Hogan suggests that this may well be because "Every single person in the community pitched in to build [the park] and who would want to destroy that which he or she has created?" (p. 28).

There is certainly no single answer to vandalism; other exciting solutions have come from involving the vandals in more constructive activities in the same setting (Clark, 1976). The involvement in growing flowers in the various people/plant programs has been particularly effective in achieving participation in seemingly unrelated domains such as sense of community and self-esteem (Lewis, 1979). The consistency of this effect is striking. The "city farms" in London ("Down on the Farm," 1979) have "spread to numerous other deprived inner-city areas throughout Britain." These self-help programs have been shown to do more than grow food and raise chickens. "Their role has an inbuilt mechanism for strengthening of mutual problems." One wonders if such programs could be as viable if the focus were on something lacking the intrinsic power of natural elements. The recommendation by Alexander *et al.* (1977, p. 25) for interlocking "fingers of farmland" in the urban design would seem to provide an exciting way to capture these advantages.

Heckscher (1977) comments on the opportunity for citizen participation with respect to urban parks. "A city's open spaces," he says, "are capable of evoking in the public a strong sense of possessiveness and a desire for involvement" (p. 7). Our studies of Liberty Plaza certainly support this contention. The community involvement in Houston's impressive park and open space program mentioned earlier further attests to the statement. The "Partnership for People" program in Portsmouth, Virginia (Greiner, 1979) demonstrates what citizens can accomplish with respect to recreation and parks and what intangible benefits such involvement has for the participants. Here residents of low-income, dis-

tressed neighborhoods have been successful in raising the funds necessary to operate their programs. Unlikely perhaps, but the recognition
that "the effectiveness of any citizen involvement program depends
upon a knowledgeable public" has led to training programs in "fund
raising, volunteer recruitment, new program ideas, conducting meetings, and understanding capital improvements" (p. 30).

Citizen involvement is equally appropriate for the planting and care
of street trees. As Dwyer (1980) points out, neighborhood associations
and homeowners are beginning to participate in this effort. In some
places they are even assuming responsibility for sharing in the cost of
the trees.

In the light of changing economic trends and the need for new
energy-efficient patterns, community involvement in the local setting
provides the opportunity for motivated environmental education. The
immediate natural environment is a shared interest of the local citizens,
an ideal focus for involvement, and a forum for regaining that lost control over direction and purpose.

SEARCH AND RESEARCH

What we do not know about the role of urban nature in people's
well-being far exceeds what we do know. As we search for ways to
improve the plight of our urban centers and their inhabitants, we must
also assess the effectiveness of these approaches.

What kind of nature and how much of it is necessary for enhancing
a sense of tranquility, an inner peacefulness, that the rush and confusion of the urban environment so readily violate? Pictures hung on walls
are frequently selected for their natural themes. Perhaps these permit
the mind to wander, providing rest from the attentional demands of the
urban cognitive load. Do the European city forests provide such solace?
Is the view out the window an important source of fascination? Is the
trip to work affected by the "greenness" of the possible alternatives?

Embedded in these questions are many unknown aspects of the role
of scale. It would seem that even a few trees, a small garden patch, a
landscaped area outside one's door, make a difference. But these small-
scale bits of nature that are immediately accessible do not replace the
role of larger expanses and buffers that one encounters less regularly. As
new communities replace the countryside, the issue of how much land
to leave wooded or open would benefit from research.

To determine what is considered nature and how close it needs to
be, one must explore the many tangible ways that nature affects well-

being. The nature that is in the mind, so to speak, also nourishes the soul. Knowing that one has the choice, that a satisfying place is readily available, may provide considerable comfort (S. Kaplan, 1973, 1976). And the contrary, the sense of having no options, of having no access to the natural environment, may be significantly detrimental to psychological health.

Participation has been shown to provide a powerful way to fulfill human needs. Gill and Bonnett (1973) suggest in their closing pages that much citizen talent and knowledge goes to waste in the way natural areas are managed. Unfortunately, citizen involvement in the management of the urban nature resource has only rarely been fostered. The frustration expressed by a park superintendent that teens kept damaging trees as soon as they were replaced might have been reduced through ways of involving these youths in their park. Interestingly enough, it was the same superintendent who frowned upon the suggestion that citizens might play a role in caring for the plants in a downtown park. We need to search for ways to enlighten those responsible for current practices in managing the urban natural environment. Bartenstein (1980) has many suggestions along these lines. As a city administrator, his suggestions and insights are particularly useful. As he points out, "partnership with local government to ensure survival or enhancement of public landscaping is not a new idea" (p. 15). The consequences of a sense of ownership that such schemes permit deserves close study.

In the long run it may be small-scale solutions, responsive to the needs of the human animal, that will prove to be most cost-effective. Many of these depend more on green foliage than on green currency. They call for recognition of humans as a resource that is integrally related to the natural resource. In reversing the denaturing of the urban environment, by preserving and enhancing the bits and pieces of nature that exist there, perhaps we can restore the people as well.

Acknowledgments

Dr. John F. Dwyer, of North Central's Urban Forestry Unit, has been particularly helpful in his continued interest in our project. Thanks also to Charles Lewis for comments on an earlier draft and infectious enthusiasm for the subject of this chapter. Stephen Kaplan and I have been a research team for a long time. The left hand does not usually thank the right hand, but the fact that they work together and depend on each other is essential to the whole.

REFERENCES

Alexander, C., Ishikawa, S., & Silverstein, M. *A pattern language*. New York: Oxford University Press, 1977.

Bartenstein, F. *The future of urban forestry*. Paper presented at the 10th Anniversary of the Consortium for Environmental Forestry Research, Longwood Gardens, Pa., May 1980 (available from Pinchot Institute, USDA Forest Service).

Burton, T. L. Review of R. J. Burby's *Recreation and leisure in new communities*. *Journal of Leisure Research*, 1978, *10*, 76–77.

Caldwell, L. K., Hayes, L. R., & MacWhirter, I. M. (Eds.). *Citizens and the environment*. Bloomington: Indiana University Press, 1976.

Clark, R. N. Control of vandalism in recreation areas—Fact, fiction, or folklore. In *Vandalism and outdoor recreation: Symposium proceedings* (USDA Forest Service General Tech. Rep. PSW-17). Berkeley, Calif.: USDA Forest Service, 1976, pp. 62–72.

Collins, J. J., & Munsell, K. Plant a tree for Marshall: A Michigan community honors its trees. *Small Town*, 1981, *11*(5), 18–23.

Cooper, C. C. *Easter Hill Village*. New York: Free Press, 1975.

Delaporte, C. T. Case report: Houston, the rising star in recreation's universe. *Parks and Recreation*, October 1980, pp. 49–51.

Down on the farm in London. *Urban Innovation Abroad* (Newsletter of the Council for International Urban Liaison, Washington, D.C.), September 1979, p. 8.

Dwyer, J. F. Managing urban forests for recreation. *Trends*, 1980, *17*(4), 11–14.

Fogel, S. Harvesting the Big Apple: Urban gardening in New York City. *The Conservationist*, May–June 1980, pp. 28–31.

Foresta, R. A. Comment: Elite values, popular values, and open space policy. *Journal of the American Planning Association*, 1980, *46*, 451.

Frey, J. E. *Preferences, satisfactions, and the physical environments of urban neighborhoods*. Unpublished doctoral dissertation, University of Michigan, 1981.

Gallagher, T. J. *Visual preference for alternative natural landscapes*. Unpublished doctoral dissertation, University of Michigan, 1977.

Gill, D., & Bonnett, P. *Nature in the urban landscape*. Baltimore: York Press, 1973.

Gold, S. M. Social benefits of trees in urban environments. *International Journal of Environmental Studies*, 1977, *10*, 85–90. (a)

Gold, S. M. Neighborhood parks: The nonuse phenomenon. *Evaluation Quarterly*, 1977, *2*, 319–327. (b)

Greiner, J. Case report: A "Proposition 13" that works for recreation. *Parks and Recreation*, June 1979, pp. 29–30.

Halkett, I. P. B. The recreational use of private gardens. *Journal of Leisure Research*, 1978, *10*, 13–20.

Heckscher, A. *Open spaces: The life of American cities*. New York: Harper & Row, 1977.

Heritage Conservation and Recreation Service (HCRS). *The Urban Park and Recreation Recovery Program* (undated).

Herzog, T. R., Kaplan, S., & Kaplan, R. The prediction of preference for unfamiliar urban places. *Population and Environment*, 1982, *5*, 43–59.

Hogan, P. The Parrish Community Park. *Mother Earth News*, 1980, *66*, 28.

Hounsome, M. Bird life in the city. In I. C. Laurie (Ed.), *Nature in cities*. Chichester, England: Wiley, 1979, pp. 179–203.

James, William. *The varieties of religious experience*. New York: Holt, 1902.

Jellicoe, G., & Jellicoe, S. *The landscape of man*. London: Thames & Hudson, 1975.

Kaplan, R. Some psychological benefits of gardening. *Environment and Behavior*, 1973, 5, 145–162.

Kaplan, R. Some methods and strategies in the prediction of preference. In E. H. Zube, R. O. Brush, & J. G. Fabos (Eds.), *Landscape assessment*. Stroudsburg, Pa.: Dowden, Hutchinson & Ross, 1975, pp. 118–129.

Kaplan, R. Preference and everyday nature: Method and application. In D. Stokols (Ed.), *Perspectives on environment and behavior*. New York: Plenum Press, 1977, pp. 235–250.

Kaplan, R. The green experience. In S. Kaplan & R. Kaplan (Eds.), *Humanscape: Environments for people*. Belmont, Calif.: Duxbury Press, 1978, pp. 186–193. (Ann Arbor, Mich.: Ulrich's, 1982) (a)

Kaplan, R. Participation in environmental design. In S. Kaplan & R. Kaplan (Eds.), *Humanscape: Environments for people*. Belmont, Calif.: Duxbury Press, 1978, pp. 427–438. (Ann Arbor, Mich.: Ulrich's, 1982) (b)

Kaplan, R. A methodology for simultaneously obtaining and sharing information. In *Assessing amenity resource values* (USDA Forest Service General Technical Report RM-68). Fort Collins, Colo.: USDA Forest Service, 1979, pp. 58–66. (a)

Kaplan, R. Visual resources and the public: An empirical approach. In *Proceedings of Our National Landscape Conference* (USDA Forest Service General Tech. Rep. PSW-35). Berkeley, Calif.: USDA Forest Service, 1979, pp. 209–216. (b)

Kaplan, R. Citizen participation in the design and evaluation of a park. *Environment and Behavior*, 1980, 12, 494–507.

Kaplan, R. *Evaluation of an urban vest-pocket park* (USDA Forest Service, North Central Forest Experiment Station Research Paper NC-195). St. Paul, Minn.: USDA Forest Service, 1981, 12 p. (a)

Kaplan, R. *Nearby nature and satisfaction with multiple-family neighborhoods*. Report to the Planning Department, City of Ann Arbor, Michigan, 1981. (b)

Kaplan, S. Cognitive maps, human needs, and the designed environment. In W. F. E. Preiser (Ed.), *Environmental design research*. Stroudsburg, Pa.: Dowden, Hutchinson & Ross, 1973, pp. 275–283.

Kaplan, S. An informal model for the prediction of preference. In E. H. Zube, R. O. Brush, & J. G. Fabos (Eds.), *Landscape assessment*. Stroudsburg, Pa.: Dowden, Hutchinson & Ross, 1975, pp. 92–101.

Kaplan, S. Adaptation, structure and knowledge. In G. T. Moore & R. G. Golledge (Eds.), *Environmental knowing*. Stroudsburg, Pa.: Dowden, Hutchinson & Ross, 1976, pp. 32–45.

Kaplan, S. Tranquility and challenge in the natural environment. In *Children, nature, and the urban environment* (USDA Forest Service General Tech. Rep. NE-30). Upper Darby, Pa.: USDA Forest Service, 1977, pp. 181–185.

Kaplan, S. Concerning the power of content-identifying methodologies. In *Assessing amenity resource values* (USDA Forest Service General Tech. Rep. RM-68). Fort Collins, Colo.: USDA Forest Service, 1979, pp. 4–13. (a)

Kaplan, S. Perception and landscape: Conception and misconceptions. In *Proceedings of our national landscape conference* (USDA Forest Service General Tech. Rep. PSW-35). Berkeley, Calif.: USDA Forest Service, 1979, pp. 241–248. (b)

Kaplan, S., & Kaplan, R. (Eds.). *Humanscape: Environments for people*. Belmont, Calif.: Duxbury Press, 1978. (Ann Arbor, Mich.: Ulrich's, 1982)

Kaplan, S., Kaplan, R., & Wendt, J. S. Rated preference and complexity for natural and urban visual material. *Perception and Psychophysics*, 1972, 12, 354–356.

Laurie, M. Nature and city planning in the nineteenth century. In I. C. Laurie (Ed.), *Nature in cities*. Chichester, England: Wiley, 1979, pp. 37–65.

Les Amis de la Terre. *Ecopolis: The new city of light.* Reprinted in *Not Man Apart* (Friends of the Earth), March 1977.

Lewis, C. A. Public housing gardens—Landscapes for the soul. In *Landscape for living.* Washington, D.C.: USDA Yearbook of Agriculture, 1972, pp. 277–282.

Lewis, C. A. Human perspectives in horticulture. In *Children, nature, and the urban environment* (USDA Forest Service General Tech. Rep. NE-30). Upper Darby, Pa.: USDA Forest Service, 1977, pp. 187–192.

Lewis, C. A. Healing in the urban environment: A person/plant viewpoint. *Journal of the American Planning Association,* 1979, *45,* 330–338.

Lingoes, J. C. A general survey of the Guttman-Lingoes nonmetric program series. In R. N. Shepard, A. K. Romney,& S. B. Nerlove (Eds.), *Multidimensional scaling* (Vol. 1). New York: Seminar Press, 1972, pp. 52–68.

Little, C. E. The double standard of open space. In J. N. Smith (Ed.), *Environmental quality and social justice in urban America.* Washington, D.C.: Conservation Foundation, 1974, pp. 73–84.

London's Hyde Park remains a quiet sanctuary. *New York Times,* May 26, 1977, p. 33.

Magill, A. W. The message of vandalism. In *Vandalism and outdoor recreation: Symposium Proceedings* (USDA Forest Service Tech. Rep. PSW-17). 1976, pp. 50–54.

Manning, O. Designing for nature in cities. In I. C. Laurie (Ed.), *Nature in cities.* Chichester, England: Wiley, 1979, pp. 3–36.

Nadel, I. B., & Oberlander, C. H. *Trees in the city.* New York: Pergamon, 1977.

Newman, O. *Defensible space.* New York: MacMillan, 1972.

Pitt, D., Soergell, K., & Zube, E. Trees in the city. In I. C. Laurie (Ed.), *Nature in cities.* Chischester, England: Wiley, 1979, pp. 205–230.

Reilly, W. K. (Ed.). *The use of land: A citizen's policy guide to urban growth.* New York: Crowell, 1973.

Rowntree, R. A., & Wolfe, J. L. *Abstracts of urban forestry research in progress—1979* (USDA Forest Service General Tech. Rep. NE-60). Upper Darby, Pa.: USDA Forest Service, 1980.

Seymour, W. N., Jr. (Ed.). *Small urban spaces.* New York: New York University Press, 1969.

Sudia, T. W. *Urban ecology series.* Washington, D.C.: Department of Interior, 1975.

Taylor, S. L. (Ed.). *The urban setting: Man's need for open space.* Symposium proceedings, Connecticut College, New London, 1981.

Thayer, R. L., & Atwood, B. G. Plants, complexity, and pleasure in urban and suburban environments. *Environmental Psychology and Nonverbal Behavior,* 1978, *3,* 67–76.

Ulrich, R. S., & Addoms, D. L. Psychological and recreational benefits of a residential park. *Journal of Leisure Research,* 1981, *13,* 43–65.

Urban parks. *Info* (Newsletter of Heritage Conservation and Recreation Service), December 1980, p. 1.

Vogt, W. Population patterns and movements. In F. F. Darling & J. P. Milton (Eds.), *Future environments of North America.* New York: Natural History Press, 1966, pp. 372–389.

Whyte, W. H. *The social life of small urban spaces.* Washington, D.C.: The Conservation Foundation, 1980.

5

Psychological Benefits of a Wilderness Experience

STEPHEN KAPLAN and JANET FREY TALBOT

> I went to the woods because I wished to live deliberately, to front only the essential facts of life and see if I could not learn what it had to teach.
>
> —Thoreau

INTRODUCTION

What does it mean to go out to the wilderness—to leave society behind and to live for a while on what one carries in a pack, devoting one's time to an exploration of the natural world?

Untouched nature is both beautiful and terrifying, both awesome and awful (Burke, 1757/1958). A person's experiences in wilderness surroundings can cause panic and fear, or they can inspire a deep sense of tranquility and peace rarely matched in other surroundings. Cultures inevitably speak of the meaning of nature and of the appropriate relationship to nature as being central human concerns (Kluckhohn, 1953). From a cultural point of view, wilderness is a particularly significant category of nature. Does wilderness offer sanctuary or danger? Should wilderness areas be preserved or plowed over? Does an individual's experience in the wilderness offer an enriched perspective on life, or does it merely tempt a person to disregard the just claims of society?

Cultural interpretations of these issues have been quite varied (Alt-

STEPHEN KAPLAN • Department of Psychology, University of Michigan, Ann Arbor, Michigan 48109. JANET FREY TALBOT • School of Natural Resources, University of Michigan, Ann Arbor, Michigan 48109. The Outdoor Challenge Program as well as the associated research effort has been funded throughout the project by the Forest Service, North Central Experimental Station, USDA.

man & Chemers, 1980; Hendee, Stankey, & Lucas, 1978; Ittleson, Proshansky, Rivlin, & Winkel, 1974; Nash, 1967). For Jews in the time of the Roman Empire, wilderness served as a sanctuary from oppressors. In the Judeo-Christian tradition, a few individuals, such as Moses, John the Baptist, and Jesus, sought isolation in wilderness in order to face God and to hear spiritual truths. Others, like Saint Paul, may not have sought spiritual experiences, but found such confrontations thrust upon them while alone in natural surroundings.

In contrast with Jewish, Roman, and Germanic traditions, which all found religious significance in wilderness surroundings and natural occurrences, the emerging Christian ideology came to see wilderness as an environment presenting earthly temptations, physical dangers, and spiritual confusion. Wilderness represented unfinished business; it was the proper function of Christians to cultivate such areas and to build the city of God. Spiritual meaning was found in built environments and in human organizations rather than in untouched natural surroundings.

Oriental traditions emphasize a third view of wilderness. In this view, wilderness encounters are instructive, and an understanding of natural processes is essential to the correct understanding of one's role in society. The natural world is not threatening or punishing; indeed, the intent is that by observing natural processes, the individual might become one with them, gaining physical comfort, spiritual insight, and worldly wisdom.

The traditional Oriental view has shifted in more modern times to an increased concern with finding one's proper place in the social community, rather than in the world of nature (Needham, 1969). At the same time, Western cultures are becoming increasingly aware of the need to understand and to adapt to the complexities of the natural world (Berry, 1979). Given such diversity and continuing change in cultural interpretations of the wilderness, it seems most useful to simply acknowledge the common cultural concern with wilderness and to explore more concretely the issues relating to the ways in which individuals respond to wilderness experiences.

Psychologists have begun to translate such speculations about the meaning of wilderness into specific research questions. Their investigations have primarily dealt with two distinct issues: first, what values are perceived in wilderness; and second, what lasting psychological impacts can result from extended encounters with wilderness.

RESEARCH ON WILDERNESS VALUES

A number of studies have focused on the issue of what people seek when they go to wilderness areas. In some studies, wilderness users have completed questionnaires or have participated in interviews concerning their motivations for visiting wilderness areas. In other studies, both users and nonusers have been asked what they would expect an experience in wilderness to be like.

The results of these studies have yielded rich but somewhat confusing evidence regarding the nature of wilderness experiences (for reviews, see Heimstra & McFarling, 1974; Iso-Ahola, 1980; and Ittleson et al., 1974). Early researchers in particular have emphasized social issues, some seeing solitude as a critical human need that was met by wilderness experience (Stankey, 1972), while others felt that the distinct character of group functioning in natural surroundings offered unique social benefits (Klausner, 1971). Different researchers have focused on stress elements, seeing the primary value of wilderness as an escape from urban pressures (Driver, 1972) or as a setting where individuals confront personal fears and physical challenges (Newman, 1980). The findings of these studies suggest that wilderness experiences incorporate a multitude of activities and feelings, but there is little agreement concerning which of these are more or less essential to the character of a wilderness encounter.

Recently, a few studies have sought to clarify such issues and to find some order among the many perceived characteristics of wilderness experience. Drawing on the earlier studies for specific items, the more recent studies have included lists of a wide variety of purported values and have obtained ratings of the extent to which these reactions would characterize wilderness experience, or the degree to which each item is viewed as adding to the satisfaction derived from wilderness experiences (Brown & Haas, 1980; Feingold, 1979; Rossman & Ulehla, 1977; Shafer & Mietz, 1969).

One finding that is consistently reported in these studies is that social concerns are of minor importance in wilderness experiences. Shafer and Mietz asked wilderness users for judgments of the relative importance of five potential wilderness benefits. In these comparisons, social benefits were given the lowest possible ranking. Brown and Haas asked wilderness users the degree to which a number of elements added to the satisfactions experienced in wilderness. Dimensional analyses yielded eight clusters of items, with the least degree of satisfaction resulting from the social dimension. Rossman and Ulehla investigated the perceived importance of a set of potential benefits and the degree to which each type of benefit would be expected in five different environments, ranging from wilderness to one's own home. Their findings revealed that social benefits were relatively unimportant to the respondents and were perceived as equally likely to occur in each of the environments studied. Similarly, Feingold found that the social dimension of vacations spent in cities and in wilderness were roughly the same.

A second consistent finding in these studies is that the enjoyment of nature is of primary value in the wilderness experience. In Shafer and Mietz's relative rankings, the aesthetic dimension had the highest ranking of the five benefits that were studied. Brown and Haas found that the enjoyment of nature contributed the most to the satisfactions resulting from wilderness experiences. Rossman and Ulehla found that enjoying the beauties of nature was perceived both as being extremely important and as much more likely to occur in wilderness than in other environments.

Beyond these areas of agreement, there is little evidence of consistency in other findings reported in these studies. The importance of physical challenges in wilderness experiences, for example, is somewhat unclear. Users' ratings of the value of physical benefits fell in the middle range of the five potential wilderness benefits studied by Shafer and Mietz (1969). Brown and Haas's study (1980) revealed two distinct physical dimensions in wilderness experience, which were assessed very differently in terms of their relationships to perceived satisfactions. In this study, a skill and achievement dimension was rated fairly high, but a dimension of items dealing with confronting hazards and risks was rated as a very low contributor to wilderness satisfactions. Perhaps the most instructive finding is in Rossman and Ulehla's study (1977) in which physical challenges were shown to be highly expected from a wilderness trip but were relatively unimportant to the respondents.

Of all the issues and potential benefits whose meaning is explored in these studies, the least resolved question concerns the exact nature of the psychological response to wilderness experiences. Early studies suggested that wilderness evokes a unitary emotional response, but in studying this possibility, Feingold (1979) failed to find evidence of one coherent emotional dimension to the wilderness experience. Instead, his results, as well as those of Rossman and Ulehla and the multiple dimensions resulting from the Brown and Haas study, suggest that there may be different kinds as well as different levels of psychological response to the wilderness. Experiences of solitude and quiet are valued, as is the sense of escape from urban life. But a variety of other responses are also evident, ranging from both good and bad feelings about one's immediate surroundings and experiences to more abstract thoughts about life in general.

What these recent studies have shown are that experiences in natural environments are highly satisfying and that the perceived benefits of these experiences are highly valued. In comparing the results of these studies, it seems evident that the primary source of these satisfactions is the wilderness environment itself. Social considerations are clearly not central to the character of this experience, and opportunities to escape urban pressures or to cope with physical difficulties are not consistently shown to be of primary importance in the enjoyment of wilderness.

RESEARCH ON THE IMPACTS OF WILDERNESS EXPERIENCES

A separate but complementary body of research on wilderness is characterized by much more practical goals. Rather than being concerned with the exact nature of the human response to wilderness, this research is based on the hypothesis that lasting changes in individuals are produced by wilderness experiences, and it looks for convincing proof that such beneficial impacts do, in fact, occur. From this perspective, wilderness experience is viewed as a powerful therapeutic tool, encouraging new behavior patterns and self-perceptions in the participants (for reviews, see Gibson, 1979; Kahoe, 1979; and Turner, 1976). This research typically deals with data on changes in individuals who take part in programs that are specifically designed to be psychologically valuable.

These studies most often evaluate existing wilderness programs that are oriented toward special client groups such as adolescents, psychiatric patients, or prison inmates. In their structure and activities, these programs often emphasize a particular facet of the experience as being essential to the personal benefits that they claim to offer. For example, some programs are led by trained therapists who conduct individual or group counseling sessions, or who supervise the deliberate working-through of conflicts that arise within the group. Other programs emphasize the physical challenges presented by the wilderness and structure the group's activities around difficult and sometimes frightening tasks that the participants must perform.

Outward Bound is the largest and best-known of this latter group of programs. The literature on Outward Bound is very specific in claiming that the benefits of this program result from having the participants face difficult tasks in frightening surroundings (Newman, 1980; Smith, 1971). Indeed, this organization has recently sought to legally defend itself from negligence claims in a number of accidental deaths by saying that exposure to real physical dangers is necessary to the enhanced self-perceptions that result from these experiences (Morganthau, 1979).

Yet for all the claims that have been made, question remain about the quality of the evidence that has been collected regarding the benefits derived from a variety of wilderness programs. Gibson (1979) assessed

21 research reports dealing with the benefits of these programs, concluding that "all of these studies suffer from minor to serious methodological shortcomings" (p. 24), such as biased or too small samples, lack of control groups or follow-up studies, or inadequate or inappropriate assessment instruments. An additional problem, given the diversity of programs studied, is that it is impossible, when significant changes have been demonstrated, to determine whether these effects are due to particular group activities, to the special needs of the participants involved, or to the nature of the wilderness environment itself. Nonetheless, the large number of studies that have found evidence of some statistically significant impacts has led Gibson and other reviewers to conclude that such programs "can and do result in positive changes in the self-concepts, personalities, individual behaviors and social functioning of the program participants" (Gibson, 1979, p. 30).

REMAINING QUESTIONS

Research on the characteristics and the impacts of wilderness experiences suggests that varied and potentially profound reactions can result from these experiences. It seems appropriate now to look more closely at the wilderness encounter itself. It is unlikely that one's appreciation of the wilderness environment is immediate or that the effects that a wilderness experience can produce occur instantly. There may be, instead, distinct and identifiable processes involved in the individual's encounter with wilderness. There may be measurable changes that occur at different points in time in the relationship between an individual and the wilderness environment. Understanding these changes may increase our understanding not only of the immediate and the lasting impacts of that experience, but it may also help clarify which qualities of the wilderness experience are responsible for the lasting changes that do emerge. What are the essential ingredients of this experience? What is the sequence of an individual's response to the natural environment? When and how does the character of this experience develop, and what makes it potentially so powerful in its impacts on the individual?

A CLOSER LOOK AT THE WILDERNESS EXPERIENCE:
THE OUTDOOR CHALLENGE RESEARCH PROGRAM

The purpose of the Outdoor Challenge Research Program, which has been carried out in collaboration with Robert Hanson and Rachel Kaplan for the past 10 years, has been first of all to find convincing evidence that extended wilderness experiences do offer considerable and lasting benefits for a variety of individuals. Once such evidence had been obtained, the purpose of this research effort has been to explore more thoroughly both the nature of the benefits that such experiences offer and the ways in which such impacts are accounted for by an individual's experience in a wilderness environment.

Hanson (1973) began the Outdoor Challenge Program in the summer of 1970. Following two summers during which Hanson took groups of adolescents through a large wilderness area, a research focus was incorporated into this program. Two independent studies were conducted during the summers of 1972 and 1973, in which program participants were compared with control groups on a variety of measures concerning activity preferences and self-perceptions. Questionnaire materials were completed at roughly six-month intervals, before and at some time after each summer's activities, by both the wilderness program participants and the control groups.

In the initial study, 10 boys between the ages of 15 and 17 participated in the wilderness program, and 25 high school boys served as the control group. The findings of this study (R. Kaplan, 1974) that dealt with the comparisons between the participants and the control group at the second testing period were most striking. While the control group's scores on the preprogram and postprogram measures reflected stable self-perceptions and interests, the Outdoor Challenge group showed changes on a number of these measures. As Kaplan reported,

> the kinds of changes found in this study are ones one would expect to be related to such an experience: A greater sense of concern for other people, a more realistic outlook of one's own strengths and weaknesses, a greater self-sufficiency in the uses of one's time and talents, and a rather positive view of oneself. (p. 115)

The following summer, the research broadened in scope. Additional groups were included to compare Outdoor Challenge with other experiences in natural environments, and the control sample was enlarged. A total of 267 high school students, both male and female, completed the initial questionnaires, and 200 of these individuals returned the second questionnaire, which was mailed out the following November. The wilderness participants in the sample took part in one of three kinds of outdoor trips: (1) Outdoor Challenge, (2) one of two backpacking trips that took place in less isolated areas, or (3) a camp program located near Lake Michigan that emphasized the development of community as well as ecological awareness.

The results of this second project again gave evidence of enduring changes in self-esteem that result from experiences in natural surroundings (R. Kaplan, 1977a,b). Participants in each of the three nature experiences were significantly more likely than control individuals to reflect positive changes on a set of measures reflecting positive self-images. In addition, on an independent group of measures that expressed negative self-assessments, Outdoor Challenge participants were more likely to demonstrate positive shifts than were individuals in any of the other samples.

Having completed these two preliminary studies, we felt that it was appropriate to shift both the focus and the methods of our research efforts. The two initial studies had compared program participants with control groups, using a variety of empirical measures. The results of these early studies gave evidence that enduring changes in self-esteem can result from wilderness experiences, that such impacts depend to some degree on the nature of the wilderness program, and that both male and female adolescents can experience the benefits offered by wilderness programs. Our efforts then shifted to a concern with the processes that unfold during the trip itself and to a more complete examination of the exact nature of the changes that individuals experience. For these further studies, which have continued since 1974, there were no control groups, as we examined in detail the reactions of the Outdoor Challenge participants throughout the course of this experience. Our earlier results had been based on questionnaires administered before and at some time after the wilderness program. For these further efforts, various instruments were developed to use during the trip itself, and participants were provided with journals to write in throughout the trip.

PROGRAM DESCRIPTION AND METHODOLOGY

The Outdoor Challenge Program consists of two weeks of backpacking through a large wilderness area in and around the McCormick Experimental Forest in Michigan's Upper Peninsula (Hanson, 1973; 1977). The trip begins with a week of group hiking, followed by a two-night solo experience, and then a final group hike without the guides.

In the seven years during which this research has been conducted, three types of groups have participated. One of these has consisted of high-school-age males, another of females of the same age, and the third has included persons of both sexes who are beyond high school age. Table 1 presents the age and sex characteristics of individuals who have participated in the Outdoor Challenge Program since this research began.

Although program participants obviously do not represent a true random sample, since they all willingly volunteered for the experience,

TABLE 1
AGE AND SEX DISTRIBUTION OF OUTDOOR CHALLENGE PARTICIPANTS

Year	Number of groups	Age range	Number of participants		
			Male	Female	Total
1972	2	15–17	10	—	10
1973	2	15–17	12	8	20
1974	1	14–16	8	—	8
1975	3	14–31	17	6	23
1976	3	14–42	8	18	26
1977	2	14–31	6	6	12
1978	3	15–33	10	9	19
1979	3	15–31	7	4	11
1980[a]	6	15–48	14	23	37
Total	25	14–48	92	74	166

[a]Trips shortened to 9 days.

efforts were made to include a wide variety of individuals in the sample. With partial funding provided by the United States Forest Service, the program has provided all necessary equipment and supplies for each trip, and participants pay only for food costs. The specific fee has varied from $50 to $100 per person, but this payment was occasionally waived to enable lower-income individuals to participate. Although most reported having gone on camping trips before, participants were not required to have any prior experience, and few had ever done wilderness orienteering or had gone on an extended backpacking trip before signing up for the program. Due in part to such considerations, almost everyone who has applied has been able to participate in the program, and the participants make up a relatively varied sample of individuals.

Most of the participants have been from Michigan's Upper Peninsula, especially from Marquette and smaller communities in the same area. Other participants have come from Ann Arbor as well as from the Detroit metropolitan area. The students are recruited primarily from the local high schools; some express interest after seeing a film about the program that has been shown to various student groups. Both students and adult participants have also responded to brochures and public announcements about the program, and some of the later participants have known about the program through a friend or relative who had taken part in an earlier year. Most of the adult participants were public school teachers from the Marquette area. Others were college students or recent graduates, housewives, office workers, and so on.

Individuals first indicate their interest in the program by mailing in a request for information and application materials. They are then sent applications and medical forms, some information about the trip activities, and a suggested exercise schedule to follow for two weeks before the beginning of their trip. These materials also explain that Outdoor Challenge is a research program and that participants will be expected to fill out a number of questionnaires.

The size of each hiking group has varied between 3 and 12, with at least two leaders accompanying each group. These leaders have generally been local outdoorsmen or individuals from the county mental health clinic. Although the leaders are also acquainted with the research nature of the program, and though some attempt has been made to encourage their sensitivity to the participants' feelings, the primary consideration in selecting these individuals has been to provide the group with capable guides and teachers.

The structure of the program has been relatively stable across the years of the study.[1] On the first day of each trip, participants complete a number of questionnaires before being driven to the wilderness area. Camp is set up, instructions in map reading and compass use are given, and the group goes on a short practice hike. On the first day each participant is also given a small spiral-bound notebook to use as a journal for the rest of the trip. The brief instructions that accompany the journals ask that individuals use them to write about their feelings, and whatever reactions they may have to their experiences on the trip.

The participants then take turns orienteering and leading on the subsequent hikes. Initially, these hikes are through dense, largely trailless forests, but after five or six days the group reaches the McCormick Tract, where the land is more open and there are some trails to follow. The solo begins early in the second week, and individuals are left at different lakes where they spend roughly 48 hours. Following the solo, the group leaders depart and the participants hike to one of the other lakes in the area and then return to base camp. They are met there two days later by the leaders for the final hike out of the area. A few questionnaires are filled out through the course of the trip, including both before and after the individual solos, and a final set of questionnaires is administered after the group has arrived back in town.

---

[1] In 1980 the trip was shortened to 9 days, beginning on a Saturday and ending on Sunday a week later. The 48-hour solo was retained, but the total hiking distance was shortened and the group hike without the leaders was dropped from the schedule. Analyses of the reentry journals from the 1980 participants suggest comparable impacts from this somewhat briefer experience.

In many respects, Outdoor Challenge is a relatively low-key program. The area itself offers few spectacular sights; for the most part, the land is heavily wooded and filled with numerous swamps and small lakes. Participants are expected to cooperate in camp chores, but although the leaders serve as examples and as sources of information on such matters as how to build a fire or where to find drinking water, most of the daily chores are simply left for the participants to divide and perform as well as they can. Similarly, the necessary wilderness skills are acquired and are constantly in use, but this is largely accomplished by imitation of the guides rather than through specific instruction. The considerable physical challenges are also intrinsic to the environment and to the demands of the trip. For example, additional food supplies are delivered twice, so the group must reach specific locations at specific times. After the solo camping, regrouping takes place a fair distance from where the participants will be picked up by the guides two days later, so in the intervening time, come what may, real progress must be made.

A number of changes have been made in the Outdoor Challenge Program over the years of this research, making it less like a typical survival course and somewhat more like a Sierra Club trip or an informal group outing. In its earliest years, this program was run very much in the style of the Outward Bound Programs, with more of an emphasis on physical hardships and on completing demanding and sometimes frightening tasks. But in reading the participants' journals, we found that some participants resented these requirements or found them to be too artificial, while others became so involved with these tasks that they seemed largely unaware of the environment around them. These more structured elements were gradually eliminated from the program and seem to have left the impacts of the program intact.

The structure that does exist in the Outdoor Challenge Program is meant to focus the participants' concerns on the environmental itself. The emphasis is on understanding one's surroundings and on being able to do what one has to do to survive comfortably in this environment: to make one's way through the woods, to recognize edible plants, to find water, to cope with physical discomforts, and to work through one's own fears.

The program also places a continuing emphasis on the opportunity for individual reflection. The research effort itself has contributed to this theme, since participants are repeatedly asked (both in the journals and in the structured questionnaires) to describe their reactions to their surroundings and to their daily experiences. The solo period is also presented as an opportunity for contemplation. The participants are given some

TABLE 2
WORRIES ABOUT THE SITUATION

Source of worries	Worry ratings[a]			Change (p-level)	
	First campsite	Second campsite	Second week	C1-C2	C2-W2
Animals	1.9	1.6	1.6	.01	—
Getting sick	2.3	2.3	2.0	—	.02
Getting hurt	2.5	2.6	2.3	—	.05
Being sore and tired	2.5	2.7	2.0	—	.001
Getting lost	2.5	2.3	2.0	.05	.01
Bugs	2.7	2.4	2.2	.05	—

[a]Worries were measured on a 5-point scale, from being "not at all" to being "very much" worried.

provisions and shelter for this experience so that this time is not spent so much in coping with physical discomforts as it is in confronting both the environment and one's own feelings.

QUESTIONNAIRE RESULTS: CHANGING REACTIONS TO WILDERNESS

One of the most striking results of this research is the finding that much of the learning that takes place in the woods occurs very quickly.[2] Despite whatever amount of previous experience they have had, all participants are somewhat anxious at the beginning of the program, feeling that they know little about how to survive in the wilderness and that the skills and knowledge needed in this environment are vast. Soon, however, people feel that they know and can do what is necessary to survive in the natural environment.

Tables 2 and 3 illustrate these changes in perceptions. As the means in Table 2 indicate, the participants were initially somewhat worried about various aspects of their situation. After the first hike, however, the environment itself became significantly less threatening; worries about the animals and insects, as well as worries about getting lost, showed significant decreases. By the beginning of the second week, the remaining items, which dealt with personal vulnerabilities and individual doubts about dealing with the physical demands of the trip, had also decreased significantly.

[2]Further details relating to the analysis of data gathered from 1974 through 1978 are available in the final project report to the Forest Service (Kaplan, Kaplan, & Frey, 1979).

TABLE 3
KNOWING THE SURROUNDINGS

Area of knowledge	Knowledge ratings[a]			Change (p-level)	
	First campsite	Second campsite	Second week	C1-C2	C2-W2
Layout of the land	2.7	3.6	3.9	.001	.001
Other group members	2.7	3.6	4.2	.001	.001
Plants and wildlife	3.1	3.4	3.6	.05	.05
Water and food sources	3.4	3.7	4.2	.01	.001
Using a compass	3.4	4.1	4.2	.001	—
Finding places on maps	3.8	4.3	4.3	.001	—

[a]Knowing was measured on a 5-point scale, from knowing very little to knowing a great deal.

Table 3 presents results in relation to the question of how knowledgeable the participants felt about various aspects of their situation. All these items increased significantly between the first two testing periods. The two items dealing with individuals' estimates of their ability to use the most essential tools in this environment—the map and the compass—showed no further change. But the more general items, dealing with understanding one's social and physical surroundings, continued to increase throughout the first week of the program.

The results presented in these two tables are complementary to each other. The experience during the first day's hike was sufficient to give the participants a feeling of competence regarding their orienteering skills and to diminish their fears about their unfamiliar surroundings. Yet more remains to be learned about the environment as a whole, and additional experience is necessary before the participants are sure that they each can cope with the physical demands of the trip.

Other sets of items in the questionnaires dealt with the participants' feelings about the solo experience and about the trip as a whole. All these evaluations were highly positive, and minimal differences in these evaluations were found by age, sex, or amount of previous experience.[3] Both in the structured items and in a number of open-ended items on the final questionnaire, the participants expressed their satisfaction with

[3]Researchers analyzing data from a variety of samples have also found that background variables made no significant differences in the response to wilderness experiences (Feingold, 1979; Wetmore, 1972).

these experiences and were glad that they had gone and had shared in what they felt was a rare opportunity to live naturally in one's surroundings.

In both the first and the final questionnaires, a set of items was included in order to explore the participants' general motivations, their preferences for different kinds of pursuits. In these items, the participants were asked to indicate how much they would prefer to be involved in different kinds of activities, if they had a month's time to do as they wished. Although these items were intended to include mutually exclusive interests, such as spending time alone and meeting new people, or taking it easy and doing something difficult, the results showed significantly greater preferences after the trip for virtually all these interests. The one item that showed no increase was the desire to be in control of one's activities. The participants' experiences seem to have left them with an increased sense of purposes in general, a desire to be intensely involved in a variety of interests. The one exception to this finding is in the area of control; the participants' need for determining their own activities was not increased by their experiences in the wilderness.

ANALYSIS OF WILDERNESS JOURNALS: EXPLORING PROCESSES, SEARCHING FOR MECHANISMS

Although the questionnaire data presented strong indications of the benefits of wilderness experiences, the eloquence of the participants' journals has led to a much broader focus of inquiry. The participants wrote in their journals about becoming acquainted with unsuspected qualities within themselves. Rather than simply learning skills and learning their way around a specific natural area, the participants felt that they were learning new ways of thinking about their place in the world and about the compelling relationship that can exist between that world and each individual.

In studying these journals, we began with a content analysis of the journals from 1976. After first defining 43 distinct categories covering the contents of the journals, coded summaries of the journals were prepared. Each summary indicated both the number of comments written by that person pertaining to each of the 43 possible categories and the day on which each category of comment first appeared in that journal, if it was mentioned at all. The coded summaries of all the journals written in 1976 were then entered into a computer file for further analysis.

These data were analyzed in two separate ways: first, the days when each of the topics were first mentioned in the journals were examined, in order to explore the time-course of the participants' reactions during the trip; second, correlations were run on the frequency measures, to determine whether common dimensions of response to a wilderness experience would emerge. The following discussion of the results of these analyses is based on only those categories that were mentioned in at least one-third of the journals studied.

Time Course of the Experience

There is a great deal of variety among the participants' journals. Although the initial instructions encouraged participants to record their reactions frequently, many participants wrote infrequently and said little when they did write. Others, including most of the adult participants, were frequent, fluid writers. Despite this variability, a clear pattern has emerged regarding the time course of individuals' reactions to the wilderness experience. In the following summary, the day that is indicated is the average day on which each group of topics was first mentioned in the journals.

Day 3: What Is It Like to Be Here?

In their earliest entries, people mention their uncertainties and fears about their surroundings, including concerns about the weather and the coming activities. But along with anxieties, they also mention how they are noticing their surroundings in a fuller way, being newly aware of the smells, sights and sounds around them. They watch gradual changes in cloud patterns, they notice subtle layers of sounds, they see an interesting species of bird or plant. More than this, people say that their new surroundings seem strangely comfortable to them, surprisingly familiar: it feels "just natural" to be here, "like in an earlier time when things were closer."

Day 4: Noticing Personal Reactions, both Good and Bad

A day later, journal entries express both personal difficulties and feelings of enjoyment. The litany of physical discomforts is long, ranging from blisters, bruises, and insect bites to the all-encompassing "torture" of the rough hiking. Yet at the same time there are strong physical enjoyments—the "terrific" sleeping, swimming, and eating, and even the hiking itself, after a while. Participants appreciate the sights around them, and feel oddly refreshed and invigorated, "feeling better than I have in a long time," laughing all the time, "having a blast."

Day 5: Awareness of Deeper Impacts

By the fifth day, people are beginning to feel that the trip is more than a comfortable, enjoyable experience. They express a new sense of self-confidence, a feeling that they can deal with whatever difficulties they may face. Individuals also express a deep sense of peacefulness and tranquility; they are "free and happy and relaxed" in their surroundings. Stresses still surface, but the difficulties now are social stresses rather than more general fears. People gossip and bicker about hiking speeds and routes, or simply feel that they need more privacy than they are getting in the group.

Day 7: New Perceptions of Self and Environment

For many participants there is eventually a surprising sense of revelation, as both the environment and the self are newly perceived and seem newly wondrous. The wilderness inspires feelings of awe and wonder, and one's intimate contact with this environment leads to thoughts about spiritual meanings and eternal processes. Individuals feel better acquainted with their own thoughts and feelings, and they feel "different" in some way—calmer, at peace with themselves, "more beautiful on the inside and unstifled." They appreciate the slow pace of things, and they appreciate their privacy and the chance to attend to their own thoughts rather than being concerned with others' activities.

The Solo: A Parallel Process of Adaptation

In many ways the solo, which occurs on days 9–11 of the trip, represents a condensed and intensified version of the processes that occur throughout the entire trip. As the solo begins, there is a sense of uneasiness, and fears intensify as night falls and sounds that seemed familiar in camp are now more ominous ("I thought I herda bare but it was a fly"). Again, as on the trip as a whole, the initially anxious observation of the physical surroundings evolves into a sense of enjoyment, and enjoyment then develops into feelings of exhilaration and awe, as well as a sense of an increased understanding of the environment and one's relationship to that surrounding reality.

PSYCHOLOGICAL DIMENSIONS OF THE WILDERNESS EXPERIENCE

Since the journals of the Outdoor Challenge participants gave ample expression to their feelings about the difficulties they faced, as well as to their perceptions of the environment and themselves, correlations among the frequency codes of the 43 content categories were computed. The clusters of topics presented in Table 4 resulted from this analysis, using the criterion that the correlation between all pairs of concepts within a cluster be at least .50. Concepts that were frequently mentioned in the journals but which did not group with any others are listed at the bottom of Table 4.

Situational Stress. There is a considerable degree of stress in coming into the woods environment. Virtually all participants expressed some feelings of discomfort, some fears and anxieties as they struggled to adjust to their new situation. In fact, the Global Fears category showed the highest mean frequency of all the topics that were examined. Participants expressed difficulties in dealing with strangers in close quarters, accomplishing cooperative tasks, and coping with unfamiliar surroundings.

Enjoyment. The Enjoyment factor reflects a general happiness within the situation. Many of the comments included here are not specific to nature, as participants said they were "enjoying this," having fun, feeling good. When opportunities came for taking it easy for a while, people found it equally enjoyable to spend "a lot of time doing nothing."

Fascination. The Fascination element speaks to a delight in sensory imputs. Watching wildlife is engaging, and innumerable sights were exciting and wonderful, leaving people eager to see and to learn more. Likewise, people relish their physical reactions to the surroundings and their activities. They enjoy the exercise, the smells, the taste of food, the soothing quality of the natural sounds around them. They enjoy being absorbed in their physical activities with no extraneous concerns and "no time for deep thoughts."

Perceptual Changes. The strongest connection between the wilderness experience and individuals' feelings about themselves is seen in the final cluster, Perceptual Changes. Individuals begin to notice small details in their surroundings—not necessarily anything new, but subtle relationships or elements they may never have appreciated before. They feel comfortable in their natural surroundings and are surprised at how easily this sense of belonging has developed. There is a growing sense of wonder and a complex awareness of spiritual meanings as individuals feel at one with nature, yet they are aware of the transience of individual

TABLE 4
DIMENSIONS OF RESPONSE TO WILDERNESS

Categories in dimension (with examples from journals)	Journal entries	
	Percentage of sample	Mean/journal
Situational stress (Alpha = .67)[a]		
Global fears (afraid, worried, want to go home)	92	4.1
Social difficulties (angry at someone, uneasy with others)	50	1.5
Enjoyment (Alpha = .80)		
Enjoying trip (feeling good, physically and mentally; happy)	85	3.0
Enjoying slow pace (nothing in a hurry, there's time to think)	62	2.1
Fascination and sensory awareness (Alpha = .67)		
Enjoying surroundings (beautiful sights; all the sounds; sun is comforting and life-giving)	89	3.4
Physical enjoyment (good sleeping, great food; hard hike, but felt great)	96	3.4
Perceptual changes (Alpha = .89)		
Notice nature details (never been aware of so very much; sounds, smells, sights)	69	3.2
Comfortable in the woods (so easy and natural, feels like coming home)	45	2.2
Awe and wonder about nature (awed and dreamy feeling; I love the wonder of everything)	42	2.2
Self-insights (learning about my thoughts and emotions; feel many different things I've never felt before)	42	2.7
Unclustered categories		
Tranquility (so relaxed and soothing; I love this peacefulness	85	3.1
Privacy (nice knowing few have been here; the lake is clean and deserted)	50	2.4
Fears overcome (conquered my fears; hardly ever think about bears)	38	1.5
Self-confidence (I can go anywhere I want; boost to ego; I made it)	58	1.7
Physical stress (sore from hiking; packs too heavy; too cold, too buggy, too steep, too wet, too fast)	73	2.6

[a]The alpha value is Cronbach's (1951) coefficient of internal consistency and represents the unity among the items within the dimension.

concerns when seen against the background of enduring natural rhythms. Individuals also come to perceive themselves differently. They "enjoy finding out about" their own feelings, they think of their futures, and they feel more sure of who they are and what they want to do.

Unclustered Categories. Five additional topics were mentioned frequently in the journals, but had low correlations with the other topics. These additional topics were people's appreciation of the tranquility in their surroundings; their appreciation of privacy; feelings of self-confidence and pride in personal accomplishments; feelings that their initial fears had been overcome; and reactions to the physical stress involved in the trip.

In understanding the interrelationships among these concepts, it is as important, from a theoretical sense, to note what categories did not correlate as it is to understand the clusters that did emerge from this analysis. Gains in self-confidence and in self-awareness, while both frequently mentioned, seem to be reactions that are totally independent of each other. And none of the three stress categories, although frequently mentioned, showed any connections with individuals' feelings about themselves. On the other hand, the environment itself is tied to these emerging self-reflections. The enjoyment of the environment is tied to individuals' appreciation of their own physical reactions to the activities with which they are occupied; they feel alive and actively engaged with the world around them. Most importantly, the way one comes to see things and to think about things in these surroundings leads to new thoughts about one's own life and purposes.

Returning to Civilization

As we became more aware of these various and sometimes powerful reactions to the wilderness experience, we began to wonder about how the participants might feel as they began to resume their normal lives and again became immersed in commonplace activities and reacquainted with more civilized surroundings. Is the wilderness experience easily left behind, or does it stay with one in persistent and frequent memories? What elements of this experience are recalled most vividly? What things seem most and least important about this experience once it is over? Does the memory of this experience make life in general more palatable, or does it make one more aware of the frustrations inherent in one's normal surroundings and activities and possibly less able or less willing to tolerate them than before?

In order to explore these additional issues, participants in recent years have been given journals to keep during the first few days back home. In these journals, the participants were asked to record various aspects of their reentry process: things that bothered or annoyed them, what they enjoyed doing, what things about Outdoor Challenge they found themselves thinking about. The participants were asked to jot down such thoughts for a few days, and then again after a week or so, and to return the journal in a stamped envelope that was provided.

The analysis of the 43 reentry journals (covering the participants between 1976 and 1979) followed procedures similar to the analysis of the 1976 journals. Comments were initially separated into a number of different categories, and each journal was then coded with the number of times that each of these topics was mentioned, if at all. Given the somewhat larger sample size, dimensional analysis procedures were then used, rather than simple correlation analysis, to explore possible groupings of these topics. Two different dimensional analysis programs· were used: the Guttman-Lingoes Smallest Space Analysis III (a non-metric factor analysis) and the ICLUST clustering program. The results of these programs were then analyzed according to procedures developed and used in a number of earlier studies (R. Kaplan, 1975a,b). Table 5 presents the clusters that emerged from this analysis, as well as two single topics that remained unclustered.

Wilderness Perspective. The Wilderness Perspective cluster expresses a sense of altered priorities—how individuals see themselves and the everyday environment in a new way. The wilderness is remembered as awesome, and is felt to have offered a compelling glimpse of a real world, and of a way of relating to one's surroundings and responding to one's daily opportunities and challenges, that was immensely satisfying. The self that individuals have become more aware of through this experience seems more closely allied with the natural environment than with the everyday environment of buildings and streets, which seem flat, ugly, and boring by comparison.

Nature Tranquility. The Nature Tranquility cluster also expresses a positive feeling about the woods. People mention the stress of dealing with the demands of their everyday lives, they remember the wilderness as a peaceful, relaxed environment, and they make plans for future trips to natural areas.

New Activities. The final cluster, New Activities, is primarily oriented toward specific pursuits, as people seek to maintain in the city the physical actions and the focus on nature which filled up so much of their time in the woods. People are newly aware of nature elements in the city; they notice birds and plants, they take frequent walks with friends, and they go on weekend trips to a campground or a cottage. They remember the group efforts in which they participated, the common

TABLE 5
Dimensions of Reentry Response

	Journal entries	
Categories in dimension (with examples from journals)	Percentage of sample	Mean/journal
Wilderness perspective (Alpha = .84)		
Reality of woods experience (everyday concerns seem trivial compared with those in the woods; learned out of necessity)	33	1.3
Awe and wonder about nature (close to God through nature; sense of where one fits in the world)	21	1.1
Enjoyed the woods (glad I went, pleasant memories; had fun)	53	1.5
Artificiality of built environment (rooms too square and boxy; kitchen too full of white)	26	1.4
Urban ugliness (obnoxious noises and smells; seems stinkier, more crowded than before)	56	1.7
Environmental concern (concern for pollution, waste, litter)	37	1.6
Self-identity feelings (feel older, wiser, less inhibited; learning how to act like myself)	49	2.5
Nature tranquility (Alpha = .67)		
Woods tranquility (felt relaxed, safe, at peace; serene, peaceful environment)	26	1.4
Plan trips to natural areas (plan backpacking and camping trips)	30	1.8
Feel harried, hurried (no time to think, always rushing; pressure, schedules, too busy)	58	2.1
New activities (Alpha = .80)		
Noticed nature in woods (could focus on nature, lack of other attention-grabbers; more interested in nature)	26	1.3
Group affiliation on trip (feelings of dependence, being needed; open, sharing atmosphere; being with people with similar interests)	40	1.7
City walks (walk during lunch; walk in the garden)	35	1.7
Nature in the city (listen to sounds, the wind, birds; smell the air)	56	1.7
Go to natural areas (camping, the beach, a cabin)	23	1.2

(continued)

TABLE 5   (*Continued*)

Categories in dimension (with examples from journals)	Journal entries	
	Percentage of sample	Mean/journal
Physical fitness concern (feel lazy, not active enough; need to stay in shape)	39	1.6
Self-confidence (nothing too big to cope with; more sure of myself)	51	1.7
Unclustered categories		
Lost impacts (fear that memories will fade; lonely, disoriented now)	44	1.8
Less worry (going to be less rushed, hurried and worried)	49	2.0

purposes, and the cooperation and mutual trust that eventually developed during their woods trip. They express a new sense of self-confidence, a desire to stay in shape and to remain physically active.

Remaining Categories. Two single topics remained after the cluster analysis. The first of these was a concern that the positive impacts and the vivid memories of the Outdoor Challenge experience would quickly fade away; individuals sensed the benefits of the experience, yet felt disoriented in their everyday surroundings, sometimes lonely and unable to cope with details and minor decisions. This category did not cluster with any of the other topics.

The second remaining topic was the feeling that concerns that had seemed urgent before the wilderness trip were less important now. This topic displayed mixed relationships with the other categories, combining both with the Wilderness Perspective cluster and with the New Activities cluster. Apparently, reactions to the wilderness experience include an increased ability to distinguish the significant from the trivial. But whether such former concerns are replaced with new activities, or with new goals and purposes, may depend on the individual involved.

It is noteworthy that many of the feelings that participants expressed after returning from Outdoor Challenge are fairly negative. Individuals have returned from an intense, enjoyable experience that made a profound impression on them. Coming back to everyday realities, they see their circumstances with newly critical eyes. They see ugliness and artificiality in their surroundings, unnecessary urgency in their activities, and superficiality in their friendships. If the only impact of wilderness experience were to make individuals feel more frustrated and alienated in their normal surroundings, one might question the value of exposing people to this other way of life. But the memory of their time in the wilderness seems to serve as an emotional benchmark for the participants. They know that tranquility is possible, that there is room in their thoughts for more than the present, for more than the immediate urgencies. They see new possibilities for disregarding some of the demands of their everyday environment, for substituting their own purposes for the goals that society urges upon them, and for choosing their own activities rather than those more commonly pursued. In many ways, the participants' view of themselves, as well as their perspective on the world, has increased in scope.

The results of these analyses shed light on some of the earlier research efforts to analyze the character of wilderness experience and its psychological impacts. The reentry diaries reveal that it is the positive aspects of a wilderness experience that are remembered and that are connected with one's later feelings about oneself and one's daily surroundings and activities. The more negative aspects of the trip—the initial anxieties, the physical stresses, the social difficulties, and the fears that had to be confronted—were frequently mentioned in the trip journals but did not emerge as commonly mentioned categories in the reentry diaries.

In contrast, the tranquility theme was frequently mentioned during the trip; when participants returned home, this remembered sense of peacefulness was highlighted by the lack of anything quite like it in the everyday environment. This sense of comfort, this opportunity for "hearing the silence," may seem unlikely to occur when one is surrounded by the hustle and bustle of career and social responsibilities rather than the patterened, soothing rhythms of the wilderness. Similarly, the focus on nature, the involvement with group activities, and the sense of self-confidence that were all part of the wilderness experience are remembered later and are correlated with the participants' continued involvement in nature-related activities when they have returned home.

The most compelling elements of the response to wilderness—the self-insights and the sense of awe and wonder about nature that emerged—are also evident in the reentry diaries, and they again emerge as a coherent dimension of response. This Wilderness Perspective dimension also includes both memories of the trip as an enjoyable and very "real" experience and a sense of the implications of that experience for one's view of the everyday environment. During the wilderness experience, people came to perceive their surroundings and themselves in new and somewhat profound ways. That these feelings persist when the participants return to their normal surroundings suggests some basic changes in their long-term view of the world and their relationship to it.

These results seem to validate the approach that was taken in conducting this program. Given the fairly unstructured nature of the Outdoor Challenge trip and the continuing focus on the physical surroundings, a rich relationship develops between individuals and the wilderness environment. It is the participants' appreciation of this relationship, their developing awareness of the environment and themselves, that seems to be largely echoed in the long-term impacts of the trip. One suspects from these results that an emphasis on social interactions or physical challenges during a wilderness trip would alter the character of such an experience, possibly obscuring the relationship between the individual and the environment and hindering the development of the kinds of benefits we have demonstrated here. The elements of fear, of physical challenges, and of interpersonal difficulties may be characteristic of many wilderness experiences, yet they do not appear to be the critical antecedents of the individual changes that occur. Rather, as Scott (1974) has suggested and as our data also indicate, it is the perceptions that occur during wilderness experiences that are essential to the benefits received. As Olson (1969) has said, seekers of a wilderness experience may

> think they go into the back country for a lark, just to test themselves, or to face a challenge, but what they really go in for is to experience at first hand the spiritual values of wilderness, . . . the opportunity of knowing again what simplicity really means, the importance of the natural and the sense of oneness with the earth that inevitably comes within it. (pp. 137; 140)

AREAS OF THEORETICAL INTEREST

The most obvious question and perhaps the most pressing issue concerning the wilderness experience is whether it in fact makes a difference, whether it in fact has a noteworthy influence on people. The findings discussed above make it clear that it does and that the sorts of effects are strikingly parallel to literary and anecdotal material treating the same topic. It thus seems appropriate to acknowledge that something of note does indeed happen and move on to some broader and more theoretically interesting issues.

Perhaps the first question of a more theoretical nature to come to mind concerns the wilderness environment *per se.* What is special about wilderness? What are the factors that make the observed effects different from what might occur in other settings? A related question concerns the reasons why people so frequently choose natural areas as the settings for restorative experiences. On a broader scale, one might look at the larger issue of how restorative environments of any type function in the mental life of the individual.

Finally, the general domain of human motivations is also relevant to this discussion. The wilderness experience obviously brings forth strong affective reactions, and many aspects of the participants' behavior during this experience could be characterized as being highly motivated. Yet at the same time, the sorts of concerns that the participants express in their journals are more the stuff of literature and religion than of traditional motivational theories. These data thus present a challenge. They raise the possibility that our conception of what people care about may have to be broadened to incorporate the full span of human experience.

BEING AWAY

There is a tendency in the recreational literature to equate the idea of a restorative experience with escape or withdrawal (cf. Driver, 1972; Driver & Knopf, 1976; Hollender, 1977; Ittelson et al., 1974; Klausner, 1971; Stringer, 1975). This interpretation has a certain intuitive appeal. People seeking a restorative experience speak of needing to "get away," and may describe the desired experience as a "change and a rest." But as a theoretical or explanatory concept it leaves much to be desired.

The term *escape* is generally employed to refer to an absence of some aspect of life that is ordinarily present, and presumably not always preferred. One might, for example, escape from crowds, noise, or routine. From an informational point of view, there are at least three different patterns that fit this description. A person might, for example, get away from distraction. Although this may bring to mind a retreat on a faraway hillside, in the literal sense of escape a quiet basement lacking a telephone could serve just as well. Another form of getting away involves putting aside the work one ordinarily does. Here the escape is from a particular content, and perhaps from anything that might serve as a reminder of that content. A third kind of escape is more internal in origin. It involves taking a rest from pursuing certain purposes, and possibly from mental effort of any kind.

A given instance of escape might, one would suppose, involve one or more of these aspects. Presumably the strongest effect would be achieved by combining all three of them. And yet it is difficult to believe that such a combination would necessarily have a restorative impact.

Certainly there is no lack of environments in which distraction is ruled out, familiar contents are absent, and one's customary purposes cannot be pursued. But such a setting might be confining, or boring, or both. Surely such absences alone cannot fully capture what we mean by a restorative environment.

FASCINATION

A crucial element missing in many discussions of escape is some source of interest or fascination. Fascinating content and fascinating process (S. Kaplan, 1978a) have been identified as key factors in the context of gardening satisfaction (R. Kaplan, 1973) and as likely to be central in the wilderness experience as well (S. Kaplan, 1977). In order to understand the restorative environment and the way it functions, it is necessary to take a closer look at fascination and at the circumstances that determine its effectiveness.

Fascination is what one experiences when attention is effortless. It coincides with what James (1892) called "involuntary attention." A listing of what people find fascinating would be long and varied. It would include sex and violence, competition and cooperation. It would include high-speed locomotion and the skillful use of tools, especially weapons. But it would also include much of what is found in nature, and especially what sustains people in nature. Thus the list would also include wild animals, sunsets and waterfalls, caves, and fires.

Fascination is important to the restorative experience not only because it attracts people and keeps them from getting bored, but also because it allows them to function without having to call on their capacity for voluntary or effortful attention. They can rely on the interest inherent in the environment to guide their behavior, making voluntary attention unnecessary. Hence they can rest that component of their mental equipment which is so susceptible to everyday stresses and pressures (S. Kaplan, 1978a).

Having difficulty concentrating, experiencing mental work as unusually effortful, and becoming irritable in the face of noise and distractions are all expressions of a voluntary attention mechanism that has been pushed beyond its effective limits. These symptoms of a fatigued voluntary attention mechanism are often interpreted as an indication that one needs a break or a vacation. Hence the vital role of fascinating environments (i.e., environments that call forth attention without effort) in restorative experiences.

Central as fascinating elements may be to recovering one's capacity for voluntary attention, they can only be part of a larger picture. Much of human fascination revolves around issues of process as well as content. Humans are fascinated by carrying out various informational activities under circumstances of some uncertainty. They are fascinated by attempting to recognize in instances where recognition is difficult but not impossible. They are also attracted to predictions of uncertain events—gambling provides a classic example. And they are fascinated by learning, by following the thread of something of interest in order to gradually acquire a bigger picture (Mueller, Kennedy, & Tanimoto, 1972), rather than by simply being taught new things. However, these process fascinations are not engaged merely by random sequences of interesting objects. An occasional fascinating element may at times challenge one's capacity for recognition, but if unconnected to a larger framework, it will be only a momentary diversion or distraction. Even an extended sequence of fascinating elements, if unrelated to each other, will not engage our process fascinations. Connectedness, or relatedness, or the existence of some larger pattern is required in order to engage this higher level human motivation to comprehend.

"OTHER WORLDS" AND THE CONCEPT OF COHERENCE

Consider for a moment what a setting that meets the criteria for fascination in both content and process would be like. On the one hand, it would be quite different from many everyday settings, where fascination is often in limited supply. On the other hand, it could not merely be a sequence of stimuli; there would have to be a suggestion of a larger framework, a suggestion of rich possibilities. Such a setting promises more than meets the eye; it suggests a domain of larger scope to anticipate, explore, and contemplate. It suggests a domain consistent enough so that it would be possible to build a mental map of it and large enough to make building such a map worthwhile (S. Kaplan, 1973, 1978b). People often refer to an experience in such a setting as being "in a whole other world." This sense of another world is a familiar one. It is employed extensively by playwrights and nightclub designers, and it can be just as familiar to an individual immersed in debugging a computer program or repairing a car.

It is clear from the Outdoor Challenge data that a wilderness experience can also constitute a vivid instance of another world. Furthermore, it is possible from these data to determine not only that such a perception occurs frequently, but also what some of the factors are that contribute to this effect. The scope of any potential other world is greatly influenced by how coherent it is, by how well the pieces fit together.

The most basic level of coherence is *pattern coherence*, which refers to the interrelatedness of the immediately perceived elements of the situation. The sense of continuity implied by pattern coherence is a matter of urgency to the novice and a source of satisfaction to the experienced naturalist. For the novice, it is important to know that the initial fragments of the mental map one is building are reasonably representative of the larger terrain. For the experienced individual, the fitting of new patterns into old knowledge serves both as an affirmation of previous knowledge and as a fresh source of fascination (Kaplan & Kaplan, 1982, Chapter 4).

Distance coherence is at a more conceptual level, encompassing the imagined as well as the seen. It requires that there be a continuation of the world beyond what is immediately perceived. In the case of wilderness, variety and sheer physical scale contribute to this sense of extent. But even a relatively small natural environment can contain certain physical features that help make it vast conceptually—such as being big enough and complex enough to get lost in, and offering numerous possibilities of what one might encounter along the way.

A further type of coherence is not a matter of extent within the setting. It is rather a consistency between what one sees and what one knows about the world as a whole. This *higher level coherence* is what gives the "other world" a sense of reality. The wilderness experience is "real" in some rather concrete ways, as well as in a somewhat more abstract sense. It is real not because it matches one's maps of the everyday world (which of course it does not do), but because it feels real[4]—because it matches some sort of intuition of the way things ought to be, of the way things really are beneath the surface layers of culture and civilization.

ACTION AND COMPATIBILITY

An environment may offer fascination and coherence but still fall short as a setting for restorative experiences. One additional component involves a degree of *compatibility* among environmental patterns, the individual's inclinations, and the actions required by the environment.

Physical actions are determined at times by an individual's purposes or intentions and at times by environmental limitations or demands. Also, the cognitive activity that guides action is sometimes stimulated by patterns in the environment; at other times, the instigation is from within the person. If these functional domains are mutually supportive—if one's purposes fit the demands imposed by the environment

---

[4]Our analysis of this issue parallels that of Brickman (1978), for whom feeling real and having real consequences are important criteria.

and if the environmental patterns that fascinate also provide the information needed for action—compatibility is fostered. In situations where this type of balance between actions and perceptions occurs, internal reflection is made possible.

The importance of compatibility in human functioning is easiest to see in its absence, that is, in terms of the costs of incompatibility. To be effective in an environment that undermines compatibility requires considerable cognitive effort. For example, one frequently encounters situations in which the most striking perceptual information is not the information needed for action. One might be looking for a crucial turn along a strip development dominated by advertising that is large, diverse, and colorful. Or one might be trying to read a difficult text in a library reading room filled with individuals who are socializing. In such cases, the inclination to pay attention to the striking information must be suppressed, and the needed information must be sought. This struggle to remain effective requires the sort of effort that James called "voluntary attention." Exerting this kind of attention requires a substantial portion of one's limited cognitive capacity (cf. Kaplan, 1983).

The human information-processing system has clear priorities concerning which domains are the most resistant to such pressures. One bias is towards action. From an evolutionary perspective, the function of cognition is not to think better thoughts but to act more effectively. Another bias is towards contact with reality. Knowing what is going on in the world is essential if action is to be based on appropriate information. The result of these biases is that reflection is the most vulnerable domain. Given much information to process and the limitations on processing capacity, opportunities for reflection are necessarily limited.

Wilderness provides a striking contrast to many other environments in its capacity to facilitate compatibility. In wilderness what is interesting to perceive tends to be what one needs to know in order to act. For many people the purposes one carries into the wilderness also fit closely with the demands that the wilderness makes: What one intends to do is also what one must do in order to survive. As Thomas (1977) has pointed out, it would hardly be surprising if our inclinations and biases tended to enhance our compatibility with the sort of environment in which we evolved.

THE EMERGENCE OF PSYCHOLOGICAL BENEFITS

The sorts of benefits one might expect people to obtain from a wilderness experience depend upon one's perspective and assumptions. At one extreme (a pure adaptation-level orientation) one might expect people to be overjoyed upon their return to civilization and its comforts. From this point of view, the primary benefit would be a greater appreciation for things previously taken for granted. If one views a wilderness experience as an escape from pressures, then one should return in some sense more rested and more capable of dealing with those pressures. Yet, literary works on wilderness—from *Walden* to *Huckleberry Finn*—tend to present a less cautious and limited perspective. From the literary context, one might anticipate far more profound changes in the individual's relation to self and to nature.

The data presented in this report suggest that there is some truth to each of these perspectives—that there are, in fact, a surprising number of benefits that can result from experiences in wilderness. These benefits appear to unfold gradually during the course of a wilderness trip and seem to include self-insights that imply lasting changes in the participants.

THE PROGRESSION OF RESPONSE TO WILDERNESS

The Outdoor Challenge data suggest a fairly orderly progression in the appearance of various benefits. Three temporal landmarks stand out, suggesting a progressive deepening of the impact of the wilderness experience in the course of a relatively short period of time. The ordering of these benefits suggests not only that some require more time to develop, but also that there may be a dependence of each successive benefit on those that preceded it. In other words, the benefits appear to build on each other, suggesting an accumulating impact through time.

Although each of these classes of benefits undoubtedly is influenced by fascination, coherence, and compatibility to some degree, one of these parameters appears to be the primary factor in each instance. Here again, the progression takes on a predictable pattern. Fascination is first to have an impact, with coherence requiring somewhat more time and compatibility the last to develop.

The first category of benefits, appearing in the journals on Days 3 and 4, involves an intense awareness of the relationship between the individual and the physical environment. The participants have left their everyday activities and surroundings behind them and have entered a setting where the physical environment has obvious implications for their comfort and safety. While initially somewhat anxious, the participants also feel a strong sense of comfort in this setting and a great sensitivity to its subtler aspects. Fascination seems to be particularly central here. First, there is the increased concentration on aspects of the natural environment, presumably based on its functional importance, as well as on the inherent attention-holding power of patterns of this kind. Correspondingly, there is less employment of effortful (i.e., voluntary) attention. The growing sense of enjoyment is likely to be a reflection of the decreased need to force oneself to attend. There is the discovery, in other words, that in addition to being comfortable and exciting it is also quite safe to attend to what one feels like attending to in the wilderness environment.

The second major category of benefits, which appears around Day 5, is at a noticeably deeper level. There is an increase in self-confidence and a sense of tranquility. Not only is there fascination, there is co-herence as well. Things are starting to fit together at many levels. There is little external distraction and, correspondingly, little internal "noise." The self-confidence that now appears suggests that fears and uncertain-ties are not simply eliminated, but that they have been replaced by a sense that one can understand and deal with whatever challenges the environment offers. The accompanying tranquility not only constitutes a highly positive experience, it also acts as a significant landmark, for some a totally new experience. Participants give the impression of hav-ing discovered something of great importance that they hope will have a place in whatever they do after their trip is completed. Hence they are led from experiencing themselves in new and rewarding ways to thoughts about the future and their own priorities and goals.

By the time the third major benefit category appears around Day 7, the concern for priorities has deepened. There is a strong inclination toward contemplation, and with it comes a feeling of relatedness to the surrounding environment that approaches awe. In theoretical terms, this level of benefit reflects a high degree of compatibility. The harmony among one's perceptions, plans, and what is necessary for one to do is so great that there is now room for internally generated perception and thought—room, in other words, for contemplation.

THE CONTENTS OF CONTEMPLATION

Given the opportunity for contemplation made possible by the high level of compatibility experienced in the wilderness, there remains the issue of what kinds of things the participants will find worth con-templating. Among the topics most likely to be compelling at this time are the self-insights that have arisen from their experiences. These dis-coveries concern both their own feelings and capacities and their rela-tionship to the natural world.

Participants are often surprised by what they learn in the wilder-ness context. They discover not only that they can function in a world very different from their usual one, they also discover that this kind of functioning has many deeply satisfying aspects. They discover a sense of peace and tranquility, some of them call it a "silence," that they have rarely if ever experienced before. This discovery of course provides information for them about a certain kind of environment. But it also provides information about themselves and about possibilities for feelings that they had not known existed.

A particularly striking discovery for a number of the participants involves a rather general stance toward any environment. There is for many individuals in our culture an implicit intent to be in control of any situation in which one finds onself (cf. Antonovsky, 1979). Although often not a conscious priority, the need for control nonetheless can be an important factor in the way an individual attempts to relate to an environment. Yet the assertion of individual control is incompatible with much of what wilderness offers and demands; rather than struggling to dominate a hostile environment, the participants come to perceive their surroundings as quite safe as long as one responds appropriately to environmental demands. There is thus a tendency to abandon the implicit purpose of control because it is both unnecessary and impossible.

This interpretation of a wilderness experience contrasts with that of Newman (1980), who argues that a major gain achieved by wilderness programs is a greater sense of control. Our findings are in the opposite direction; administered both before and at the end of the program, a set of measures of how individuals would like to spend their time showed significant increases in all measures except for the participants' desire for control. This finding parallels the pattern of results obtained by Feingold (1979). His "aesthetic-transpersonal" factor, one of three major components of wilderness benefits that he obtained, "related to feeling less in control or dominant in the environment" (p. 58).

Although this finding is in striking contrast with what one might expect from reading certain segments of the psychological literature, it is not totally surprising in the context of both literary and empirical studies of human reactions to the wilderness. There may indeed be, as Newman argues, a reduced sense of helplessness as a result of a wilderness experience. Yet in its place there appears not a greater sense of control, but a greater sense of competence, relatedness, or participation. Central to so many characterizations of the wilderness experience is a sense of awe and wonder. Not only are such feelings not conducive to a sense of control, they put the whole issue in a new perspective. It is no longer so important to remain in control at all times; in fact, some of the Outdoor Challenge participants come to recognize their concern about control as a costly and disturbing preoccupation. Thus, individuals who had spent many of their waking hours struggling to gain, or to maintain, control now felt that they could relax and pay attention to something other than their immediate circumstances. They discovered unanticipated possibilities within themselves, and found that they could function quite comfortably in a more unassuming fashion as an integral part of a larger whole.

Such an experience can have a far-reaching influence on individuals' priorities. They come to feel quite strongly that the natural environment deserves a more prominent place in their lives. They have discovered a different self in the wilderness setting—a self less conflicted, more integrated, more desirable. They fear losing this valued aspect of themselves and consider continued commerce with nature essential to its preservation. But their concern to retain contact with nature is not motivated solely by the self that they see emerging in the wilderness setting. While they may not have paid much attention to their surroundings in the past, they come to find themselves fascinated by their environment. They are attracted to it and wish to become related to it in a meaningful way. They feel a sense of union with something that is lasting, that is of enormous importance, and that they perceive as larger than they are. While psychology has at times tended to look the other way when spiritual dimensions of human experience are at issue, it is difficult to ignore this aspect of the data. There are a sufficient number of such instances in the data to make them readily recognizable, and the importance the participants attach to them attests to their psychological significance.

CONCLUDING COMMENTS

A Perspective on Restorative Environments

Our analysis of the benefits of wilderness programs has led us to look at a number of factors that are not in themselves unique to the wilderness setting. One is thus tempted to look beyond this particular setting to any environment in which similar factors operate and in which similar benefits might accrue. We have termed this presumably diverse class of beneficial settings *restorative environments*. While environments undoubtedly differ in restorative value, our analysis of the way people function in and benefit from wilderness suggests that one or more of the four critical factors identified must be involved in at least some degree in any restorative environment.

1. The first factor is *being away*. Although it is easy to overemphasize the importance of this factor, and though it cannot by itself create a

restorative effect, the benefits we have studied seem to require having been away from at least some aspect of the everyday environment.

2. The second factor is *fascination*, or interest. Being away from the usual and at the same time being totally bored is as unrestorative as it is easy to achieve. Padded cells would presumably be far more popular than they are if escape alone were sufficient.

3. The third factor is *coherence*. The addition of coherence suggests an alternative environment of considerable scope, one that can function as "another world." Here at last is an environment with enough in the way of regularities that one can become deeply involved in it; here is an environment that is big enough to absorb one's imaginings and one's energy. And finally, here is an environment that does not break the spell by violating what we know and believe about the way things work in the world.

4. Undoubtedly, there are substantial benefits available in an environment in which these three factors are present. Both the extent of benefit, however, and very likely the quality of benefit one receives, depend on the presence of a fourth and final factor, the *compatibility* across domains of human functioning. In the wilderness environment, the activities that are required seem to fit well with people's inclinations. Activities revolve around the basics: food, shelter, fire building, and locomotion. This consonance between the necessary and the desirable suggests that some ancient resonance is at work, that the wilderness setting calls on predispositions that became part of the human psychological makeup in the course of evolution. But the sense of simplicity to which this leads is by no means restricted to wilderness. There are parallels in the vacations people spend in rustic cabins and in the uncluttered life a monastery offers to someone in search of peace of mind.

This theoretical framework for dealing with restorative environments, preliminary and sketchy as it is, suggests a number of interesting directions for further research.

1. *Generality.* Are the factors identified here in fact characteristic of settings people choose for rest and recovery? Or, viewed the other way, do settings with these characteristics inevitably yield benefits of the kind identified here? Is there some proportionality between the degree to which these factors are present and the quantity or quality of benefits? Are certain of these factors critical for certain of the benefits?

2. *Levels of Benefits and Their Possible Interaction.* One of the most unexpected findings of this research has been the existence of benefits more profound and far-reaching than we had anticipated. Clearly not all restorative settings operate at this level. One is led to wonder what the relationship might be between experiences of a more profound sort and

experiences that yield more modest benefits. More specifically, might these "smaller" experiences serve a maintenance function, prolonging the effects of benefits received from more major ones? Might there be a meaningful role of what might be called "microrestorative" experiences in the psychic economy of the individual? Perhaps there are great advantages of some mix. Interaction effects may exist that make the combination of different restorative experiences more beneficial than the simple sum of their effects.

3. *Application to Environments Lacking Any Restorative Pretensions.* If the presence of these four factors tends to be restorative, does their absence make an environment costly? Is there a relationship between such deficiencies and the stress-producing aspects of an environment? Do environments lacking these factors hasten the need for a restorative environment? If such a balanced relationship exists, it might be possible to identify areas of stress and perhaps even to propose mitigating interventions.

Does the Natural Environment Make a Difference?

A central question regarding the psychological benefits of wilderness involves the wilderness environment itself. If the activities characteristic of wilderness programs were carried out in some other setting, would the results be the same, or is the environment in fact a critical factor? Does research of this kind tell us about the natural environment, or does it merely reflect the interactions of group, leaders, and strenuous physical activities? There are several kinds of evidence bearing on this issue.

We have already alluded to one sort of evidence. During the years of this research, the Outdoor Challenge Program evolved from an emphasis on physically difficult and demanding activities into an increased opportunity to simply be in and interact with the wilderness environment. These changes have in no way reduced the benefits gained by the participants, suggesting a primary role not for any particular set of activities, but for the environment in which they occur.

A second source of evidence involves the very character of the benefits. There are both indirect and direct data bearing on this issue. The indirect data are based on a contrast between wilderness and more traditional recreational settings. Feeling more fit and better rested are benefits common to many recreational experiences. The more profound benefits, however, such as contemplation and self-insight, are not typical accompaniments of most recreational activities. The role that wilderness plays is expressed not only in the fact that such reflections occur, but in their content as well. Participants discover that they can cope with an environment that they considered difficult and challenging. They find that they feel competent in an environment that has come to take on considerable importance for them. Yet at the same time, they feel small relative to the forces they see around them. They abandon any illusion of control in favor of a less dominant but more trusting relationship, and in the process they are likely to reassess their place in the world and their relationship to the natural world in particular. In all these respects the wilderness environment plays a specific content role in the contemplative process of the participants.

This rather complex line of reasoning might be viewed as indirectly supporting the proposition that the natural environment makes a difference. On the other hand it might be viewed as simply constituting a hypothesis, namely that there is a particular pattern of benefits that is more likely to arise from natural environment experiences than from other sorts of vacation environments. Fortunately this hypothesis has been tested. One such study looked at expectations persons had of obtaining different benefits in different environments. Rossman and Ulehla (1977) found that certain benefits, such as experiencing "tranquility" and "a different perspective on life," were considered vastly more likely to occur in natural than in built environments, and even within natural settings, they were substantially more likely to occur in wilderness. One might wonder, however, whether reality in fact matches these expectations. Does a vacation in the city, for example, yield different benefits than a wilderness outing? This direct comparison has been made in Feingold's (1979) imaginative study. Comparing their vacation environments with their home surroundings, wilderness vacationers experienced a wide variety of benefits not reported by city vacationers. Given the findings of the Outdoor Challenge research, two categories of benefits in which the wilderness vacationers enjoyed a significant advantage were of particular interest. The first of these, "health-related experiences," included "mental relaxation" and "feelings of receptivity and harmony with the environment." The second, which Feingold labeled "aesthetic-transpersonal experiences," included "awareness of beauty and flux of the natural world," "perceptual alertness," "personal insight," and "expanded identity." Across various studies, then, these themes have strong parallels. There is growing evidence that nature in general and wilderness in particular do make a substantial difference in the benefits obtained. There are certain characteristic patterns of benefits which occur in wilderness surroundings, and these are not the same as those enjoyed by urban vacationers.

A third source of argument supporting the special role of the environment in the benefits characteristic of wilderness experience depends upon a theoretical analysis at a fairly abstract level. In the context of this analysis the natural environment can be seen as having a special relationship to human functioning. It offers unending fascination, it tends to be experienced as coherent, and it enhances compatibility. The wilderness environment is one in which natural elements are particularly forceful and particularly influential. It is an environment in which fascination, coherence, and compatibility are not undermined by distraction and discrepancy. We have thus reached a point where it is possible to suggest a psychologically oriented definition of what wilderness must be:

1. *There is a dominance of the natural.* There are relatively few human and human-constructed elements with which to contend.
2. *There is a relative absence of civilized resources for coping with nature.* Nature must be dealt with on what one might be tempted to characterize as "its own terms."
3. *There is a relative absence of demands on one's behavior that are artificially generated or human imposed.* A primary activity is the meeting of one's vital needs.

This definition of wilderness as not simply a background but as a way of functioning as well seems to account for the sort of environment in which Muir delighted, but what of Thoreau? He built his cabin not very far from the farms of his New England neighbors. Were there not "civilized resources" readily available? The answer, of course, is that they were not available because Thoreau had decided not to use them. He rightly understood wilderness not only as a kind of environment, but as a way of relating to it. There is an implied trade-off here. One can compensate conceptually for what otherwise would be limitations within the physical environment.

An amusing and thought-provoking analysis of the role of the conceptual in outdoor experiences is provided by Frisbie (1969) in his colorful book, *It's a Wise Woodsman Who Knows What's Biting Him.* He argues that being in the right frame of mind is crucial in transforming relatively local natural area adventures into wildernesslike experiences. His examples suggest the importance of paying close attention to the natural patterns that are present and of organizing one's plans to be compatible with the natural setting and its demands. He also focuses on the story one tells oneself, the interpretation one makes of what one is doing, as being especially vital to a successful small-scale outdoor experience. His examples show that he is sensitive to distance coherence and higher level coherence, two factors particularly susceptible to conceptual manipulations.

The question of the role that the wilderness environment itself plays in the benefits discussed here raises a number of issues for future research. The idea that more major natural environment experiences and smaller microrestorative experiences might complement each other raises the question of the minimum environment required for each. Although it is unlikely that a full-blown wilderness environment is necessary for a microrestorative experience, it is likely that natural elements would still play an important role.

WILDERNESS AND HUMAN NATURE

The research program described here covers a period of a full decade. During that time we have received an extensive education in wilderness and its influences on people. At the same time we have been educated in the ways of human nature as well. We have been introduced to some deeply felt human concerns that broadened our conception of human motivations and priorities. Exactly how these concerns cluster is not entirely clear at this point. The proposed grouping that follows must be considered suggestive rather than in any sense definitive:

1. *Tranquility, peace, silence.* While it is widely recognized at some intuitive level that people at least sometimes desire "peace and quiet," the concept seems not to have received much serious attention in the psychological literature. In a religious context, of course, serenity is often a central theme.
2. *Integration, wholeness.* This concept is related to the idea that the achievement of self-identity is a significant developmental goal. Here the emphasis is more on the coherence of the identity than on its distinctiveness. There is an interesting interaction between this idea and the tranquility concept. The greater the self-integration, the less the internal noise and hence the greater the tranquility. Conversely, tranquility is a state that makes contemplation possible, and contemplation may be necessary for the achievement and maintenance of integration.
3. *Oneness.* The sense of being at one with the universe is not foreign to the psychological literature; it is in fact a central concept in James's (1902) *The Varieties of Religious Experience.* The research reported here suggests that the concept has not become obsolete in the ensuing years and that its usefulness is not restricted to religious content. Indeed, this seems to be another case of what might be called a spiritual dimension of human experience, to which psychology has given relatively little attention.

Our investigation of the psychological benefits of wilderness experiences has led us on a rather devious course. We have looked at data collected in the wilderness and we have proposed mechanisms of mental functioning that may explain the benefits that modern humans can derive from life under rather primitive conditions. Further, we have explored the theoretical implications of data dealing with individuals' responses to wilderness experiences, both as this relates to other kinds of restorative environments and in terms of some previous assumptions about human nature and human needs. We had not expected the wilderness experience to be quite so powerful or pervasive in its impact. And we were impressed by the durability of that residue in the human makeup that still resonates so strongly to these remote, uncivilized places.

Acknowledgments

Without the good efforts of two individuals over a span of ten years, the research reported in this chapter could not have taken place. Robert Hanson developed the wilderness program described here, guided it, and managed its gradual evolution. Rachel Kaplan designed the research program, kept it on track, and contributed to many of the ideas discussed here. It is a pleasure to acknowledge our indebtedness to them both. Needless to say, without the stable source of support by the Forest Service, North Central Experimental Station (USDA), the entire effort could not have taken place.

REFERENCES

Altman, I., & Chemers, M. *Culture and environment.* Monterey, Calif.: Brooks/ Cole, 1980.

Antonovsky, A. *Health, stress and coping.* San Francisco: Jossey-Bass, 1979.

Berry, W. The gift of the good land. *Sierra Club Bulletin,* 1979 (Dec.), *12,* 20–26.

Brickman, P. Is it real? *Journal of Experiential Learning and Simulation,* 1978, *2,* 39–53.

Brown, P. J., & Haas, G. E. Wilderness recreation experiences: The Rawah case. *Journal of Leisure Research,* 1980, *12,* 229–241.

Burke, E. *A philosophical inquiry into the origin of our ideas on the sublime and beautiful.* London: Routledge & Paul, 1958. (Originally published, 1757.)

Cronbach, L. J. Coefficient alpha and the internal structure of tests. *Psychometrika,* 1951, *16,* 297–335.

Driver, B. L. Potential contributions of psychology to recreation resource management. In J. F. Wohlwill & D. H. Carson (Eds.), *Environment and the social sciences.* Washington, D.C.: American Psychological Association, 1972, pp. 233–244.

Driver, B. L., & Knopf, R. C. Temporary escape—One product of sport fisheries management. *Fisheries,* 1976, *1*(2), 24–29.

Feingold, B. H. *The wilderness experience: The interaction of person and environment* (Doctoral dissertation, California School of Professional Psychology, 1979). University Microfilms No. 8000914.

Frisbie, R. *It's a wise woodsman who knows what's biting him.* New York: Doubleday, 1969.

Gibson, P. M. Therapeutic aspects of wilderness programs: A comprehensive literature review. *Therapeutic Recreation Journal*, 1979, *13*, 2, 21–33.

Hanson, R. A. Outdoor Challenge and mental health. *Naturalist*, 1973, *24*, 26–30.

Hanson, R. A. An Outdoor Challenge program as a means of enhancing mental health. In *Children, nature, and the urban environment: Proceedings of a Symposium Fair* (USDA Forest Service General Tech. No. Rep. NE-30). Upper Darby, Pa.: USDA Forest Service Northeastern Experimental Station, 1977, pp. 171–173.

Heimstra, N. W., & McFarling, L. H. *Environmental psychology.* Monterey, Calif.: Brooks/Cole, 1974.

Hendee, J. C., Stankey, G. H., & Lucas, R. C. *Wilderness management* (USDA Forest Service Miscellaneous Publication No. 1365). Washington, D.C.: USDA Forest Service, 1978.

Hollender, J. W. Motivational dimensions of leisure experience. *Journal of Leisure Research*, 1977, *9*, 133–141.

Iso-Ahola, S. E. *The social psychology of leisure and recreation.* Dubuque, Iowa: William C. Brown, 1980.

Ittleson, W. H., Proshansky, H. M., Rivlin, L. G., & Winkel, G. H. *An introduction to environmental psychology.* New York: Holt, Rinehart & Winston, 1974.

James, W. *Psychology: The briefer course.* New York: Holt, 1892.

James, W. *The varieties of religious experience.* New York: Holt, 1902.

Kahoe, R. D. (Ed.). Wilderness therapy. *Wilderness Psychology Newsletter*, 1979, *2*, 1–20.

Kaplan, R. Some psychological benefits of gardening. *Environment and Behavior*, 1973, *5*, 145–162.

Kaplan, R. Some psychological benefits of an Outdoor Challenge program. *Environment and Behavior*, 1974, *6*, 101–116.

Kaplan, R. A strategy for dimensional analysis. In D. H. Carson (Ed.), *Man–Environment interactions* (Environmental Design Research Association). Stroudsburg, Pa.: Dowden, Hutchinson & Ross, 1975, pp. 66–68. (a)

Kaplan, R. Some methods and strategies in the prediction of preference. In E. H. Zube, R. O. Brush, & J. G. Fabos (Eds.), *Landscape assessment.* Stroudsburg, Pa.: Dowden, Hutchinson & Ross, 1975, pp. 118–129. (b)

Kaplan, R. Patterns of environmental preference. *Environment and Behavior*, 1977, *9*, 195–216. (a)

Kaplan, R. Summer outdoor programs: Their participants and their effects. In *Children, nature, and the urban environment: Proceedings of Symposium Fair* (USDA Forest Service General Tech. Rep. NE-30). Upper Darby, Pa.: USDA Forest Service Northeastern Experimental Station, 1977, pp. 175–179.

Kaplan, R., Kaplan, S., & Frey, J. *Final report: Assessing the benefits of a natural area experience, and orientation to a wilderness area experience* (Cooperative agreements 13-451 and 13-452). USDA Forest Service North Central Forest Experimental Station, 1979.

Kaplan, S. Cognitive maps in perception and thought. In R. M. Downs & D. Stea (Eds.), *Image and environment.* Chicago: Aldine, 1973, pp. 275–283.

Kaplan, S. Tranquility and challenge in the natural environment. In *Children, nature, and the urban environment: Proceedings of a Symposium Fair* (USDA Forest Service General Tech. Rep. NE-30). Upper Darby, Pa.: USDA Forest Service Northeastern Experimental Station, 1977, pp. 181–185.

Kaplan, S. Attention and fascination: The search for cognitive clarity. In S. Kaplan & R.

Kaplan (Eds.), *Humanscape: Environments for people.* Belmont, Calif.: Duxbury Press, 1978, pp. 84–90. (Ann Arbor, Mich.: Ulrich's, 1982) (a)

Kaplan, S. On knowing the environment. In S. Kaplan & R. Kaplan (Eds.), *Humanscape: Environments for People.* Belmont Calif.: Duxbury Press, 1978, pp. 54–58. (Ann Arbor, Mich.: Ulrich's, 1982) (b)

Kaplan S. A Model of person–environment compatibility. *Environment and Behavior,* 1983.

Kaplan, S., & Kaplan, R. *Cognition and environment: Functioning in an uncertain world.* New York: Praeger, 1982.

Klausner, S. L. *On man in his environment.* San Francisco: Jossey-Bass, 1971.

Kluckhohn, F. R. Dominant and variant value orientations. In C. Kluckhohn, H. A. Murray, & D. M. Schneider (Eds.), *Personality in nature, culture and society.* New York: Knopf, 1953, pp. 342–357.

Morganthau, T. Risky or reckless. *Newsweek,* Dec. 3, 1979, p. 72.

Mueller, E., Kennedy, J. M., & Tanimoto, S. Inherent perceptual motivation and the discovery of structure. *Journal of Structural Learning,* 1972, *3,* 1–6.

Nash, R. *Wilderness and the American mind.* New Haven: Yale University Press, 1967.

Needham, J. *The grand titration.* London: George Allen & Unwin, 1969.

Newman, R. S. Alleviating learned helplessness in a wilderness setting: An application of attribution theory to Outward Bound. In L. J. Fyans, Jr. (Ed.), *Achievement motivation: Recent trends in theory and research.* New York: Plenum Press, 1980, pp. 312–345.

Olson, S. F. The spiritual aspects of wilderness. In W. Schwartz (Ed.), *Voices for the wilderness.* New York: Ballantine, 1969, pp. 131–142.

Rossman, B. B. & Ulehla, Z. J. Psychological reward values associated with wilderness use. *Environment and Behavior,* 1977, *9,* 41–66.

Scott, N. R. Toward a psychology of wilderness experience. *Natural Resources Journal,* 1974, *14,* 231–237.

Shafer, E. L., Jr., & Mietz, J. Aesthetic and emotional experiences rate high with northeast wilderness hikers. *Environment and Behavior,* 1969, *1,* 187–197.

Smith, M. A. W. *An investigation of the effects of an Outward Bound experience on selected personality factors and behaviors of high school juniors* (Doctoral Dissertation, University of Oregon, 1971). University Microfilms No. 72-08601.

Stringer, P. The natural environment. In D. Canter & P. Stringer (Eds.), *Environmental interaction.* London: Surrey University Press, 1975, pp. 281–319.

Stankey, G. H. A strategy for the definition and management of wilderness quality. In J. V. Krutilla (Ed.), *Natural Environments: Studies in Theoretical and Applied Analysis.* Baltimore, Johns Hopkins University Press, 1972, pp. 88–114.

Thomas, J. C. *Cognitive psychology from the perspective of wilderness survival* (IBM Research Report RC 6647, #28603). Yorktown Heights, N.Y.: IBM, 1977.

Turner, A. L. The therapeutic value of nature. *Journal of Operational Psychiatry,* 1976, *7,* 64–74.

Wetmore, R. C. *The influence of Outward Bound school experience on the self-concept of adolescent boys* (Doctoral Dissertation, Boston University, 1972). University Microfilms No. 7225475.

6

Recreational Needs and Behavior in Natural Settings

RICHARD C. KNOPF

INTRODUCTION

Do humans require nature? The query has bounded for decades throughout the literature, seemingly without resolution.

The affirmative response clearly has its constituency. The popular scenario features an organism evolving over millions of years in nature—growing and organizing in response to it, even becoming fascinated by it (S. Kaplan, 1978). Out of this process emerged the human design, a mix of senses and psyche genetically programmed for operation in the natural world (Dubos, 1968). The basic tenet is that humans function optimally in environments that possess attributes of the natural settings in which they evolved. To allow otherwise would be contrary to principles of natural selection (S. Kaplan, 1977). Humans, the argument states, are best suited for acting in the environment that engineered the script.

Others dispute this implied essentiality of nature. They point to the demonstrated neutrality of children to natural stimuli (Holcomb, 1977), the strong cultural influences on affect toward nature (Chemers & Altman, 1977), and the apparent human proclivity for adaptation (Wohlwill & Kohn, 1976). The belief is that natural environments, like all environments, assume different values for people with different life experiences (Moore, 1979; Tuan, 1977).

RICHARD C. KNOPF • North Central Forest Experimental Station, USDA Forest Service, Saint Paul, Minnesota 55108.

Even while discounting the role of nature as an innately required stimulus, proponents of this second view are quick to expound upon its virtues. Some feel natural environments offer respite from overly complex, chaotic stimulation in everyday life spaces (Knopf, Driver, & Bassett, 1973; Stillman, 1977). Others suggest that natural environments are valued because they heighten the individual's sense of control, competency, and esteem (Ladd, 1978; Lewis, 1973). Or it may be that people turn to nature simply for diversity. Fueled by the need to investigate, people are lured by nature's promise for information (R. Kaplan, 1977) and stimulation that departs from the routine (Parr, 1965). All these virtues notwithstanding, the argument remains that nature is not essential. Many other vehicles (e.g., music, art, and travel) offer the same virtues. Nature, then, is only one of many means upon which humans can draw to reach states of optimality.

Riddled with disparate notions, the debate leaves us with few points of consensus. We are unable to establish whether nature is innately required or instrumentally useful. And if nature is indeed useful, it is not precisely clear what use it has. It seems that discussions have been more speculative than anchored in empiricism.

Our purpose here is to search the emerging outdoor recreation literature for data potentially useful in describing human linkages with nature. The recreation discipline is not equipped to resolve the debate, but it does offer a growing empirical base for evaluating what people are responding to in nature.

The first task is to acquaint ourselves with the current state of motivational research in outdoor recreation. We will examine the style of research now underway to determine why people engage in particular activities or visit particular outdoor settings. Having done that, we will sort through the accumulating maze of detail in an attempt to extract principles, concepts, and themes potentially of value in constructing a theoretical perspective on how people relate to nature. The message that seems to emerge is that people use natural environments largely for their instrumental potential rather than for their innate properties. Moreover, the functions these environments perform vary widely from individual to individual.

RECREATION, NATURE, AND EXPECTED OUTCOMES

THE EVOLUTION OF INQUIRY

Even recent literature might lead one to conclude that little is known concerning the reasons why people use natural environments for recreation (Crandall, 1980; Stokols, 1978). Yet, aggressive data-building efforts have been housed within forestry and other natural-resource management disciplines since the mid-1960s (Driver & Tocher, 1970; Hendee, Catton, Marlow, & Brockman, 1968).

This research thrust was stimulated when government agencies such as the USDA Forest Service began to question traditional approaches to backcountry recreation planning, which focused primarily on strategies for accommodating the swelling number of backcountry visitors (Douglas, 1975, pp. 69–93). As use pressures escalated, so did construction of new facilities and other support services. But added services, in turn, were drawing more people into the backcountry. Managers became concerned about congestion (Nash, 1977), visitor conflict (Driver & Bassett, 1975), exceeded site capacity (Stankey, 1973), displacement of veteran visitors (Knopf & Lime, 1981) and, in general, changes in the overall character of backcountry experiences (Schreyer, 1980). The weakness of traditional planning methodologies was being revealed—they stopped short of addressing the complex issue of recreation quality. Resource–management agencies, then, began to switch from a policy of accommodating increasing volumes of use to one of offering appropriate mixes of desired experiences (Brown, Driver, & McConnel, 1978). The call to the research community was to quantify what these experiences might be (Driver & Brown, 1975; Hendee, 1974).

Early research activities concentrated on identifying reasons why recreationists participated in backcountry recreation (Knopf, 1972). Psychometric inventories were developed to describe motive strengths relating to such diverse themes as escape, achievement, affiliation, social recognition, and exploration (Crandall, 1980; Driver, 1977; Hendee, 1974; Knopf *et al.*, 1973). By the mid-1970s it was common practice to construct and compare motive profiles for recreationists engaging in different activities (Driver, 1976; Tinsley, Barrett, & Kass, 1977). Figure 1 presents abbreviated data that convey the spirit of these early analyses. In an Ann Arbor sample, nature walkers, picnickers, and sailors all valued the opportunity to escape, but sailors distinguished themselves in the search for achievement and control. In addition, picnickers deviated from nature walkers in their desire to affiliate with others.

Three basic tenets emerged from these kinds of comparative analyses. First, motive structures were seen as being activity dependent—that is, people doing different things seemed to be searching for different mixes of outcomes (Driver & Brown, 1978). Second, people were seen as visiting natural environments largely to alleviate stress. In virtually every analysis, escape was identified as particularly important irrespective of the activity (Driver & Knopf, 1976). Third, people were seen as valuing the psychological products of the activity more than the activity itself. For example, anglers don't go fishing as much for the food as for

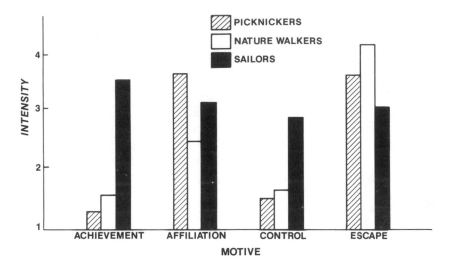

Figure 1. Selected outcomes desired by a sample of picnickers ($N = 53$), nature walkers ($N = 62$), and sailors ($N = 25$) in Ann Arbor, Michigan. (Intensity is based on a five-point Likert response format, with 1 representing "not important" and 5 representing "extremely important.")

the opportunity to relax, achieve, and socialize (Hendee, Clark, & Dailey, 1977; Knopf *et al.*, 1973). Similarly, hunters tend to be more interested in escape, companionship, and exercise than in harvesting or displaying game (More, 1973; Potter, Hendee, & Clark, 1973).

As research progressed into the late 1970s, it became clear that motive profiles lacked homogeneity even among recreationists participating in the same activity. Recreationists engaging in the same activity could often be divided into motivationally distinguishable groups (Brown & Haas, 1980; Hautaluoma & Brown, 1979; Knopf & Barnes, 1980). Moreover, it was discovered that recreationists in these various groups reacted differently to environmental features, looked for different sources of satisfaction, and felt differently about what the priorities of management should be. Recreation motives were being established as important predictors of environmental perception and attitudes.

Illustrative of this activity is our 1978 study of overnight backpackers in the Allegheny National Forest (Bowley, 1979). Employing cluster analytic methodology (Tyron & Bailey, 1970), we found the population of Allegheny backpackers to be a composite of five motivationally distinguishable groups. Two of these groups are shown in Figure 2. The first group, labeled Type 1 backpackers, made up 15 percent of the backpacking population. The profile shows a strong orientation toward

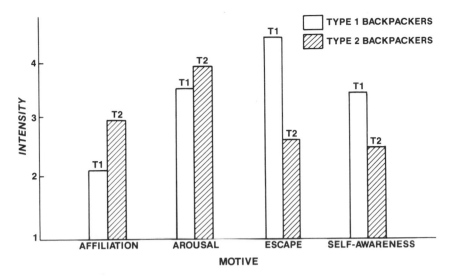

Figure 2. Selected outcomes desired by two motivationally distinguishable groups of Allegheny National Forest backpackers in 1978. (Intensity is based on a five-point Likert response format, with 1 representing "not important" and 5 representing "extremely important.")

escape. The second group, labeled Type 2, made up 23 percent of the population. They were interested more in an arousing social experience than in escape. The profiles also show a marked difference between the groups in desire to gain self-awareness, with a more intense desire for Type 1 individuals.

The two groups were also found to differ in important ways both in their recreation behavior and in their management preferences. For example, those oriented toward escape (Type 1) tended to hike in small groups (average of three members), while those in Type 2 preferred larger groups (average of five members). Type 1 people tended to be veteran users of the area (average of four prior hikes), while Type 2 individuals were relative newcomers (average of one prior hike).[1] Type 2 people on the average would accept encountering up to 20 hikers per day on the trail, while Type 1 individuals would accept seeing only eight other people. Not surprisingly, the escape-oriented group also reported higher levels of crowding.

[1]This finding is consistent with other research suggesting that, in recreation areas of increasing popularity, new visitors are more likely to be socially oriented than are repeat visitors (Clark, Hendee, & Campbell, 1971; Knopf & Lime, 1981).

Perhaps the most impressive data arose as these two groups were asked their opinions on 17 management regulations intended to control personal behavior or restrict backcountry use (e.g., "prohibit camping within 200 feet of stream," "restrict number of hiking groups"). For 15 of the 17 regulations, Type 1 and Type 2 respondents had significant differences of opinion. The message was clear: In nearly every case, the socially oriented Type 2 newcomers were more opposed to management regulation[2] than were the escape-oriented Type 1 veterans.

These kinds of analyses were revealing to natural resource managers, for they demonstrated the fallacy of designing environments to meet expectations of the "average" visitor (Shafer, 1969). Thinking flourished on the value of partitioning resources into zones and then managing the zones differently to provide a spectrum of opportunities (Brown et al., 1978; Griest, 1975). These analyses are also revealing to us here, for they hint at the diversity of reasons why people migrate to natural environments, and they demonstrate how these reasons may influence perception of what the optimal character of those settings should be.

There are now literally scores of in-depth analyses of outcomes desired from recreation experiences in natural environments. Target populations have included backcountry hikers (Shafer & Mietz, 1969), campers (Dorfman, 1979), cross-country skiers (Ballman, 1980), anglers (Hendee et al., 1977), hunters (Hautaluoma & Brown, 1979), National Park visitors (Wellman, Dawson, & Roggenbuck, 1982), off-road vehicle users (Watson, Legg, & Reeves, 1980), river runners (Schreyer & Roggenbuck, 1978), second-home owners (Marans, Wellman, Newman, & Kruse, 1976), snowmobilers (McLaughlin & Paradice, 1980), tourists (Gratzer, Sutherland, & Throssell, 1979), and wilderness users (Rossman & Ulehla, 1977). Pursuant to the earlier described views on the meanings of nature, themes of stress mediation (Knopf et al., 1973), competence building (Bryan, 1979), and the search for environmental diversity (Hendee et al., 1968) dominate the literature.

Although data abound, theory does not. The normal process seems to be for the researcher to collect as much descriptive data as possible and then search through it in hopes of finding revelations about preference. With notable exceptions (Bryan, 1979; Driver, 1976; R. Kaplan, 1977; Lee, 1972) data collection has taken precedence over confirmation or disconfirmation of theoretical postulates. In this context, it becomes difficult to draw upon even our vast reservoir of recreation studies to

---

[2]The only exception was that Type 1 visitors were more opposed to prohibiting dogs and horses in the backcountry.

assemble systematically a holistic model of recreation preference. As a discipline, we continue to suffer from an inability to predict *in advance* of data how and why recreationists are likely to relate to a setting. This is not a moot issue for recreation planners, who frequently are forced to make decisions without the benefit of available data (Knopf & Lime, 1981).

THE RECREATIONIST AS A PURPOSIVE ACTOR

While the recreation literature might fail us in offering quick theoretical perspective, its broadening empirical base is beginning to offer significant clues about the relationship between humans and nature. Our task now is to sense what these clues might be. In effect, we are looking for empirical scaffolding around which a model of human–nature relations might be constructed.

The perspective from which this task is approached is offered by Knopf *et al.* (1973). Basically the behavior of recreationists is viewed as problem-solving behavior (Howard & Scott, 1965; Miller, Galanter, & Pribram, 1960). That is, they use recreation time to resolve gaps between normal states and ones that are preferred (Knopf, 1972). Thus, we view the recreating human not as a passive creature, but as *purposive actor*, systematically operating on his or her environment to bring about states of optimality (Stokols, 1978). Given this perspective, the task of recreation research is to understand what these states of optimality might be and to understand how people organize recreation experiences to bring them about. As this is accomplished, the role natural environments play in the search for optimality will become clear.

So what can be said about the actor? Four broad themes are beginning to emerge.

The Actor Is Stressed

This quality captured our attention by the late 1960s when evidence was mounting that natural areas were being used heavily for escape (Driver & Tocher, 1970). The early motive analyses were riddled with testimony about desires to reduce tension by withdrawing from noise (Lucas, 1964), crowding (Lime & Cushwa, 1969), the city (Hendee *et al.*, 1968), unpredictability (Catton, 1969), role overload (Knopf, 1972), and social restriction (Etzkorn, 1965).

Perhaps the most convincing early data were gained from a national household survey conducted by Mandell and Marans (1972). They asked household heads to identify their favorite outdoor activity and then asked them to rate the relative importance of 12 possible reasons for wanting to participate in it. For the nation's populace as a whole, the most important reason was "to relieve my tensions." A hefty 60 percent of the people sampled rated it "very important." The population was then stratified according to the type of activity designated as favorite. Impressively, the opportunity to relieve tensions was rated as the most important reason for participating in all but one of the eight most popular activities.[3]

Other studies in the early 1970s produced similar findings. While most motives were found to vary widely in intensity across activities, the escape motive remained dominant (Davis, 1973; Knopf, 1972), providing strong evidence that a large share of outdoor recreation behavior is, in fact, coping behavior. Some researchers, however, wondered if these data might not only be reflecting psychometric artifact (see Wellman, 1979). It may have been, for example, that most responses were reflecting impressions that were in vogue (or had social consensus) during the sixties and seventies. In other words, with media emphasis on environmental reform and urban adversities, it may have become fashionable to feel compelled to leave the city. Or, even if not fashionable, the impression may have entered the mainstream of public consciousness to the point where it was readily delivered as a reason for recreating.

In reaction to such contentions, some of us began to explore whether the stress response was indeed linked to adversities experienced in nonleisure settings. In 1973, we found campers from more urbanized environments showing stronger orientations toward privacy, security,[4] and escaping physical stresses such as noise, bright lights, and crowding (Table 1). Parallel findings were unveiled by Knopp (1972), who found orientations toward solitude positively related to both housing-unit density and average number of social contacts per day at work. And, indicative of a host of studies linking recreation preferences to occupation, Bishop and Ikeda (1970) found people in occupations requiring high energy expenditure tended to seek recreation activities requiring low energy expenditure.[5]

---

[3]The exception was outdoor swimming, for which the item "to spend more time with the family" received a higher rating.

[4]As used in our research (Knopf, 1976), the "security" scale taps a motive dimension elucidated by Catton (1969): "the desire to live in a morally and socially dependable world for a time." Constituent items include: "to be where people are considerate, to be where things are relatively safe, to be where people can be trusted, to be where people are respectful of one another."

[5]An excellent review of the apparent relation between occupation style and recreation behavior is offered by Cheek and Burch (1976).

TABLE 1

RELATION BETWEEN SIZE OF HOME COMMUNITY AND STRENGTH OF STRESS-
RELATED OUTCOMES DESIRED BY A SAMPLE OF MICHIGAN CAMPERS[a]

		Desired outcome[b]		
Size of home community	N	Escape physical stress	Security	Privacy
Central area of large city (more than 500,000 people)	8	4.9	4.2	3.7
Central area of medium city (100,000–500,000 people)	10	3.5	3.2	3.3
Suburb of medium or large city	23	3.4	3.2	3.3
Small city (50,000–100,000 people)	13	3.4	3.3	3.3
Town (5,000–50,000 people)	15	3.1	3.3	2.0
Rural area, or village (less than 5,000 people)	31	2.4	2.4	1.9

[a]Adapted from Knopf (1973).
[b]Based on six-point response format, with 1 representing "not important" and 6 representing "extremely important."

Following the lead of life-satisfaction literature, we recognized that
personal judgments of adversity levels in nonleisure environments may
be more useful indicators of stress than objective measures (Marans &
Mandell, 1972) and began focusing attention on relating desired recreation outcomes to perceived home and work quality (Driver & Knopf,
1976; Grubb, 1975; Mandell & Marans, 1972). Table 2 draws on results
from one of Driver and Knopf's (1976) analyses and serves to illustrate
the rather convincing relationships that emerged.

But even these kinds of analyses were vulnerable to criticism if used
to support the proposition that recreationists are under stress. The findings may be tautological. For example, one could not expect those residing in rural areas to attach importance to escaping urban stressors (Iso-
Ahola, 1980, p. 282). Or, one would not expect those who rate their
neighborhood conditions as poor to be less interested in leaving them
behind (Knopf, 1976).

To deal with this dilemma, Knopf (1976) conducted household surveys of Lakewood, Colorado, residents living in close proximity, but in
microneighborhoods differing in traffic noise, housing-unit density, and
burglary rates. The aim was to see if the effects of these neighborhood
stressors were being manifested in outdoor recreation preference. The

TABLE 2

RELATION BETWEEN PERCEIVED NEIGHBORHOOD QUALITY AND STRENGTH OF
STRESS-RELATED OUTCOMES DESIRED BY A SAMPLE OF MICHIGAN RECREATIONISTS[a]

Perceived neighborhood quality[b]	N	Desired outcome[c]		
		Escape physical stress	Security	Autonomy
1. (High)	88	2.5	2.6	2.4
2.	104	2.8	2.8	2.8
3.	65	3.1	3.0	2.9
4. (Low)	26	4.1	3.2	3.3

[a]Adapted from Driver and Knopf (1976). The sample included 40 anglers, 50 canoeists, 45 picnickers, and 95 campers.
[b]From semantic differential ratings of neighborhood noise, green space, traffic, lights, temperatures, and general attractiveness.
[c]Based on six-point response format, with 1 representing "not important" and 6 representing "extremely important."

sample was tightly controlled for consistency in mean family income, stage in life cycle, housing market value, and level of neighborhood upkeep. Respondents were asked to rate the importance of a variety of reasons for participating in their most frequent outdoor activity. While the noise variable was found not to be a useful predictor, the density and crime variables were. For example, people from neighborhoods with greater housing-unit density were more inclined to state that recreation activity was a means of "getting out of their neighborhood for a while."[6] Those who were more likely to be victimized by home burglary attached more importance to the opportunity to experience a secure, trustful social environment (Table 3). This latter motive is not of incidental value to many outdoor recreationists. As Catton (1969) concluded from his analysis of campground behavior, a major motivation for outdoor recreation may be to experience for a while a morally, socially dependable world.

Finally, Wellman (1979) managed to avoid the potential pitfalls of psychological inventories altogether by searching for overt behavioral

[6]Respondents were asked to rate the importance of "to get out of the neighborhood for a while" on a six-point (extremely important–not important) scale. Those residing in high-density neighborhoods (greater than 4.0 dwelling units/acre) reported a mean score of 4.1 ($N = 33$), while those in low-density neighborhoods (less than 2.0 units/acre) registered a mean score of 3.2 ($N = 31$). Reduction in response uncertainty (Hays, 1963, p. 405) was 7 percent, an impressively high figure given the multiplicity of factors known to influence neighborhood satisfaction (Lansing & Marans, 1969).

TABLE 3
RELATION BETWEEN NEIGHBORHOOD
BURGLARY RATE AND DESIRE TO EXPERIENCE
SECURITY FOR A SAMPLE OF COLORADO
RECREATIONISTS[a]

Average annual number of break-ins in home neighborhood[b]	N	Desire for security[c]
<6	13	2.3
6–10	79	2.8
11–15	54	3.1
>15	16	3.5

[a]Adapted from Knopf (1976). The sample included 200 Lakewood, Colorado, residents.
[b]The average annual number of residential break-ins from 1973–1975 within the half-mile square locale of the respondent's residence.
[c]Based on a six-point response format, with 1 representing "not important" and 6 representing "extremely important." Level of importance was evaluated in terms of reasons for participating in the respondent's most frequent outdoor recreation activity.

manifestations of the stress response. He examined the fishing behavior of 826 seasonal visitors to residences in northern Michigan lakeshore communities. Among the findings: those who indicated that escaping distractions was an important motive for their trip to northern Michigan spent an average of 22 minutes longer fishing each day than those for whom it was not an important reason. And incredibly, renters who felt that their vacation microneighborhood lacked privacy spent over twice as much time fishing as those who felt it offered privacy.

For their recreation experiences, people have relative freedom to choose the environments that they prefer (Driver & Tocher, 1970). While not incontrovertible, evidence is mounting that what they prefer is shaped strongly by attributes of home and work environments. The contention is that recreation experiences are being used in large part to resolve problems not resolvable in more restrictive nonrecreational environments (Knopf et al., 1973). So, in our analysis of the recreator as an actor in the natural environment, we find action strongly influenced by the state of affairs in environments left behind.

The Actor Has a Personality

Thus far, the actor has been cast largely as a mere respondent to external forces. But the actor also must be recognized as an enduring organism with distinguishable features, as a system with its own organization, dynamics, and propensities, as an individual with a personal style. The premise is that an individual's own character influences response (Allport, 1937; Wiggins, 1973). In a sense, each of us is programmed to respond in a certain, consistent manner across a broad range of situations (Murray, 1938).

The thrust of personality research has been to develop measures capable of describing interpersonal differences in behavioral style (Craik, 1976). Early recreation researchers cast a curious eye toward developments in this discipline. It seemed that trait measures were useful forecasters of a wide range of outcomes, such as vocational choice, life satisfaction, marital stability, participatory style, delinquency, and managerial success. It was reasonable to anticipate a link between personality and recreation choice.

To these early researchers, the readily available, easily administered trait scales were appealing devices for easing into the unfamiliar territory of psychological inquiry (Havighurst, 1957; Moss, Shackelford, & Stokes, 1969). Much of this work was housed in sports research, where a plethora of trait studies blossomed in the late 1960s and 1970s (Alderman, 1974). We learned, for example, that a sample of competitive fencers were aggressive, achievement-oriented exhibitionists generally not interested in socializing or offering assistance to others (Williams, Hoepner, Moody, & Ogilivie, 1970). And, while basketball players were similar to sports-car drivers in having strong needs for achievement and aggression, the drivers were searching for dominance while the basketball players were not (Ogilvie, 1967).

This interest in applying trait scales eventually spilled into the outdoor recreation literature, where theoretically logical relationships between trait scores and activity participation were found (Knopf, 1972). Hunters, for example, may be more dominant, traditional, and dogmatic than nonhunters (Moss et al., 1969; Moss & Lamphear, 1970). Backcountry campers may tend to be distinguishable by low scores on harm avoidance and high scores on autonomy, endurance, and tolerance for ambiguity (Howard, 1976; Knopf, 1972). The same may be said of participants in high-risk activities such as mountain climbing and skydiving, but these groups may also be typified by strong needs for dominance (Huberman, 1968; Martin & Myrick, 1976).

The tenet underlying these analyses is that people with similar trait profiles tend to be attracted to similar kinds of recreation activities. Trait scores then are seen as useful predictors in multivariate models of recreation choice (Driver, 1976; Knopf, 1972). While trait scores have been entered only rarely into such models, there is encouraging evidence of their discriminating power (Granzin & Williams, 1978). Howard (1976), for example, found that trait scores cut uncertainty in half while forecasting individuals likely to favor nature-oriented recreation experiences.

Primarily through the influence of Hendee (1967) and McKechnie (1970), the focus of recreation–personality research began to move away from strict reliance on the traditional trait measures. Interest began to grow in developing measures that differentiate people according to the ways in which they comprehend or make use of the physical environment. Hendee's (1967) wilderness–urbanism scale, for example, describes the degree to which individuals value urban amenities during outdoor experiences. Scale scores have been linked to both recreation site selection (Loder, 1978; Wohlwill & Heft, 1977) and management preferences (Schreyer, Roggenbuck, McCool, Royer, & Miller, 1976; Stankey, 1972).[7] Similarly, McKechnie (1974) found scale scores on the Environmental Response Inventory aligned with patterns of recreation activity.

While these studies capture our interest, they do little more than whet our curiosity about how specific recreation preferences may be manifestations of general disposition. Forecasting measures now rampant in the environmental psychology literature are virtually unemployed in recreation research (Craik, 1976). Potentially powerful predictors include locus of control (Rotter, Chance, & Phares, 1972), cognitive flexibility (Harvey, 1966), cognitive complexity (Bieri, 1955), privacy orientation (Marshall, 1974), and arousal (Mehrabian and Russell, 1974) or sensation-seeking (Zuckerman, 1971) tendencies. Since high-arousal seekers find more pleasure in complex environments than low-arousal seekers (Mehrabian & Russell, 1974), it seems logical to propose that high-arousal seekers will search out more complex recreation experiences (Loder, 1978; Loy & Donnelly, 1976). And since the magnitude of a stress response is linked to locus of control (Baron, Mandel, Adams, & Griffen, 1976), we would expect that externals would be less bothered by backcountry crowding than internals (Kempf, 1978; Kleiber, 1979). Or, since cognitively complex people differentiate their environment to a higher degree (Moore, 1979), they may be more perceptive of and affected by subtle environmental changes in their recreation locales (Williams, 1980).

---

[7]Schreyer et al. (1976) found river runners with more urban dispositions more likely to desire support facilities such as picnic tables, sleeping shelters, self-guided nature trails, and water spigots. And they tended to be more opposed to restrictive management policies such as rationing use and assigning campsites.

Other unplowed but fertile ground in recreation–personality research stems from the increasingly popular interactionist perspective (Mischel, 1973; Morgan, 1980). Under this perspective the effects of person disposition are recognized as important, but the particular nature of these effects is seen to be largely dictated by the environmental situation. Behavior then reflects the attributive confluence of the person and the setting. In fact, evidence suggests that person X setting interactions explain more behavioral variables than either personal or environmental variables alone (Bowers, 1973; Moos, 1969).

This is not a new perspective. Murray's (1938) early trait measures were accompanied by the argument that behavior is determined not only by personal traits, but also by the degree to which the environment satisfies or frustrates the expression of these traits. And Mischel (1968, 1973) developed the notion of behavior–contingency units to emphasize how expression of disposition is cued by properties of the setting. Under the interactionist perspective, having a personality is having the tendency to respond in certain ways under certain circumstances (Wiggins, 1973).

Recreation–personality research, through its strong reliance on trait models, has largely avoided examining the role of situational influences in the expression of personal character (Knopf, 1972). But our descriptions of the actor under stress clearly suggest that recreation choices are not made in a vacuum. And there is strong evidence that measures of frustrated behavioral propensities are more powerful forecasters of recreation choice than traditional trait measures (Bishop & Witt, 1970; Knopf, 1972). Adams and Stone (1977), for example, found achievement-oriented recreation behavior more successfully predicted by a measure of work-related achievement deprivation than by a measure of need for achievement. Interestingly, Davis (1973) found an inverse relation between achievement orientation and income among inner-city Detroit anglers. It may be that low-income groups are more frustrated in fulfilling achievement needs and attach more importance to this dimension of the fishing experience. Or, put in an interactionist frame, fishing environments may stimulate expression of achievement behavior, and low-income groups may be more responsive to the cue (Mischel, 1973).

So the literature points to the need to expand our personality paradigm to one that acknowledges the contingency nature of character expression. As research under the person X situation model begins to unfold, it seems imperative that recreation researchers fully recognize what is meant by "situation." In one sense, situation is a resultant state, one that is shaped by prior experience, such as the nature of conditions experienced at work. This is perhaps the most traditional interpretation

(Cofer & Johnson, 1960; Murray, 1938). Yet in another sense, situation can be defined strictly in terms of contemporaneous stimuli. The immediate environment itself has behavior-setting properties (Barker, 1968; Mischel, 1973). Thus, each recreation site offers cues that spark the expression of particular forms of action (Lee, 1972). The task of personality research under this perspective is to understand how personal character mediates response to these cues.

Future research will benefit from joint efforts under each of these perspectives. But at the moment we are impaired from elucidating the nature of person X situation interaction in recreation due to absence of data. What we have learned in recreation research is that our actor has tendencies for relating in a personal way to the environment. What we do not yet know is how these tendencies are situationally mediated or induced.

The Actor Is Socialized

The recreating actor does not act alone. The actor must respond not only to the regulatory principles and adjustment mechanisms of a larger society, but also to the will of the group with whom the experience is shared.

And the outdoor experience is indeed a group experience (Field & O'Leary, 1973). Cheek and Burch (1976, p. 24) found 96 percent of visitors to parks, beaches, lakes, and rivers participating as members of a group. Even our stereotypic notion of the solitary wilderness journeyer is rapidly dissipated by data (Lee, 1977; Stankey, 1973). As few as two percent of visitors to the wilderness are alone (Cheek, Field, & Burdge, 1976).

So our preliminary image of the actor, which has largely implied a self-determined, freely choosing organism, must be altered. We now envision an actor having to reconcile his or her own ambition with that of others around him. The reconciliation pressures may be strong: Cheek and Burch (1976, p. 162) found park visitors more often than not were present at the wish of someone else. Kelly (1976) found 26 percent of recreation activities performed under "some obligation to others," plus a rather impressive 29 percent performed under "considerable obligation."

For these reasons, outdoor-recreation inquiry is seen by many largely as a sociological problem (Burch, 1971; Cheek et al., 1976). Under this perspective, the social group is the fundamental unit around which behavior is organized. Behavior is more a manifestation of group properties than of features inherent in the recreation site (contrast Cheek and

Burch, 1976, p. 117, with Driver, 1976). What people do and what is gained will depend upon the particular combination of people participating (Field, Burdge, & Burch, 1975).

Recreation sociology as a discipline was born in the onslaught of demographic analyses that typified recreation research in the sixties (Meyersohn, 1969). It was then we began to notice the behavioral influences of culture (Burch, 1970), gender (Brewer & Gillespie, 1966), life cycle (Burch, 1966), race (ORRRC, 1962), and other sociocultural variables. Peterson, Hanssen, and Bishop (1971) found variables such as race and gender more predictive of outdoor behavior than supply variables. And childhood experiences seemed important. Behavior was linked to childhood recreation patterns (Yoesting & Burkhead, 1973), family style of upbringing (autocratic vs. democratic; Kenyon & McPherson, 1970), parental attitudes toward nature and recreation (Aiello, Gordon, & Farrell, 1974), and perhaps even the nature of children's reading materials (More, 1977). Although these early studies have in retrospect been denounced as superficially correlational (Bultena & Field, 1980; Lee, 1977), they did point to the powerful role of social forces in shaping preference. The message was that one's sociocultural background predisposes action.

But the focus in this early work was on the individual and on what shapes individual preference. The transitions that occur as these individuals form recreating groups were largely unexplored until the works of Burch (e.g., 1971), Lee (e.g., 1972), and Cheek et al. (e.g., 1976). For many, however, the unexpected was being revealed: social groups act not only to constrain recreation behavior, but to catalyze it. As we began to understand that the social group has motivational properties of its own, the search became to reveal what these properties might be.

As the fruits of this search are summarized elsewhere (Cheek & Burch, 1976), we will concentrate here on extracting points of understanding helpful in assessing how outdoor recreationists relate to nature. Three messages are particularly germane.

First, the social group may be an end in itself. The commitment to any one style of interacting with the environment may be low relative to commitment to the group. In observations of park behavior, Field (1976) noted how recreating groups freely moved from activity to activity during their outings. O'Leary, Field, and Schrouder (1974) demonstrated that for particular social groups a wide variety of activities were considered interchangeable. But as the nature of the group changes, so does the perception of what activities are appropriate (Field & O'Leary, 1973). Family groups participate in a different repertoire of activities than friendship groups, even in the same setting (Burch, 1965; Cheek, 1971).

If members of a family group return to the same recreation site as members of a friendship group, they are likely to participate in a completely different stream of activity (Field, 1976). Furthermore, the satisfactions they seek would likely differ (Hendee et al., 1977). These kinds of data suggest that outdoor-recreation behavior is linked less to supply variables than to the configuration of the participating group. Behavior in the out-of-doors, then, becomes less an end in itself and more a means of optimizing interaction among members of the participating group.[8]

Second, individuals seem to be searching for cues from their social environment on how to behave. Many receive cues from status groups that they are attempting to emulate (Kornhauser, 1965). Recreation activities are chosen as a symbol of transition from one reference group to another (Moore, 1979). In a provocative time–series analysis, West (1977) discovered that outdoor-recreation patterns of upper-income strata are emulated and eventually adopted by lower-income strata. At the same time, upper-income classes are continually striving to separate themselves through the adoption of unique activity styles that demonstrate social distance (Burch, 1964).[9] People also turn to significant others for cues on how to behave (Ajzen & Fishbein, 1973). Kelley (1979), for example, found recreationists in Montana's Rattlesnake Backcountry engaging in behavior meant to comply with what was held important by significant others back home. And, people even read the recreation site itself for enduring implicit social cues that prescribe what forms of behavior are appropriate (Lee, 1972). Each recreation locale carries its own normative order—what is socially acceptable behavior in one setting may violate the behavioral code of another (Heberlein, 1977). Individuals not concurring receive cues that direct them to more appropriate recreation settings (Lee, 1972). Park managers frequently are heartened by the way in which groups with potentially conflicting normative structures purposively and voluntarily segregate into distinct territories (Westover & Chubb, 1980).

Third, social groups exhibit a life of their own. Group behavior, over time, develops regularities of action distinguishable from the behavioral propensities of individuals comprising the group (Field et al.,

---

[8]Under this perspective, systems that inventory recreation potential would evaluate resources in terms of abilities to facilitate different styles of group interaction (Cheek & Burch, 1976, p. 155). In contrast, inventory schemes presently adopted by federal land-management agencies such as the Forest Service evaluate resources in terms of abilities to deliver resource-dependent satisfactions (Brown et al., 1978).

[9]The popularity cycles of numerous fad activities such as surfing (Irwin, 1973) and karate (Doeren & Gehlen, 1979) can be explained by the status-emulation process.

1975). Bultena and Field (1980), for example, found the rates of visitation to national parks to be higher for middle-income communities than working-class communities. Socioeconomic status thus appears to be a predictor of national park visitation (Bultena & Field, 1978). But working-class people in the predominantly middle-income community showed substantially higher rates of visitation than people of the same socioeconomic status in the predominantly working-class community. The data suggest that visits to national parks reflect not so much individual propensities as the corporately held activities, values, and norms of the prevailing social system. The study is powerful in being one of the few to empirically demonstrate the emergent properties of social systems. Even during the momentary paucity of research, there seems to be no question that the social group causes behavior to emerge that may not coincide with the personal disposition of the individual (Kelley, 1979). A clear task of recreation research is to identify what these behaviors are, what the underlying norms might be, how they come into being, under what conditions they operate, and what the regulatory mechanisms of enforcement and reward are (Cheek & Burch, 1976, p. 183; Iso-Ahola, 1980, p. 129).

We conclude from these broad observations that our recreating actor in the out-of-doors is an organism remarkably responsive to, even aligned with, social forces. Nature as a goal is important to this person, but it is primarily important as a setting for social interaction, adjustment, and bonding (Cheek & Burch, 1976, p. 167). Human meanings associated with outdoor-recreation places are only indirectly linked to conditions of the physical environment; the myriad of social groups present are perhaps more forceful determinants of meaning.

The Actor Interprets the Environment

Thus far we have imagined an actor responsive to social milieu, home and work conditions, and even his or her own personality. But we have yet to consider how the actor receives input from the recreation setting itself.

In recreation research, we have been tempted to assume that what is perceived corresponds to physical properties of the environment (Schreyer, 1980). Thus, different recreation locales offering similar environmental features will be seen by the recreationist as offering essentially equivalent experiences (Brown et al., 1978). And, shifts in the environmental array will bring about corresponding shifts in environmental perception.

This perspective holds true only if people respond passively to their environments. Clearly, they do not (Kates & Wohlwill, 1966). People transform reality by imposing their own order on incoming stimuli. They filter it (Downs & Stea, 1973), attach meaning to it (Harrison & Sarre, 1971), associate past experience with it (Moore, 1979), organize it (Kaplan, 1976), choose to attend to only parts of it (Taylor & Fiske, 1978), and indeed even create it themselves (Stokols, 1978). So the environments that people actually "see" are not the same environments that recreation planners strive to define objectively. The environments people see are, in part, created by the mind (Moore & Golledge, 1976).

Environment, to a person, means more than a collection of physical attributes—it means a history of past experiences, an accumulation of emotion and meaning (Ittelson, Franck, & O'Hanlon, 1976; Tuan, 1974). Thus, the way people conceive of an environment depends on the way people have experienced it. An urban residential area can be imaged as a slum by one person and seen by another as a positive source of stimulation and haven from fear (Gans, 1962). A wilderness area can be imaged as a source of tranquility and inspiration by one and as a threatening wasteland by another (Nash, 1973). In constructing images of what the environment offers, people impose an array of impressions from past experience upon the collection of stimuli actually present.

The same process occurs as recreationists evaluate recreation settings. Recreationists bring to each setting an image of what the environment offers (Schreyer & Roggenbuck, 1980), and the image creates more information about the environment than the environment actually carries. They see more than what is there. To understand, then, what recreation settings deliver to the individual, we have to move away from strict reliance on objective analyses of environmental attributes and begin looking at the environment from the eyes of the experiencer.

Research on environmental cognition in recreation, like research on cognition in general, is in its infancy (Williams, 1980). From the limited research that does exist we can construct a few principles that confirm the tenets posited above.

First, different recreationists can look at the same collection of stimuli and see different things. The same campsite can be viewed as too secluded or too open, depending on the visitor (Foster & Jackson, 1979). The same recreation locale can be imaged by some visitors as a natural reserve and by others as an arena for social interaction (Knopf & Lime, 1981; McCool, 1978). Further, what is perceived in the out-of-doors can even be related to disciplinary training. Buhyoff and Leuschner (1978) found forestry students focusing on different environmental attributes than recreation students while viewing backcountry landscapes.

Second, what starts out as physically undifferentiated space becomes mentally differentiated space as recreationists impose meaning on it. It may take only a name. Designation of a locale as "wilderness," "national park," or "wild river" generates imagery that is not instilled by contiguous resources that are physically indistinguishable (Nash, 1973; Schreyer, 1980). Reed (1973) demonstrated how symbolic labels such as "national park" and "national forest" evoke images of desirability even when nothing else is known about the environment. But people need not rely on linguistic cues to differentiate recreation spaces. Stankey (1973) described wilderness visitors as mentally stratifying the otherwise homogeneous backcountry into three zones: portal, travel, and destination. Even while all zones were essentially equivalent, visitors experienced more crowding upon encountering others in the destination zones than in the transitory zones.[10] Stankey's work suggests the fallacies of inventorying recreation supply by objective measures of what the environment offers. While the inventory may record one environment, the visitors in fact see many.

Third, use history as an important determinant of how an environment is represented. Limited empirical evidence suggests that repeated visitation to a setting forms an affective bond that sets the resource apart from others (Williams, 1980). As the bonding process develops, the recreationist represents the environment less by its physical character and more by its record of endowed rewards (Tuan, 1974) and its capacity to deliver predictable experiences (Lee, 1977). This could lead one to maintain a participation pattern in an environment even after environmental change had made the realization of desired outcomes more difficult than in other locales (Schreyer, 1980). Use history is also important in shaping the frame of reference upon which visitors draw to evaluate how an environment is performing (Parducci, 1968). Veteran users of a resource see the environment not only as it is, but how it has been (Nielsen, Shelby, & Hass, 1977; Schreyer *et al.*, 1976). First-time visitors image the environment more in terms of its present state. We have found curious manifestations of these differences in research: In areas receiving escalating use, veteran users feel more crowded and see more environmental damage than first-time users (Knopf & Lime, 1981; Schreyer *et al.*, 1976; Vaske, Donnelly, & Heberlein, 1980). It seems that first-time visitors are more susceptible to defining what they see as normal and appropriate for the setting (Heberlein, 1977).

---

[10]Stankey's findings strikingly support Stokols' (1976) conception that environmental stressors impose differential effects depending upon whether they are experienced in primary or transitory settings.

Finally, and most important from a modeling perspective, images held by recreationists affect their behavior. We construct this principle largely through anticipation, as systematic research in this area is largely nonexistent (Christy, 1970; Lee, 1972; Schreyer & Roggenbuck, 1980). From the tourism literature, however, we do glean evidence that (1) images of the environment are typically distorted (Hunt, 1975), (2) these images affect decisions to visit environments (Mayo, 1973), and (3) these images are vulnerable to reconstitution by advertising campaigns (Perry, 1975). In spite of this enticing evidence of the mediating role of image, the variable has yet to surface saliently in outdoor-recreation research.

So we turn to our actor for a final time, and cautiously propose that what he or she sees goes beyond what the environment has to offer. Caution is in order, as the proposal is founded more in speculation than empiricism. With notable exceptions (e.g., Lee, 1972), outdoor-recreation researchers have concentrated on (a) quantifying person or group attributes, (b) quantifying setting attributes, and (c) searching for fit between the two sets. What typically has been missed is the mediating role of the mind—its ability to interpret, adapt, adjust, define, and organize the environment for its own purposes. This is not to suggest that the physical environment has little influence on the individual and his or her recreation behavior (Wohlwill, 1973). But it does suggest that prior experience can modulate what the nature of that influence will be. And it suggests that recreation research has focused on the objective environment to the extent that the experienced environment has been largely ignored as topic of inquiry. We need to consider both, and put the latter in relationship with the former (Wohlwill, 1976).

We have avoided studying the effects of mind on the environment because they have not been accessible to direct observation. But as the work of Lee, Schreyer, Stankey, and others have revealed, these effects are being manifested in behavior and thus are subject to quantification. If we are to assess fully the roles that the natural stimuli play in the human life space, we have little alternative to exploring the mediating effects of the mind. As Tuan (1977) might suggest, if people agree on what nature has to offer it is because they have been taught in the same school.

THE ACTOR NEEDS MORE STUDY

We return to the query which sparked this paper—do humans require nature? A review of the outdoor-recreation literature leaves us with a resounding theme: people recreating in the out-of-doors seem to be responding to things other than properties unique to natural stimuli.

The values people ascribe to outdoor experiences are diverse, and they vary across individuals, activities, and time. While recreating in nature, people seem to be responding to the influence of their home environments, the dictates of their personality, the will of a social milieu, and cognitive structures that impose their own interpretation of what the environment is offering. Of course, the literature we have reviewed does not disprove the possibility that people in fact do require nature. But the relationships that are revealed seem to be more fluid and individualistic than consistent and pervasive.

We have constructed an image of the outdoor recreationist as being subject to four systems of influence: (1) home and work environments, (2) personality, (3) social forces, and (4) cognitive processes. The schema in Figure 3 has been developed to imply that all the systems are interrelated. There are no simple linear cause–effect relationships; all variables simultaneously can serve both independent and dependent roles (Chemers & Altman, 1977). It becomes impossible, then, to make substantive progress in research that focuses on the effects of one system at the exclusion of others.

As with most images, the image we have constructed is probably distorted. Its structure may do little more than reflect the current organization of recreation research, which strongly adheres to traditional disciplinary lines. Recreation sociologists concentrate almost exclusively on developing appreciation for the social system. Those with a natural-resource management perspective in their efforts to understand demand for backcountry experiences have tended to focus on the motivating effects of conditions in nonleisure environments. Researchers with

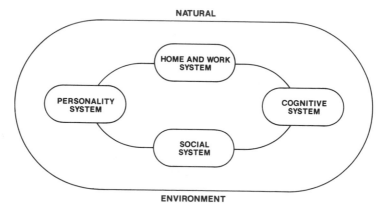

Figure 3. Systems affecting relations with nature.

physical education and recreation health perspectives have concentrated on the personality system as they seek to understand the mental health benefits of leisure participation. Only infrequently does collaboration reach across these disciplinary lines; it is rare to find cross-citation between the three bodies of literature. One might wonder how the character of Figure 3 would have been different had inquiry been organized to study recreation behavior from a more holistic perspective (Peterson, 1973).

Because of this disciplinary fragmentation, we have at our disposal no global theory of outdoor-recreation action. Conceptual frameworks do exist, but they relate to independent problems of a disciplinary nature without reference to unifying theory (Driver & Knopf, 1981). Disagreements over how specific concepts should be defined and measured even seem to follow disciplinary lines. Recreation satisfaction, for example, has tended to be defined by those with backgrounds in natural resources management as the degree to which the environment facilitates goal accomplishment (Peterson, 1974; Stokols, 1978). A recreation sociologist might define the same construct as the degree to which the environment promotes a shared scheme of social order (Lee, 1977). Although the differences between these conceptions are intriguing, we leave the recreationist confused as to how satisfied he or she really is!

So, like our recreating actor, outdoor-recreation researchers carry images that tend to impose artificial structures on reality. The images we hold, and the kinds of structures we impose, are related to the way we are trained. At first blush, this is quite unsettling. But to have varying, even discrepant, points of view can be an asset to the discipline. The environmental psychology literature, for example, is riddled with widespread debate and lack of consensus. Yet it is precisely this process of debate that articulates the issues needing research attention, clarifies the fundamental differences of view, and generates alternatives to the present course of inquiry. It is the process of debate that causes us each to adapt and reformulate the structures we hold, reducing their artificiality and elevating them toward the status of theory.

To date, unfortunately, the diversity of perspective in the outdoor-recreation discipline has not blossomed into rich, intense debate. Lines of inquiry have been remarkably disjointed; there has been relatively little critical evaluation of the research effort. Rather than engaging in open, revealing debate on the nature of human motivation, we have done little more than collect information on reasons why people visit recreation areas.

The dangers inherent in this lack of debate are two-fold. First, the inferential process becomes overly distorted by the perspective of individual investigators. As students of the recreation literature, our image of why people visit recreation areas differs according to who is doing the teaching—a sociologist, a forester, a psychologist, or a personologist. Without the benefit of debate and critique, individual investigators have not been inclined to place their information in the context of that being generated by others, leaving us with a view of the recreationist that is disjointed, incomplete, and possibly erroneous. Second, research becomes deficient in testing alternate hypotheses about behavior. Revelations about behavior tend to be more incidental than designed to converge on principles through systematic testing of alternatives. Lacking such purposiveness, the larger goals or directions of research become muddled. The volume of data grows, but it remains difficult to identify the issues being addressed, the points of agreement and disagreement, and the directions that should be taken to provide insights about behavior.

We draw on the theoretical perspective of this chapter to pose specific themes around which the needed debate might be organized. These themes, posed as research questions, are structured to command the attention of all who are interested in the broad area of recreation motivation and are capable of drawing discussion from diverse lines of inquiry in the discipline. They are:

1. What states of optimality are people trying to achieve?
2. How do people operate within recreation environments to bring them about?
3. From the standpoint of environmental planning and design, what intervention strategies are available to facilitate movement toward these optimal states?

As the debate begins, we will enjoy a sharpened definition of the issues that confront the discipline and clearer impressions of the directions of needed research.

What are the states of optimality? Identifying the states toward which people are attempting to migrate is a fundamentally different research problem than identifying why people make use of particular environments. The latter has been the hallmark of traditional recreation research. It has enabled us to become adept in describing categories of needs salient in various environmental settings, but it has not enabled us to evaluate the forms of experience that are most important to people. The issue becomes one of establishing, from a motivational perspective, the relative values of different forms of recreation experience. In short, we have to do more than identify the experiences people are capable of gaining—we have to identify the experiences that people need most.

So we must turn to the broader question of what humans are striving for. The issues that emerge provide exciting challenges and directions for inquiry. How does one operationalize the concept of optimality? What are the relevant dimensions? What shapes its character? Is the character stable or situationally defined? Are there indicators of optimality? Is expressed satisfaction a valid indicator? Can we model the optimization process (Stokols, 1976)? Can we quantify progress made in moving toward states of optimality?

Such questions may seen excessively abstract for an applied discipline like outdoor recreation. For recreation resource administrators, however, the answers to these questions are important. They too need to understand the nature of optimality and the process by which it can be achieved. Without this orientation, they can do little more than accommodate needs presently expressed by people as they appear at recreation sites. But these needs are a function of existing design and may not reflect optimal use of the resources. By studying instead what people are seeking, resource administrators can discover the forms of experience that people require but are not gaining either in everyday life or through existing forms of recreation opportunity. Thus, planning becomes founded in the need to deliver essential human experiences, rather than in the need to deliver more of what has been offered in the past (Knopf et al., 1973).

How do people operate within recreation environments? This question forces us to articulate the relationship between people and their recreation environments. As a logical extension of the first theme, the task is to define how recreation environments fit in the optimization process.

Again we are confronted with a wave of unanswered questions. How do people organize their time in recreation environments? What kinds of environmental features are needed? What are the functions of different environments? How do particular settings act in facilitating or thwarting different forms of goal accomplishment? What do people perceive recreation environments as offering? How do they mentally organize the array of recreation opportunities available to them? How do people get to know recreation environments? How do they learn where to gratify their needs? While some of these questions have indeed captured the attention of researchers, alternate conceptions and methodologies have not been forcefully advanced and evaluated through debate.

The theoretical perspectives of this chapter can be used to construct a framework for approaching the problem of specifying how people operate in their recreation environments. As noted earlier, the recreating actor responds not only to stimulation from the recreation environ-

SETTING

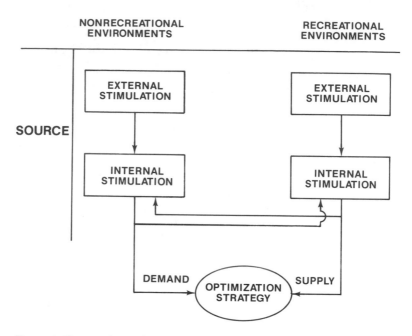

Figure 4. Classes of stimulation affecting outdoor-recreation decision making.

ment, but also to stimulation from the nonrecreational environments left behind. The actor also responds to stimulation generated internally. As Figure 4 suggests, these dimensions can be employed in classifying sources of influence on decision making. In brief, behavior is organized to bring about experiences that are (a) judged to be optimal (demand), and (b) capable of being delivered by the environment (supply). Demand, in turn, emanates from the interaction of internal (e.g., personality) and external (e.g., neighborhood) stimulation in nonrecreational environments—but it is also influenced by supply. Conversely, supply emanates from the interaction of internal (e.g., schemas) and external (e.g., social groups) stimulation in recreational environments—but, given the abilities for people to shape their own environments (Stokols, 1976), it is also influenced by demand.

The task of future research is to expand the schema in Figure 4 by revealing the dimensions of stimulation represented by each cell. We need to know what the specific sources of stimulation are, how influential they are, and how they interact. This review has offered some direction, by specifying a number of influential factors such as personality, culture, peer groups, neighborhood, work environment, and mental representation. But we now need to advance beyond these generalities and to specify the dimensions most germane in shaping recreation behavior. Which dimensions of personality are most relevant, and under what conditions? What aspects of home and work environments bear most strongly on recreation choice, and precisely what forms of social influence become manifested in behavior? To what dimensions of the physical environment in outdoor settings are people responding? What forms of internally stored information mediate response to a recreation environment? And, having reached this level of specificity, what are the relative weights of these diverse sources of influence? What patterns of interaction exist? We suspect, for example, that personality affects not only response to home and work conditions, but also one's representation of what the environment delivers. Yet even preliminary discussion on how to establish the flows of causality among these complex and diverse sources of stimulation has eluded us to date.

What intervention strategies are available to planners? The schema of Figure 4 is particularly useful for defining the scope of the problem that recreation administrators must address. Clearly, the bounds of influence on a recreationist extend well beyond the bounds of the recreation site itself. Thus, perspectives on how to administer to the needs of a recreationist must also extend beyond the bounds of the recreation site. Environmental planners can service recreation demand by introducing appropriate designs in recreation environments, but they can also service it by manipulating the character of stimulation in nonrecreation environments. They can influence recreation supply by reconstituting the character of the physical setting, but they can also influence it by shifting people's image of what it has to offer (Perry, 1975).

The schema suggests, then, the variety of points at which planners might intervene to affect what is being demanded of and supplied by recreation resources. The issue becomes one of identifying how planners should intervene: What is the most effective way to aid recreationists in their quest for optimality? Elsewhere, for example, we have questioned the wisdom of developing backcountry resources to help people resolve problems that simply reappear as they return home (Knopf *et al.*, 1973). But the issue has been treated so inadequately that it is even difficult to know what specific questions should be posed. We suspect that they would include the questions of whether recreation needs can be met before they become expressed at a recreation site and whether these needs can be serviced at substitute sites that may differ in environmental character while being perceived to be psychologically equivalent by the recreationist. Figure 4 leads us to believe that there are many other questions that have not yet been articulated. What it makes clear is that recreation planners, in their task of meeting recreation needs, have more to work with than the character of the physical setting in recreation areas.

CONCLUSION

Recreation research has progressed to the point where general classes of influence upon decision making in the out-of-doors can be posited. The discipline has become quite proficient in amassing data useful in describing why people visit particular recreation sites. But we now need to address the more fundamental questions of what constitutes optimality for the goal-striving human and how can it best be accomplished. Recreation researchers need to abandon the tendency to work isolated from one another, and should begin to engage in active critique and debate. Only then will the issues become clear and will new directions for research emerge. Until we begin to draw on each other more fully, our view of the outdoor recreationist will continue to be disjointed and incomplete.

REFERENCES

Adams, A. J., & Stone, T. H. Satisfaction of need for achievement in work and leisure time activities. *Journal of Vocational Behavior*, 1977, *11*, 174–181.

Aiello, J. F., Gordon, B., & Farrell, T. S. Description of children's outdoor activities in a suburban residential area: Preliminary findings. In D. H. Carson (Ed.), *Man–environment interactions: Evaluations and applications—The state of the art in environmental design research* (Vol. 12). Stroudsburg, Pa.: Dowden, Hutchinson & Ross 1974, pp. 187–196.

Ajzen, I., & Fishbein, M. Attitudinal and normative variables as predictors of specific behaviors. *Journal of Personality and Social Psychology*, 1973, *27*, 41–57.

Alderman, R. B. *Psychological behavior in sport*. Philadelphia: W. B. Saunders, 1974.

Allport, G. W. *Personality: A psychological interpretation*. New York: Holt, 1937.

Ballman, G. Operationalizing the cross-country skiing opportunity spectrum. *Proceedings, North American symposium on dispersed winter recreation*. St. Paul: University of Minnesota, Office of Special Programs, Educational Series 2–3, 1980, pp. 31–35.

Barker, R. B. *Ecological psychology: Concepts and methods for studying the environment of human behavior*. Stanford, Calif.: Stanford University Press, 1968.

Baron, R. M., Mandel, D. R., Adams, C. A., & Griffen, L. M. Effects of social density in university residential environments. *Journal of Personality and Social Psychology*, 1976, *34*, 434–446.

Bieri, J. Cognitive complexity—Simplicity and predictive behavior. *Journal of Abnormal and Social Psychology*, 1955, *51*, 263–268.

Bishop, D. W., & Ikeda, M. Status and role factors in the leisure behavior of different occupations. *Sociology and Social Research*, 1970, *44*, 190–208.

Bishop, D. W., & Witt, P. A. Sources of behavioral variance during leisure time. *Journal of Personality and Social Psychology*, 1970, *16*, 352–360.

Bowers, K. B. Situationism in psychology: An analysis and critique. *Psychological Review*, 1973, *80*, 307–336.

Bowley, C. S. *Motives, management, preferences, and perceptions of crowding of backcountry hiking trail users in the Allegheny National Forest of Pennsylvania*. Unpublished master's thesis, Pennsylvania State University, 1979.

Brewer, D., & Gillespie, G. A. *Socioeconomic factors affecting participation in water-oriented outdoor recreation* (Missouri Agricultural Experiment Station Publications ERS-403). Columbia: University of Missouri, 1966.

Brown, P. J., & Haas, G. E. Wilderness recreation experiences: The Rawah case. *Journal of Leisure Research*, 1980, *12*, 229–241.

Brown, P. J., Driver, B. L., & McConnel, C. The opportunity spectrum concept and behavioral information in outdoor recreation resource supply inventories: Background and application. *Proceedings, Integrated inventories of renewable natural resources workshop* (USDA Forest Service General Tech. Rep. RM-55). Fort Collins, Colo.: Rocky Mountain Forest and Range Experiment Station, 1978, pp. 73–84.

Bryan, H. *Conflict in the great outdoors*. Birmingham, Ala.: Birmingham Publishing, 1979.

Buhyoff, G. J., & Leuschner, W. A. Estimating psychological disutility from damaged forest stands. *Forest Science*, 1978, *24*, 424–432.

Bultena, G. L., & Field, D. R. Visitors to national parks: A test of the elitism argument. *Leisure Sciences*, 1978, *1*, 395–409.

Bultena, G. L., & Field, D. R. Structural effects in national parkgoing. *Leisure Sciences*, 1980, *3*, 221–240.

Burch, W. R. *Nature as a symbol and expression in American social life*. Unpublished doctoral dissertation, The University of Minnesota, 1964.

Burch, W. R. The play world of camping: Research into the social meaning of outdoor recreation. *American Journal of Sociology*, 1965, *70*, 604–612.

Burch, W. R. Wilderness—The life cycle and forest recreational choice. *Journal of Forestry*, 1966, *64*, 606–610.

Burch, W. R. Recreation preferences as culturally determined phenomena. In B. L. Driver (Ed.), *Elements of outdoor recreation planning*. Ann Arbor, Mich.: University Microfilms International, 1970, pp. 61–88.

Burch, W. R. *Daydreams and nightmares: A sociological essay on the American environment*. New York: Harper & Row, 1971.

Catton, W. R. Motivations of wilderness users. *Pulp and Paper Magazine of Canada*, December 19, 1969, *70*, pp. 121–126.

Cheek, N. H. Toward a sociology of not-work. *Pacific Sociological Review*, 1971, *14*, 245–258.

Cheek, N. H., & Burch, W. R. *The social organization of leisure organization of leisure in human society*. New York: Harper & Row, 1976.

Cheek, N. H., Field, D. R., & Burdge, R. J. *Leisure and recreation places*. Ann Arbor, Mich.: Ann Arbor Science, 1976.

Chemers, M., & Altman, I. Use and perception of the environment: Cultural and developmental processes. In *Children, nature, and the urban environment* (USDA Forest Service General Tech. Rep. NE-30). Upper Darby, Pa.: Northeastern Forest Experiment Station, 1977, pp. 43–54.

Christy, F. T. Elements of mass demand for outdoor recreation resources. In B. L. Driver (Ed.), *Elements of outdoor recreation planning*. Ann Arbor, Mich.: University Microfilms International, 1970, pp. 99–103.

Clark, R. N., Hendee, J. C., & Campbell, F. L. Values, behavior, and conflict in modern camping culture. *Journal of Leisure Research*, 1971, *3*, 143–159.

Cofer, L., & Johnson, W. Personality dynamics in relation to exercise and sport. In W. Johnson (Ed.), *Science and medicine of exercise and sports*. New York: Harper Brothers, 1960, pp. 47–69.

Craik, K. H. The personality research paradigm in environmental psychology. In S. Wapner, S. B. Cohan, & B. Kaplan (Eds.), *Experiencing the environment*. New York: Plenum Press, 1976, pp. 55–79.

Crandall, R. Motivations for leisure. *Journal of Leisure Research*, 1980, *12*, 45–54.

Davis, R. L. *Selected motivational determinants of recreational use of Belle Isle Park in Detroit*. Unpublished master's thesis, University of Michigan, 1973.

Doeren, S. E., & Gehlen, F. L. Karate instruction as a type of craze: An application of Smelser's determinants. *Leisure Sciences*, 1979, *2*, 155–172.

Dorfman, P. W. Measurement and meaning of recreation satisfaction: A case study in camping. *Environment and Behavior*, 1979, *11*, 483–510.

Douglas, R. W. *Forest recreation*. New York: Pergamon Press, 1975.

Downs, R. M., & Stea, D. Cognitive maps and spatial behavior: Process and products. In R. M. Stea & D. Stea (Eds.), *Image and environment: Cognitive mapping and spatial behavior*. Chicago: Aldine, 1973, pp. 8–26.

Driver, B. L. Quantification of outdoor recreationists' preferences. In B. van der Smissen (Ed.), *Research camping and environmental education*. State College: College of Health, Physical Education, and Recreation, The Pennsylvania State University, 1976, pp. 165–188.

Driver, B. L. *Item pool for scales designed to quantify the psychological outcomes desired and expected from recreational participation*. Unpublished manuscript, USDA Forest Service Recreation Project. Fort Collins, Colo.: Rocky Mountain Forest and Range Experiment Station, 1977.

Driver, B. L., & Bassett, J. R. Defining conflict among river users: A case study of Michigan's Ausable River. *Naturalist*, 1975, *26*, 19–23.

Driver, B. L., & Brown, P. J. A social-psychological definition of recreation demand, with implications for planning. In *Assessing demand for outdoor recreation*. Washington, D.C.: National Academy of Sciences, 1975. (Appendix A)

Driver, B. L., & Brown, P. J. The opportunity spectrum concept and behavioral information in outdoor recreation resource supply inventories: A rationale. *Proceedings, Integrated inventories of renewable natural resources workshop* (USDA Forest Service General Tech. Rep. RM-55). Fort Collins, Colo.: Rocky Mountain Forest and Range Experiment Station, 1978, pp. 24–32.

Driver, B. L., & Knopf, R. C. Temporary escape: One product of sport fisheries management. *Fisheries*, 1976, *1*, 21–29.

Driver, B. L., & Knopf, R. C. Some thoughts on the quality of outdoor recreation and other constraints on its application. In K. Chilman (Ed.), *Proceedings, Social research in national parks and wildland areas*. Atlanta: USDI National Park Service. Southeast Regional Office, 1981, pp. 85–98.

Driver, B. L., & Tocher, S. R. Toward a behavioral interpretation of recreation, with implications for planning. In B. L. Driver (Ed.), *Elements of outdoor recreation planning*. Ann Arbor, Mich.: University Microfilms International, 1970, pp. 9–31.

Dubos, R. *So human an animal*. New York: Charles Scribner's Sons, 1968.

Etzkorn, K. R. Leisure and camping: The social meaning of a form of public recreation. *Sociology and Social Research*, 1965, *49*, 76–81.

Field, D. R. The social organization of recreation places. In N. J. Cheek, D. R. Field, & R. J. Burge (Eds.), *Leisure and recreation places*. Ann Arbor, Mich.: Ann Arbor Science, 1976.

Field, D. R., & O'Leary, J. T. Social groups as a basis for assessing participation in selected water activities. *Journal of Leisure Research*, 1973, *5*, 16–25.

Field, D. R., Burdge, R. J., & Burch, J. S. *Sex roles and group influences on sport fishing behavior*. Paper presented at Annual Meeting of the Rural Sociological Society, San Francisco, California, February 1975.

Foster, R. J., & Jackson, E. L. Factors associated with camping satisfaction in Alberta provincial park campgrounds. *Journal of Leisure Research*, 1979, *4*, 292–306.

Gans, H. J. *The urban villagers: Group and class in the life of Italian-Americans*. New York: Free Press, 1962.

Granzin, K. L., & Williams, R. H. Patterns of behavioral characteristics as indicants of recreation preferences: A canonical analysis. *The Research Quarterly*, 1978, *49*, 135–145.

Gratzer, M. A., Sutherland, J. E., & Throssell, R. T. *Recreation in the Poconos: Images and perceptions*. Syracuse: New York College of Environmental Science and Forestry, 1979.

Greist, D. A. Risk zoning—A recreation area management system and method of measuring carrying capacity. *Journal of Forestry*, 1975, *73*, 711–714.

Grubb, E. A. Assembly line boredom and individual differences in recreation participation. *Journal of Leisure Research*, 1975, *7*, 256–269.

Harrison, J., & Sarre, P. Personal construct theory in the measurement of environmental images: Problems and methods. *Environment and Behavior*, 1971, *3*, 351–374.

Harvey, O. J. System structure, flexibility and creativity. In O. J. Harvey (Ed.), *Experience, structure and adaptability*, New York: Springer, 1966, 39–65.

Hautaluoma, J., & Brown, P. J. Attributes of the deer hunting experience: A cluster-analytic study. *Journal of Leisure Research*, 1979, *10*, 271–287.

Havighurst, R. J. The leisure activities of the middle-aged. *American Journal of Sociology*, 1957, *63*, 152–162.

Hays, W. L. *Statistics for the social sciences*. New York: Holt, Rinehart, & Winston, 1963.

Heberlein, T. A. Density, crowding, and satisfaction: Sociological studies for determining carrying capacities. *Proceedings, River recreation management and research symposium* (USDA Forest Service General Tech. Rep. NC-28). St. Paul, Minn.: North Central Forest Experiment Station, 1977, pp. 67–76.

Hendee, J. C. *Recreation clientele—The attributes of recreationists preferring different management agencies, car campgrounds or wilderness in the Pacific Northwest*. Unpublished doctoral dissertation, University of Washington, 1967.

Hendee, J. C. A multiple-satisfaction approach to game management. *Wildlife Society Bulletin*, 1974, *2*, 104–113.

Hendee, J. C., Catton, W. R., Sr., Marlow, L. D., & Brockman, C. F. *Wilderness users in the Pacific Northwest—Their characteristics, values, and management preferences* (USDA Forest Service, Research Paper PNW-61). Portland, Ore.: Pacific Northwest Forest and Range Experiment Station, 1968.

Hendee, J. C., Clark, R. N., & Dailey, T. E. *Fishing and other recreation behavior at high-mountain lakes in Washington State* (USDA Forest Service, Research Note PNW-304). Portland, Ore.: Pacific Northwest Forest and Range Experiment Station, 1977.

Holcomb, B. The perception of natural vs. built environments by young children. In *Children, nature, and the urban environment* (USDA Forest Service General Tech. Rep. NE-30). Upper Darby, Pa.: Northeastern Forest Experiment Station, 1977, pp. 33–38.

Howard, A., & Scott, R. B. A proposed framework for the analysis of stress in the human organism. *Behavioral Science*, 1965, *10*, 141–160.

Howard, D. R. Multivariate relationships between leisure activities and personality. *Research Quarterly*, 1976, *47*, 226–237.

Huberman, J. *A psychological study of participants in high-risk sports*. Unpublished doctoral dissertation, University of British Columbia, 1968.

Hunt, J. D. Image as a factor in tourism development. *Journal of Travel Research*, 1975, 13, 1–7.

Irwin, J. Surfing: The natural history of an urban scene. *Urban life and culture*, 1973, 2, 131–160.

Iso-Ahola, S. E. *The social psychology of leisure and recreation.* Dubuque, Iowa: Wm. C. Brown, 1980.

Ittelson, W. H., Franck, K. A., & O'Hanlon, T. J. The nature of environmental experience. In S. Wapner, S. B. Cohen, & B. Kaplan (Eds.), *Experiencing the environment.* New York: Plenum Press, 1976, pp. 187–206.

Kaplan, R. Down by the riverside: Informational factors in water-scape preference. *Proceedings, River recreation management and research symposium.* (USDA Forest Service General Tech. Rep. NC-28). St. Paul, Minn.: North Central Forest Experimental Station, 1977, pp. 285–289.

Kaplan, S. Adaptation, structure and knowledge. In G. T. Moore & R. G. Golledge (Eds.), *Environmental knowing: Theories, research, and methods.* Stroudsburg, Pa.: Dowden, Hutchinson & Ross, 1976, 32–45.

Kaplan, S. Tranquility and challenge in the natural environment. In *Children, nature, and the urban environment* (USDA Forest Service General Tech. Rep. NE-30). Upper Darby, Pa.: Northeastern Forest Experiment Station, 1977, pp. 181–186.

Kaplan, S. Attention and fascination: The search for cognitive clarity. In S. Kaplan & R. Kaplan (Eds.), *Humanscape: Environment for people.* North Scituate, Mass.: Duxbury Press, 1978, pp. 84–90.

Kates, R. W., & Wohlwill, J. F. Man's response to the physical environment. *Journal of Social Issues*, 1966, 224, 15–20.

Kelley, M. D. *Individual and social motive factors influencing recreation participation in the Rattlesnake backcountry.* Unpublished master's thesis, University of Montana, 1979.

Kelly, S. R. *Two orientations of leisure choices.* Paper presented at the Annual American Sociological Association Convention, New York, September 1976.

Kempf, M. *Variations in size of territory exhibited by groups of picnickers in central Pennsylvania.* Unpublished master's thesis, Pennsylvania State University, 1978.

Kenyon, G. S., & McPherson, B. D. *An approach to the study of sport socialization.* Paper presented at the Seventh World Congress of Sociology, Varna, Bulgaria, 1970.

Kleiber, Douglas A. Fate control and leisure attitudes. *Leisure Sciences*, 1979, 2, 239–248.

Knopf, R. C. *Motivational determinants of recreation behavior.* Master's thesis, University of Michigan, 1972. (Xerox University Microfilms, No. M-4224).

Knopf, R. C. *Uses of outdoor recreation resources in the Northeastern Lower Peninsula of Michigan for the purposes of stress mediation.* Rogers City, Mich.: Northeast Michigan Regional Planning and Development Commission, 1973.

Knopf, R. C. *Relationships between desired consequences of recreation engagements and conditions in home neighborhood environments.* Unpublished doctoral dissertation, University of Michigan, 1976.

Knopf, R. C., & Barnes, J. D. Determinants of satisfaction with a tourism resource: A case study of visitors to Gettysburg National Military Park. In D. E. Hawkins, E. L. Shafer, & J. M. Rovelstad (Eds.), *Tourism, marketing, and management issues.* Washington, D.C.: George Washington University Press, 1980, 217–238.

Knopf, R. C., & Lime, D. W. *The national river recreation study: An aid to recreation management* (USDA Forest Service, River Recreation Research Project Paper 1901-79-03). St. Paul, Minn.: North Central Forest Experiment Station, 1981.

Knopf, R. C., Driver, B. L., & Bassett, J. R. Motivations for fishing. In *Transactions of the 28th North American wildlife and natural resources conference.* Washington, D.C.: Wildlife Management Institute, 1973, pp. 191–204.

Knopp, T. B. Environmental determinants of recreational behavior. *Journal of Leisure Research*, 1972, 4, 129–138.

Kornhauser, A. *Mental health of the industrial worker: A Detroit study*. New York: Wiley, 1965.

Ladd, F. C. City kids in the absence of legitimate adventure. In S. Kaplan & R. Kaplan (Eds.), *Humanscape: environments for people*. North Scituate, Mass.: Duxbury Press, 1978, 443–447.

Lansing, J. B., & Marans, R. W. Evaluation of neighborhood quality. *Journal of American Institute of Planners*, 1969, 35, 195–199.

Lee, R. G. The social definition of outdoor recreation places. In W. R. Burch, N. H. Cheek, & L. Taylor (Eds.), *Social behavior, natural resources, and the environment*. New York: Harper & Row, 1972, pp. 68–84.

Lee, R. G. Alone with others: The paradox of privacy in wilderness. *Leisure Sciences*, 1977, 1, 3–19.

Lewis, C. A. People–plant interaction: A new horticulture perspective. *American Horticulturist*, 1973, 5261, 18–25.

Lime, D. W., & Cushwa, C. T. *Wildlife aesthetics and auto campers in the Superior National Forest* (USDA Forest Service Research Paper NC-32). St. Paul, Minn.: North Central Forest Experiment Station, 1969.

Loder, A. W. *Relationship of camper characteristics and choice of a campground*. Unpublished master's thesis, Pennsylvania State University, 1978.

Loy, J. W., & Donnelly, P. Need for stimulation as a factor in sport involvement. In T. M. Craig (Ed.), *Humanistic and mental health aspects of sports, exercise, and recreation*. Chicago: The American Medical Association, 1976, pp. 80–89.

Lucas, R. C. *The recreational carrying capacity of the Quetico-Superior Area* (USDA Forest Service Research Paper LS-15). St. Paul, Minn.: Lake States Forest Experiment Station, 1964.

Mandell, L., & Marans, R. *Participation in outdoor recreation: A national perspective*. Ann Arbor, Mich.: Institute for Social Research, 1972.

Marans, R. W., & Mandell, L. *Proceedings of the American Statistical Association, Social Statisticians Section*. The American Statistical Association, New York, 1972, pp. 360–363.

Marans, R. W., Wellman, J. D., Newman, S. J., & Kruse, J. A. *Waterfront living: A report on permanent and seasonal residents in northern Michigan*. Ann Arbor, Mich.: Institute for Social Research, 1976.

Marshall, N. J. Dimensions of privacy preferences. *Multivariate Behavioral Research*, 1974, 9, 255–272.

Martin, W. S., & Myrick, F. L. Personality and leisure time activities. *Research Quarterly*, 1976, 47, 246–253.

Mayo, E. J. Regional images and regional travel behavior. *Proceedings of the Fourth Annual Conference of the Travel Research Association*, 1973, 211–218.

McCool, S. F. Recreational activity packages at water-based resources. *Leisure Sciences*, 1978, 1, 163–174.

McKechnie, G. E. Measuring environmental dispositions with the environmental response inventory. In J. Archea & C. Eastman, (Eds.), *Proceedings, Second Annual EDRA conference*. Stroudsburg, Pa.: Dowden, Hutchinson, & Ross, 1970, 320–326.

McKechnie, G. E. The psychological structure of leisure: Past behavior. *Journal of Leisure Research*, 1974, 6, 27–45.

McLaughlin, W. J., & Paradice, W. E. J. Using preference information to guide dispersed winter recreation management for cross-country skiing and snowmobiling. *Proceedings, North American symposium on dispersed winter recreation*, St. Paul: University of Minnesota, Office of Special Programs, Educational Series 2–3, 1980, pp. 64–72.

Mehrabian, A., & Russell, J. A. *An approach to environmental psychology.* Cambridge, Mass.: MIT Press, 1974.

Meyersohn, R. The sociology of leisure in the United States: Introduction and bibliography 1945–1965. *Journal of Leisure Research,* 1969, *1,* 53–79.

Miller, G. A., Galanter, E., & Pribram, K. H. *Plans and the structure of behavior.* New York: Holt, Rinehart, & Winston, 1960.

Mischel, W. *Personality and assessment.* New York: Joseph Wiley & Sons, 1968.

Mischel, W. Toward a cognitive social learning reconceptualization of personality. *Psychological Review,* 1973, *80,* 252–283.

Moore, G. T. Knowing about environmental knowing: The current state of theory and research on environmental cognition. *Environment and Behavior,* 1979, *11,* 33–70.

Moore, G. T., & Golledge, R. G. Environmental knowing: Concepts and theories. In G. T. Moore & R. G. Golledge (Eds.), *Environmental knowing: Theories, research, and methods,* Stroudsburg, Pa.: Dowden, Hutchinson & Ross, 1976, pp. 3–24.

Moos, R. H. Source of variance in responses to questionnaires and in behavior. *Journal of Abnormal Psychology,* 1969, *74,* 405–412.

More, T. A. Attitudes of Massachusetts hunters. In J. C. Hendee & C. Schoenfeld (Eds.), *Human dimensions in wildlife programs,* Rockville, Md.: Mercury Press, 1973, pp. 72–76.

More, T. A. An analysis of wildlife in children's stories. In *Children, nature, and the urban environment* (USDA Forest Service (Gen. Tech. Rep. NE-30). Upper Darby, Pa.: Northeastern Forest Experiment Station, 1977, pp. 89–94.

Morgan, W. P. The trait psychology controversy. *Research Quarterly,* 1980, *51,* 273–289.

Moss, W. T., & Lamphear, S. L. Substitutability of recreational activities in meeting stated needs and drives of the visitor. *Journal of Environmental Education,* 1970, *1,* 129–131.

Moss, W. T. Shackelford, L., & Stokes, G. L. Recreation and personality. *Journal of Forestry,* 1969, *67,* 182–184.

Murray, H. A. *Explorations in personality.* New York: Oxford University Press, 1938.

Nash, R. *Wilderness and the American mind.* New Haven: Yale University Press, 1973.

Nash, R. River recreation: History and future. *Proceedings, River Recreation Management and Research Symposium* (USDA Forest Service General Tech. Rep. NC-28). St. Paul, Minn.: North Central Forest Experiment Station, 1977, pp. 2–7.

Nielsen, J. M., Shelby, B., & Hass, J. E. Sociological carrying capacity and the last settler syndrome. *Pacific Sociological Review,* 1977, *20,* 568–581.

Ogilvie, B. C. The personality of the male athlete. *American Academy of Physical Education Papers,* 1967, *1,* 45–52.

O'Leary, J. T., Field, D. R., & Schrouder, G. Social groups and water activity clusters: An exploration of interchangeability and substitution. In D. R. Field, J. C. Barron, & B. F. Long (Eds.), *Water and community development: social and economic perspectives,* Ann Arbor, Mich.: Ann Arbor Science, 1974, pp. 195–215.

Outdoor Recreation Resource Review Commission. *Participation in outdoor recreation: Factors affecting demand among American adults.* Washington, D.C.: U.S. Government Printing Office, 1962.

Parducci, A. The relativism of absolute judgments. *Scientific American,* 1968, *219*(12), 84–90.

Parr, A. E. City and psyche. *Yale Review,* 1965, *55,* 71–85.

Perry, M. Planning and evaluating advertising campaigns related to tourist destinations. In S. P. Ladany (Ed.), *Management science applications to leisure-time operations.* New York: American Elsevier, 1975, pp. 116–123.

Peterson, G. L. Psychology and environmental management for outdoor recreation. In W. F. E. Preiser (Ed.), *Proceedings, Environmental Design Research Association Conference IV.* Stroudsburg, Pa.: Dowden, Hutchinson, & Ross, 1973, pp. 161–173.

Peterson, G. L. Evaluating the quality of the wilderness environment: Congruence between perception and aspiration. *Environment and Behavior*, 1974, *6*, 169–193.

Peterson, G. L., Hanssen, J. U., & Bishop, R. L. Toward an explanatory model of outdoor recreation preference. *Paper presented at Symposium on consumer behavior*, American Psychological Association, Washington, D.C., September 3, 1971.

Potter, D. R., Hendee, J. C., & Clark, R. N. Hunting satisfaction: Games, guns or nature? In J. C. Hendee & C. Schoenfeld (Eds.), *Human Dimensions in Wildlife Programs*, Rockville, Md.: Mercury Press, 1973, pp. 62–71.

Reed, H. P. *A prestige hierarchy of recreation land classification.* Unpublished master's thesis, Utah State University, 1973.

Rossman, B. B., & Ulehla, Z. J. Psychological reward values associated with wilderness use: A functional-reinforcement approach. *Environment and Behavior*, 1977, *9*, 41–66.

Rotter, J. B., Chance, J., & Phares, E. *Applications of a social learning theory of personality.* New York: Holt, Rinehart, & Winston, 1972.

Schreyer, R. *Succession and displacement in river recreation* (USDA Forest Service, River Recreation Research Project Paper 1901-78-07). St. Paul, Minn.: North Central Forest Experiment Station, 1980.

Schreyer, R., & Roggenbuck, J. W. The influence of experience expectations on crowding perceptions and social-psychological carrying capacities. *Leisure Sciences*, 1978, *4*, 373–394.

Schreyer, R., & Roggenbuck, J. W. Visitor images of national parks: The influence of social definitions of places upon perceptions and behavior. *Proceedings of the second conference on scientific research in the national parks, Sociology, Vol. 6.* Washington, D.C.: USDI National Park Service, 1980, pp. 460–477.

Schreyer, R., Roggenbuck, J. W., McCool, S. F., Royer, L. E., & Miller, S. *The Dinosaur National Monument whitewater river recreation study.* Logan: Institute for the Study of Outdoor Recreation and Tourism, Department of Forestry and Outdoor Recreation, Utah State University, 1976.

Shafer, E. L. *The average camper—who doesn't exist* (USDA Forest Service Research Paper NE-142). Upper Darby, Pa.: Northeastern Forest Experiment Station, 1969.

Shafer, E., & Mietz, J. Aesthetic and emotional experiences rank high with northeast wilderness hikers. *Environment and Behavior*, 1969, *1*, 187–197.

Stankey, G. H. A strategy for the definition and management of wilderness quality. In J. V. Krutilla (Ed.), *Natural environments: Studies in theoretical and applied analysis.* Baltimore: The Johns Hopkins University Press, 1972, pp. 88–114.

Stankey, G. H. *Visitor perception of wilderness recreation carrying capacity* (USDA Forest Service Research Paper INT-142). Ogden, Utah: Intermountain Forest and Range Experiment Station, 1973.

Stillman, C. W. On the meanings of "nature." In *Children, nature, and the urban environment* (USDA Forest Service General Tech. Rep. NE-30). Upper Darby, Pa.: Northeastern Forest Experiment Station, 1977, pp. 25–32.

Stokols, D. The experience of crowding in primary and secondary environments. *Environment and Behavior*, 1976, *8*, 49–86.

Stokols, D. Environmental psychology. *Annual Review of Psychology*, 1978, *29*, 253–295.

Taylor, S. E., & Fiske, S. T. Salience, attention, and attribution: Top of the head phenomena. In L. Berkowitz (Ed.), *Advances in experimental social psychology* (Vol. 2). New York: Academic Press, 1978, pp. 249–288.

Tinsley, H. E. A., Barrett, T. C., & Kass, R. A. Leisure activities and need satisfaction. *Journal of Leisure Research*, 1977, *9*, 110–120.

Tuan, Y. F. *Topophilia: A study of environmental perception, attitudes, and values.* Englewood Cliffs, N.J.: Prentice Hall, 1974.

Tuan, Y. F. Experience and appreciation. In *Children, nature, and the urban environment* (USDA Forest Service General Tech. Rep. NE-30). Upper Darby, Pa.: Northeastern Forest Experiment Station, 1977, pp. 1–6.

Tyron, R. C., & Bailey, D. E. *Cluster analysis.* New York: McGraw-Hill, 1970.

Vaske, J. J., Donnelly, M. P., & Heberlein, T. A. Perceptions of crowding and resource quality by early and more recent visitors. *Leisure Sciences,* 1980, *3,* 367–381.

Watson, S. W., Legg, M. H., & Reeves, J. B. The enduro dirt-bike rider: Empirical investigation. *Leisure Sciences,* 1980, *3,* 241–255.

Wellman, J. D. Recreational response to privacy stress: A validity study. *Journal of Leisure Research,* 1979, *11,* 61–73.

Wellman, J. D., Dawson, M. S., & Roggenbuck, J. W. Park managers' predictions of the motivations of visitors to two National Park Service areas. *Journal of Leisure Research,* 1982, *14,* 1–15.

West, P. L. A status group dynamics approach to predicting participation rates in regional recreation demand sites. *Land Economics,* 1977, *53,* 196–211.

Westover, T., & Chubb, M. Crime and conflict in urban recreation areas. *Proceedings of the second conference on scientific research in the national parks, Sociology, Vol. 6.* Washington, D.C.: USDI National Park Service, 1980, pp. 408–425.

Wiggins, J. S. *Personality and prediction: principles of personality assessment.* Reading, Mass.: Addison-Wesley, 1973.

Williams, D. R. *Relationship to place as a determinant of outdoor recreation preferences.* Unpublished master's thesis, Utah State University, 1980.

Williams, J. M., Hoepner, B. J., Moody, D. L., & Ogilvie, B. C. Personality traits of champion level female fencers. *Research Quarterly,* 1970, *41,* 446–453.

Wohlwill, J. F. The environment is not in the head. In W. Preiser (Ed.), *Environmental design research* (Vol. 2). Stroudsburg, Pa.: Dowden, Hutchinson, & Ross, 1973, pp. 166–182.

Wohlwill, J. F. Searching for the environment in environmental cognition research: A commentary on research strategy. In G. T. Moore & R. G. Golledge (Eds.), *Environmental knowing: Theories, research, and methods.* Stroudsburg, Pa.: Dowden, Hutchinson, & Ross, 1976, pp. 385–392.

Wohlwill, J. F., & Heft, H. A. A comparative study of user attitudes towards development and facilities in two contrasting natural recreation areas. *Journal of Leisure Research,* 1977, *9,* 264–280.

Wohlwill, J. F., & Kohn, I. Dimensionalizing the environmental manifold. In S. Wapner, S. B. Cohen, & B. Kaplan (Eds.), *Experiencing the environment.* New York: Plenum Press, 1976, pp. 19–53.

Yoesting, D. R., & Burkhead, D. L. Significance of childhood recreation experience on adult leisure behavior: An exploratory analysis. *Journal of Leisure Research,* 1973, *5,* 25–36.

Zuckerman, M. Dimensions of sensation seeking. *Journal of Consulting and Clinical Psychology,* 1971, *36,* 45–62.

7

Affective, Cognitive, and Evaluative Perceptions of Animals

STEPHEN R. KELLERT

INTRODUCTION

The lack of systematic investigation of human perceptions of animals is surprising given the theoretical and practical significance of the topic. The theoretical aspect is suggested by the role that animals have played in diverse aspects of human commerce and communication for as long as such things have been measured. For example, the cave paintings of primitive peoples remind us of the ancient symbolic importance of animals as modes of thought and belief. Klingender (1971) remarked in this regard, "the history of animal art must begin with the beginning of all art, for animals were the first subject to challenge the artistic faculties of men" (p. 3). Unfortunately, the conceptual significance of this finding, as well as the impact of domestication some 10,000 years ago, have only been lightly considered by the great majority of social theorists and researchers. One might postulate that the dearth of such investigation is, in itself, a social statement on a society regarded by some as particularly anthropocentric and detached from considerations of human relatedness and dependence on the nonhuman world.

STEPHEN R. KELLERT • School of Forestry and Environmental Studies, Yale University, New Haven, Connecticut 06520.

The practical importance of understanding human perceptions of animals has been repeatedly stressed. In 1943, Leopold suggested, "the real problem [of wildlife management] is not how we shall handle the [animals] . . . the real problem is one of human management. Wildlife management is comparatively easy; human management difficult . . ." (Flader, 1974, p. 188). More recently, Norris (1978) remarked:

> Wildlife management is largely a matter of human management. . . . How we behave in relation to natural populations is largely a human affair tightly interwoven with the needs, competitions, and frivolities of humans—and with the social institutions they build. (p. 320)

Although the practicality of comprehending human valuations of animals has been articulated, its yield in empirically substantiated and scientifically standardized benefits has been lacking. Most efforts have amounted to little more than vague, although often eloquent, urgings and subjectively articulated philosophies.

Unfortunately, in a world governed by numbers and commensurable units of evaluation, inspiring "calls-to-arms" bear marginal practical significance. The need to assess costs and benefits and to evaluate trade-offs of environmental protection and economic development mandate clearly defined measures of human valuations of animals and natural habitats. Although empirical work is not completely lacking, the available literature is limited and has been primarily oriented to assessing the consumptive uses of wildlife, mainly hunting.

This chapter examines the state of our scientific understanding of human perceptions of animals, although primarily in the context of American society. In considering perception, three components of human thought and feeling will be described—affective, cognitive, and evaluative perceptions. The affective component refers primarily to the feelings and emotions that people attach to animals; the cognitive aspect, refers to knowledge and factual understanding of animals; the evaluative, refers to beliefs and values associated with animals. These three aspects of human perception of animals will be variously related to four areas of concern: (1) basic attitudes toward animals, (2) attitudes toward specific animal-related issues, (3) knowledge and awareness of animals, and (4) symbolic perceptions of animals. Interestingly, if the two attitude areas are combined (i.e., basic attitudes and attitudes toward specific issues), the three areas of concern can be roughly distinguished according to their primary, secondary, and tertiary relationship to affective, cognitive, and evaluative perceptions of animals. For example, knowledge and awareness of animals can be regarded as involving cognitive perceptions primarily, evaluative views secondarily, and least of all, affective perceptions. Symbolic views of animals, on the

TABLE 1
RELATION OF PERCEPTION OF ANIMALS TO COMPONENTS OF
HUMAN PERCEPTION

Perceptions of animals	Primary, secondary, and tertiary components of perception		
	Evaluative	Affective	Cognitive
Attitudes	1	3	2
Knowledge	2	3	1
Symbolic	2	1	3

other hand, are mainly affective, evaluative in a secondary sense, and least subject to cognitive understandings of animals. Finally, attitudes appear to fall in between the other two areas—that is, they are most strongly influenced by values and beliefs of animals (the evaluative perspective), but also reflect cognitive and affective perceptions. Schematically, the three areas of concern are diagramatically related to the three aspects of perception in Table 1.

Although this chapter focuses on perceptions of animals, this topic in many respects is relevant to an understanding of broader relationships between humans and nature. In this regard, animals may represent a metaphorical device for people to express basic perceptions and feelings about the nonhuman world. As the most sentient and evident characteristic of the natural world, animals often function as a symbolic barometer of people's fundamental beliefs and valuations of nature. Additionally, most discussions of animal species lead to considerations of natural habitat and, as a consequence, wildlife issues often become basic land-use questions. Thus, as metaphorical expressions of meanings attached to nature, and as a basis for prompting considerations of various land-use practices, perceptions of animals often reflect broader facets of the relationship between humans and nature.

BASIC ATTITUDES TOWARD ANIMALS

The development of a taxonomy of basic attitudes toward animals has been attempted. The primary deficiency of most efforts has been a lack of both comprehensiveness and empirical measurement. The best summarization of existing systems is that of Steinhoff (1980), as reflected in Table 2. The primary limitations of the systems reviewed are their

TABLE 2

CLASSIFICATION SYSTEMS PROPOSED FOR WILDLIFE VALUES OR RELATED VALUES[a]

Author of system	Basis of system	Categories of value		
King (1947)	The experience	Recreational Social	Biological Educational	Aesthetic Commercial
Hendee (1969)	The experience	Appreciative Passive free-play Active-expressive	Consumptive Sociable learning	
Hendee (1974)	The experience	Backcountry hunt Meat hunt General season party hunt	Cast-drifting Boat-drifting	Plunking Fly only
Shaw (1974)	The experience	Utility or nuisance Aesthetic or existence	Consumptive recreational	
Hendee (1974)	Elements of experience	Solitude Outdoor skill Nature appreciation	Companionship Escapism	Trophy Exercise
Nobe & Steinhoff (1973)	Economic interest	Direct users Primary beneficiaries Alternative resource user	Vicarious user Secondary beneficiaries Environmentalist Option holder	Altruist

Swartzman & Van Dyne (1975)	Quality of life	I. Economic
		  1. Income per capita
		  2. Employment stability
		  3. Net regional product change
		  4. Income distribution		

II. Ecological
  5. Ecological degradation
  6. Environmental quality
  7. Percentage use of renewable resources
  8. Annual percent usage of non-renewable resources
  9. Man-initiated energy consumption
III. Sociocultural
  10. Population size
  11. Social differentiation
  12. Cultural heterogenity
  13. Sociopsychological
  14. Information advantage
IV. Political
  15. Scope of governmental services
  16. Uses of government services
  17. Political participation
  18. Property tax base
  19. Political power advantage
  20. Dollar investment

Kellert (1978)	Attitude	Utilitarian	Moralistic	Naturalistic
		Negativistic	Dominionistic	Knowledge of animals
		Humanistic	Scientistic	Ecologistic
		Aesthetic		
More (1973)	Attitude	Display	Kill	Esthetic
		Exploration	Affiliation	Challenge
				Pioneering

(continued)

TABLE 2 (Continued)

Author of system	Basis of system	Categories of value		

Langford & Cocheba (1978)	Sources of activities	I. Current period values
		  A. Sensory perception values
		    1. Recreational hunting activity
		    2. Nonhunting recreational activity
		      a. Wildlife-based activity
		      b. Wildlife-related activities
		      c. Endemic wildlife activities
		      d. Recording-based wildlife activities
		  B. Existence values
		    1. Contemplative wildlife activities
		II. Future period values
		  A. Option values
		    1. Option demand activities		

Rolston (1979)	Philosophical criteria	Economic Recreational Stability–freedom	Life intelligibility Plurality–unity Dialectic environmental	Life support Scientific Aesthetic Sacramental
Raths et al. (1966)	Educational criteria	Money Family Religion and morals	Work Love and sex Character traits Politics and social organizations	Friendship Maturity Leisure

[a]From Steinhoff, 1980.

generality, lack of empirical substantiation, and orientation largely to the extractive uses of wildlife (mainly, hunting).

The most widely used and perhaps best articulation is King's (1947), which identified the recreational, aesthetic, educational, biological, social, and commercial values of wildlife. No attempt has been made, however, to measure these values, to assess their relative importance in American society, nor to demonstrate their significance as motivational aspects of personal behavior. On the other hand, the categorization by Hendee (1969) and Potter, Hendee, and Clarke, (1973) of the hunting experience provided some basis for understanding human desires and actions in relation to wildlife. Among the motivational elements of the hunting experience identified were solitude, companionship, escapism, nature appreciation, outdoor skill, obtaining a trophy, and exercise. The primary limitations of the system, however, as Hautaloma and Brown (1978) described, are a lack of distinctiveness of the motivational categories and their questionable applicability to other areas of human/animal experience. The system also appears to specify particular satisfactions rather than basic value or attitudinal constellations.

The primary challenges, thus, in developing a comprehensive system of wildlife values are:

1. Isolating basic valuations and attitudes that encompass all elements of human perceptions of animals
2. Developing a standardized procedure for their empirical and numerical assessment

A preliminary system of basic attitudes toward animals was initially developed in 1974 (Kellert, 1974) and subsequently modified and slightly expanded (Kellert, 1976, 1980c). This system is based on a typology of 10 attitudes or valuations, and one-sentence definitions are provided in Table 3, although more lengthy descriptions are available elsewhere (Kellert 1980b). While the independence of the attitudes has not been sufficiently demonstrated, a partial validation has occurred. In-depth personal interviews of 67 individuals resulted in subjects being assigned primary, secondary, and tertiary attitude classifications. These subjects answered a closed-ended questionnaire concerning various animal-related issues not used as a basis for their attitudinal designations. Multiple discriminant analysis of the closed-ended question responses confirmed the differentiating power of the typology and the tendency of similarly classified individuals to cluster together.

A modified version of the typology was used in two national studies of American attitudes, knowledge, and behaviors toward animals (Kellert, 1976, 1980d). The first investigation was largely exploratory and

TABLE 3
ATTITUDES TOWARD ANIMALS

Naturalistic:	Primary interest and affection for wildlife and the outdoors
Ecologistic:	Primary concern for the environment as a system, for interrelationships between wildlife species and natural habitats
Humanistic:	Primary interest and strong affection for individual animals, principally pets
Moralistic:	Primary concern for the right and wrong treatment of animals, with strong opposition to exploitation or cruelty toward animals
Scientistic:	Primary interest in the physical attributes and biological functioning of animals
Aesthetic:	Primary interest in the artistic and symbolic characteristics of animals
Utilitarian:	Primary concern for the practical and material value of animals or the animal's habitat
Dominionistic:	Primary interest in the mastery and control of animals typically in sporting situations
Negativistic:	Primary orientation toward an active avoidance of animals due to dislike or fear
Neutralistic:	Primary orientation toward a passive avoidance of animals due to indifference

included a relatively small sample ($N = 553$). In 1978, a far more comprehensive study was conducted involving personal interviews with 3,107 people residing in the 48 contiguous states and Alaska. Scales were developed to measure attitudes, although an adequate aesthetic scale was not obtained, and it proved impossible to differentiate the negativistic and neutralistic attitudes.

The attitude scales were standardized on a 0 to 1 range and mean scores, frequency distributions, regression lines, and slopes computed. This analysis resulted in an estimate of the relative prevalence of the attitudes in the American population, as indicated in Figure 1. According to this analysis, the most prevalent attitudes were the humanistic, negativistic, moralistic, and utilitarian. Interestingly, these attitudes are roughly distinguishable into two relatively antagonistic pairs suggesting some reason for the considerable tension and conflict in attitudes toward animals in contemporary American society. The humanistic and negativistic attitudes diverge in their affective response to animals; the former are characterized by strong emotional attachment to individual animals and the latter by feelings of alienation, indifference, and often dislike of the nonhuman world. The dynamic tension of the moralistic and utilitarian viewpoints is their respective perspectives on exploiting animals, especially if death is inflicted for the sake of enhancing human material benefit. The moralistic viewpoint objects to pain or harm to animals or the denial of animal rights not rationalized by absolute necessity. In contrast, the utilitarian perspective assumes the positive value of exploiting and utilizing animals and their habitats if some practical benefit results, omitting situations of obvious cruelty or suffering.

The distribution of the attitudes among various demographic and animal-related activity groups was also examined (Kellert, 1980a; Kellert & Berry, 1980). As an illustration of the potential value of employing these distinctions, educational results are presented in Figure 2. Attitude differences were highly significant, with progressive variations from one educational group to another. A comparison of the college-educated with respondents of less than a sixth-grade education revealed the two groups to be nearly opposites. Respondents of less education were characterized by a relative lack of appreciation, concern, affection, and knowledge of animals. In contrast, the college educated were far more protective, emotionally attached, actively involved, and factually informed about animals and the natural environment. Interestingly, a comparison of college-educated respondents, distinguished according to disciplinary concentration in college, revealed insignificant attitude

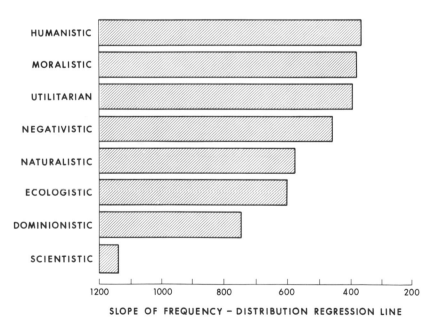

Figure 1. Relative variability of attitudes toward animals in a U.S. sample.

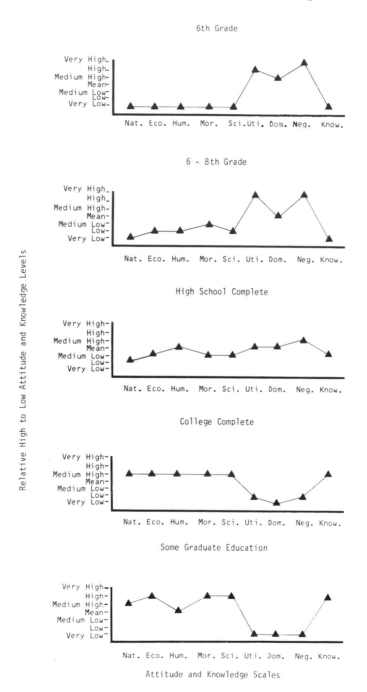

Figure 2. Positions on selected attitude and knowledge scales by Educational level.

scale differences among science, liberal arts, education, and social science majors. These latter results suggested the experience of a college education, regardless of the disciplinary focus, has a positive, sensitizing impact on interest and concern for animals. Additionally, far less impressive income than educational-group differences suggested that educational results could not be solely attributed to the higher socioeconomic status and presumably greater outdoor recreational opportunities of more highly educated persons.

THE SPECIAL CASE OF HUNTING

Although the subject of human attitudes toward animals has received comparatively little scientific attention, the perceptions of hunters and antihunters have been the focus of a number of inquiries. Reviews of relevant literature have been compiled by Potter, Sharpe, and Hendee (1973) and, more recently, by Langenau (1980). Most research has emphasized satisfactions and experiences derived from the activity and, relatedly, presumed motivations rather than considering basic attitudes. Perhaps the most frequently cited study of hunters is one conducted by Potter, Hendee, and Clark (1973) which identified eleven satisfactions related to the hunting experience. Hendee (1974) was particularly concerned with the possibility of identifying specific satisfactions that could be used "for more explicit management . . . to produce the variety and quality of hunting experiences . . . desired" (p. 104). Potter, Hendee, and Clark's study of 5,540 Washington state hunters found major differences among big game and other hunters, although all hunters appeared to value satisfactions associated with nature, escapism, companionship, vicariousness, harvesting game, and shooting.

Additional work by Kennedy (1970, 1974), Stankey, Lucas, and Ream, (1973), Schole, Glover, Sjorgren, and Decker (1973), and others has distinguished a variety of hunt-related rewards. Game-dependent satisfactions included success, challenge, trophy, and meat, while some non-hunt-related rewards were the outdoor recreational experience, aesthetics, exercise, camping, and a variety of social opportunities. More (1973) attempted to further group these satisfactions and emphasized the importance of aesthetics and affiliation and challenge, while depreciating the significance of challenge, display, and kill. Additional studies by Heberlein and Laybourne (1978), Langenau and Mellon-Coyle (1977), Langenau, Moran, and Terry (1981), Jackson, Norton, and Anderson (1981), Applegate (1977), and others have provided further insight regarding the satisfactions and motivations of hunters.

At a more philosophical and less empirical level, Leopold (1968), Ortega Y Gasset (1972), Clarke (1958), Shepard (1974), Madsen and Kozicky (1964), and others have tried to understand the meaning of the hunting experience and its value for human society. Much attention has focused on the opportunities for atavistic recall, for experiencing an intimacy and participatory involvement with nature, for exercising predatory urges, for living off the land, for partaking in the interaction of life and death, and for understanding historical and cultural origins.

Our research (Kellert, 1978), based on the previously described attitude typology, identified three types of hunters. Hunters who cited the opportunity to be close to nature as their primary reason for hunting tended to have especially high naturalistic, ecologistic, and knowledge-of-animals scale scores. This nature hunting group valued the activity primarily for the close contact and familiarity with the natural world it affords. Hunters who indicated obtaining meat as their primary reason for hunting had especially high utilitarian scale scores. This group was mainly oriented toward the practical and material benefit of the activity; thus, the major focus, in contrast to the nature hunter, was on the dead rather than living animal. Finally, persons who cited sport and recreation as their major reason for hunting had very high dominionistic scale scores. This latter group primarily valued the hunting experience as a competitive and social activity involving mastery and conquest of the prey animal.

Far less attention has been devoted to understanding the antihunter. Most studies have focused instead on the extent of antihunting sentiment (which will be considered in a later section) rather than on the motivations and attitudes of the antihunter. Perhaps the best study to date is William Shaw's (1975). Shaw interviewed 463 members of an antihunting organization (Michigan Fund for Animals), a prohunting organization (Michigan Deer Hunters), and an organization with no stand on the issue (Michigan Audubon Society). He found opposition to hunting mainly related to dislike of killing for pleasure, opposition to denying animals their freedom, and concern about cruelty to animals. Dale Shaw (1973) additionally reported objections to hunting stemming from opposition to trophy hunting, wasting meat, endangering species, and taking pleasure in killing. A study by the National Shooting Sports Foundation (Rohlfing, 1978) concluded that most people did not object to hunting but rather to the unethical and antisocial conduct of many hunters.

Our research (Kellert, 1978) identified two basic types of antihunters: humanistic and moralistic. The latter particularly objected to the notion of killing for sport and emphasized the philosophic right of animals to live free from human interference and exploitation. The humanistic antihunter, on the other hand, was characterized by strong affection for individual animals and tended to regard hunting as incompatible with a feeling of love for animals. Very little support was found for the notion that persons objected to hunting because of opposition to firearms or undue concern for the disrespectful and unethical conduct of hunters.

This kind of analytical scrutiny of hunters needs to be extended to other animal-related activities. Some consideration of birdwatching and zoological park visitation has occurred, although most analyses have focused on specific management issues (e.g., nongame funding, animal displays) rather than basic attitudes and motivations. Illustrative of the potential for obtaining useful and illuminating information is research that found birdwatchers to have among the highest naturalistic, ecologistic, knowledge, and lowest negativitistic attitude scale scores (Kellert, 1981). The humanistic and moralistic scores of birdwatchers, however, were not unusual, suggesting that this group was more oriented toward wildlife and natural habitats than toward domestic animals, strong affection for individual animals, or particular concern about cruelty issues (Figure 3). Three characteristics of birdwatching may partially explain the especially high knowledge, ecologistic, and naturalistic scores of this group. First, birdwatching tends to focus attention on species rather than individual animals. This emphasis may encourage a broader, ecological perspective. Second, the specialized interrelationship of many bird species and their habitats may foster a more ecological understanding of nature. Finally, greater awareness among birdwatchers of environmental issues may stem from adverse pollution impacts that have affected a variety of bird species.

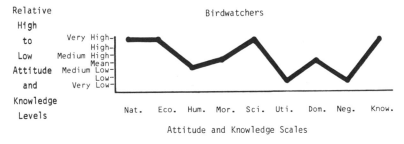

Figure 3. Positions on selected attitude and knowledge profiles by birdwatchers.

KNOWLEDGE OF ANIMALS

In contrast to examining how people value animals, perceptual research has also focused on knowledge of the nonhuman world. This issue of cognitive perception is particularly relevant to interpreters, naturalists, and educators, although surprisingly little empirical research has documented people's factual understanding of animals. An additional need exists to distinguish kinds of cognitive understanding; at least three types can be identified. One type of cognitive understanding focuses on simple statements of factual knowledge such as "Is the manatee an insect?" "Is the iguana a mammal?" Another form of knowledge relates to basic principles or relationships between animals and nature. For example, one may inquire about the concept of habitat, population dynamics, or ecosystem dependence. Finally, a third kind of cognitive understanding concerns awareness of conservation issues and problems, as well as management principles and practices.

Most research has focused on knowledge in the simple factual sense and has been largely directed at children. These studies have revealed some interesting differences among children of varying demographic and experiential backgrounds. For example, Giles (1959) found that white secondary school students knew significantly more about animals than black students, and these differences tended to increase with age. Pomerantz (1977) distributed a questionnaire to 2,362 Michigan public school children in a study of "Young People's Attitudes Toward Wildlife." She reported significantly greater wildlife and conservation knowledge among rural students, especially those participating in outdoor recreational activities such as hunting and fishing.

TABLE 4
MEAN CORRECT SCORE FOR TYPES OF
KNOWLEDGE QUESTIONS[a]

Human injury	63.4
Biological characteristics	55.3
Domestic animals	53.4
Predators	47.1
Wildlife management/history	43.6
Taxonomic characteristics	38.5
Invertebrates	34.7
Superstition/myth	33.2
Endangered species	27.4

[a]Scoring range is 0–100.

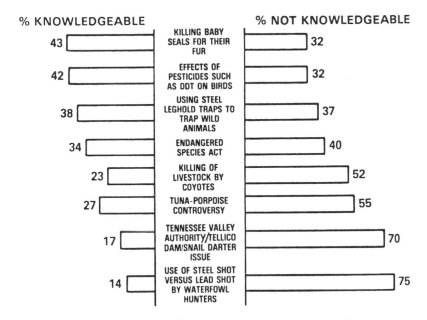

Figure 4. Awareness of selected wildlife issues. *Note:* The Knowledgeable category combines the very and moderately knowledgeable groups; the Not Knowledgeable category combines the very little knowledge group and the group that never heard of the issue.

Our research (Kellert & Berry, 1980) focused on factual knowledge and awareness of prominent management issues. Factual-knowledge results revealed that Americans were most knowledgeable about animals known to inflict human injury and disease, as well as domestic animals (Table 4). On the other hand, relatively limited knowledge was found of endangered species, invertebrates, and animals commonly associated with superstition and myth.

Research on awareness of animal-related issues (Stuby, Carpenter, & Arthur, 1979; Kellert, 1980c) has revealed a number of surprising results. Perhaps most important, the American public appears to be only moderately familiar with even the most popular wildlife issues, suggesting the limited salience of most animal-related issues to the great majority of Americans (Figure 4). Secondly, issues of greatest familiarity were either highly emotional or associated with a human health hazard. For example, the most recognized issue was the baby seal controversy, notable for its association with presumed cruelty, its focus on a large, attractive animal, and the exploitation of the newborn. In contrast, the least recognized issues generally involved indirect impacts on wildlife, primarily due to habitat loss. For example, the presumably well-known TVA/Tellico Dam/Snail Darter issue was unfamiliar to 70 percent of the American public, despite its extensive media coverage. It appears the average person has difficulty understanding wildlife problems involving adverse impacts due to the elimination of natural areas.

ATTITUDES TOWARD ANIMAL-RELATED ISSUES AND PROBLEMS

Most research on attitudes toward specific animal-related issues has been descriptive and, for the most part, unrelated to any theoretical perspective of human–animal relations. If one examines the range of attitude issues covered, four major types dominate: (1) human socioeconomic development versus animal and habitat protection; (2) animal rights and welfare issues, particularly involving presumed cruelty; (3) attitudes toward consumptive and extractive uses of animals; and (4) wildlife-management practices and procedures.

Attitudes toward socioeconomic development versus animal protection has become an increasingly prominent consideration due to the promulgation of various laws mandating the mitigation of human impacts on wildlife habitat and, relatedly, the widespread emergence of social impact analysis in a diversity of land-use contexts. Many policymakers and political leaders have presumed a widespread public reluctance to inhibit socioeconomic development to protect wildlife or natural habitat. Recent research, however, has revealed a far greater willingness to make these sacrifices than had been assumed, particularly for the sake of certain animal species.

The protection of endangered wildlife is a good illustration. For example, data reported by Mitchell (1980) in a national survey conducted for the Council on Environmental Quality reported a willingness among a significant majority of the American public to protect endangered wildlife despite potentially adverse socioeconomic impacts. Moreover, the 1,576 adults interviewed indicated, in a variety of contexts, "that environmental protection enjoys continued strong backing." (p. 2) Our 1978 national study (Kellert, 1980b) explored four hypothetical conflicts between human activity and endangered-species protection, including impacts on energy development, water use, forestry, and commercial activities in wetlands. The results indicated a willingness to protect endangered and threatened wildlife, except in situations where relatively obscure species conflicted with relatively important human benefits such as agricultural production, energy development, and increasing drinking supplies. An assessment of these and other results hypothetically suggested the following factors as substantially influencing public attitudes toward modifying human activities in order to protect vanishing and threatened wildlife:

1. Aesthetic value of the species
2. Degree of socioeconomic impact involved in protecting the species
3. Phylogenetic relation (similarity) of the species to human beings
4. Presumed threat of the species to human health and productivity
5. Cultural and historical importance of the species
6. Potential and actual economic value of the species

No research has determined the relative importance of each factor, although the development of a predictive model will depend on this type of study.

A second type of issue has focused on cruelty and animal welfare considerations. A variety of findings regarding attitudes toward trapping, rodeos, dog fighting, cock fighting, bullfighting, killing seals, dog racing, horse racing, trophy hunting, and the killing of elephants and rhinoceroses for tusks and horns have revealed strong opposition to presumably painful or lethal practices not serving important social purposes. On the other hand, more ambivalent results were obtained regarding such activities as animal medical research, livestock slaughtering, or controlling animal damage to livestock and crops. These latter results suggested a greater willingness to accept harm or death to animals when relatively important social purposes were served. Nevertheless, even in the latter situations, the desire to minimize presumed suffering and the extent of animal loss was evident. For example, in studies of attitudes toward controlling coyote livestock predation (Arthur, Gum, Carpenter, & Shaw, 1978; Buys, 1975; Kellert, 1980c), the public strongly favored control procedures that maximized humaneness and focused on the individual offending animal rather than on the entire species. Specifically, large majorities objected to indiscriminate reductions of coyote populations and the use of poisons.

A third type of attitude-issue research has focused on the consumptive or extractive uses of animals. Major considerations have been public attitudes toward the recreational and utilitarian exploitation of animals and, relatedly, the ethical and legal rights of animals. Various results of studies on harvesting of furbearers, whaling, fishing, and hunting suggest that most people support these activities if a significant degree of practical justification is involved and cruelty is not evident. On the other hand, only a minority of persons of higher socioeconomic status, females, and residents of urban areas approve of these practices.

Views for and against hunting are particularly illustrative of research in this area. Among the most valuable studies have been the longitudinal work done by William Shaw (1974; Shaw, Carpenter, Arthur, Gum, & Witter, 1976) and Applegate (1973, 1975, 1979) in New Jersey. Although these studies have yielded important information, widely varying results somewhat limit their generalizability. One possible explanation for this diversity may be that public attitudes toward hunting vary with different reasons for hunting. Our 1978 national study (Kellert, 1980c) considered this factor by confronting the respondent with five reasons for hunting (Table 5). Overwhelming support was expressed for the two most utilitarian forms—subsistence hunting by Native Americans and hunting exclusively for the animal's meat regardless of the ethnic identity of the hunter. On the other hand, nearly 90 percent of the national sample objected to trophy hunting, and over 60 percent disapproved of waterfowl or big-game hunting pursued solely for recreational or sporting enjoyment. When hunting for recreation and sport was combined with utilizing the meat, however, nearly two-thirds approved of hunting. These results suggested most Americans approved of hunting if some practical utilization is involved.

A fourth area of issue-related research has emphasized wildlife-management practices and policies. For the most part, little theory has informed this inquiry, with the primary interest being a descriptive determination of support for or against a particular management procedure. Among the topics receiving attention have been wildlife law enforcement, controlling bear–people conflicts in the national parks, clear-cutting and other habitat manipulations, perceptions of wildlife-management agencies, predator reintroduction programs, and the funding of public wildlife management. Research on the latter topic has been primarily motivated by the interest to determine public support for obtaining additional revenues to manage nongame, especially endangered wildlife. Historically, the bulk of management funds has been obtained from taxes on hunters and fishermen. The major consequences of this funding procedure have been an inordinate degree of power and attention bestowed on sportsmen by public wildlife agencies. For example, one study conducted by the Wildlife Management Institute (1975) estimated that 97 of 100 management dollars were directed at largely game species. Diversification of funding would, thus, result in not only increasing attention to nongame wildlife but, inevitably, also a sharing of power with the nonconsumptive wildlife user. The most recent studies of pub-

Table 5

Distribution of Responses by General Public to the Question: "Of the Following Reasons For Hunting, Which do you Approve or Oppose?"[a]

Reason for hunting	Response categories						Total	
	Strongly approve	Approve	Slightly approve	Slightly disapprove	Disapprove	Strongly disapprove	Approve	Disapprove
A. Traditional native hunting such as done by some Indians and Eskimos	(397) 16.2	(1166) 47.5	(453) 18.4	(145) 5.9	(167) 6.8	(51) 2.1	(82)	(15)
B. Hunting game mammals such as deer for recreation and sport	(108) 4.4	(457) 18.6	(333) 13.6	(268) 10.9	(671) 27.3	(580) 23.6	(37)	(62)
C. Hunting waterfowl such as ducks for recreation and sport[b]	(113) 4.6	(470) 19.1	(388) 15.8	(292) 11.9	(636) 25.9	(526) 21.4	(40)	(59)
D. Hunting for meat	(542) 22.1	(1143) 46.5	(408) 16.6	(135) 5.5	(125) 5.1	(76) 3.1	(85)	(14)
E. Hunting for recreation and meat[c]	(227) 9.2	(779) 31.7	(573) 23.3	(288) 11.7	(342) 13.9	(208) 8.5	(64)	(34)
F. Hunting for a trophy, such as horns or a mounted animal	(49) 2.0	(190) 7.8	(207) 8.4	(230) 9.4	(655) 26.7	(1081) 44.1	(18)	(80)

[a]Note the following format procedures: (1) numbers in parenthesis indicate the actual number of people who responded in a particular way; (2) other numbers refer to the percentage of respondents who answered in a particular way.
[b]Difference between approve and disapprove: $Z = 9.81$, $p = \leq .0001$.
[c]Difference between approve and disapprove: $Z = 15.07$, $p = \leq .0001$.

lic attitudes toward this issue have been Shaw, Witter, King, and Richards (1978) and Kellert (1980c), both demonstrating strong public support for funding diversification, as well as a surprising degree of distrust
among nonconsumptive users of public wildlife-management agencies.

SYMBOLIC PERCEPTIONS OF ANIMALS

This section on symbolic perceptions will primarily emphasize affective, emotional relationships to animals, focusing attention on the
likes, fears, attractions, and subjective feelings that people possess of
animals. Relatedly, the symbolic factor emphasizes the human capacity
to employ animals as metaphorical devices for enhancing communication and thought. The immediate practical significance of this subject is
implied by the previously cited endangered species results indicative of
how the destiny of many animals will depend on people's subjective
feelings toward particular species.

At a more indirect level, the importance of symbolic perceptions of
animals is suggested by the role that animal symbols play in a variety of
human growth and communication functions. Indeed, this process may
reflect animal contributions to human society as important as the better
known utilitarian, ecological, and scientific values of animals. In this
regard, Shepard (1978) remarked:

> There is a profound, inescapable need for animals for which no substitute
> exists. . . . It is the peculiar way that animals are used in the growth and
> development of the human person. . . . It is the role of animal images and
> forms in the shaping of personality, identity, and social consciousness. . . .
> The mind and its organ, the brain, are in reality that part of us most depen-
> dent on the survival of animals. (p. 2)

Shepard, in his provocative and sometimes profound book, *Thinking Animals*, endeavored to describe how animals are employed as devices for thought, metaphor, communication, and differentiation, thereby providing the basis for much human expression, feeling, and ideas.
By offering opportunities for taxonomic distinction, for expressing basic
dilemmas of selfhood, and by communicating complicated thoughts and
feelings through analogy and abstraction, animals provide a number of
fundamental symbolic functions. For example, in research on 150 randomly selected preschool children's books, over 91 percent were found
to include animal characters (Sokolow, 1980). For the most part, these
animals were used to instruct children in classifying and differentiating
or were portrayed as disguised humans in the context of expressing
various psychosocial issues and dilemmas.

Additionally, Bettelheim (1977) in his study of children's stories and, to some extent, Levi-Strauss (1966), Jung (1964) and Lopez (1978) in their research on myths, describe diverse situations of animals used to confront fundamental human conflicts (e.g., incest, patricide, fears of parental abandonment). In these and other contexts, animal species are symbolically employed to express particular feelings and motives. For example, the wolf—a predatory animal associated with dusk and twilight—is typically invoked as a malevolent sexual symbol (Lopez, 1978). In contrast, the bear—a creature of as much if not more practical danger—is usually associated with positive attributes, a treatment possibly related to the bear's diurnal, omnivorous, and aesthetically pleasing character. Without question, much needs to be learned and empirically investigated about the symbolic importance of varying species. Contemporary advertising certainly reflects an intuitive understanding of the symbolic power of particular species, as the names and promotion of many products suggests. This linguistic importance of animals may even extend to more obscure realms of language. Leach (1964), for example, provocatively noted the role of domesticated animals in the development of profane and forbidden vocabularies (e.g., cock, bitch, swine, etc.).

Klingender (1971) in his study of animals in art and thought invoked Freud's ideas to elucidate the often paradoxical role of animals in diverse symbolic situations. He suggested, these varying uses of animals "illustrate the distinction, often used by Freud, between the reality principle and the pleasure principle" (p. xxv). The former principle is typically manifest in symbolic conflicts between man and beast, whereas the latter allows humans to take aesthetic delight in animals

> so far as we ignore the realities of struggle and exploitation . . . , thus transplanting [animals] into a dream-world of wish-fulfillment where all creatures are friends. [In either situation,] it clearly transforms the real animal by turning it into a symbol on to which human feelings and wishes may be projected. (pp. xxv–xxvi)

Unfortunately, most empirical research on the symbolic role of animals has limitedly considered people's likes and dislikes of particular species (Arthur, 1981; Bart, 1972; Dagg, 1974; Badaracco, 1973; La Hart & Tillis, 1974; More, 1977). An interesting study was conducted by Paulhus and Dean (1977) in an attempt to provide empirical criteria for determining which animals were most socially suitable for laboratory research. Based on discriminate analysis results, they found that the most significant influences on people's protective feelings toward animals were the intelligence, size, perceived harmfulness, and aesthetic appeal of the animal.

Our 1978 national study (Kellert & Berry, 1980) also assessed the relative preference for 33 animals based on a seven-point like/dislike scale. This analysis revealed domestic, aesthetically attractive and game species to be the most preferred types of animals. The least preferred types were biting and stinging invertebrates, aesthetically unattractive animals, animals associated with human injury and damage, and invertebrates in general. Based on these and other results, the following factors appear importantly to influence symbolic perceptions of animals: aesthetics, presumed intelligence of the animal, size of the animal, the animal's perceived dangerousness to human beings, predatory tendencies of the animal, its skin texture and morphology, and the relationship of the animal to human society (e.g., companion, work, farm and livestock, game, pest, native or exotic animal).

POLICY AND MANAGEMENT IMPLICATIONS

The views of Norris (1978) and Leopold (Flader, 1974) were cited at the outset regarding the practical need for developing a better understanding of people's perceptions of animals as an essential element in effective wildlife-management programs. Specifically, information on human perceptions may be useful in at least five management contexts: (1) constituency identification, (2) multiple-satisfactions management, (3) resource allocation, (4) social impact and trade-off analysis, and (5) public awareness and environmental education.

The area of constituency identification emphasizes the need to better understand the motivations and values of various wildlife interest groups, a knowledge particularly relevant given major changes that have occurred in the clientele of wildlife-management agencies. Historically, sportsmen and rural groups were overwhelmingly the dominant constituency of the management field. Since World War II, however, the number of people interested in direct contact and observation of wildlife has expanded dramatically, particularly in the nonconsumptive use of wildlife resources. Moreover, a large fraction of these new interest groups have voiced strong concern for the protection of wildlife and natural habitats. Various studies have suggested that this new clientele consists of predominantly urban and higher socioeconomic groups traditionally possessing little access to public wildlife management. Inevitably, these changes have produced considerable tension and confusion and, as servants of the entire American public, the management agencies require a far better understanding of this new constituency. Studies of the animal-related perceptions and attitudes of the nonconsumptive user, as well as the values and concerns of traditional groups, should provide much of the information needed.

A related value of perceptual research is the evolution of a multiple-satisfacions approach to management. Historically, when wildlife management was primarily oriented toward the sportsmen and the regulation of overharvest, effective management was largely measured in terms of harvest limits and sportsmen days-afield. In today's situation, with new, primarily nonconsumptive groups appearing, and with a better understanding of the interests of sportsmen emerging, a more deliberate multiple-satisfactions approach is increasingly possible. From this perspective, as Hendee (1974) described, the wildlife user's satisfactions and interests become a direct focus and product of management. In other words, assuming a knowledge of the values, needs, and desires of various wildlife interest groups, opportunities can be provided to enhance the probability of achieving the desired satisfactions. The multiple-satisfaction approach, thus, represents a marketing approach to management, with the empirical assessment of particular target groups presumably resulting in a product designed to satisfy the desires of these groups.

Constituency identification and multiple-satisfactions management should provide a better basis for the third value of human dimensions research: the equitable allocation of wildlife resources. To enhance the likelihood of scarce resources being distributed in an efficient and appropriate manner, information on the characteristics and interests of various wildlife groups should prove helpful. This information could enhance standards of fairness as well as provide a better basis for defending administrative decisions. Additionally, information on public preferences for varying species and the public's willingness to allow socioeconomic sacrifices to protect wildlife should enable managers to assign conservation priorities in the absence of unlimited funds and unqualified support for protecting all wildlife.

An additional benefit of human dimensions data is in the assessment of social impacts and the analysis of costs and benefits of wildlife-habitat protection versus human development. This information can provide a better understanding of the wildlife values at risk when particular habitats or wildlife populations are adversely affected by human activities. Additionally, this understanding may suggest opportunities for resolving conflicts among competing groups by offering intelligent bases for compromise. For example, information on public willingness to accept socioeconomic trade-offs should suggest mitigating measures that recognize legitimate human needs while minimizing adverse environmental effects.

Ultimately, the most important value of human perceptions research is helping to develop public awareness and environmental education programs. Only by better understanding public attitudes toward and appreciation of wildlife will it be possible to improve these perceptions. The true measure of wildlife-education programs, however, will not be the amount of factual information imparted, but the evolution of an ethic of respect and concern for wildlife and the environment. As Leopold remarked (1968),

> perception is the only truely creative act of [environmental] engineering. . . .
> Let no man jump to the conclusion that Babbitt must take his Ph.D. in
> ecology before he can "see" his country. On the contrary, the Ph.D. may
> become as callous as an undertaker to the mysteries at which he officiates. (p.
> 174)

Environmental education will need to move beyond simply emphasizing affection for animals to a broader ecological understanding of species in relation to their land base. As Joseph Wood Krutch once remarked (1970), "love is not enough" (p. 192). The prevalence of the humanistic perspective of animals signified a broad affection for animals in our society, but emotional attachment is not without its problems, as suggested by the public's greater familiarity with the baby seal than snail darter issue. Developing a meaningful wildlife ethic will require an empathy not only for the individually exploited animal but also for the plight of the species. Love for animals is not the essential ingredient in this understanding; rather, it is respect, awe, and an affinity for the whole ecosystem as something as precious as its constituent parts. A sense of beauty and the aesthetic qualities of animals are not so important as is an appreciation of the immense complexity and intricacy of the overall biosphere. Most of all, an awareness of the need to save the various functioning elements must not be based solely on an ethic of short-term self-interest, but on a visceral knowledge that the well-being of animals is ultimately related to the long-term survival of man.

Regardless of the shape and form of such education programs, their successful design will require a far greater knowledge of human perceptions of animals. The information presented in this paper reflects only the tip of the iceberg of the data needed. Far more empirical study is required of valuations of animals, attitudes toward specific management issues, knowledge and understanding of wildlife, and symbolic perceptions of animals. Just a few of the specific research topics needing attention include: public perceptions of invertebrates, attitudes toward snakes, valuations of animals among third-world nations, characteristics and attitudes of the owners of exotic pets, preferences and values of zoological park visitors, wildlife-related attitudes and concerns among private landowners, the relationship of moral valuations of people to moral valuations of animals, the importance of animals in child development, and the symbolic meaning of animals in literature and myth. The research agenda may appear formidable, but the chance to affect the development of a potentially meaningful and practically useful field is a worthy incentive for proceeding.

REFERENCES

Applegate, J. E. Some factors associated with attitudes toward deer hunting in New Jersey residents. *Transactions of the North American Wildlife and Natural Resources Conference,* 1973, *38,* 267–273.

Applegate, J. E. Attitudes toward deer hunting in New Jersey: A second look. *Wildlife Society Bulletin,* 1975, *3,* 3–7.

Applegate, J. E. Dynamics of the New Jersey hunter population. *Transactions of the North American Wildlife and Natural Resources Conference,* 1977, *42,* 103–116.

Applegate, J. E. Attitudes toward deer hunting in New Jersey: A decline in opposition. *Wildlife Society Bulletin,* 1979, *7,* 127–129.

Arthur, L. M. Measuring public attitudes toward natural resource issues. *USDA Economic Research Service Technical Bulletin,* No. 1657, 1981.

Arthur, L. M., Gum, R. L., Carpenter, E. H., & Shaw, W. W. Predator control: The public viewpoint. *Transactions of the North American Wildlife and Natural Resources Conference,* 1978, *42,* 137–145.

Badaracco, R. J. Scorpions, squirrels or sunflowers. *The American Biology Teacher,* 1973, *35,* 528–530.

Bart, W. M. A hierarchy among attitudes toward animals. *Journal of Environmental Education,* 1972, *3,* 4–6.

Bettelheim, B. *The uses of enchantment.* New York: Vintage Books, 1977.

Buys, C. J. Predator control and ranchers' attitudes. *Environment and Behavior,* 1975, *7,* 81–98.

Clark, C. H. D. Autumn thoughts of a hunter. *Journal of Wildlife Management,* 1958, *22,* 420–427.

Dagg, A. I. Reactions of people to urban wildlife. In J. H. Noyes & D. R. Progulske (Eds.), *Wildlife in an urbanizing environment.* Amherst: University of Massachusetts, Holdsworth Natural Resources Center, Planning and Resource Development Series No. 28, 1974, pp. 163–165.

Flader, S. L. *Thinking like a mountain.* Columbia: University of Missouri Press, 1974.

Giles, R. H., Jr. The conservation knowledge of Virginia school pupils. *Transactions of the North American Wildlife and Natural Resources Conference,* 1959, *24,* 488–499.

Hautaloma, J., & Brown, P. Attributes of the deer hunting experience: A cluster analysis study. *Journal of Leisure Research,* 1978, *10,* 271–287.

Heberlein, T. A., & Laybourne, B. *The Wisconsin deer hunter: Social characteristics, attitudes and preferences for proposed hunting season changes.* University of Wisconsin Working Paper No. 10, School of Natural Resources, 1978.

Hendee, J. C. Appreciative versus consumptive uses of wildlife refuges: Studies of who gets what and trends in use. *Transactions of the North American Wildlife and Natural Resources Conference,* 1969, *34,* 252–264.

Hendee, J. C. A multiple satisfaction approach to game management. *Wildlife Society Bulletin,* 1974, *2,* 104–113.

Jackson, R. M., Norton, R., & Anderson, R. The resource manager and the public: An evaluation of historical and current concepts and practices. *Transactions of the North American Wildlife and Natural Resources Conference,* 1981, *46,* 208–222.

Jung, C. G. *Man and his symbols.* New York: Doubleday, 1964.

Kellert, S. R. *From kinship to mastery: A study of American attitudes toward animals.* A Report to the U.S. Fish and Wildlife Service, Yale University, 1974.

Kellert, S. R. Perceptions of animals in American society. *Transactions of the North American Wildlife and Natural Resources Conference,* 1976, *41,* 533–545.

Kellert, S. R. Attitudes and characteristics of hunters and anti-hunters. *Transactions of the North American Wildlife and Natural Resources Conference,* 1978, *43,* 412–423.

Kellert, S. R., *Activities of the American public relating to animals.* Springfield, Va.: National Technical Information Service PB-80-194525, 1980. (a)

Kellert, S. R. Contemporary values of wildlife in American society. In W. W. Shaw & E. H. Zube (Eds.), *Wildlife values.* Fort Collins, Colo.: Center for Assessment of Noncommodity Natural Resource Values, Report No. 1, 1980, 31–61. (b)

Kellert, S. R. Public attitudes, knowledge and behaviors toward wildlife and natural habitats. *Transactions of the North American Wildlife and Natural Resources Conference,* 1980, *45,* 111–124. (c)

Kellert, S. R. *Public attitudes toward critical wildlife and natural habitat issues.* Springfield, Va.: National Technical Information Service PB-80-138332, 1980. (d)

Kellert, S. R. Birdwatchers score well in wildlife study. *Birdwatchers Digest,* 1981, *4,* 7–9.

Kellert, S. R., & Berry, J. K. *Knowledge, affection and basic attitudes toward animals in American society.* Springfield, Va.: National Technical Information Service PB-81-173106, 1980.

Kennedy, J. J. *A consumer analysis approach to recreational decisions: Deer hunters as a case study.* Unpublished doctoral dissertation, Virginia Polytechnical Institute, 1970.

Kennedy, J. J. Attitudes and behaviors of deer hunters in a Maryland forest. *Journal Wildlife Management,* 1974, *38,* 1–8.

King, R. T. The future of wildlife in forest use. *Transactions of the North American Wildlife Conference,* 12, 1947, 454–466.

Klingender, F. *Animals in art and thought.* Cambridge, Mass.: MIT Press, 1971.

Krutch, J. W. *The best nature writing of Joseph Wood Krutch.* New York: Pocket Books, 1970.

La Hart, D. E., & Tillis, C. R. Using wildlife to teach environmental values. *Journal of Environmental Education,* 1974, *6,* 43–48.

Langenau, E. E., Jr. *Human dimensions in the management of white-tailed deer: A review of concepts and literature.* Lansing, Mich.: Department of Natural Resources, Wildlife Division Report No. 2846, 1980.

Langenau, E. E., Jr., & Mellon-Coyle, P. M. *Michigan's young hunter.* Lansing, Mich.: Department of Natural Resources, Wildlife Division Report No. 2800, 1977.

Langenau, E. E., Moran, R. J., & Terry, J. R. Relationship between deer kill and ratings of the hunt. *Journal of Wildlife Management,* 1981, *45,* 956–964.

Leach, E. Anthropological aspects of language: Animal categories and verbal abuse. In E. H. Lenneberg (Ed.), *New directions in the study of language.* Cambridge, Mass.: MIT Press, 1964, pp. 23–63.

Leopold, A. *Sand County almanac.* New York: Oxford University Press, 1968.

Levi-Strauss, C. *The savage mind.* Chicago: University of Chicago Press, 1966.

Lopez, B. H. *Of wolves and men.* New York: Charles Scribner's Sons, 1978.

Madsen, J., & Kozicky, E. The Hunting Ethic. *Rod and Gun,* 1964, *66,* 12; 24.

Mitchell, R. *Public opinion on environmental issues.* Washington, D.C.: U.S. Government Printing Office, Pub. No. 329-221/6586, 1980.

More, T. A. Attitudes of Massachusetts hunters. *Transactions of the North American Wildlife and Natural Resources Conference,* 1973, *38,* 230–234.

More, T. A. *The formation of wildlife perceptions.* Paper presented at the Northeast Wildlife Conference, Boston, Mass., April 6–9, 1977.

Norris, K. S. Marine mammals and man. In H. P. Brokaw (Ed.), *Wildlife and America.* Washington, D.C.: Council on Environmental Quality, 1978, pp. 320–338.

Ortega Y Gassett, J. *Mediations on hunting.* New York: Charles Scribner's Sons, 1972.

Paulhus, D., & Dean, R. *Scaling the ethical acceptability of animal research in semantic space.* Paper presented at the meetings of the American Psychological Association, San Francisco, August 26–30, 1977.

Pomerantz, G. A. *Young people's attitudes toward wildlife.* Lansing, Mich.: Department of Natural Resources, Wildlife Division Report 2781, 1977.

Potter, D. R., Hendee, J. C., & Clarke, R. N. Hunting satisfaction: Game, guns or nature? *Transactions of the North American Wildlife and Natural Resources Conference, 1973, 38,* 220–229.

Potter, D. R., Sharpe, K. M., & Hendee, J. C. *Human behavior aspects of fish and wildlife conservation: An annotated bibliography.* Portland, Ore.: USDA Forest Service General Tech. Rep. PNW-4, 1973.

Rohlfing, A. H. Hunter conduct and public attitudes. *Transactions of the North American Wildlife and Natural Resources Conference, 1978, 43,* 404–411.

Schole, B. J., Glover, F. A., Sjorgren, D. D., & Decker, E. Colorado hunter behavior, attitudes and philosophies. *Transactions of the North American Wildlife and Natural Resources Conference, 1973, 38,* 242–248.

Shaw, D. L. *The hunting controversy: Attitudes and arguments.* Unpublished doctoral dissertation, Colorado State University, 1973.

Shaw, W. W. Meanings of wildlife for Americans: Contemporary attitudes and social trends. *Transactions of the North American Wildlife and Natural Resources Conference, 1974, 39,* 151–155.

Shaw, W. W. *Attitudes toward hunting: A study of some social and psychological determinants.* Lansing, Mich.: Department of Natural Resources, Wildlife Division Report No. 2740, 1975.

Shaw, W. W., Carpenter, E. H., Arthur, L. M., Gum, R. L., & Witter, D. J. The American disposition toward hunting in 1976. *Wildlife Society Bulletin, 1978, 6,* 33–35.

Shaw, W. W., Witter, D. J., King, D. A., & Richards, M. T. Nonhunting wildlife enthusiasts and wildlife management. *Transactions of the 58th Western Association Fish and Wildlife Agencies, 1978,* 255–263.

Shepard, P., Jr. *The tender carnivore and the sacred game.* New York: Charles Scribner's Sons, 1974.

Shepard, P., Jr. *Thinking animals.* New York: Viking Press, 1978.

Sokolow, J. E. S. *The role of animals in children's literature.* Unpublished manuscript, School of Forestry and Environmental Studies, Yale University, 1980.

Stankey, G. H., Lucas, R. C., & Ream, R. R. Relationships between hunting success and satisfaction. *Transactions of the North American Wildlife and Natural Resources Conference, 1973, 38,* 234–242.

Steinhoff, H. W. Analysis of major conceptual systems for understanding and measuring wildlife values. In W. W. Shaw & E. H. Zube (Eds.), *Wildlife values.* Fort Collins, Colo.: Center for Assessment of Noncommodity Natural Resource Values, Rocky Mountain Forest and Range Experiment Station, 1980, pp. 4–22.

Stuby, R. G., Carpenter, E. H., & Arthur, L. M. *Public attitudes toward coyote control.* Washington, D.C.: USDA Economic Statistics Cooperative Service, No. 54, 1979.

Wildlife Management Institute. *Current investments, projected needs and potential new sources of income for nongame fish and wildlife programs in the U.S.* Washington, D.C., 1975.

8

Social and Behavioral Aspects of the Carrying Capacity of Natural Environments

WILLIAM R. CATTON, JR.

THE MULTIDIMENSIONED ENVIRONMENT–USER RELATIONSHIP

"Yellowstone Campgrounds Full" in big letters on a huge plywood sign at the park entrance was the welcome encountered by many visitors arriving on summer afternoons in recent years at the world's oldest national park. In view of the apparent stress-mediating value of outdoor recreation in an "age of anxiety" (Driver, 1972, pp. 236–237), and in view of other functions of play behavior not specific to humans (Fagen, 1981), the predicament of these visitors is not unimportant. It typifies many situations that call for new forms of inquiry extending beyond conventional patterns of social-psychological research on effects of density and crowding. These new lines of investigation require clear comprehension of a concept not yet common in the vocabulary of traditional social-psychological research: *carrying capacity*.

The phrase "carrying capacity" represents something unusually

WILLIAM R. CATTON, JR. • Department of Sociology, Washington State University, Pullman, Washington 99164.

fundamental about the relationship between an environment and its users. Environments are finite; users and uses multiply and compete. Carrying capacity means the extent to which an environment can tolerate a given kind of use by a given type of user.[1] From overuse, environments lose usability. Inevitably, then, past and present overuse of an environment must alter future user opportunities and thus change future behavior.

To protect natural environments from damage, the National Park Service (NPS) has long had to restrict all camping in the parks to designated sites. Not just a resource–management agency, this government bureau had unavoidably become an organization striving to manage the behavior of its human clientele. Just as university libraries reduce book losses by the strategic placement of coin-operated photocopy machines, the Park Service has sought to reduce environmental damage by furnishing ample visitor facilities, such as campgrounds (see National Park Campgrounds, 1980). In Yellowstone, apart from backcountry locations where limited numbers of hikers bearing ranger-issued permits might camp, the NPS made available to automobile tourists a total of 2,235 campsites in 12 campgrounds ranging in size from Slough Creek (with 30 sites) to Bridge Bay (with 438).

However, the capacity of the national parks to provide their "incomparable benefit of enriching the mind and spirit" (Everhart, 1972, p. 39) was severely challenged by the tide of visitors (National Park Service, 1979; Stottlemeyer, 1975, pp. 359–361). Toward sunset, when 2,235 parties had already pitched their tents or parked their recreation vehicles for the night, stark redundancy heaped further discouragement on anyone arriving who might scan the park map portion of the big signboard at Yellowstone's entrances, hoping forlornly to find somewhere in the park a campground with a remaining vacancy. Below each of the dozen names on the map indicating the campground locations was a pair of hooks; from these hooks were hung, before the end of most summer afternoons, small plaques reiterating (12 separate times) the sad news: FULL.

---

[1]Carrying capacity is often defined as a *population* ceiling, but the concept is much more general. It can refer not only to an environment's limited rate of sustenance provision but also to its limited ability to absorb and recycle effluents, to accommodate recreational activities, and so on. Defining carrying capacity in terms of environmental tolerance of *use* also enables the concept to cover different types of users—from different species to different cultural types among the human species, different interest groups within a given human population, or different roles particular humans may perform—each entailing characteristic environmental impacts. Thus *biological carrying capacity* (as understood by range scientists) and *recreational carrying capacity* (as understood by park administrators) can be seen as equally legitimate special instances of the general concept.

Regulation of visitor use "on the basis of what an area can stand without serious damage" came to be seen (after decades of trying to have it otherwise) as "probably the only longterm solution" to the dilemma bestowed on the National Park Service by the legislation that created it (Haines, 1977, p. 386). The mission assigned in 1916 by the 64th Congress to this new bureau of the Interior Department was to "provide for the enjoyment" of the national parks "in such manner and by such means as will leave them unimpaired for the enjoyment of future generations" (Ise, 1961, p. 192). The full significance of these words was scarcely apparent to members of that legislative body, nor to the public, for years afterward. Implicit in this language of the National Parks Act, as hindsight reveals, was the ecological concept of carrying capacity, which subsequent accumulation of knowledge enables us to define as

1. the amount of use (of a given kind)
2. a particular environment can endure,
3. year after year,
4. without degradation of its suitability for that use.

As is suggested by breaking this definition into phrases, carrying capacity is a multidimensional relation (between environments and users). Corresponding to four of the definition's phrases, we can speak of: (1) the per capita impact dimension, (2) the environmental deficiency dimension, (3) the time dimension, and (4) the degradation dimension. Each part of the complex relationship will be carefully examined in later sections of this paper, and the common tendency (in various disciplines) to overlook several of these dimensions will become evident. As we shall also see, familiarity with *all* of the dimensions of carrying capacity can illuminate much more than the disappointments of vacationers; in the 1980s the same multidimensioned concept also reveals fundamental aspects of the increasingly desperate predicament facing large portions of the human race living on an overloaded planet. In places like sub-Saharan Africa, for example, "the earth's capacity to support life is being seriously damaged" already—by the efforts of present populations just to survive. There is worse to come, but even now the *consequences of exceeding carrying capacity* can be seen:

> People who have no other choice for getting their living plant crops on poor soils that will soon wash away, graze their stock on land that is turning to desert from overuse, cut trees that are needed to stabilize soils and water supplies, burn dung needed to fertilize and condition agricultural soils. (Council on Environmental Quality and United States Department of State, 1981, p. xii)

That one ecological concept (carrying capacity) is applicable across such a vast range of human experience—from recreation to "desertification"—means that it has become possible for studies of leisure behavior in natural environments to clarify certain aspects of even our most serious global problems. What we can begin to see in either context is that nature exacts penalties when loads exceed carrying capacity. A clear grasp of this principle, so crucial to what carrying capacity means, will enable us to see that *Homo sapiens* is not exempt from fates that befall other species. Human attributes, in fact, can cause our species to behave in response to problems arising from surpassed carrying capacity in ways that aggravate such problems. Social organization can be weakened or broken by the effects of inadequate or malfunctioning life-support systems; social disorganization may, in turn, impede types of behavior needed for ecological damage control.

CARRYING CAPACITY EXCEEDED: TWO EXAMPLES

Before looking at ways in which these points may be illuminated by studies of recreational use of natural environments, the comparison of two *non*-recreation instances where loads grew to exceed carrying capacity will establish the core meaning of the carrying-capacity concept. It is essential to see that the concept refers not to the maximum load that may exist briefly in a given environment, but to the amount of use that can be exceeded only by impairing that environment's future suitability for accommodating that use. After these two examples are compared and their implications noted, distractions that impede social science attention to carrying-capacity issues will be briefly considered. The origins and early development of the concept carrying capacity in the fields of ecology and range management will be reviewed next, after which its special applications in the realm of wildland recreation will be examined and its generalizability explored.

Easter Island

The first of our two instances occurred on a 116-square-kilometer volcanic triangle with a mild temperate-subtropical climate, lying 3,700 kilometers west of the Chilean coast. This area is so remote from other human settlement and so obviously finite that it renders unusually visible the limits that an environment's carrying capacity has for a particular kind of life. Today, with a jet airstrip, tourist hotel facilities, electricity, and piped water, Easter Island serves as a stepping stone in travel across the southern Pacific. But until discovered by a Dutch ship (on Easter Sunday) in 1722, it was unknown except to the descendants of perhaps no more than a few Polynesian refugees who had chanced upon this colonizable speck of land nearly 20 centuries ago.

For some 16 centuries, natural increase by these Polynesian inhabitants required them to exploit increasingly the resources of the island. As the human load increased, protective bush had to be cleared to put even marginal land under cultivation. Human society came to dominate the once-natural environment as effectively as it does in any modern nation (Mulloy, 1974). But even in their originally well-endowed habitat, and even with their remarkable culture, the people of Easter Island were subject to carrying-capacity limits, and *crash* was the sequel of exuberant growth. In the process, the enormous and distinctive statues these islanders had carved and erected were maliciously toppled.

Behavior based on religious concepts that the settlers shared with other Polynesian peoples had been channeled by the particular geological characteristics of this island into a pattern of enormous and obsessive building and sculpturing. Religious monument construction led the Easter Islanders to develop a surprisingly complex culture despite their isolation; it came to include a written language not shared by other Polynesians (and still undeciphered) and a class structure with sufficient coercive power to bring together large crews of laborers to accomplish spectacular public-works projects. An extensive network of roads was built, mainly for transporting huge stone statues from hilltop quarries to seaside altars. Dwellings, refuges, crematory platforms, and masonry-walled agricultural terraces to conserve limited soil were built.

The amount of labor represented by all these achievements had to be enormous. To support it, food had to be grown on the volcanic land or harvested from the adjacent sea. If some people were to specialize in religious construction, others had to specialize in food production. Social norms presumably existed that required the gardeners to support the sculptors and builders. But such norms were vulnerable. According to archaeological research (Mulloy, 1974, p. 25), much of the 116-square-kilometer area was wooded originally. But irrupting descendants of the settlers became so numerous that they eventually cut down even trees that needed to be left in place to stabilize soils and water supplies. The results interfered seriously with the continuation of the people's accustomed activities.

The fallibility of social organization under ecological pressure turned out to be a major manifestation of the constrictive effects of natural-resource depletion. The population crash that began around 1680 (as shown by radiocarbon dating and genealogical evidence) started with a devastating war between two distinct groups into which the islanders had become differentiated. After the war, in which one group virtually exterminated the other, human numbers continued declining due to persistently disrupted food-producing activities, mutual depradation, and disease—the last factor being aggravated later by European contact.

The maximum population before onset of the crash may have been about 12,000.[2] By 1722, less than two generations after the genocidal war, there were still an estimated 3,000 to 4,000 Easter Islanders; by 1877 only 111 remained (Mulloy, 1974, p. 31). Population decrease of this order of magnitude (99 percent) marks this as one of the human race's more tragic encounters with the penalties that nature exacts when loads surpass carrying capacity.

St. Matthew Island

To understand how and why this fate befell the human population of Easter Island, it is essential to note that it has many counterparts among other kinds of creatures, from mammals to insects, from weeds to protozoa (Catton, 1978, 1980). A vivid mammalian example occurred in the north central Bering Sea on St. Matthew Island, an arctic tundra area of 331 square kilometers where in 1944 United States Coast Guardsmen abandoned a loran station. Before leaving the island, however, they imported and released 29 yearling reindeer (Klein, 1968). As in the human colonization of Easter Island, descendants of these fortunate animals were destined to suffer from their forebears' exuberant response to welcome opportunity. Conditions on St. Matthew were virtually ideal for the 29 colonizing reindeer. The herd increased at a pace that probably approached the maximum rate theoretically possible for *Rangifer tarandus*—numbering 1,350 in 1957 and reaching an estimated 6,000 in 1963.

---

[2]Captain Jacques Cousteau, the undersea explorer, during an hour-long television documentary, "Blind Prophets of Easter Island," drew from Mulloy tentative assent to an estimated maximum figure of "15,000 to 20,000." I can find no estimate in print that high. But suppose the overall precrash density had reached a level comparable to that of peasant Ireland just before crash hit that country (when potato blight eliminated the sustenance base relied upon by most of its people); simply multiplying the 1845 Irish population density figure by the area of Easter Island yields a figure of about 12,000. Moreover, had the number landing in the original canoes been no more than 50, and had they proceeded to increase no faster than one-fifth of the rate of increase Birdsell (1957) found among other island populations, their living descendants would have numbered 12,000 only 11 centuries later.

For land and climate comparable to St. Matthew Island, estimates of carrying capacity for this species have varied from about five to seven head per square kilometer (Klein, 1968, p. 364). So this 331-square-kilometer environment presumably could have supported up to 2,300 reindeer in perpetuity. Under a load no larger than 2,300, the vegetation required for sustaining the reindeer could have escaped being damaged beyond annual recovery. The 1963 population of 6,000 was at least 2.6 times the sustainable carrying capacity. There was thus an excess of at least 3,700 animals. The crash that followed (in February or March of 1964) did more, however, than simply reduce the herd by that many. The environment had been severely damaged by overuse, so the number of animals still living after the crash was far less than 2,300. The survivors were, in fact, fewer than three percent of even the lower (five per square kilometer) estimate of the island's original carrying capacity.

In winter, drifting snow made the vegetation of many parts of St. Matthew Island unavailable to the reindeer. Aerial observations showed the reindeer concentrated in winter on two windswept areas on one end of the island (Klein, 1968, p. 360). Winter range determines carrying capacity, for typically it can deteriorate from rising population pressure even when summer range may be still unimpaired. Skeletal material was collected after the population crash, and evidence of an absence of fat in the marrow of the animals indicated starvation as the cause of death (Klein, 1968, p. 354).

DIFFERENCES AND SIMILARITIES

From colonization, through irruption, to crash, the reindeer experience on St. Matthew Island took less time than the human experience on Easter Island, for a reindeer generation is much shorter than a human generation. Winter, not war, was the agent of calamity. In the two cases, however, the numbers colonizing, the numbers at maximum, and the numbers after crash were approximately comparable. Moreover, the severe environmental effects of overuse by both populations were comparably manifest.

The reindeer episode strengthens the view that the people on Easter Island came to grief not because of something peculiarly human—moral malfeasance or some quirk of history—but because of the pressure of their burgeoning numbers upon the carrying capacity of an inexorably finite environment. Neither the religion of these people, their written language, nor their impressive engineering achievements protected them. As Mulloy (1974, p. 29) pointed out, their lives and culturally prescribed activities were "dependent on the uninterrupted maintenance of what must have been a highly coordinated social mechanism. Even slight disruption might have been expected to be sharply felt by many people."

Among the reindeer, on the other hand, it was impossible for social differentiation and religious beliefs to induce half the herd to slaughter the other half, nor would there have been chronic fratricidal behavior among those surviving the initial episode of the crash process. Quantitatively, the reindeer crash was as severe as the human crash, but the suffering was not prolonged for generations; the die-off occurred quite suddenly (Klein, 1968, pp. 354–355). On Easter Island, there was eloquent evidence (e.g., tools abandoned in the quarries beside statues in various stages of incompletion) that the social breakdown put a comparably abrupt stop to public works (Mulloy, 1974, p. 30). But in this human instance, social chaos, demoralization, and iconoclastic destruction continued long after the war, and for a century and a half deaths exceeded births. For the nonhuman species that built no icons, crash involved no iconoclastic behavior.

The important differences, then, between these impressively similar encounters of two burgeoning populations with constraints from carrying capacity scarcely suggest any intrinsic advantage for the human as compared with the nonhuman species.

Penchant for Discounting Ecological Omens

Social science thought has been persistently skeptical about generalizing from animals to humans (see, e.g., Freedman, 1975, pp. 24–54). Social scientists have been keen to notice any inconsistencies in the animal studies and have insisted on a need "to do research on humans to understand the issue of crowding and population density" (Altman, 1978, p. 5). Preoccupation with human subjects, however, seems to obscure the ecological essence of any adequate idea of carrying capacity. More specifically, whether or not *crowding* is distinguished from *density* (Choi, Mirjafari, & Weaver, 1976; Rapoport, 1975; Stokols, 1978), studies of human density or crowding characteristically neglect the time dimension of carrying capacity. Even when attention to "long-term" crowding is called for (Zlutnick & Altman, 1972, p. 51), it is not the impact an overload may have *on the environment* (and thereby on future generations of users instead of present users) that the writers have in mind. Questions of the *sustainability* of use of an environment in a given manner and to a given extent *year after year* are simply not considered.

These ingredients of the carrying-capacity relationship have been overlooked not only by psychologists but also by sociologists. Some of the latter have neglected the effects of overload upon natural environments because they were interested in strain (physiological, psychological, and social) *among people,* arising from overstimulation due to density. Others have followed too simplistically the Durkheimian view, seeing high population density chiefly as a "prerequisite for the development of division of labor" (Winsborough, 1965, p. 121).

The ecological ingredients of the carrying-capacity relationship also eluded demographers. Concern for the relation between user load and environment was preempted among demographers more than half a century ago by the inadequately equivalent concept of "optimum population." The pattern was set by the eminent British student of population, Carr-Saunders (1922, p. 200), who wrote that in any given circumstances "if the population fails to reach [the optimum] number or if it exceeds it, the return per head will not be so large as it would be if it attained that number." Dublin (1926, p. 68) called the optimum "the most productive ratio between population and natural resources," but he almost achieved the concept of carrying capacity when he added that the economic desideratum was attainment of "the largest, permanently practicable, per-capita product." But the importance of that phrase *permanently practicable* was not widely grasped.

The Indian sociologist Mukerjee (1933, p. 688) sought to shift the concept of optimum population away from its economic emphasis (that number which can produce and consume the most goods); he defined optimum density as the density "which when overstepped leads to a decrease of the span of life." This again approached comprehension of carrying capacity, but Wolfe (1934) argued against it, insisting that because longevity was valuable only insofar as life was rich in content and most "welfare" variables tended to be highly correlated with material income, we should stay with the concept that had the virtue of simplicity—the economic optimum. And so it was done. Just after midcentury, a United Nations document defined an "economic optimum population" as "that size of population which, given the technical and economic conditions existing in a given country, allows maximum *per capita* output" (Population Division, 1953, p. 233). The four dimensions of carrying capacity were missing then, and were neglected again very recently when an economist repeatedly and forcefully argued that, despite much "false bad news," population growth has no long-run negative effect on standard of living (Simon, 1977, 1980).

Even the few most ecologically sensitive sociologists continued to be distracted by "optimum population" from focusing sharply on the central elements in the relation between load and environment specified by carrying capacity. In *Human Ecology,* his ground-breaking textbook,

Hawley (1950, p. 171) defined the optimum as "that population size which yields the best quality of life." For him it was also "the number without which necessary forms of behavior cannot be maintained." Unlike carrying capacity, then, "optimum population" was *not* the number above which required *environmental conditions* cannot be maintained.

Commenting on city size, Duncan (1957, p. 772) took note of various *kinds* of optima that would need somehow to be weighted, equilibrated, balanced, or compromised to yield "an unequivical figure for *the* optimum population." Impressionistic weighting systems or subjective value preferences were, he felt, inescapable.

CONCEPTUAL DEVELOPMENT

Although Price (1967, p. 27) seemed to be reaching out for the idea of carrying capacity by observing that industrial societies find it necessary to spend an increasing portion of income "for things that were formerly free or available at much lower proportionate costs, such things as clean air, pure water, and outdoor recreation facilities," the phrase he persisted in using was "optimum population." He cited a colleague's opinion that "for most purposes the United States has already exceeded its optimum population."

Accompanying that opinion's emergence was the growing acknowledgment that optimum population was not synonymous with carrying capacity (Freeman, 1970, p. 145; Singer, 1971, p. 400), but few seemed yet to recognize the major flaw in the demographer's concept—its emphasis on the idea that departures from optimum merely entailed reduced per capita wealth for the existing population. The notion of optimum population failed to make explicit "both the environmental dependence and the environmental impact" of a demographic load. Unlike carrying capacity, optimum population ignores the fact that overuse reduces *the environment's capability of continuing to provide* (Catton, 1978, p. 232).

HIGHLIGHTS OF THE IDEA'S EMERGENCE

Some people long ago must have begun to sense the vulnerability of their environment's ability to provide. Accordingly, the following paragraphs sketch a few highlights in the emergence of a consciousness of the problem of environmental overuse. Later, the explicit development of the four specific dimensions of the scientific concept of carrying capacity in the literature of range management and ecology, and its use in studies of human behavior, will be explored.

Because the bounty of even the most Eden-like ecosystem was finite, Neolithic peoples must have encountered hardships when land and biotic communities were overused. Soon after techniques of plant cultivation began to anchor human communities to particular locations, hunters would have diminished the supply of game in the vicinity of their villages (McNeill, 1963, pp. 3–28). This would have led to at least a vague awareness that the capacity of local animal populations to provide meat was limited. Reliance on hunting had to decline—as a trade-off for the advantages of horticulture. In time, however, some members of our species would have become sensitized to even the soil's limited carrying capacity, when local soil exhaustion compelled people to abandon an overworked tract of land to allow nature some years for restoring its fertility.

By the 6th century B.C., the danger of destroying a valuable natural resource by exploiting it too rapidly was metaphorically expressed in Aesop's fable about the cottager and his wife who stopped the welcome flow of (golden) eggs by unwisely killing the hen that laid them. What they sought was to obtain all at once the yet-to-be-ovulated wealth they supposed the hen already contained.

Many centuries later, the idea that environments have only finite capacities to support living things, as discussed by Malthus, became a premise for Darwin's solution of the riddle of evolution. The premise had practical meaning for a contemporary of Darwin, Samuel Butler, less well known now for his efforts in science than for his novels *Erewhon* and *The Way of All Flesh*. On his way to New Zealand to raise sheep when Darwin's *Origin of Species* came out, Butler (1923, p. 95) was aware by 1860 that "land laid down in English grass is supposed to carry about five or six sheep to the acre." Because he presumably knew that a run more heavily stocked than this would be degraded by overgrazing, he was able in an 1862 newspaper article to convey succinctly to non-scientists the Darwinian premise: "all plants and animals increase very rapidly, and . . . unless they were in some manner checked, the world would soon be overstocked" (1923, p. 190).

A similar practical concern about environmental overstocking was voiced in 1912 by an American president, Theodore Roosevelt. The sportsman-conservationist, responding to a thirty-year crusade to save game populations in Yellowstone National Park, wrote to the superintendent (see Haines, 1977, pp. 77, 82), pointing out that elk, for example, "are hardy and prolific" and could "double in numbers every four years" so that "where natural checks are removed" the elk would increase to the limit of the food supply, with the result that "either disease or starvation must come." It seemed to Roosevelt unwise to have killed the predators that controlled elk populations in the park, and he deplored well-meaning proposals to help get the enlarged herds through Yellowstone's winters by feeding them hay. Instead, he thought "hunting them should be permitted right up to the point of killing each year on an average what would amount to the whole increase." It turned out in later years that officials at Yellowstone did have to resort to herd reduction as a means both to protect elk from winter starvation and to protect park flora from overbrowsing.

The time was almost ripe for the crystallization of carrying capacity as a scientific concept. By 1922 a government publication on reindeer in Alaska defined grazing capacity as "the number of stock which range will support for a definite period of grazing without injury to the range" (quoted in Edwards & Fowle, 1955, p. 590). Similarly, but very recently, in reference to Yellowstone's bears, Craighead wrote that "Carrying capacity is the average number of grizzlies a given area can support year after year without deterioration or adverse changes in the environment" (1979, p. 139).

COMPONENTS OF CARRYING CAPACITY

What remained to be appreciated was the inadequacy of head-count definitions of the carrying capacity idea. The sheer number of organisms of a given kind was not the only dimension. Even range managers and ecologists had to develop their present understanding of carrying capacity bit by bit, and each of the several parts of the concept has had its own history.

The Per Capita Impact Dimension

Writing of African mammals, Eltringham (1979, p. 85) noted that six duiker (a small antelope species) would have much less environmental impact than six elephants and suggested thinking in terms of "the weight of living matter . . . per unit area." An environment, as Elton (1927/1966, p. 115) recognized in 1927, can support more small animals than big animals. It was an advance, therefore, to think of carrying capacity not as a permanently supportable number of organisms but as the maximum biomass (of a given kind) that could be continually supported. Fisheries biologists, for example, began to consider not *how many* fish an environment was capable of producing but *how much* fish (Edwards & Fowle, 1955, p. 591). In general, the amount of environmental pressure per capita differs according to the organism's size.

Even biomass was of limited use as an ecological metric, however, since animals differ in the ratio of their basic metabolic rate to their weight (Benedict, 1938). Because "a tonne of mice use up much more energy than a tonne of buffaloes," then in order "to estimate the carrying capacity of an area, it is necessary to take energy utilisation into consideration" (Eltringham, 1979, p. 85).

Later (pp. 294–295) we shall see how especially important these considerations become in understanding human carrying capacity, due to the exosomatic "metabolism" that varies so greatly among human populations endowed by different cultures with different technologies.

The Deficiency Dimension

Meanwhile, another aspect of carrying capacity was increasingly discerned. In 1927 it was pointed out that "an animal is limited by the things at which it is least efficient" (Elton, 1927/1966, p. 42). No animal population, consequently, ever fully utilizes all aspects of its environment; it is limited by some particular attribute of the environment least favorable to its activity. Just as the factor limiting one species will differ from what restricts another, so for any given species the most deficient (and hence limiting) aspect of one environment will differ from what is least propitious elsewhere. One important implication of this point was recognized by Leopold:

> If . . . all the kitchens were situated within one quarter of a given city, all the bedrooms in another quarter, all the restaurants and dining-rooms in a third, and all the parks and golf courses in the last quarter, the human population which it would be capable of supporting would be considerably reduced. The extent of the reduction would vary inversely to the mobility of the inhabitants. In fact, it is only the recent artificial extension of the human cruising radius by means of mechanical transportation that would allow such a city to be inhabited at all. (1933, p. 128)

It was likewise with game animals, said Leopold. Since an animal must usually be able to reach food, cover, and water each day, "The maximum population of any given piece of land depends, therefore, not only on its environmental types or composition, but also on the *interspersion* of those types in relation to the cruising radius of the species." In thinking of carrying capacity, it was clear to Leopold that:

> Every range is more or less out of balance, in that some particular aspect of food or cover is deficient, and thus prevents the range from supporting the population which *the other aspects would be capable of supporting*. Management consists in detecting that deficiency and building it up. This once done, some *other* aspect will be found to be out of balance, and in need of building up. (1933, p. 135)

Further, Leopold realized, deficiencies tend to be seasonal. Effective range management must offset the deficiencies of the least favorable season. Thus, for example, according to Errington (1934, p. 111), the carrying capacity of an environment for quail was the maximum number of such birds it could support through a winter.

The Time Dimension

For about two centuries, foresters have contributed to our understanding of carrying capacity by speaking of *sustained yield* forest management. To achieve sustained yields of merchantable timber, mere piecemeal efforts at forest regeneration do not suffice. Forest management has to follow two comprehensive procedures: each year's harvest has to be strictly limited to the amount of annual growth, and the age-structure and species composition of the forest must be arranged so that the annual growth can be constant (Heske, 1938, pp. 28–29). As these forestry practices influenced ecological ideas, eventually the term carrying capacity came to be understood in ecosystem management as the maximum sustained yield of a given biological resource (Bishop, Toth, Crawford, & Fullerton, 1973, p. 194).

The word *sustained* refers, of course, to the time dimension; carrying capacity is the load that can be supported not just briefly but year after year. Another phrase that has come into use to denote this dimension is *steady state*. One writer on natural-resource management expressed in ecosystem language the question put by Malthus, asking "At what level of human population is a steady state possible?" (Schultze, 1967, p. 155). Odum and Odum (1976) define carrying capacity for animals such as deer or quail as "the population . . . that the food chains of the ecosystem can support in a steady state" (p. 32).

However, this sustainability element has been foreign to the Western world view (Corbet, 1978, p. 3). More specifically, neglect of this element by sociologists has enabled their discipline to hold too sanguine a view of the effects of technology and organization and to overlook environmental degradation by overuse (Wisniewski, 1980). But even an entomologist (Berryman, 1981, pp. 44, 78) can forget to give the steady state idea consistent emphasis. At one point in his important book on *Population Systems,* he defines carrying capacity as "the total population that the resources in a given environment can support," omitting any explicit time reference like "indefinitely" or "on a long-term basis." Later, by referring to carrying capacity as "the equilibrium density," he *implicitly* embraces the steady state idea.

The Degradation Dimension

As a journal editor (Clay, 1971) has commented, "It took 75 years of overgrazing and soil erosion before range managers in the West began adding to their definition [of carrying capacity] the vital qualifying phrase '. . . without ruining the pasture.'" Eventually, however, the qualifying phrase was incorporated as part of the concept. Some examples: "the maximum number . . . that can be maintained in good flesh year after year on a grazing unit without injury to the range forage growing stock or to the basic soil resource" (Dasmann, 1945, p. 400); "the maximum stocking rate possible without inducing damage to vegetation or related resources" (Range Term Glossary Committee, 1974, p. 5); "the maximum number of animals that can be supported . . . without causing habitat deterioration" (Eltringham, 1979, pp. 88–89).

After the metaphor of Spaceship Earth became popular, two ecologists (Odum & Franz, 1977, p. 264) described natural ecological systems as "the Earth's life-support module" and defined carrying capacity in space-age terms as "the maximum population that can be sustained in a habitat without degradation of the life-support system."

The importance of this aspect was underscored by Garrett Hardin's mirroring of the definition when he insisted in an interview that "you can *deduce* the carrying capacity by looking at the environment. If the environment is becoming degraded, you can assume the species has exceeded carrying capacity" (Hayes, 1981, p. 66). When officials at Yellowstone in 1955 regretfully began killing elk to reduce the herds in the park to a size commensurate with winter range capacity, they were responding to an overload that was leading to "damage of a serious, perhaps even irreversible nature" (Haines, 1977, pp. 381–382).

FURTHER BASIC CONSIDERATIONS

Every species "uses" the environments upon which it depends in three basic ways: (1) as a *place* in which to carry on its activities, (2) as a *source* of supplies required for those activities, and (3) as a *repository* for the material products of those activities (e.g., effluents). For any of these three types of use, the amount that any finite environment can sustain indefintely has to be finite. If carrying capacity in biological literature usually implies source and repository limits, "recreational carrying capacity" may connote mainly place limits. Because environments are finite, however, these three basic ways species use them can interfere with each other as user numbers rise. There may indeed be "different kinds" of carrying capacity, but they are not unrelated to each other. Likewise, for any of the three use types, the demands of one user species may, within a finite environment, interfere with the demands of another species.

Of course, the capacity of physical environments to sustain a load of a given type is not fixed, but certain considerations are fundamental if we are to avoid misconstruing this lack of fixity. Some human activities can enlarge or reduce an environment's capacity for those or other activities (Catton, 1980, pp. 17–33). We live on a planet that we have repeatedly "filled" with human users and uses, but time and again human ingenuity and circumstances (e.g., development of horticulture, retreat of ice sheets, discovery of a second hemisphere) have enabled people to devise new ways of using the planet or have made additional parts of it usable, thus enlarging its carrying capacity. Genetic selection of crop species, shifting styles of recreation, changing forms of human organization, shrewd methods of managing land or channeling human activities can and do enable intensity of use of a fixed environment to increase. But changed forms of use (and changes wrought in an environment by use of it) can also *diminish* the amount of use it can sustain. Accumulated historical achievements have led us to expect carrying capacity to increase as needed, and we have grown unmindful of both the fact that use may (at our peril) temporarily exceed capacity and that (by overuse) an environment's capacity can be reduced.

Although the range of our species has become global in its extent, some societies have more or less deliberately retained certain parts of the earth as wilderness. Some members of some societies visit these remnant natural environments in pursuit of unregimented opportunities to be uncrowded witnesses of nature's forces operating with minimal human redirection. When a natural environment in the United States is "managed as wilderness," a major aim (as mandated by the Wilderness Act of 1964) is to permit sustained yields of that sort of human experience. Such experiences depend on three conditions:

1. The naturalness of the environment
2. A very low level of development of facilities for users
3. Infrequent contact with other humans in that environment

All three conditions are vulnerable. If they are prerequisites for a "wilderness experience," then even the nonconsumptive forms of recreation conforming to the motto "Take only pictures, leave only footprints" can be engaged in excessively. The truest devotees can overuse an environment, thereby reducing its "productivity" of true "wilderness quality" experiences (Hendee, Stankey, & Lucas, 1978, pp. 179–180). The concept of carrying capacity thus applies even to "nonharvest" forms of leisure behavior. Let us never forget, though, that if people seeking enjoyment can overuse a wilderness, people seeking all manner of things can overuse a planet.

RECREATIONAL CARRYING CAPACITY

Just after World War II, apprehension that wildland environments could be subjected to more use pressure even from human recreational activity than they could withstand led a professor of forest recreation and game management to suggest a way of minimizing that pressure. His proposal envisioned interpretive programs in forest settings to teach minimal-impact techniques of outdoor living (J. V. K. Wagar, 1946). His concern was based on the implicit premise that natural environments have limited carrying capacities even for such "nonharvest" recreational activities as hiking, boating, and wildlife observation.

Not quite two decades later, his son (J. A. Wagar, 1964) worked out in detail much of the meaning of the term "carrying capacity" as applied to wildland recreation, offered a systematic array of management suggestions for maximizing the visitor load that an environment might "withstand while providing a sustained quality of recreation," and tested some techniques for predicting the durability of biotic communities under stress from recreational use. At about this time, the associate director of the Wilderness Society called attention to the need for "managing people in wilderness" in order to avoid the increasing threat of excessive or inappropriate use of these natural environments (Brandborg, 1963).

As we shall see, however, the concept of carrying capacity began to be distorted as social inquiry on the topic was undertaken. This will become apparent even when we look at an exemplary specimen of such research.

A decade ago, resource managers in the National Park Service were faced with the prospect that rapidly increasing recreational use of the Colorado River either soon would exceed or perhaps already had exceeded the capacity of the ecosystem in the bottom of the Grand Canyon to adjust to changes in the river resulting from completion of the Glen Canyon Dam upstream (Johnson, Carothers, Dolan, Hayden, & Howard, 1977, p. 13). Accordingly, a comprehensive Colorado River Research Program was begun, comprising some 30 contract studies to answer such questions as:

- How rapidly are the physical and biological resources of the riparian (streamside) zone adjusting to the new river regime?
- How is the increased visitation affecting the riparian and aquatic resources?
- And what are the sociological effects of different visitor use levels

and patterns on the nature and quality of the river running experience?

A two-year research project on the river-running experience was carried out by a team of sociologists from the University of Colorado. Not surprisingly, they interpreted their topic and their findings according to the premise that

> Crowding is a social-psychological phenomenon, and the effects of density are mediated by such other situational variables as definition of the activity, crowding norms associated with that activity, social and psychological aspects of the situation, and individual personality traits. (Shelby & Nielsen, 1976, p. 21)

To convey the plausibility of this premise, they noted how the density of people might be perceived as inappropriately small if only 500 spectators were seated in a football stadium where such "low" density could detract from enjoyment of the game. In contrast, 500 people in an area of several acres within the Grand Canyon would be perceived as an "overcrowded" situation and this high density would detract from enjoyment of the wilderness.

Although as recently as the early 1950s only 200 people had ever floated down the Colorado River through the Grand Canyon, by 1967 the trip was being made by 2,100 people per year. River running became a thriving business. In 1973 at least 21 commercial boating companies and private outfitters got into the act, and more than 15,000 people made the trip through the canyon (Johnson *et al.*, 1977, p. 14).

In 1975, with cooperation from both the staff of Grand Canyon National Park and the commercial boatmen, and enjoying excellent rapport with river passengers, the Colorado sociologists were able not only to have observers accompany a considerable sample of the groups running the river, taking notes and administering questionnaires; they were also actually able to manipulate departure schedules in order to arrange considerable variation in weekly river traffic density for experimental purposes (equivalent to season traffic totals ranging from 4,800 to 16,500 persons).

During that season there was an average of 26 trips per week down the river, involving an average of 3.4 encounters per day with another party on the river. There were also some encounters with other parties during stops at "attraction sites." On the river, an average of 39 minutes per day were spent in sight of another party, and an average of 72 other-party persons were seen per day. Comparing the arranged "low-use" condition with arranged "high use," there were 13 versus 32 trips per week, an average of 1.1 river contacts per day versus 4.7, some 13 minutes per day in sight of another party versus 50 minutes, and an average of 17 versus 100 other-party persons seen per day.

Even in the "low-use" condition, there were usually more encounters than the number specified as a preferred upper limit by a majority of respondents. Ninety percent also expressed a preference for spending their nights during the river trip at campsites "out of sight and hearing of others." Only about one-fourth of the respondents, however, said that they "would have enjoyed the trip more if there hadn't been so many boats going by" or felt that "the places we stopped . . . were often too crowded."

The volume of use had been increasing by 59 percent per year during the past decade, but 91 percent of the respondents in this study considered the canyon a wilderness. After the canyon experience, river passengers were asked how they rated their trip. There was a statistically significant but very small negative correlation between self-rated trip satisfaction and *perception* of crowding ($r = -.14$). Whether respondents *perceived* the canyon as crowded was unrelated, however, to overall use level, number of contacts per day with other parties, number of other people seen per day, and time in sight of other parties ($r \leq .05$ on each variable). Twenty-nine percent (of 984 respondents) rated their 1975 trip "perfect," and another 55 percent said that it was "excellent." Only five percent rated it less than "very good." Seventy-eight percent felt that the canyon was relatively unaffected by human presence in it.

Apart from the fact that upward-gazing visitors in the bottom of so vast a canyon would often be literally *over*looking whatever evidence of human impact there might be at river level, the research team offered two major explanations for the finding that user satisfaction was substantially uncorrelated with crowding (perceived or actual). One was that most river passengers were doing the trip for the first time, and therefore had no clearly established frame of reference for evaluating the degree of crowding they experienced (Nielsen, Shelby, & Haas, 1977). The second explanation consisted of a number of shortcomings that these sociologists recognized in the crowding model itself (Nielsen, 1976). Many other variables besides the particular crowding measures used in this study, they argued, could be expected to influence user satisfaction. User definitions of *wilderness* may have been softened to embrace not only zero-contact wilderness but also moderate-contact semiwilderness. Since the river passengers were self-selected and river running was voluntary behavior, potential users less tolerant of existing use densities may well have gone elsewhere (Nielsen & Endo, 1977; cf. Cheek & Burch, 1976, p. 175), and these Grand Canyon passengers' perceptions of their experience would tend to be in accord with their (self-fulfilling) expectations of "having a good time."

From these and other considerations, the researchers concluded that "Any carrying capacity, then, is based on values" (Shelby & Nielsen, 1976, p. 37). They encouraged park officials to make one value judgment rather than another, however, by suggesting that it was "reasonable to manage for the character of the experience" rather than "to attempt to manage for satisfaction." They also suggested a number of ways for avoiding "concentration of use" so as to minimize (for a given use level) the perception of crowding. But they were unable to specify for the Park Service what maximum use level would be acceptable.

In short, they did not determine the human carrying capacity of the canyon or the river. Moreover, they implied that it could not be determined. They did suggest, however, that it could be enhanced by clever management.

Sociologically, this was a well-planned and well-executed study; for park administrators, it provided useful management suggestions plus detailed knowledge of the characteristics, values, and experiences of a large sample of visitors who were overwhelmingly pleased with their river-running experience. The study was clearly worthwhile. But if, in the end, it did not ascertain the river's human carrying capacity, perhaps this was partly due to the fact that:

1. The research looked at visitors' effects upon each other and *not upon the natural environment.*
2. It made no attempt to measure *environmental* deficiencies.
3. It did not investigate visitor-caused degradation *of the natural environment.*
4. It focused chiefly on possible effects of perceived crowding upon the visitors' satisfaction with their present trip, and only by indistinct implication was it at all concerned with the effects of present use-volume upon *future* cohorts of river passengers.

In other words, conceived as it was in accord with contemporary sociological and psychological ideas about the effects of density and crowding *upon people,* this study scarcely addressed any of the four dimensions of carrying capacity elucidated earlier in the chapter. This was not noticed because, in leisure research, carrying capacity tends to be understood as "the use level at which total satisfactions or benefits are maximized" (Greist, 1976).

To be true to the meaning of carrying capacity in ecology, so-called "recreational carrying capacity" should be defined as the maximum intensity of use an area can take continually "without inducing permanent change in the biotic environment" (Burden & Randerson, 1972, p. 440).

In contrast, environmental psychologists, for example, have focused their attention not upon costs to the environment from human load imposed on it but rather upon costs *to people* from adapting to particular environmental circumstances (e.g., Wohlwill, 1974, p. 141). A group of ecologically knowledgeable authors employed by the United States Forest Service (Hendee *et al.*, 1978, p. 171), taking their cue from the management goals mandated by the Wilderness Act of 1964, have come closer to the mark by seeing "wilderness carrying capacity" as meaning those "use configurations [that are] consistent with long-term maintenance of opportunities for wilderness-dependent experiences."

In short, behavioral scientists studying wildland recreation have too often reverted to mistaking "optimum population" for carrying capacity (see, e.g., Fisher & Krutilla, 1972; cf. Bury, 1976, p. 57; Duncan, 1957, p. 772). The present writer, in fact, has to confess that when he served as a consultant to the sociological team doing the Grand Canyon river-contact study, his own understanding of carrying capacity was still too nascent to prevent just that error.

Recalling now what Hardin said about deducing from environmental degradation that carrying capacity has been exceeded, let us consider what else was happening within the Grand Canyon. Current recreational use levels *are* producing irreversible physical and biological changes (Johnson *et al.*, 1977). River beaches are used by float-trip passengers for camping, with 30 or 40 people per night camping on each of the more desirable sites during a five- or six-month season. Charcoal, human waste, and other debris become incorporated into the sedimentary deposits, producing a "sandbox" condition at the most heavily used places—with contaminants accumulating faster than the river can purge them. As a result, higher densities of harvester ants appear at the heavily used sites, together with increased populations of flies. The ants have a painful and toxic sting, and the flies can be a disease vector. Clearly, human recreational use of these river beaches is reducing their suitability for the continuation of such use. In other words, their recreational carrying capacity (at least on certain dimensions) has been exceeded—by actions that have incidentally *raised* their fly and ant carrying capacities.

For recreational purposes, driftwood is an important component of the beach ecosystem, but its rate of natural replenishment is less than its rate of consumption (e.g., in campfires). Careless burning of refuse at campsites has sometimes resulted in burnt vegetation. This diminishes at least temporarily the nesting and foraging opportunities for wildlife in places where visitors might otherwise have opportunities to observe native species.

At some of the "attraction sites" along the river, foot traffic has eroded some trails into trenches, sometimes as much as .75 to 1.25 meters deep. As visitors wander about, multiple trails are formed, and this tends to accelerate soil loss and cause marked changes in vegetation.

Thus the most important finding by the sociologists in the Grand Canyon may well have been *visitor nonrecognition* of the environmental impact of their own presence and activity. Evidence that use can exceed carrying capacity without user awareness is not unique to the Grand Canyon. In a study of a pair of state parks in Texas (Willard, 1971, p. 123), a campground in what visitors viewed as a "healthy" and shady forest was ecologically a desert because of the very absence of undergrowth that made camping easy. New growth was unavailable to replace trees that would die. Soil compaction from heavy recreational use had changed the moisture-retention qualities so that increased runoff was removing organic material.

Likewise, substantial visitor-induced change in the behavior of native animals can occur. This indicates that the recreational use of a natural environment has surpassed its carrying capacity. This has happened, for example, at Glacier National Park, where grizzly bears are a part of the natural ecosystem. Seeing them, or knowing they were there, has been part of the recreational value of park visits. In 1967, however, bears killed visitors for the first time since the park was established in 1910. With increased human visitation, and especially with an upsurge in backcountry use, the risk has since continued to rise. Not only did bear–human encounters increase, but bear behavior has changed. Maulings began to be inflicted not only by female grizzlies with cubs, as earlier, but also by adolescent or subadult grizzlies recently "turned loose by their mothers" and, in an ever less sufficient habitat, "apparently in search of a home range for themselves" when they ventured into developed areas such as campgrounds (Hanna, 1978, p. 136).

In Yellowstone, originally also a wildlife sanctuary as well as a destination for human recreational travel, the once commonly seen black bear has been subjected (along with the grizzly) to controls in the interest of visitor safety. Over the last decade, the chance that a tourist visiting the park will be able to see a bear has all but vanished. The park has been sadly described as "no longer functioning as a refuge to wildlife" (Craighead, 1979, pp. 207, 247). More accurately, Yellowstone has become a place where visitors must be content with seeing elk or bison instead of seeing bears.

It appears that the feasibility of two species as different as grizzlies and humans using the same habitat diminishes with any increase in the number or activity of either species. Insofar as their respective ways of using the environment are incompatible with each other, the environment's carrying capacity for either is limited by the abundance of the other. This is an important departure from the biologist's "competitive exclusion" principle. That principle says, in effect, that *the more similar* the demands of two competing populations, the less feasible their coexistence (Hardin, 1960). The departure merits further study.

A considerable literature on recreational carrying capacity has accumulated, some of it concerned specifically with this fact that an increase in any particular use diminishes a finite environment's suitability for any other incompatible use. Various writers have explored the way in which incompatible uses of an environment come into intensified competition with each other as the abundance of each use increases. There is, for example, the conflict between snowmobiling and cross-country skiing (Knopp & Tyger, 1973). More generally, there can be conflict between mechanized and nonmechanized recreation, as well as conflicts between small parties of backpackers and larger parties, or between hikers and horse riders (Lucas & Stankey, undated). Still more broadly, there is ecological antagonism between nonrecreational uses of an environment (such as mining or timber harvesting) and recreational uses (Brockman & Merriam, 1979, pp. 18–19). Some conflicts between alternative uses involve the problem of exosomatic metabolism mentioned earlier. Humans using elaborate technology tend to do more to the environments they use than unaugmented humans would.

If we compare a type of use that has less environmental impact versus a type that has greater environmental impact, the former commonly tends to be displaced by the latter, rather than vice versa. When the same environment has the potential for being used in a number of more or less incompatible ways, the user type least prone to defer to other types likely will obtain by default an exclusive claim on that environment. "To prevent all opportunities from being reduced to the lowest common denominator," says J. A. Wagar (1974, pp. 276; cf. 1964, p. 12), "and to prevent rare and unique opportunities from being converted to conditions that are already abundant [elsewhere], the obvious solution is to create an integrated and highly visible *system* of areas and zones." Wagar here suggests an application of a principle subtly similar to Leopold's (1933, p. 128) principle of "interspersion." More recreationists, with more varied interests, can be accommodated if some zoning scheme ensures a diversity of environmental opportunities rather than permitting every recreational environment to become adapted to serving just the most prevalent form of use.

A number of writers have sought mainly to prescribe methods for estimating, or management practices for maximizing, an environment's capacity to withstand recreational use (e.g., Barkham, 1975; Catton, 1979, pp. 110–115; Greist, 1976; Heberlein & Shelby, 1977; Hendee *et al.*, 1978; Jaakson, Buszynski, & Botting, 1976; Penz, 1975; Stankey, 1974; Stottlemeyer, 1975). User impressions of what constitutes overuse and whether an environment has in fact been overused have been studied and found to differ among different user categories (Echelberger, Deiss, & Morrison, 1974). Professionals, too, continue to work with various and sometimes contradictory criteria for what types or amounts of overuse constitute a surpassing of carrying capacity (Irland, 1979, p. 160). Possibly because of such lack of consensus, some researchers have apparently lost the courage of their previous convictions and have begun to doubt the wisdom of thinking about carrying capacity at all. For example, J. A. Wagar (1974, p. 275), arguing that a value choice rather than a technical assessment is involved in defining what consequences of a high use-level are "unacceptable," has ventured to suggest that terms like "use-limits" or "use–intensity–quality relationships" might be better than carrying capacity.

ANTHROPOLOGISTS AND CARRYING CAPACITY

No such loss of nerve seems to have beset the anthropologists, however, with their professional commitment to the study of peoples who live in smaller aggregates and maintain life by means of simpler technologies. Perhaps because of the nature of their subject matter, anthropologists seem to have been less tempted than other social scientists to imagine that humans are exempt from ecosystem constraints (Hardesty, 1980). Over the years, a number of anthropologists have seen environmental carrying capacity as an important determinant of human opportunity and activity (e.g., Ammerman, 1975; Birdsell, 1953; Shawcross, 1970; Thompson, 1949, 1970; Weiner, 1972; Zubrow, 1971). Being apparently less compulsively anthropocentric than other social scientists, anthropologists have retained an awareness of the interdependence of humans with other species of organisms. Thus, even the joint effect of human and nonhuman predation in keeping a prey population within the carrying capacity of its environment has been investigated (B. D. Smith, 1974). And some anthropologists have confidently ventured to devise quantitative indicators of human carrying capacity (e.g., Brush, 1975; Casteel, 1972).

As elsewhere, in the anthropological literature the carrying-capacity concept has been subject to unwitting distortion. Thus, for example, even though Bennett (1976, 1980) was clearly well acquainted with problems of environmental change resulting from use, he neglected to include explicit reference to either the time dimension or the environmental degradation dimension when he defined carrying capacity as "the maximum number . . . that can be supported at a given level of nutrition by the forage produced with a particular technique" (1980, p. 260). However, the environmental deficiency dimension, at least, has been plainly evident to anthropologists (e.g., Bennett, 1976; Birdsell, 1953; Hardesty, 1980; Shawcross, 1970; Thompson, 1949). Liebig's "law of the minimum" has been recognized as applicable to humans, so that load limits are known to be set "not by the mean conditions but by the extremes . . . not by the factors that are present in excess but by the essential factor that is present in minimal quantity" (P. E. L. Smith, 1972, p. 8).

For anthropology, with its focus on the study of cultural evolution, it has perhaps been easier than for other social sciences to recognize why carrying capacity needed to be taken into account. As Bayliss-Smith (1974, p. 259) has put it,

> If one can assess the maximum carrying capacity of a population's environment under a given system of resource management, then one can also define the limits beyond which the population could not grow *without cultural changes taking place*. (emphasis added)

As "the engine which sets in motion adaptive changes in a set of related technological and social variables" (P. E. L. Smith, 1972, p. 15), the ratio of load to carrying capacity has produced important results:

> More than any other animal species, man has developed a vast array of means to exploit his environment for survival. He has done so in niches ranging from the arctic tundra to tropical rain forests, from low-lying Pacific atolls to the high mountain valleys of the Andes. (Laughlin & Brady, 1978, p. 23)

In short, by means of culture, developed in response to the oft-recurrent stimulus of carrying-capacity deficits, the "range" of *Homo sapiens* has been extended to all parts of the earth.

FUTURE DIRECTIONS OF RESEARCH

Some of the pitfalls to be avoided and some of the lines that future inquiry needs to follow can be discerned by drawing some major inferences from the basic proposition implicit in the generalized carrying-capacity concept: For *any* use of any environment there is a use intensity that cannot be exceeded without reducing that environment's suitability for continuation of that use.

As the Grand Canyon study showed, even with effort and ingenuity it may not be possible to assign a precise number to the carrying capacity of a given environment for a given type of use and user. This hardly justifies supposing, however, that an environment's carrying capacity is infinite (or infinitely expandable); it never is. Nor is it really necessary to know the numerical value of an environment's carrying capacity. What matters is the investigation and understanding of patterned differences in the ways in which people are likely to behave—depending on whether they face the kind of conditions that prevail when there is a substantial carrying-capacity surplus awaiting use or the conditions that result when their environment's carrying capacity has been appreciably surpassed. This kind of difference, of course, is why the discovery of a "New World" awaiting European exploitation had monumental importance for reshaping human institutions and why, subsequently, the "closure of the frontier" was considered another profoundly fateful turning point in history (Webb, 1952).

In future research and analysis we must keep in mind all four dimensions of the carrying-capacity relationship between environments and their users. Further important inferences can be drawn regarding each of these dimensions, and these inferences will highlight some needed kinds of further inquiry.

Homo Colossus: The Per Capita Impact Dimension

First, consider what we noted previously: that mechanized forms of recreation, which have greater environmental impact than non-mechanized forms, can crowd out the latter. We must recognize that this is a special case of a major trend in human history—the displacement of peoples using less advanced technology by other peoples deriving competitive advantage from more advanced technology. What needs to be seen (and can be seen when we think in terms of carrying capacity) is that the apparent triumph of mechanization may be a Pyrrhic victory. High-technology life-styles will not be feasible for all the world's peoples—for the same reason that Africa can support fewer elephants than antelope. Here we confront the factor that makes inadequate a mere head-count definition of carrying capacity, and it becomes especially important in human application of the concept. For most other species, defining carrying capacity in head-count terms almost does suffice because the variation in metabolism (energy consumption) between one adult member of the population and another is not large, usually within a 2 to 1 ratio, rarely more than 3 to 1 (Benedict, 1938). We are thus not much misled by attributing unit value to each individual and defining carrying capacity for such species as "the maximum *population* that a given resource base can sustain indefinitely" (Wisniewski, 1980, p. 55, emphasis added).

For human beings, who augment their bodily apparatus with technological extensions and thereby enable themselves to do vastly more than could be done without such equipment, the variation in per capita energy consumption (food for the body plus fuel for that "exosomatic metabolism") is more than 1,000 to 1 between the most mechanized and least mechanized cultures (Lenski & Lenski, 1978, p. 260). It does not suffice just to count individuals as equal units; we must learn to consider the maximum permanently sustainable *load*, where load = population × per capita resource appetite. Had it been some genetic mutation that endowed a portion of our species with a resource hunger a thousand times greater than the normal rate of consumption by nonmutants, we would then easily see that the world would support fewer such *Homo colossus* than ordinary *Homo sapiens*. The mutation was not genetic but cultural, so it has been deemed an achievement instead of a disaster. Nevertheless, in view of the meaning of carrying capacity, a population can find itself more severely beset with problems of overload and intensified competition when its resource appetites are colossal than when they are modest. One important line of future study, therefore, should be devising measures of per capita environmental pressure (including per capita demand for a limiting resource) in order to give us an index of (variable) human "colossalness."

On the other hand, if industrial populations find they have overshot the planet's carrying capacity by the joint irruption of their numbers and their technology, they may have an option that was not available to the Easter Islanders. It will be an unwelcome option, but we should investigate factors that might increase or decrease resistance to "de-development"—scaling down the resource-hungry mechanized life-styles of the developed countries, a conceivable alternative form of "crash" that can postpone or mitigate real die-off.

TRADE AND AIR-CONDITIONING: THE DEFICIENCY DIMENSION

Until recently, most peoples (as studied by anthropologists) have lived in narrowly circumscribed areas and in intimate association with their biophysical environments. "The model of the closed ecosystem is very nearly approximated under such conditions" (Hawley, 1973, p. 1198). With further elaboration of culture and the rise of modern technology, however, a "thickening web of exchange relations . . . has spread across the world [and] created a social environment between each local population and the physical environment."

In the future it will be essential to recognize just what this network of exchange relations has done to change the scope of application of Liebig's law of the minimum. Local populations and life-styles need not, when trade is possible, be limited by local shortages of some necessary resource—if that resource can be supplied from another locality's surplus. The *composite carrying capacity* of several different environments combined by trade relations can thus exceed the sum of their separate carrying capacities (Catton, 1980, pp. 158–161), though the extent of the gain will still be limited (in accordance with Liebig's law) by whatever factor remains most deficient *in the composite environment.*

Expansion of carrying capacity by webs of trade can be studied as a human manifestation of what Leopold (1933, p. 128) called "interspersion," which he said was relative to the "cruising range" of the species in question. Our species has attained enormous mobility by technological means. The effectiveness of exchange webs in achieving the enlargement of composite carrying capacity depends on the feasibility of transporting resources from place of origin to place of use. When a transportation network that has been functioning for a while deteriorates or becomes unworkable, the consumer load that had in the meantime expanded to fill the increment of carrying capacity can be faced with loss of viability. Some human redundancy is therefore an expectable consequence of rising transportation costs in an age of fossil-fuel depletion. Careful studies of the way in which redundancy-induced stress can fracture the social web (as it did on Easter Island) will be needed, and it will be important to study feedback processes by which responses to the stress and social chaos may exacerbate the shrinkage of carrying capacity.

It is not enough, then, simply to search for the effects of overcrowding of finite environments through experiments based on the idea that density is just another "aversive stimulus" like an electric shock or a loud noise. The experimenter who reasons from a paradigm that omits concepts like carrying capacity and interspersion may unwittingly so reduce effective density among his laboratory subjects that he precludes any possibility of discovering high density's influence upon their behavior. In an effort "to investigate the effects of high density per se, and not the effect of other factors," Freedman, Klevansky, & Ehrlich (1971, p. 13) deliberately excluded possible influences from lack of air, physical discomfort, high temperature, odors, and so forth, by carefully air-conditioning even the smallest room into which they packed their task-performing subjects—not recognizing the air-conditioner as a device for enhancing environmental interspersion. It effectively rendered the dimensions of the room irrelevant, enlarging the real denominator of the density ratio by importing comfort for the subjects from an environment outside the walls between which they were seated. Because it was thus misinterpreted, the experiment did not actually show what it purported to show, that "density per se" has no effect on human task performance. It might therefore be worthwhile to repeat the experiment without air-conditioning and to remain ecologically sophisticated enough to desist from "explaining away" whatever impairment of task performance might result from the environmentally imposed discomfort.

Correction would also be advisable for the ecological myopia reflected in Esser's (1972, p. 17) curious misinterpretation of an experiment in which the air-conditioning relationship was reversed—with effluents instead of resources being imported. Water that had contained a large number of tadpoles was transferred to another aquarium in which there was a single tadpole, which reacted as if it were crowded (e.g., its growth was inhibited). From this result, Esser inferred not only that "the absolute amount of space available to the animal is of no importance" but more astoundingly that "crowding disrupts behavior only through its subjective experience" in the central nervous system. What Esser should have concluded was merely that the behavioral effects of *extrametabolites* given off by other organisms apparently can be observed apart from the physical presence of the organisms that produce them. Acid rain that falls on Canadian lakes is made no less harmful by the fact that it is formed partly from air pollution generated outside Canada (i.e., in the United States).

Although symbols and social definitions of the situation do indeed have mediating effects upon human responses to crowding, and these must not be neglected (Klausner, 1972), it is at least as important not to neglect the straightforwardly ecological causes of the responses. We must refrain from forcing ecologically important data into conceptual molds that distort their meaning. In future research it must be recognized that a space shortage is by no means the only deficiency that may limit an environment's carrying capacity. And unlike the devout New Yorker who scoffs at any thought of national or global overpopulation as long as there are places less densely built up than Manhattan, we must learn to see the dependence of modern life-styles on carrying capacities derived from vital but precarious (and often unseen) interactions between local environments and their hinterlands.

DIACHRONIC COMPETITION: THE TIME DIMENSION

Because the research team in the Grand Canyon worked from an idea of carrying capacity that did not clearly embrace the time dimension, river passengers were only asked to rate *their own* experience on a scale of satisfaction. It would have been unrealistic to have asked them to rate posterity's enjoyment of the river-running experience; yet they were not even asked to think about how the pleasures or frustrations of future visitors might be affected by the impact of the present users on the environment.

When we learn the real ecological nature of the carrying capacity aspect of the environment–user relationship, however, one startling fact becomes evident: as load approaches or surpasses carrying capacity, present users actually *compete* with future users. The National Parks Act embodied remarkable foresight and sensitivity to the possibility of such diachronic competition when it prescribed in 1916 that the enjoyment of these congressionally dedicated natural environments should be managed so that future generations would not be deprived of opportunities for equivalent enjoyment.

All industrial societies today, because they depend on the ravenous use of nonrenewable resources, are increasingly involved in diachronic competition. Present human gratification is being achieved at the cost of environmental changes that ensure future human deprivation. Explicit studies of diachronic competition are needed. These could range from studies of the motivations for and against abortion to studies of economic discount rates. There should also be studies of changing conceptions of justice. Opinions regarding the obligations that one generation may have toward another may be changing and should be specifically investigated. It may be found that for ecological reasons it is even harder to attain equity between living and unborn generations than between social classes living at one time. Clearly there is here an array of topics demanding, and beginning to receive, serious inquiry (e.g., Hubbard, 1978; Lippit & Hamada, 1977; Morrison, 1978)—whether or not we share the view of Heilbroner (1974, pp. 142–143) that "by choosing the present over the future" the people now living are likely to condemn to nonexistence portions of posterity "whose claim to life can be honored only by sacrificing present enjoyments."

AVOIDANCE OF OVERSTOCKING: THE DEGRADATION DIMENSION

"Choosing" to prosper by robbing posterity of a usable environment is, in effect, what both the Easter Islanders and the St. Matthew Island reindeer did. Similarly, when Yellowstone National Park became so manifestly overstocked with elk that its management one winter had to have 5,000 of them shot, this was a consequence of the fact that elk thriving temporarily (without control by their former predators) were, so to speak, "choosing" to proliferate without regard for their environment's carrying capacity, thereby "condemning" some of their posterity. An overloaded environment was losing its ability to nourish descendants of the animals that overgrazed it. Adequate predation would have prevented this. Various human parallels deserve to be studied, and conventional trepidation about pursuing "analogies" must be overcome. In particular, it would be useful to know how decisions are made that result in the avoidance of overstocking an environment and what factors tend to prevent similar decisions in regard to human overstocking of nations, continents, or the planet.

Some species of animals *prevent themselves* from becoming too numerous. Throughout the world, every animal species is either resource limited, predator limited, or self-limited. Predator-limited species *become* resource limited if insulated from predation (e.g., if their predators are destroyed). Resource-limited populations tend to overshoot carrying capacity, degrade their range, and crash. But in nature, self-regulation is very common, and one very common behavioral means of regulation is territoriality. Density-dependent patterns of defense of exclusive territorial claims serve as a mechanism of population homeostasis and thus function to prevent populations from exceeding carrying capacity (Wynne-Edwards, 1962, pp. 1–22). Animals simply competing directly for sustenance tend sooner or later to degrade their environment. When animals instead contest for exclusive claims to adequate sustenance-yielding territories, each successful claimant can forage in peace and reproduce freely. Unsuccessful contestants may starve or fail to leave progeny. If each territory claimed is large enough to provide sufficient sustenance for the claimant throughout the cycle of seasons without being overgrazed, the number of contest winners is held approximately steady by the constancy of the number of such territories into which the environment can be partitioned, and *the environment is protected from overuse.*

Unfortunately, studies of human "territorial" behavior have muddied the concept and have overlooked this ecological function of preventing environmental degradation. Among humans, claims to space are taken to be simply means of reducing opportunities for conflict, or devices for regulating social interaction (Brower, 1980). Once again, attention needs to be focused not only on how the behavior affects people, but also on how it affects their environments. What has been investigated is such matters as the utility of territories in regard to the "primary or secondary motivational states" of individuals or groups concerned with hunger, reproduction, child rearing, and maintenance of identity or integrity (Altman, 1970). Despite a tendency to preface studies of human territorial behavior with citations of classic animal studies, the conventional disclaimer about innate patterns being overshadowed in human life by social learning seems to abort any chance of considering the nature of the fundamental ecological challenge that requires a solution—

to which territoriality has been a common response among animals. *Some* human response to that challenge has become no less imperative.

Even a social psychologist who cites Wynne-Edwards can miss the point; thus, conceiving the right kinds of inquiry will not come easily. By construing animal territoriality as only a source of analogies for human behavior patterns, and by not looking to the animal studies for explanation, Edney (1976) can dismiss the density-regulation function as "questionable in humans" because humans frequently do not get their food from the territory they occupy. Instead of regarding territorial behavior as the phenomenon to be explained, we need to see that, among territorial animals, territoriality is a *means*. What needs to be explained for any population (animal or human) is how it can keep itself from surpassing carrying capacity. Studies ought to be deliberately designed to ascertain whether, when, or how aversion to present crowding may function to avert the kinds of overuse that diminish future carrying capacity.

Anthropologists tell us that hunter-gatherer societies often did gain real advantages by somehow maintaining their populations at numbers well below their environment's carrying capacity (Clinton, 1979; Freeman, 1970; Hayden, 1972). By contrast, modern societies like the United States seem to have lost either the power or the desire to keep loads below carrying capacity. These countries revere growth but may have "lower carrying capacities than do many less industrialized countries" (Maserang, 1976, p. 255) because they ravenously consume fossil fuels and mineral materials instead of relying on sustained yields of renewable resources. Recalling the statue-toppling action by Easter Islanders, newly won ecological sophistication ought to foster the application of an unorthodox framework to studies of vandalism and other deviant behavior—a framework that will highlight any iconoclastic themes. We may thereby discover indications that the incidence of such behavior is being stimulated by ecological pressures.

For *Homo colossus*, the day of reckoning implied by the concept of carrying capacity is nearer than most people have recognized. Studies of peoples who have already encountered the consequences of surpassed carrying capacity (e.g., the studies assembled by Laughlin & Brady, 1978) will be increasingly vital and should be multiplied and systematized with all deliberate urgency. The insights that emerge from such efforts will doubtless remind us of an idea anticipated in Jeremiah 2:7,20:

> And I brought you into a plentiful land
>   to enjoy its fruits and its good things.
> But when you came in you defiled my land,
>   and made my heritage an abomination. . . .
> For long ago you broke your yoke and burst your bonds

Acknowledgments

The author is grateful to Robert L. Wisniewski and John Wardwell for a number of very stimulating discussions of ideas pertinent to the topic of this paper.

REFERENCES

Altman, I. Territorial behavior in humans: An analysis of the concept. In L. A. Pastalan & D. H. Carson (Eds.), *Spatial behavior of older people*. Ann Arbor: The University of Michigan-Wayne State University Institute of Gerontology, 1970, pp. 1–24.

Altman, I. Crowding: Historical and contemporary trends in crowding research. In A. Baum & Y. M. Epstein (Eds.), *Human response to crowding*. Hillsdale, N.J.: Lawrence Erlbaum, 1978, pp. 3–29.

Ammerman, A. J. Late pleistocene population dynamics: An alternative view. *Human Ecology*, 1975, *3*, 219–233.

Barkham, J. P. Carrying capacity and ecological research. In R. Hey & T. Davies (Eds.), *Science, technology, and environmental management*. New York: Saxon House, 1975, pp. 9–16.

Bayliss-Smith, T. Constraints on population growth: The case of the Polynesian outlier atolls in the precontact period. *Human Ecology*, 1974, *2*, 259–295.

Benedict, F. G. *Vital energetics: A study in comparative basal metabolism*. Washington, D.C.: Carnegie Institution of Washington, 1938.

Bennett, J. W. *The ecological transition: Cultural anthropology and human adaptation*. New York: Pergamon Press, 1976.

Bennett, J. W. Human ecology as human behavior: A normative anthropology of resource use and abuse. In I. Altman, A. Rapoport, & J. F. Wohlwill (Eds.), *Human behavior and environment: Advances in theory and research* (Vol. 4), *Environment and culture*. New York: Plenum Press, 1980, pp. 243–277.

Berryman, A. A. *Population systems: A general introduction*. New York: Plenum Press, 1981.

Birdsell, J. B. Some environmental and cultural factors influencing the structuring of Australian Aboriginal populations. *American Naturalist*, 1953, *87*, 171–207.

Birdsell, J. B. Some population problems involving pleistocene man. *Cold Spring Harbor Symposium on Quantitative Biology*, 1957, *22*, 47–69.

Bishop, A. B., Toth, R., Crawford, A. B., & Fullerton, H. H. The concept of carrying capacity. In A. Neuschatz (Ed.), *Managing the Environment* (Socioeconomic environmental studies, U.S. Environmental Protection Agency). Washington, D.C.: U.S. Government Printing Office, 1973, pp. 193–202.

Brandborg, S. M. On the carrying capacity of wilderness. *The Living Wilderness*, 1963, *84*, 28–33.

Brockman, C. F., & Merriam, L. C., Jr. *Recreational use of wild lands* (3rd ed.). New York: McGraw-Hill, 1979.

Brower, S. N. Territory in urban settings. In I. Altman, A. Rapoport, & J. F. Wohlwill (Eds.), *Human behavior and environment: Advances in theory and research* (Vol. 4), *Environment and culture*. New York: Plenum Press, 1980, pp. 179–207.

Brush, S. B. The concept of carrying capacity for systems of shifting cultivation. *American Anthropologist*, 1975, *77*, 799–811.

Burden, R. F., & Randerson, P. F. Quantitative studies of the effects of human trampling on vegetation as an aid to the management of semi-natural areas. *Journal of Applied Ecology*, 1972, *9*, 439–457.

Bury, J. L. Recreation carrying capacity: Hypothesis or reality? *Parks and Recreation*, 1976, *11*, 22–25; 56–58.

Butler, S. *A first year in Canterbury settlement and other early essays*. (Vol. 1 of the Shrewsbury edition of the works of Samuel Butler.) London: Jonathan Cape, 1923.

Carr-Saunders, A. M. *The population problem: A study in human evolution*. Oxford: The Clarendon Press, 1922.

Casteel, R. W. Two static maximum population-density models for hunter-gatherers: A first approximation. *World Archaeology*, 1972, *4*, 19–40.

Catton, W. R., Jr. Carrying capacity, overshoot, and the quality of life. In J. M. Yinger & S. J. Cutler (Eds.), *Major social issues: A multidisciplinary view*. New York: Free Press, 1978, pp. 231–249.

Catton, W. R., Jr. The recreation visitor: Motivation, behavior, impact. In C. F. Brockman & L. C. Merriam, Jr., *Recreational use of wild lands* (3rd ed.). New York: McGraw-Hill, 1979, pp. 91–117.

Catton, W. R., Jr. *Overshoot: The ecological basis of revolutionary change*. Urbana: University of Illinois Press, 1980.

Cheek, N. H., Jr., & Burch, W. R., Jr. *The social organization of leisure in human society*. New York: Harper & Row, 1976.

Choi, S. C., Mirjafari, A., & Weaver, H. B. The concept of crowding: A critical review and proposal of an alternative approach. *Environment and Behavior*, 1976, *8*, 345–362.

Clay, G. Carrying capacity. *Landscape Architecture*, 1971, *61*, 117.

Clinton, R. L. Population dynamics and future prospects for development. In D. W. Orr & M. S. Soroos (Eds.), *The global predicament: Ecological perspectives on world order*. Chapel Hill: University of North Carolina Press, 1979, pp. 56–74.

Corbet, P. S. *Introductory remarks*. Paper presented in a session on population and resources at the Fourth Annual Conference of the New Zealand Demographic Society, Victoria University of Wellington, June 30, 1978.

Council on Environmental Quality, and United States Department of State. *Global future: Time to act* (Report to the president on global resources, environment and population). Washington, D.C.: U.S. Government Printing Office, 1981.

Craighead, F. C., Jr. *Track of the grizzly*. San Francisco: Sierra Club Books, 1979.

Dasmann, W. A method for estimating carrying capacity on range lands. *Journal of Forestry*, 1945, *43*, 400–402.

Driver, B. L. Potential contributions of psychology to recreation resource management. In J. F. Wohlwill & D. H. Carson (Eds.), *Environment and the social sciences: Perspectives and applications*. Washington, D.C.: American Psychological Association, 1972, pp. 233–244.

Dublin, L. I. *Population problems*. Boston: Houghton Mifflin, 1926.

Duncan, O. D. Optimum size of cities. In P. K. Hatt & A. J. Reiss (Eds.), *Cities and society: The revised reader in urban sociology*. Glencoe, Ill.: Free Press, 1957, pp. 759–772.

Echelberger, H. E., Deiss, D. H., & Morrison, D. A. Overuse of unique recreation areas: A look at the social problems. *Journal of Soil and Water Conservation*, 1974, *29*, 173–176.

Edney, J. J. Human territories: comment on functional properties. *Environment and Behavior*, 1976, *8*, 31–47.

Edwards, R. Y., & Fowle, C. D. The concept of carrying capacity. *Transactions of the North American Wildlife Conference*, 1955, *20*, 589–602.

Elton, C. *Animal ecology*. New York: October House, 1966 (First published, 1927.)

Eltringham, S. K. *The ecology and conservation of large African mammals*. London: Macmillan, 1979.

Errington, P. L. Vulnerability of Bob-White populations to predation. *Ecology*, 1934, *15*, 110–127.

Esser, A. H. A biosocial perspective on crowding. In J. F. Wohlwill & D. H. Carson (Eds.), *Environment and the social sciences: Perspectives and applications*. Washington, D.C.: American Psychological Association, 1972, pp. 15–28.

Everhart, W. C. *The national park service*. New York: Praeger, 1972.

Fagen, R. *Animal play behavior*. New York: Oxford University Press, 1981.

Fisher, A., & Krutilla, J. V. Determination of optimal capacity of resource-based recreation facilities. *Natural Resources Journal*, 1972, *12*, 417–444.

Freedman, J. L. *Crowding and behavior*. New York: Viking Press, 1975.

Freedman, J. L., Klevansky, S., & Ehrlich, P. R. The effect of crowding on human task performance. *Journal of Applied Social Psychology*, 1971, *1*, 7–25.

Freeman, M. M. R. Not by bread alone: Anthropological perspectives on optimum population. In L. R. Taylor (Ed.), *The optimum population for Britain*. New York: Academic Press, 1970, pp. 139–149.

Greist, D. A. The carrying capacity of public wild land recreation areas: Evaluation of alternative measures. *Journal of Leisure Research*, 1976, *8*, 123–128.

Hanna, W. L. *The grizzlies of Glacier*. Missoula, Mont.: Mountain Press, 1978.

Haines, A. L. *The Yellowstone story: A history of our first national park*. Yellowstone National Park, Wyo.: Yellowstone Library and Museum Association, 1977.

Hardesty, D. L. The ecological perspective in anthropology. *American Behavioral Scientist*, 1980, *24*, 107–124.

Hardin, G. The competitive exclusion principle. *Science*, 1960, *131*, 1292–1297.

Hawley, A. H. *Human ecology: A theory of community structure*. New York: Ronald Press, 1950.

Hawley, A. H. Ecology and population. *Science*, 1973, *179*, 1196–1201.

Hayden, B. Population control among hunter/gatherers. *World Archaeology*, 1972, *4*, 205–221.

Hayes, H. A conversation with Garrett Hardin. *The Atlantic Monthly*, 1981, *247*, 60–70.

Heberlein, T. A., & Shelby, B. Carrying capacity, values, and the satisfaction model: A reply to Greist. *Journal of Leisure Research*, 1977, *9*, 142–148.

Heilbroner, R. *An inquiry into the human prospect*. New York: Norton, 1974.

Hendee, J. C., Stankey, G. H., & Lucas, R. C. *Wilderness management*. (USDA Forest Service Miscellaneous publication No. 1365), Washington, D.C.: USDA Forest Service, 1978.

Heske, F. *German forestry*. New Haven: Yale University Press, 1938.

Hubbard, F. P. Justice, limits to growth, and an equilibrium state. *Philosophy and Public Affairs*, 1978, *7*, 326–345.

Irland, L. C. *Wilderness economics and policy*. Lexington, Mass.: Lexington Books/D. C. Heath, 1979.

Ise, J. *Our national park policy: A critical history*. Baltimore: Johns Hopkins University Press, 1961.

Jaakson, R., Buszynski, M. D., & Botting, D. Carrying capacity and lake recreation planning: A case study from north central Saskatchewan, Canada. *Town Planning Review*, 1976, *46*, 359–373.

Johnson, R. R., Carothers, S. W., Dolan, R., Hayden, B. P., & Howard, A. Man's impact on the Colorado River in the Grand Canyon. *National Parks and Conservation Magazine*, 1977, *51*, 13–16.

Klausner, S. Z. Some problems in the logic of current man–environment studies. In W. R. Burch, Jr., N. H. Cheek, Jr., & L. Taylor (Eds.), *Social behavior, natural resources, and the environment*. New York: Harper & Row, 1972, pp. 334–363.

Klein, D. R. The introduction, increase, and crash of reindeer on St. Matthew Island. *Journal of Wildlife Management*, 1968, *32*, 350–367.

Knopp, T. B., & Tyger, J. D. A study of conflict in recreational land use: Snowmobiling vs. ski-touring. *Journal of Leisure Research*, 1973, *5*, 6–17.

Laughlin, C. D., Jr., & Brady, I. A. Introduction: Diaphasis and change. In C. D. Laughlin, Jr., & I. A. Brady (Eds.), *Extinction and survival in human populations*. New York: Columbia University Press, 1978, pp. 1–48.

Lenski, G., & Lenski, J. *Human societies: An introduction to macrosociology* (3rd ed.). New York: McGraw-Hill, 1978.

Leopold, A. *Game management*. New York: Charles Scribner's Sons, 1933.

Lippit, V. D., & Hamada, K. Efficiency and equity in intergenerational distribution. In D. C. Pirages (Ed.), *The sustainable society: Implications for limited growth*. New York: Praeger, 1977, pp. 285–299.

Lucas, R. C., & Stankey, G. H. Social carrying capacity for backcountry recreation. In *Outdoor recreation research: Applying the results*. Papers from a workshop held by the USDA Forest Service at Marquette, Mich., June 19–21, 1973 (Forest Service Tech. Rep. NC-9). St. Paul, Minn.: USDA Forest Service, North Central Forest Experiment Station, undated, pp. 14–23.

Maserang, C. H. Factors affecting carrying capacities of nation-states. *Journal of Anthropological Research*, 1976, *32*, 255–275.

McNeill, W. H. *The rise of the west: A history of the human community*. Chicago: University of Chicago Press, 1963.

Morrison, D. E. Equity impacts of some major energy alternatives. In S. Warkov (Ed.), *Energy policy in the United States: Social and behavioral dimensions*. New York: Praeger, 1978, pp. 164–193.

Mukerjee, R. The criterion of optimum population. *American Journal of Sociology*, 1933, *38*, 688–698.

Mulloy, W. Contemplate the navel of the world. *Americas*, 1974, *26*, 25–33.

National Park Campgrounds—1980. *National Parks and Conservation Magazine*, 1980, *54*, 13–20.

National Park Service. *National Park Statistical Abstract*. Denver: Statistical Office, National Park Service, 1979.

Nielsen, J. M. Crowding models, stress, and wilderness. *Mass Emergencies*, 1976, *1*, 249–260.

Nielsen, J. M., & Endo, R. Where have all the purists gone? An empirical examination of the displacement hypothesis in wilderness recreation. *Western Sociological Review*, 1977, *8*, 61–75.

Nielsen, J. M., Shelby, B., & Haas, J. E. Sociological carrying capacity and the last settler syndrome. *Pacific Sociological Review*, 1977, *20*, 568–581.

Odum, E. P., & Franz, E. H. Whither the life-support system? In N. Polunin (Ed.), *Growth without ecodisasters*. London: Macmillan, 1977, pp. 263–274.

Odum, H. T., & Odum, E. C. *Energy basis for man and nature*. New York: McGraw-Hill, 1976.

Penz, A. J. Outdoor recreation areas: Capacity and the formulation of use policy. *Management Science*, 1975, *22*, 139–147.

Population Division, United Nations Department of Social Affairs. *The determination and consequences of population trends*. New York: United Nations, 1953.

Price, D. O. (Ed.). *The 99th hour: The population crisis in the United States.* Chapel Hill: University of North Carolina Press, 1967.

Range Term Glossary Committee. *A glossary of terms used in range management* (2nd ed.). Denver, Society for Range Management, 1974.

Rapoport, A. Toward a redefinition of density. *Environment and Behavior,* 1975, *7,* 133–158.

Schultz, A. M. The ecosystem as a conceptual tool in the management of natural resources. In S. V. Ciriacy-Wantrup & J. J. Parsons (Eds.), *Natural resources: Quality and quantity.* Berkeley: University of California Press, 1967, pp. 139–161.

Shawcross, W. Ethnographic economics and the study of population in prehistoric New Zealand: Viewed through archaeology. *Mankind,* 1970, *7,* 279–291.

Shelby, B., & Nielsen, J. M. *Use levels and crowding in the Grand Canyon* (River Contact Study Final Report, Part 3). Report to the Superintendent of the Grand Canyon National Park, 1976. (Contract #CX821040104)

Simon, J. L. *The economics of population growth.* Princeton, N. J.: Princeton University Press, 1977.

Simon, J. L. Resources, population, environment: An oversupply of false bad news. *Science,* 1980, *208,* 1431 1437.

Singer, S. F. (Ed.). *Is there an optimum level of population?* New York: McGraw-Hill, 1971.

Smith, B. D. Predator–prey relationships in the southeastern Ozarks—A.D. 1300. *Human Ecology,* 1974, *2,* 31–43.

Smith, P. E. L. Changes in population pressure in archaeological explanation. *World Archaeology,* 1972, *4,* 5–18.

Stankey, G. H. Criteria for the determination of recreational carrying capacity in the Colorado River basin. In A. B. Crawford & D. F. Peterson (Eds.), *Environmental management in the Colorado River basin.* Logan: Utah State University Press, 1974, pp. 82–101.

Stokols, D. A typology of crowding experiences. In A. Baum & Y. M. Epstein (Eds.), *Human response to crowding.* Hillsdale, N.J.: Lawrence Erlbaum, 1978, pp. 219–255.

Stottlemeyer, R. Estimating carrying capacity for the national parks. In B. van der Smissen (Compiler), *Indicators of change in the recreation environment—A national research symposium* (Penn State HPER Series No. 6). University Park, Pa.: College of Health, Physical Education and Recreation, The Pennsylvania State University, 1975, pp. 359–372.

Thompson, L. The relation of men, animals and plants in an island community (Fiji). *American Anthropologist,* 1949, *51,* 253–267.

Thompson, L. A self-regulating system of human population control. *Transactions of the New York Academy of Sciences* (Series 2). 1970, *32,* 262–270.

Wagar, J. A. *The carrying capacity of wild lands for recreation* (Forest Science Monograph No. 7). Society of American Foresters, 1964.

Wagar, J. A. Recreational carrying capacity reconsidered. *Journal of Forestry,* 1974, *72,* 274–278.

Wagar, J. V. K. Services and facilities for forest recreationists. *Journal of Forestry,* 1946, *44,* 883–887.

Webb, W. P. *The great frontier.* Boston: Houghton Mifflin, 1952.

Weiner, J. S. Tropical ecology and population structure. In G. A. Harrison & A. J. Boyce (Eds.), *The structure of human populations.* Oxford, England: The Clarendon Press, 1972, pp. 393–410.

Willard, D. E. How many is too many? Detecting the evidence of over-use in state parks. *Landscape Architecture,* 1971, *61,* 118–123.

Winsborough, H. The social consequences of high population density. *Law and Contemporary Problems*, 1965, *30*, 120–126.

Wisniewski, R. L. Carrying capacity: Understanding our biological limitations. *Humboldt Journal of Social Relations*, 1980, *7*, 55–70.

Wohlwill, J. F. Human adaptation to levels of environmental stimulation. *Human Ecology*, 1974, *2*, 127–147.

Wolfe, A. B. On the criterion of optimum population. *American Journal of Sociology*, 1934, *39*, 585–599.

Wynne-Edwards, V. C. *Animal dispersion in relation to social behavior*. Edinburgh: Oliver & Boyd, 1962.

Zlutnick, S., & Altman, I. Crowding and human behavior. In J. F. Wohlwill & D. H. Carson (Eds.), *Environment and the social sciences: Perspectives and applications*. Washington, D.C.: American Psychological Association, 1972, pp. 44–58.

Zubrow, E. B. W. Carrying capacity and dynamic equilibrium in the prehistoric southwest. *American Antiquity*, 1971, *36*, 127–138.

9

Contributions of Behavioral Scientists to Recreation Resource Management

BEVERLY DRIVER and PERRY J. BROWN

INTRODUCTION

Visitation to publicly administered outdoor-recreation areas in the United States has increased across all activities at about five percent annually during the past several decades. The use of many backcountry areas and areas designated as wilderness has shown an average annual rate of increase of about 20 percent per year, and the use of wild rivers has increased even faster during the past decade (USDA Forest Service, 1980). Furthermore, tourism is an important industry, especially in those states with outstanding scenic beauty, varied outdoor settings, and rich cultural histories (Owen, 1980). Thus, tastes for outdoor opportunities appear to be well established; appreciation of natural areas seems to have become more widespread and intense since the environmental movement of the late 1960s; and opportunities to enjoy outdoor recreation are valued highly for their contribution to satisfaction with life in America (Driver, Rosenthal, & Peterson, 1978). Outdoor recreation is important socially—and is big business—in American society.

BEVERLY DRIVER • Rocky Mountain Forest and Range Experiment Station, USDA Forest Service, Fort Collins, Colorado 80526. PERRY J. BROWN • Department of Resource Recreation Management, School of Forestry, Oregon State University, Corvallis, Oregon 97331.

Undoubtedly, use of public outdoor-recreation areas will continue to increase in the near future. However, energy constraints and shifts toward an older age structure in the population will influence the types of use and perhaps concentrate use closer to centers of population (Marcin & Lime, 1977).

As public use of outdoor-recreation opportunities has increased, so have demands to produce timber, water, and minerals. At the same time, pressures have increased to allocate public resources for other purposes, such as education and national defense.

These growing demands for outdoor-recreation opportunities, and rapidly increasing competition between demands for scarce public resources, have intensified the problems involved in managing outdoor-recreation resources. Also, much recent environmental legislation has mandated that recreation (and related amenity) values be considered more fully in decisions involving allocation of public resources. This legislation has added to the challenges facing outdoor-recreation policymakers and managers because of the difficulty of defining and quantifying these less-tangible values and because of the lack of market price indices of the economic worth of the social benefits created.

This chapter looks at the responsibilities of outdoor-recreation policymakers and managers from the perspective of two behavioral scientists who have worked closely with outdoor-recreation practitioners in research and research application efforts over the past 10 years. In this chapter, we develop an applied perspective for defining recreation policy and management issues, share with other social and behavioral scientists our perceptions of those issues that social and behavioral research can help resolve, explain how that research is relevant, give some examples of past successes, and outline some needs for future research. Our purpose is to encourage more social and behavioral scientists to devote their attention to the issues raised.

This chapter focuses on policy and management problems related to outdoor recreation that are faced by federal agencies; but the problems faced by other public, or even private, outdoor-recreation agencies are similar. No attempt will be made to separate policy issues from management issues other than to say that policy issues relate to the establishment of decision guidelines, including budgetary guidelines, within an organization. Management decisions must be made within these guidelines and generally relate to the production of some type of good or service. Outdoor-recreation policy decisions, therefore, are made at all levels of a recreation agency, while management decisions are made only at those levels that actually "manipulate" the environment to provide recreation opportunities.

The words "outdoor recreation" will refer to leisure activities that take place in open green spaces away from one's home and backyard and that generally refer to the hinterland rather than to outdoor settings in urban areas. Also included are problems related to the recreational use of areas that make up the nation's wilderness-preservation system.

SKILLS NEEDED BY RECREATION POLICYMAKERS AND MANAGERS

All issues involving outdoor-recreation policy and management reflect one or more of the following five general responsibilities of outdoor-recreation policymakers and managers:

1. To determine how many scarce public resources (e.g., land, labor, and capital) will be allocated to outdoor-recreation programs, when, where, for whom, and at what price to the users
2. To provide appropriate, high-quality recreation opportunities once basic allocations have been made
3. To protect the biophysical and cultural-historical recreation resources from unacceptable change or damage
4. To reasonably protect the users from harm
5. To evaluate the effectiveness of the results of the above actions

These five general classes of responsibilities cover a diverse variety of more specific responsibilities that weave a complex web of interactions between outdoor-recreation demand and supply.

To meet their diverse responsibilities, outdoor-recreation policymakers and managers must be professional jacks-of-all-trades (Driver, 1975; Driver & Brown, 1978). They must understand the social-institutional settings from which recreation demand and agency decrees are derived as well as understand the historical evolution and current implications of these demands and mandates. They must know how to inventory and classify biophysical and cultural resources for their recreational potential and understand how recreational use will adversely affect those basic resources and alternative uses. They must be able to measure the economic and other values of the recreation goods and services provided, so that allocations are economically efficient, equitable, and responsive to the public. In addition, managers must have other skills, such as personnel administration, along with analytical skills for handling data. Finally, managers must have some skills in the behavioral sciences in order to understand recreation demand, consumption, satisfaction, and other aspects of recreation behavior. Such understanding helps managers to provide quality recreation opportunities, minimize depreciative behavior of users (such as littering), reduce conflicts between different user groups, and protect users from themselves and from potentially hazardous situations.

Many challenges and issues are inherent in the responsibilities and skill requirements of recreation policymakers and managers. In keeping with the theme of this volume, this chapter focuses on those issues that the social and behavioral sciences can help to resolve.

AN APPLIED PERSPECTIVE

To identify policy and management issues relevant to behavioral science, we have chosen to view management of outdoor-recreation areas as a production process that converts basic resources into human benefits. This viewpoint gives an applied perspective for discussing those problems and issues that the behavioral sciences can help to resolve.

A simplified variation of the outdoor-recreation production process is shown in Figure 1. This model is elaborated more fully by Driver and Rosenthal (1982). Basically, it indicates how relationships between the inputs and outputs of recreation programs can be displayed to indicate three related production processes: (1) production of recreation opportunities from basic resources, (2) production of recreation experiences from use of recreation opportunities, and (3) production of recreation benefits from recreation experiences or directly from opportunities. The first production process involves the efforts of managers, the second the efforts of managers and recreationists, and the third the efforts of managers, recreationists, and society at large.

Boxes 1, 2, and 3 of Figure 1 show the first production process. In that process, recreation opportunities (box 3) are produced from basic resources (box 1) through management actions (box 2). These recreation opportunities generally are viewed by managers as sites or settings that are provided for participation in specific types of recreation activity.

Boxes 3, 4 and 5 in Figure 1 show the second production process. From a behavioral perspective, the reason that a person uses (box 4) a specific recreation opportunity (box 3) is to realize desired types of satisfying experience (Driver & Brown, 1975; Driver & Tocher, 1970; Hendee, 1974). Therefore, by using recreation settings, recreationists produce various types of experiences (box 5) for themselves. For example, some recreationists attempt to experience affiliation with other people, others

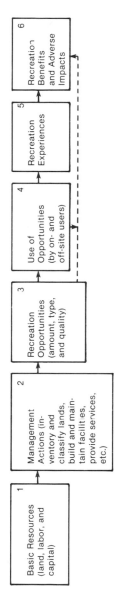

Figure 1. The recreation production processes.

to experience privacy or solitude, still others to experience challenges, and so forth (Driver, 1975, 1976).

It should be noted that the users, and not the managers, produce the experiences. Management actions contribute substantially to the production of "experience opportunities", however, through the management of settings to permit different levels of use (which enhances opportunities to experience affiliation or solitude), the provision of different levels and types of visitor information (learning), the control of noise levels (tranquility), the provision of challenging settings such as expert ski runs (skill testing and exhilaration), the protection of visual resources (scenic enjoyment), and in other ways.

Boxes 5 and 6 in Figure 1 show the third production process. Having recreation experiences (box 5) fits into the process of producing recreation benefits (box 6). Although little systematically documented information is available on these benefits, it seems reasonable to assume that benefits of some type are realized by the users of the opportunities provided. These benefits to users could include better physical and mental health, increased environmental awareness, and such improved social relations as enhanced family solidarity. Benefits also accrue to "off-site" users, who value the existence of the opportunities or resource protection but might not ever go on site. Beyond benefits to the user, recreation opportunities also produce benefits to society, including increased economic stability and growth. Therefore, benefits can arise directly from both the process of producing opportunities and the use of those opportunities.

In addition to benefits, adverse impacts (box 6) also accompany the production and use of recreation opportunities. These impacts include those that affect people and those that affect the environment.

The remainder of this chapter shows how the social and behavioral sciences can continue to help resolve the policy and managerial problems and issues associated with each of the three production processes.

POLICY AND MANAGEMENT ISSUES RELATED TO BEHAVIORAL RESEARCH

Behavioral scientists can help improve outdoor-recreation policy making and management in two fundamental ways. First, they can contribute to the basic body of knowledge about recreation and its many values. Such knowledge has its greatest payoffs in advancing the profession and in constructing a firmer foundation on which other research can build. This increased basic knowledge offers as many intellectual, thought-structuring, intrinsic benefits to decisionmakers as it does extrinsic benefits realized from the application of that knowledge. These intrinsic benefits are particularly important to members of an embryonic profession such as recreation.

Second, behavioral scientists can help to improve outdoor-recreation management by assisting practitioners in their use of knowledge that has not yet been applied or by carrying out applied research. Those efforts would be concerned primarily with resolving practical-applied problems, with the testing of theories being a secondary consideration. However, such research need not, and generally should not, be without conceptual-theoretical underpinnings.

Because of its applied orientation, this chapter concentrates on the second type of contribution by behavioral scientists. To maintain a perspective that is relevant to management, we have organized the subsections around the production processes identified by Figure 1. The scope of issues discussed and the amount of useful research already done prevents any attempt to be comprehensive in the references cited for a particular issue. The illustrative references selected, however, generally offer longer lists of citations on each subject.

PRODUCING AND MEASURING USE OF RECREATION OPPORTUNITIES

The conversion of basic resources (box 1 in Figure 1) to recreation opportunities (box 3) is a complex task that involves many issues that social and behavioral scientists have helped to resolve, but it is also a task that requires more investigation. The most significant issues are: establishing a clear definition of a recreation opportunity; quantifying the demand for recreation; determining the type, amount, and quality of opportunities to be provided; determining interactions between recreation and other uses (timber, minerals, range, water, etc.) under multiple-use management; and measuring use of the opportunities provided.

Defining Recreation Opportunities

Recreation opportunities are commonly accepted as the outputs, products, or goods and services produced through the management of recreation resources. Until recently, however, the concept of a recreation opportunity was not clearly defined; the idea persisted that it was an opportunity for people to engage in a recreation activity. Although this activity definition of a recreation opportunity was widely used, it was also widely viewed as inadequate. For example, the names of some activity opportunities (e.g., camping or driving for pleasure) are vague, and the activity definition of an opportunity provides little information about what goods or services are being produced. Furthermore, this definition induces the belief that recreation is a behavior rather than an end state, just as education and health are end states, not behaviors.

Recreation social and behavioral scientists (Driver, 1975; Driver & Brown, 1975; Driver & Tocher, 1970; Hendee, 1974, Wager, 1964) helped clarify and resolve the definitional issue by viewing recreation as an experience. That perspective led to changing the restricted, one-dimensional definition of the products (or outputs) of recreation programs from an opportunity to engage in an activity to the enlarged three-dimensional definition that a recreation opportunity is the opportunity to engage in an activity in a specific setting to realize desired experiences (Driver & Brown, 1978).

As mentioned, the *activity* dimension of a recreation opportunity is well established, and little elaboration is needed concerning users' desires for opportunities to hike, fish, hunt, picnic, etc. The *setting* dimension is also well understood and reflects users' preferences for different types of places to recreate, such as beginning or expert ski slopes with powder snow and few skiers. However, the concept of an *experiential* dimension of a recreation opportunity is more abstract. It realistically reflects the desires of users for opportunities to realize different types of satisfaction from recreation, such as the satisfaction received from solitude, social interaction, skill development, challenge, physical rest, exhilaration, risk taking, study of natural phenomena, or mental relaxation. As elaborated in subsequent sections of this chapter, the broader definition of a recreation opportunity, which uses all three dimensions, is based on research by social and behavioral scientists on the preferences of users for specific activity, setting, and experience opportunities.

Quantifying Demand for Recreation Opportunities

Before managers can effectively provide or supply recreation opportunities such as defined above, they need estimates of the demand for these opportunities—because demand, resource protection, and user protection are the driving forces of management. However, the concept of recreation demand in recreation policy and management decisions is not a clear one. Behavioral scientists continue to play an important role in clarifying this concept and in developing techniques to measure demand.

Confusion in the terminology of demand and the lack of adequate techniques for measuring the demand for outdoor recreation exist because:

1. The word *demand* is confusingly used to denote different things: economic demand, use of opportunities provided, and recreation preferences. To avoid confusion in this chapter, demand will refer to recreation preferences. The words *economic demand* will be used to refer only to a schedule that relates prices that users (actual or potential) are willing and able to pay for different quantities of recreation goods and services.

2. Although information on economic demand is necessary to determine the efficiency of outdoor-recreation allocation decisions, it has been quite difficult to determine that demand. For example, most outdoor-recreation opportunities are provided by public agencies and are not allocated and valued by competitive market prices. Also, there are demands for which it is difficult or impossible to assign an indisputable dollar measure of worth because of the "exclusion principle" (e.g., indivisibility of the products of recreation management into units that can be sold only to the user who is willing to pay). Also, there are other problems with economic indexing of demand for recreation because of confounding factors that influence users' perceptions of whether they should have to pay at all. These factors include: historical-cultural mores regarding outdoor-amenity resources; past traditions on pricing (i.e., high public subsidization); perceptions of rights to low-priced amenity resources; and philosophical interpretations about the extent to which humans should exploit, conserve, or preserve natural environments and about whether individuals or society at large should pay for conservation and preservation efforts.

3. Users with varying social, economic, demographic, and experiential characteristics have different demands for different opportunities. It has been difficult to appraise the different demands of these different types of users.

4. Although many types of opportunities are demanded, it has been difficult for managers to obtain needed information to determine which "packages" of opportunities should be provided for different types of users.

5. Demands of individuals and segments of society might not be the demands of society at large. Nor do demands of current generations necessarily reflect those of future users.

6. Demands exist for off-site as well as for on-site users. The value

to these off-site users reflects what have been called option, existence, and bequest demands (Greenley, Walsh, & Young, 1981; Krutilla, 1967; Tombaugh, 1971). It is quite difficult to identify and quantify each of these types of demand.

7. Finally, most demand analyses lack clear specification of what is demanded; this is caused, in part, by the wide variety of opportunities available. For example, a wide variety of activity opportunities (boating, fishing, and hunting of many types, alpine and cross-country skiing, picnicking, swimming, hiking, etc.) are demanded—and frequently from the same area. Also, the variety of setting attributes demanded is mind-boggling, given the great diversity of recreation activities, regional diversity (mountains, coasts, plains, etc.), and biophysical-historical, social, and managerial features involved. When demands for different types of satisfying experiences are added to the list of variables needed to specify demand for recreation opportunities, the problems of specifying what is demanded can be appreciated even more fully.

Despite these difficulties of quantifying the demand for recreation, considerable progress has been made recently by social and behavioral scientists. For example, recreation economists have made contributions by developing techniques, such as the travel-cost and contingent-valuation methods, for estimating the economic demand for publicly provided outdoor-recreation opportunities (Clawson & Knetsch, 1966; Dwyer, Kelley, & Bowes, 1977; National Academy of Sciences, 1975; U.S. Water Resources Council, 1979). Working with social and behavioral scientists, economists such as Miller, Prato, and Young (1977) and King (1980) also have begun to integrate measures of most-highly-desired recreation experiences with measures of users' economic willingness to pay for the types of opportunities that provide those experiences.

Despite the progress made in improving measures of economic demand, behavioral economists and other behavioral scientists can make additional contributions. The travel-cost method (whereby schedules of demand for sites or opportunities are derived from information on travel and time costs) and the contingent-valuation approach (which uses iterative bidding techniques employing survey research) can be refined as means of estimating user willingness to pay. Results of that research can help guide studies of the willingness of users to bear, through higher user fees, a larger share of the variable (i.e., operating and maintenance) costs of providing recreation opportunities. At least one study (USDI

Bureau of Outdoor Recreation, 1976) suggests that such willingness exists for most users and that higher user fees are supported by even larger numbers of nonparticipants.

Future research on economic demand and more responsive management decisions can also be enhanced by past and future studies of relationships between demand for and use of different types of activity opportunities. For example, Witt and Bishop (1970) have helped define how participation in one activity is related to participation in other activities, thus forming activity clusters; and Bryan (1979) has categorized fishing activities into discrete types of fishing. Results of these types of studies can be used in the specification of recreation products in demand analyses.

Managerially useful studies also have been made of the demands for different types of recreation settings. For example, Lucas (1964) identified what people considered to be the wilderness in the region of the Boundary Waters Canoe Area; Peterson (1974) identified desired and undesired attributes of the recreation setting in the same area. However, additional research could focus on demands for other setting attributes and on ways of managing those features to best meet those demands. The list of such setting attributes is lengthy and necessitates continued research on preferences: for visual-scenic resources (Daniel & Boster, 1976; Shafer, Hamilton, & Schmidt, 1969; Wellman & Buhyoff, 1980; Wohlwill, 1979); for different types of services, such as sanitation, safety, and informational-educational services; for limitations on the number of other users who will be encountered on-site (Lime, 1972; Lucas, 1964, 1980; Stankey, 1973); for different species of wildlife, both for consumptive uses, such as hunting and fishing, and nonconsumptive uses, such as viewing, photographing, and studying (Daniel, Zube, & Driver, 1979; Hautoluoma & Brown, 1978; Hendee & Schoenfeld, 1973; Kellert, 1978; Shaw & Zube, 1981); for vegetation and other natural characteristics of the recreation environment (Knopp, Ballman, & Merriam, 1979; Peterson, 1974); and for particular settings to engage in winter sport activities (Rosenthal, Driver, & Rauhauser, 1980).

Since 1970, several studies have been reported that focused on identifying and measuring the importance of specific experiences or kinds of satisfactions expected, desired, or realized by recreationists engaging in different activities in different environmental settings. For example, Potter, Hendee, and Clark (1973), More (1973), and Brown, Hautaluoma, and McPhail (1977) considered hunting; Driver and Knopf (1976) and Driver and Cooksey (1977) examined fishing; Haas, Driver, and Brown (1980a) and Brown and Haas (1980) studied wilderness backpacking; Haas, Driver, and Brown (1980b) investigated cross-country skiing, and

Schreyer and Nielson (1978) focused on white-water floaters. The list of such studies is growing yearly as attempts are being made to define more completely the experiential component of the demand for outdoor recreation.

Finally, work is needed also on other facets of demand. Little is known about the demands of the off-site and passive users (Ulrich & Addoms, 1981). These users might not ever go on site, but they value the existence of recreation and other areas, such as those designated for preservation. For certain types of areas (e.g., designated wildernesses), the number of off-site users far exceeds the number of users who actually visit those areas.

In summary, although recreation behavioral scientists, including behavioral economists, have already made useful contributions to the quantification of specific demands for recreation, the current state of the art for estimating the demand for outdoor recreation places severe limits on the realization of the normative ideal of meshing demand and supply. Because of these constraints on knowledge, most decisions involving allocation of public outdoor-recreation resources are still guided largely by "supply-side management," which relies mostly on feedback about past on-site use to regulate what is to be supplied in the future. Such a supply-oriented approach, although required because of limited information on the demand for recreation, can be quite inefficient; it is difficult to evaluate the effectiveness and responsiveness of such management and to compare in economic terms the social benefits obtained from recreation programs with those obtainable from alternative uses of the public funds. There will be little change in the situation until improved estimates of the demand for recreation, especially economic demand, are obtained.

Determining the Type, Amount, and Quality of Opportunities to Be Provided

Once the demand for recreation is quantified in economic and other terms, including the demands of off- and on-site users and the demands of users with different social, economic, demographic, and experiential characteristics, the policymaker and manager must decide what type, amount, and quality of opportunities should and can be provided given available resources. What *should* be provided is determined largely by the demand for recreation. What *can* be provided is determined by the managerial and natural resources available and by competing nonrecreation demands such as the need for timber or minerals.

Type of Opportunities. To relate recreation supply to demand, all the complexities and components of demand analysis discussed above must be integrated and greatly simplified (or reduced) into a taxonomy that is useful to managers by permitting definition of demand and supply in equivalent terms.

Meeting needs for a simple, but inclusive, taxonomy that integrates the terminologies of the demand for and supply of recreation opportunities is no easy task and involves two basic steps. First, relationships between the activity, setting, and experiential dimensions of recreation demand need to be established. Specifically, what types of satisfying experiences (under managerial influence) are most probable from specific types of settings and particular activities? Relating experiences and activities to settings is needed because managers inventory and manage settings to provide recreation opportunities. Once these relationships are established, the second task is to identify patterns in these relationships, so that they can be grouped and reduced into useful recreation opportunity categories, rather than to define a practically unlimited number of outdoor-recreation activity, setting, and experience opportunities. These categories must not overlap greatly, however, and each category must be supported logically and empirically.

The taxonomy recommended must be readily understandable without undue qualifications, and it should be intuitively acceptable to managers and users. Also, the opportunity categories must be generalizable, in order to assure similarity of management output across different administrative regions for budgetary aggregation and disaggregation purposes and to assure comparability of output measures across agencies. In addition, the recommended reduced number of categories of opportunities or outputs must be defined in such a way that managers can inventory natural resources, or landscapes, in terms of their potential to provide these categories of outputs and then take actions to produce those outputs. Finally, the measures of output defined must be subject to economic valuation and to other types of quantification (such as linear programming) required in multiple-use land management planning.

In sum, the burden on behavioral scientists doing applied studies of recreation does not start or end with quantifying user preferences for a large number of recreation activity, setting, and experience opportunities. Rather, these scientists must define the relationships between these dimensions of recreation demand and classify them in ways that meet the managerial needs specified.

Input from social and behavioral scientists into development and implementation of the Recreation Opportunity Spectrum (ROS) system for inventorying, planning, and managing outdoor-recreation resources has contributed greatly to meeting the above needs (Brown, Driver, & McConnell, 1978; Brown, Driver, Bruns, & McConnell, 1979; Clark &

Stankey, 1979; Driver & Brown, 1978; Stankey & Brown, 1981). In fact, the limited empirical support available for the ROS system (which has been adopted nationwide by the USDA Forest Service and the USDI Bureau of Land Management) came from behavioral research on the preferences of outdoor recreationists. Research can now begin to refine and extend that system and to evaluate the economic worth of the recreation opportunities defined by that system.

Amount of Opportunities. The amounts of opportunities that will be supplied are determined by: demand; the resources available, including funds appropriated for personnel and facilities; the social benefits created; the needs to protect the basic biophysical and cultural-historic resources and the users from damage or harm; and the responsibilities of a particular agency to supply different types of opportunity.

Behavioral scientists studying recreation can continue to help managers make decisions on the amount of opportunities to supply by improving the estimates of demand in ways discussed above, by developing inventory and management systems, such as the ROS, and by determining the recreation benefits and adverse impacts (which will be considered later in this chapter).

Decisions about supply are also related to the quality of opportunities that can be provided. This is demonstrated in the next section, which includes a discussion of area carrying capacity.

Quality of Opportunities. A third basic challenge associated with providing recreation opportunities involves developing management systems to determine the quality of the outputs provided.

Currently, managers use three types of systems to assess the quality of recreation opportunities. The first, and most pervasive, is based on the manager's subjective appraisals of how well the settings under management meet the desires and expectations of the users. These judgments of the "degree-of-user-satisfaction" by managers are important and needed; they should, however, be enhanced by systematic research by behavioral and social scientists on the preferences and satisfaction of users, since it has been found that the managers' perceptions of the users' preferences are not always accurate (e.g., Clark, Hendee, & Campbell, 1971a; Hendee & Harris, 1970; Lucas, 1964).

The second system in use focuses on quantifying the scenic or aesthetic attractiveness of the "visual resources" of rather large areas that are either proposed for or under management. Several techniques now in use (e.g., the visual resource management systems employed by the USDA Forest Service, 1974, and by the USDI Bureau of Land Mangement, 1980) have helped managers quantify and protect the physical attractiveness of natural resources under recreation and multiple-use management. Those systems provide general guidelines for environmental design and engineering in wildlands, so that necessary development and utilization of resources can be achieved with minimal adverse impact on the visual aspects of the area. Such guidelines exist for the development and maintenance of utility corridors and highways, for other physical developments, and for those practices of timber harvesting, such as clear cutting, that can be quite obtrusive visually when consideration is not given to the visual impacts of the shape, size, and location of the units cut.

Social and behavioral scientists have contributed to the development of many systems for assessing the visual quality of resources (Cherem & Driver, in press; Daniel & Boster, 1976; Litton, 1968; Schroeder & Daniel, 1981). These studies have also increased basic understanding of human perception and of what is and is not scenic and why (Daniel, Zube, & Driver, 1979; Elsner & Smardon, 1979; Peterson & Neumann, 1969; Shafer & Meitz, 1969; Shafer & Richards, 1974; Zube, Brush, & Fabos, 1975). All the problems are not solved, however, and research is needed to show managers how to make needed developments in ways that minimize undesirable visual impacts (Wohlwill, 1979).

The third system being used by managers to appraise the quality of the recreation opportunities provided somewhat overlaps the purposes of the techniques for assessing visual resources, but it focuses on the quality of specific recreation sites rather than on broad areas or landscapes. That system is concerned with those specific features or attributes of the recreation setting that influence the quality of the recreation opportunities either being provided or considered for provision. In that system, attention must be given to features of the basic biophysical and cultural-historic resources. Examples include the depth and quality of snow for winter sports activities, the amount, quality, and duration of flow of water for water-based activities, the type and condition of soils and vegetation, the types and number of wildlife species present, the natural hazards present, the slope aspect of the area, its topography, insects, cultural artifacts, and so on. Also, attributes of the social setting must be considered. These include the number and behavior (e.g., littering, destruction of recreation facilities, noise, etc.) of users, the things (e.g., pets, equipment, etc.) users bring to the site, the conflicts between users with different demands, and the social influences on the setting from nearby areas and land uses. Included too in these quality appraisals must be those attributes that define the results of management actions that affect quality. The list of such features is long and includes all the facilities and services provided (e.g., picnic tables, water, and sanitation facilities, including frequency of cleaning the toilets and litter pickup, electrical hookups, roads, hazard reduction safety programs, interpretative-informational programs, visitor centers, insect and dust control programs, and the provision of shops and vehicle service stations). Other managerial factors influencing the quality of the opportunities provided include the user fees charged and how they are administered, regulations on use and on users, and types of maintenance equipment (power saws, etc.) used, especially in wilderness areas.

Not only must managers consider those setting attributes that affect the quality of recreation opportunities, they must also develop clearly specified management standards to show what amount and type of management actions must be taken to assure the desired level of quality for each attribute under managerial control.

It takes little imagination to appreciate how difficult it is to develop and apply these level-of-service (or level-of-quality) standards, given the wide variety of setting attributes that must be considered and given that the quality of the opportunity provided will vary for the same attribute (such as user density, level of facility or basic resource development, level of safety-risk management, or amount of information provided) because of the different demands and values of different types of users.

Social and behavioral recreation researchers have worked on the definition of the qualitative aspects of many attributes of recreation settings (e.g., LaPage & Bevins, 1981; LaPage & Ragain, 1974; Lime, 1971; Lucas, 1970; Peterson, 1974; Shelby, 1980; Stankey, 1973; Willis Canavan, & Bond, 1975).

However, the above partial list of attributes and managerial needs indicate that even greater contributions are possible.

The role of behavioral scientists in quality appraisals is critical, for several reasons. Any determination of recreation quality is ultimately based on the users' perceptions of the psychological effects of the setting attribute under evaluation on their recreation satisfaction. In addition, much of the needed research must deal with the effects of the behavior of one type of user on another. Finally, economic measures are needed of the costs and economic worth of implementing level-of-service standards to assure different levels of quality. In fact, the job cannot be done without the assistance of social and behavioral researchers. But to be of value to managers, that research must give results they can use generally and not just with respect to isolated instances. Doing the research is only the first step toward the development of specific standards that must be applied widely to other similar setting conditions.

The concept of the carrying capacity of recreation areas represents a good example of the approach of behavioral scientists to research on the quality of recreation opportunities. That concept has been discussed widely in the literature (Brown, 1977; Brown, Driver, & Stankey, 1976; Frissell & Stankey, 1972; Lime & Stankey, 1971; Lucas & Schecter, 1977; Shelby, 1980; Stankey, 1973; Towler, 1977). Carrying capacity can be defined as the number of a particular type of users, having specified "packages" of experience preferences (e.g., for solitude, tranquility, etc., or for affiliation, exhilaration, etc.), that an area can accommodate under given biophysical and cultural resource conditions and specified management inputs, including location and types of trails, information programs, and other types of actions that regulate use. It is presumed that assurance is given to the manager that: high-quality experience opportunities will be provided, the basic biophysical and/or cultural-historic resources and recreation facilities will be protected from un-acceptable change or damage, and allocated levels of managerial re-sources (including budgets and personnel) will not be exceeded. From this definition, it can be seen that any particular recreation area does not have one carrying capacity but several capacities depending on the types of experience opportunities to be provided, the nature and condition of the basic resources being managed, and the operating resources avail-able to the managers. Therefore, level-of-use standards must be based on consideration of these three sets of variables, and each set involves complex subsets of interactions.

Behavioral research can further contribute to the definition of social-psychological dimensions of area carrying capacity. That research must identify and quantify the "experience packages" preferred by different types of users (Driver, 1976; Driver & Brown, 1975, 1978; Driver & Tocher, 1970; Hendee, 1974) and determine how the satisfaction of users is influenced by different setting attributes, especially attributes of the social setting. Of particular concern is the number and type of encoun-ters made with other users (e.g., Lime, 1972; Lucas, 1964; Shelby, 1980; Stankey, 1973). Such concerns must address whether the encounters are made at trailheads or at campsites and the size of parties encountered (Lucas, 1980). For instance, Stankey (1973) found that hikers in the wil-derness preferred to encounter few other parites, and, when they did encounter parties, they preferred to encounter parties of hikers rather than parties using horses.

To be most useful to managers, the results of research on carrying capacity must be generalizable and should not define conditions for only one area. This means making many replications of the same basic re-search design to determine predictable patterns of response for similar but not necessarily identical situations.

Along with the need to determine the aesthetic and other impacts of human-made developments and modifications of the natural environ-ment and the need to determine area carrying capacity, social and behavioral scientists are faced with another research challenge related to recreation quality. With acceptance by the USDA Forest Service and the USDI Bureau of Land Management of the ROS system for inventorying, planning, and managing outdoor-recreation resources, and with interest shown in that system by other public outdoor-recreation agencies, there is growing use of the concept of experience-based management of recreation settings (Driver & Rosenthal, 1982).

Essentially, the experience-based approach takes the view that managers cannot provide recreation experiences, but that they can manage settings to *increase the probability* that specified types of recreation experiences (such as solitude, tranquility, group interaction, nature study, risk taking, exploration, exercise, physical challenge, etc.) can be realized.

Such an approach is now possible, given our definition of an outdoor-recreation opportunity and the state of the art for psychometrically identifying and quantifying those types of satisfying experiences (Brown & Haas, 1980; Clark *et al.*, 1971a; Driver, 1975, 1976; Driver & Cooksey, 1980; Haas *et al.*, 1980; Hautaluoma & Brown, 1978) that are valued most highly within the package of specific experiences desired from a particular recreation activity and setting opportunity by a specified type of user.

The approach requires:

1. Defining the experience opportunity preferences of different types of users
2. Defining the setting attributes (including management actions) on which specific types of experiences are dependent
3. Developing level-of-service (and level-of-quality) standards necessary for determining the management inputs required for different types, amounts, and qualities of experience opportunity to be provided
4. Specifying management objectives directed toward providing different types of experience opportunities within different subareas of the area under management
5. Writing management prescriptions to increase the probability that the planned objectives of experience-based management can be met
6. Monitoring whether supply has been meshed with demand by providing the type, amount, and quality of opportunities demanded, given limited resources

Much more social and behavioral science input is needed to accomplish each of these steps. These needs are growing because an increasing number of outdoor-recreation planners and managers are accepting the experience-based concept of managing settings and many more are now being trained to think that way in colleges and universities.

Determining Interactions between Recreation and Other Multiple-Use Resources

The continued help of social and behavioral scientists is also needed to solve problems concerning relationships between inputs and outputs under conditions of multiple-use management. When the natural resources of an area are managed for timber, range, water, mineral, wildlife, or fishery outputs, the recreational values of the area can either be enhanced or reduced. Removal of overstory trees can stimulate vegetative reproduction that can enhance wildlife habitats. Creation of openings in expanses of forested landscapes can improve visual amenity values. Timber sale access roads can be used for access to recreation areas and to prevent the spread, or aid in the suppression, of wildfires. Also, reservoirs created for flood control, water supply, or hydroelectric power frequently offer opportunities for various types of recreation.

On the other hand, timber-management operations can adversely affect the quality of the recreation setting if the results of roads and cutting practices are visually obtrusive, if streams become silted, if too many wildlife den and food (mast) tress are removed, or if reduced vegetative screening of live streams raises water temperatures beyond those tolerable to certain species of fish, such as trout. The development of water-resource projects also frequently conflicts with, as well as supplements, recreation values, especially when opportunities for more highly valued types of recreational use of free-flowing streams in essentially undeveloped natural areas are lost because of impoundments.

Very little research has been undertaken into these joint production processes. We do know that some recreation uses conflict with other uses, such as motorboating and canoeing (Lucas, 1964) and snowmobiling and cross-country skiing (Rosenthal *et al.*, 1980) and that some uses are complementary, such as camping, and photography. Not many of these relationships have been studied, however. Therefore, social and behavioral scientists can continue to play a role in these types of appraisals. They also can provide additional useful information on the aesthetic impact of other uses and their associated developments, on how alterations and degradations of the environment (noise, air and water pollution, erosion, forest fires, etc.) created by other uses affect the quality of recreation opportunities provided on these and nearby areas, and on which mixes of multiple uses optimize net economic returns.

Managers need to be able to specify clearly the type, amount, and quality of the recreation opportunities made available. They also need to understand better how management of basic resources for other than recreation uses both adversely affects and enhances recreation values. Behavioral and social scientists continue to have an important role in resolving these issues.

Measuring Use of Opportunities

Information on use of recreation opportunities and on unused opportunities serves many purposes in policy and management decisions. Use information, along with measures of the economic value of the opportunities provided, is needed in budget and other resource-allocation decisions to compare the social worth of one type of public recreation program with another and to compare recreation with alternative uses. Analyses of trends in use over time are needed to help estimate future demands and use levels for different types of opportunities. Data on different types of users help managers and policymakers understand the recreation-related needs and preferences of their clients. Use data by subareas are needed to help make output quality determinations and to set management objectives, such as those related to determination of area carrying capacity or amount of a particular type of service (e.g., sanitation, water, information, safety, etc.) to provide. Information on use is also needed to determine the amount of unused opportunities, which can reflect inefficient management decisions.

Reasonably good data exist for the overall use of areas at which a user fee is charged. But even at these areas, the amount of use of different types of opportunities within the area is not measured very well. Poor use data generally exist for the remote-backcountry types of use, which represent opportunities with the fastest rates of growth. Statistics for different types of off-site use and for passive (e.g., seeing but not entering) use are practically nonexistent, even though the number of on-site users could not come close to justifying the creation and management of many areas. Furthermore, except for those obtained from household surveys, use statistics that describe use by the socioeconomic and demographic characteristics of the users are not generally available. These household survey statistics are problematic though, because they tend to combine use by all types of public agencies. Therefore, the use of opportunities provided by a particular agency generally cannot be distinguished. Lastly, most of the existing techniques for measuring use are not cost-effective, given the budget constraints facing most public recreation agencies, and once these data are collected, improved systems for processing and interpreting them are needed.

Social and behavioral scientists have been involved in developing counting and recording procedures for measuring use of developed recreation sites (e.g., Wagar & Thalheimer, 1969) and for backcountry recreation opportunities (e.g., James, 1971; Lucas, Schreuder, & James, 1971). They have completed baseline studies that describe the use of specific areas and enable the comparison of use across several areas (e.g., Lucas, 1980). For selected areas, these studies have provided good descriptions of use levels and of the activities and behaviors of recreationists. The techniques so far developed, however, are not generally applicable for measuring off-site use or use of large areas of desert or forest land with very dispersed forms of recreation.

Social and behavioral scientists can continue to help develop better techniques for measuring the on-site, passive, and off-site use of recreation and other amenity resources. Special attention is needed in identifying: which types of visitors use which types of opportunities; who are the off-site users and what is the magnitude of their use; how and how much are areas used by people who drive by, fly over, or otherwise passively use the area; what amount of unused opportunities exist; how is actual use (and idle capacity) distributed over time of day, day of the week, and season; can more cost-effective use-measurement techniques be developed; and how can the data be collected, stored, processed, and used more efficiently and effectively.

PRODUCING AND MEASURING RECREATION EXPERIENCES

Recreation experiences are the immediate consequences of using recreation opportunities. They are what people realize when participating in specific activities in specific recreation settings. Some recreation experiences are desirable and some are undesirable, in the same ways that other kinds of experiences are good and bad.

The production of opportunities for recreation experiences is done by managers as they maintain and improve recreation settings. The actual production of experiences is done by the recreationist, however. They are produced when a recreationist, having specific dispositions, knowledge, skills, and equipment uses recreation opportunities.

Understanding the user experience production process and the results of that process is important to managers. Experiences are what recreationists seek, and experience opportunities are what managers need to supply. This understanding can come from modeling the user experience-production process and testing to determine which variables in the process are important and how they interact. Social and behavioral scientists have made some contribution in this area, although there remains much work that could be done. Basically, the factors studied so far in defining the types of experiences that users desire and expect or realize can be classified as characteristics of individuals, characteristics of other people, characteristics of natural resources, characteristics of activities, and characteristics of management.

Some studies have identified socioeconomic characteristics of users (e.g., ORRRC, 1962), with a lesser number identifying personality characteristics (e.g., Driver & Knopf, 1977; Moss & Lamphear, 1969) and the processes of developing individual preferences and desires (Kelly, 1974). Although we know much about socioeconomic groupings of recreationists, we know quite a bit less about other antecedents of their recreation behavior. Fewer studies yet have looked at the characteristics of information processing, such as cognitive mapping (Knopf & Barnes, 1980), and at dimensions such as mood (More & Payne, 1978).

Many studies have reported on the effects of other people on recreation experiences. Some have dealt with the general socialization of leisure (e.g., Kelly, 1974), while others have dealt with persons outside one's recreation group (e.g., Lucas, 1964; Stankey, 1973). The in-group studies have often indicated that recreation behaviors are regulated to a considerable extent by other members of the recreation group. For instance, many people who prefer to do backpack camping frequently switch to camping near their auto when accompanied by young children. Studies of the effects of persons outside one's group have focused on the number and the behaviors of other users present. For example, it has been reported that wilderness backpackers object to encountering large numbers of other users groups on horseback, and loud and boisterous people (C. Harris, 1979; Lucas, 1980; Stankey, 1973).

Social and behavioral scientists also have made contributions to studying the effects of natural resources on the realization of recreation experiences. For instance, Peterson (1974) described the effect of many characteristics of the environment of the Boundary Waters Canoe Area Wilderness on the experiences of area users; Shafer and Mietz (1969) studied the effects of characteristics of scenery on recreation experiences. These kinds of studies have been important in development of the ROS system.

Several studies have been made of the perceived and actual effects of management on recreation experiences. For instance, Willis, Canavan, and Bond (1975) studied the effect of campsite pricing on choice of campsites; Hendee, Catton, Marlow, and Brockman (1968) and Lucas (1980) studied the effects of different wilderness-management actions on user satisfaction. Similar studies have been made for users in many other recreation activities, including camping, hiking, cross-country skiing, river running, fishing, hunting, off-road vehicling, and snowmobiling.

Although useful research has been done by recreation behavioral scientists in defining the types of experiences wanted and not wanted by outdoor recreationists, additional research could help identify the types of experiences desired by different types of users and how management systems can influence the realization of the experiences desired.

PRODUCING AND MEASURING RECREATION BENEFITS

Benefits are realized from the production and use of recreation opportunities and the realization of satisfying recreation experiences. Both recreation policymakers and managers need information about these benefits. Such information would help managers understand more completely the general nature and ultimate social ends and values of the systems they manage. It would aid managers in meeting the recreation needs of their users. It would also help advance their professionalism by filling gaps in the current professional body of knowledge about what recreation is, what it is not, and why it is what it is.

Although useful to recreation managers, information on the benefits of recreation would be of greater utility to policy analysts and policymakers responsible for deciding what piece of the public "national resource pie" will go to recreation or to alternative uses and which types of recreation opportunities will be emphasized. Without objective information on the social benefits of public outdoor-recreation programs, including valid estimates of the economic worth of these programs, there are no rational ways of knowing whether the benefits exceed the costs or of objectivity comparing expenditures for outdoor-recreation programs.

Five possible types of benefits from the production and use of recreation opportunities and the preservation of natural areas have been identified (Driver & Rosenthal, 1982). These are: overt (observable) beneficial changes in behavior (or improved functioning or performance) resulting from recreation participation; psychological benefits (or users' subjective appraisals of improved mental states); national, regional, and local economic development benefits; "spinoff" benefits (beyond the user) to society; and resource-preservation benefits. Except for the psychological (and some of the economic) benefits, little objective information is available about these benefits of outdoor-recreation opportunities.

The task of obtaining systematic and objective measures of the benefits of outdoor-recreation programs rests primarily with social and behavioral scientists. In fact, all the benefits, except for the ecological benefits of preserving resources, must be identified, specified, classified, and quantified by social and behavioral scientists. The job simply cannot be done without their help. Until more help is forthcoming, policymakers will have to continue to rely on informed intuition about the nature and scope of these benefits.

A few attempts have been made to determine beneficial changes in behavior caused by recreation participation. Included are studies of the role of recreation participation in relieving job-caused boredom (Grubb, 1975), mental patients' responses to outdoor-recreation experiences (Barcus & Bergeson, 1972), and the effects of outdoor-challenge programs on improved self-concept (Harris, 1975). However, these studies usually do not relate directly to recreation opportunities provided by public agencies, and most of them evaluate perceived changes in states of mind, or cognitions, rather than overt behavior. There have been few, if any, studies of beneficial changes in behavior caused by use of recreation opportunities. Therefore, only inferences can be made about that type of benefit by using results from studies of the psychological benefits, from self-concept studies, and possibly from research on the health-related benefits of persistent aerobic exercise. This void of hard conclusions about behavioral-change benefits can be explained in large part by the scientific complexity of quantifying these benefits, the need for costly longitudinal studies, and the lack of adequate resources to do the research.

Little research, too, has focused directly on the psychological benefits realized from outdoor recreation. However, very strong inferences can be made from the research described earlier on the types of satisfying recreation experiences desired by different types of users. For example, recreation satisfactions related to family togetherness, learning, exploring, being creative, resting physically and mentally, sharing skills with one's children, building other social friendships, being challenged, exercising, and escaping temporarily a wide variety of adverse conditions experienced in physical and social environments at work and home, logically suggest improved states of mind of the users realizing these types of satisfaction.

Techniques for measuring the national, regional, and local benefits of economic development derived from public outdoor-recreation projects are fairly well advanced; economists have developed most of these techniques (U.S. Water Resource Council, 1973). Studies of the desired economic impacts of tourism and tourist-related enterprises (Rajender, Harmston, & Blood, 1967) on local communities have also helped to define these economic benefits more comprehensively. Yet too little is still known about how public investments in programs for outdoor recreation and resource preservation facilitate and promote private recreation enterprises, which represent important industrial sectors in most states.

As with benefits derived from changes in behavior, little is known objectively about spinoff benefits (i.e., those realized beyond the user), even though it is widely believed that spinoff benefits (e.g., better citizens, more productive workers, closer families) result from the use of public outdoor-recreation opportunities. Despite these pervasive beliefs and the large public subsidies for financing outdoor-recreation programs (subsidies justified in large part because of these beliefs), research is needed to test the existence and magnitude of recreation benefits of this type. Social and behavioral scientists must take the lead in this research if needed answers are to be found.

Although there is also little objective documentation available on the benefits of preservation, it is possible to recognize that these benefits fall into several categories of positive impacts. The first category is that of benefits to human survival and well-being, including the mental satisfaction derived from knowing that actions have been taken to preserve germ plasm and to preserve opportunities for natural systems to function with limited, purposeful modification by human activity. The concept of right to live and recognition of the delicate interdependencies between human survival and continued functioning of natural ecosystems are involved here. These dimensions include any ecological benefits to human survival of the preservation of plants and animals and the psychological benefits associated with those human values and preferences.

The second category of possible benefits derived from preservation, which perhaps is a subcategory of the first, represents benefits realized by preserving areas for scientific study.

The third category is related to the first two. It can be defined as any benefits realized by preserving options for future choices. Included are the option, existence, and bequest demands defined by economists (Krutilla, 1967; Tombaugh, 1971), as well as the satisfaction that current generations may take in the knowledge that they have been good stewards of the resources of the earth. This class of benefits includes the sheer knowledge that one has the option temporarily to escape, if one desires, from a less-desirable life or work space into a natural environment. There is some indication that "just knowing the opportunity exists" has psychological value to some people even though the option has never been exercised (Ulrich & Addoms, 1981).

The fourth category of possible benefits derived from preservation relates to protecting unique historical and natural features (as contrasted with the germ plasm and gene pools covered under the first benefit category) from unacceptable levels of damage or change.

The fifth category is a catchall of those preservation benefits not covered in the other categories and includes the possible contribution of preservation efforts to a sense of national pride or social cohesion. For example, most Americans are proud to know that the whooping crane, the grizzly bear, Yellowstone and the Grand Canyon, the giant red-woods, Gettysburg Battlefield, the Liberty Bell, the Statute of Liberty, and many million acres of wilderness areas and wildlife preserves are being maintained in perpetuity as other events of everyday life rush by.

Except for the research of ecologists on the benefits of the preserva-tion of natural resources (Breuer, 1980; Soulé & Wilcox, 1980), a few economic studies of people's willingness to pay for some types of amenity resource preservation (Krutilla, 1970; Randall, 1979; Brookshire, 1979; Greenley et al., 1981) and a few studies of the psychological bene-fits of options for future choices (Ulrich & Adomms, 1981), the benefits of preservation represent a largely unexplored area scientifically, despite the great amount of public support for such preservation. For this rea-son, most of the benefits of the preservation of resources are defined intuitively by public policymakers based on the limited information available to them, especially that provided in the political process by public involvement of groups interested in preservation. That process should and will play the prominent role in the preservation of these resources. Social and behavioral scientists, however, can offer much help in defining more objectively the nature of the previously men-tioned types of benefits to be derived from preservation, particularly those benefits that are not ecological in nature. Thereby, the rationality of the allocation decisions can be enhanced.

REDUCING AND MEASURING ADVERSE IMPACTS

Although the production of recreation opportunities can lead to benefits for individuals and society, there are also costs associated with these production processes. Recreation behavioral scientists can con-tinue to help policymakers and managers understand how some of these costs arise and how to mitigate and, in some cases, prevent them.

Adverse impacts of providing recreation opportunities include all the adverse ecological consequences (forest fires, pollution, damage to vegetation and soils, etc.), depreciative behaviors (littering, poaching, destruction of equipment and facilities), negative impacts on local com-munities, and opportunity costs (e.g., benefits foregone from feasible alternative uses) associated with management of an area for recreation. Appraisals of these and other negative impacts are needed to determine the nature and magnitude of unwanted consequences and how they can be reduced or eliminated.

Useful research could focus on a number of issues. Studies are needed on the environmental and social costs of managing outdoor-recreation resources. Other studies are needed to augment past research on depreciative behavior (Alfano & Magill, 1976; Christensen & Clark, 1978; Clark, Hendee, & Campbell, 1971b). Still other research could emphasize uses that have a low impact, including the use of energy-efficient opportunities. Also, more needs to be known about how use can be distributed or redistributed in order to reduce adverse ecological impacts and to reduce congestion (Lloyd & Fischer, 1972). Additional information on the differential impacts of different types of use (horse, mechanical, or foot travel) would be helpful, especially for backcountry and wilderness areas where hardening the site (e.g., asphalt trail surfaces) to reduce adverse impacts may not be a feasible or permissable managerial option (e.g., Firssell, 1973; McQuaid-Cook, 1978; Weaver & Dale, 1978).

Behavioral research can also help determine the effectiveness of different types of on- and off-site educational programs in reducing adverse impacts of use (Krumpe, 1979). Similarly, opportunities exist to study the effectiveness of other, soft, nonauthoritative techniques of management, which are preferable to the heavy-handed regulation of people.

Needed too are additional economic studies of the costs of the adverse impacts, including the opportunity costs of the economic benefits foregone because of the allocation of public resources to recreation rather than to the alternative uses.

This chapter has attempted to show that considerable social and behavioral science research has already contributed to the resolution of many issues involved in recreation and wilderness resource policy and management. However, more applied research is needed before all the issues raised in this chapter will be resolved.

REFERENCES

Alfano, S. S., & Magill, A. W., (Eds.). *Vandalism and outdoor recreation: Symposium proceedings* (USDA Forest Service General Tech. Rep. PSW-17). Berkeley, Calif.: Pacific Southwest Forest and Range Experiment Station, 1976.

Barcus, C. F., & Bergeson, R. G. Survival training and mental health: A review. *Therapeutic Recreation Journal*, 1972, *6*, 3–7.

Breuer, G. *Air in danger: Ecological perspectives of the atmosphere*. Cambridge, England: Cambridge University Press, 1980. (rev. English ed.).

Brookshire, D. S. Issues in valuing visibility: An overview. In D. G. Fox, R. S. Loomis, & T. C. Green (Technical Coordinators), *Proceedings of the Workshop in Visibility Values*

(USDA Forest Service General Tech. Rep. WO-18). Washington, D.C.: USDA Forest Service, 1979, pp. 130–139.

Brown, P. J. Information needs for river recreation planning and management. *Proceedings of the River Recreation Management and Research Symposium* (USDA Forest Service General Tech. Rep. NC-28). St. Paul, Minn.: North Central Forest Experiment Station, 1977, pp. 193–201.

Brown, P. J., & Haas, G. E. Wilderness recreation experiences: The Rawah case. *Journal of Leisure Research*, 1980, *12*, 229–241.

Brown, P. J., Driver, B. L., & Stankey, G. H. Human behavioral science and recreation management. In *Proceedings, World Congress*. Oslo, Norway: International Union of Forestry Research Organizations World Congress, 1976, *16*, 53–63.

Brown, P. J., Hautaluoma, J. E., & McPhail, S. M. Colorado deer hunting experiences. *Transactions of the Forty-second North American Wildlife and Natural Resources Conference*. Washington, D.C.: Wildlife Management Institute, 1977, *42*, 216–225.

Brown, P. J., Driver, B. L., & McConnell, C. The opportunity spectrum concept and behavioral information in outdoor recreation resource supply inventories: Background and application. In G. H. Lund *et al.* (Technical Coordinators), *Integrated Inventories of Renewable Natural Resources: Proceedings of the Workshop* (USDA Forest Service General Tech. Rep. RM-55). Fort Collins, Colo.: Rocky Mountain Forest and Range Experiment Station, 1978, pp. 73–84.

Brown, P. J., Driver, B. L., Bruns, D. H., and McConnell, C. The outdoor recreation opportunity spectrum in wildland recreation planning: Development and application, Vol. 2. *Recreation planning and development: Proceedings of the First Annual National Conference*. New York: American Society of Civil Engineers, 1979.

Bryan, H. *Conflict in the great outdoors* (Sociological Studies No. 4). University, Ala.: Bureau of Public Administration, The University of Alabama, 1979.

Cherem, G., & Driver, B. L. *Visitor employed photography: A technique for measuring common perceptions of natural environments*. Fort Collins, Colo.: Rocky Mountain Forest and Range Experiment Station, in press.

Christensen, H. H., & Clark, R. N. Understanding and controlling vandalism and other rule violations in urban recreation areas. *Proceedings of the Urban Forestry Conference*. Syracuse, N.Y.: School of Forestry, State University of New York, 1978, pp. 63–84.

Clark, R. N., & Stankey, G. H. *The recreation opportunity spectrum: A framework for planning, management, and research* (USDA Forest Service General Tech. Rep. PNW-98). Portland, Ore.: Pacific Northwest Forest Experiment Station, 1979.

Clark, R., Hendee, J. C., & Campbell, F. Values, behavior, and conflict in modern camping culture. *Journal of Leisure Research*, 1971, *3*, 143–159. (a)

Clark, R. N., Hendee, J. C., & Campbell, F. C. *Depreciative behavior in forest campgrounds: An exploratory study* (USDA Forest Service Research Note PNW-16). Portland, Ore.: Pacific Northwest Forest Experiment Station, 1971. (b)

Clawson, M., & Knetsch, J. *Economics of outdoor recreation*. Baltimore, Md.: Johns Hopkins Press, 1966.

Daniel, T. C., & Boster, R. S. *Measuring landscape aesthetics: The scenic beauty estimation method* (USDA Forest Service Research Paper RM-167). Fort Collins, Colo.: Rocky Mountain Forest and Range Experiment Station, 1976.

Daniel, T. C., Zube, E. H., & Driver, B. L. (Technical Coordinators). *Assessing amenity resource values* (USDA Forest Service General Tech. Rep. RM-68). Fort Collins, Colo.: Rocky Mountain Forest and Range Experiment Station, 1979.

Driver, B. L. Quantification of outdoor recreationists' preferences. In B. Van der Smissen & J. Myers (Eds.), *Research: Camping and environmental education* (HPEP Series No. 11). University Park, Pa.: The Pennsylvania State University, 1975, pp. 165–187.

Driver, B. L. Toward a better understanding of the social benefits of outdoor recreation participation. *Proceedings of Southern States Recreation Research Applications Workshop* (USDA Forest Service General Tech. Rep. SE-9). Asheville, N.C.: Southeastern Forest Experiment Station, 1976, pp. 163–189.

Driver, B. L., & Brown, P. J. A social-psychological definition of recreation demand, with implications for recreation resource planning. *Appendix A, Assessing demand for outdoor recreation.* Washington, D.C.: National Academy of Sciences, 1975, pp. 63–88.

Driver, B. L., & Brown, P. J. The opportunity spectrum concept and behavioral information in outdoor recreation resource supply inventories: A rationale. In G. H. Lund *et al.* (Technical Coordinators), *Integrated inventories of renewable natural resources: Proceedings of the Workshop* (USDA Forest Service General Tech. Rep. RM-55). Fort Collins, Colo.: Rocky Mountain Forest and Range Experiment Station, 1978, pp. 24–31.

Driver, B. L., & Cooksey, R. W. Preferred psychological outcomes of recreational fishing. In R. A. Barnhart & T. D. Roelofs (Eds.), *Catch and release fishing as a mangement tool: A national sport fishing symposium.* Arcata, Calif.: Humboldt State University, 1977, pp. 27–40.

Driver, B. L., & Knopf, R. C. Temporary escape: One product of sport fisheries management. *Fisheries,* 1976, *1,* 21–29.

Driver, B. L., & Knopf, R. C. Personality, outdoor recreation, and expected consequences. *Environment and Behavior,* 1977, *9,* 169–193.

Driver, B. L., & Rosenthal, D. H. *Measuring and improving the effectiveness of public outdoor recreation programs.* Washington, D.C.: George Washington University Press, 1982.

Driver, B. L., & Tocher, S. R. Toward a behavioral interpretation of recreational engagements, with implications for planning. In B. L. Driver (Ed.), *Elements of Outdoor Recreation Planning.* Ann Arbor, Mich.: University of Michigan Press, 1970, pp. 9–31.

Driver, B. L., Rosenthal, D. H., & Peterson, G. Social benefits of urban forests and related green spaces in cities. *Proceedings of the National Urban Forestry Conference* (Environmental Science and Forestry Publication 80-003). Syracuse, N.Y.: College of Environmental Science and Forestry, State University of New York, 1978, *1,* 98–113.

Dwyer, J. F., Kelly, J. R., & Bowes, M. D. *Improved procedures for valuation of the contribution of recreation to national economic development* (Water Resources Center Report 128). Urbana-Champaign, Ill.: University of Illinois, 1977.

Elsner, G. H., & Smardon, R. C. (Technical Coordinators). *Proceedings of Our National Landscape: A conference on applied techniques for analysis and management of the visual resource* (USDA Forest Service General Tech. Rep. PSW-35). Berkeley, Calif.: Pacific Southwest Forest and Range Experiment Station, 1979.

Frissell, S. S. *The impact of wilderness visitors on natural ecosystems* (Completion report for the USDA Forest Service). Missoula, Mont.: Intermountain Forest and Range Experiment Station, 1973.

Frissell, S. S., & Stankey, G. H. Wilderness environmental quality: Search for social and ecological harmony. *Proceedings, National Convention of the Society of American Foresters.* Hot Springs, Ark.: 1972, pp. 170–183.

Greenley, D. A., Walsh, R. G., & Young, R. A. Option value: Empirical evidence from a case study of recreation and water quality. *Quarterly Journal of Economics,* 1981, *95*(4), 657–673.

Grubb, E. A. Assembly line boredom and individual differences in recreation participation. *Journal of Leisure Research,* 1975, *7,* 256–269.

Haas, G. E., Driver, B. L., & Brown, P. J. Measuring wilderness recreation experiences. *Proceedings of the Wilderness Psychology Group Annual Conference.* Durham, N.H.: University of New Hampshire, 1980, pp. 20–40. (a)

Haas, G. E., Driver, B. L., & Brown, P. J. A study of ski touring experiences on the White

River National Forest. *Proceedings of the North American Symposium on dispersed winter recreation.* St. Paul, Minn.: College of Forestry University of Minnesota, 1980, pp. 25–30. (b)

Harris, C. *Crowding in a wilderness setting.* Unpublished master's thesis, Colorado State University, 1979.

Harris, D. V. Perceptions of self. In B. van der Smisson (Compiler), *Research: Camping and environmental education* (Pennsylvania State HPER Series No. 12). University Park: The Pennsylvania State University, 1975, pp. 153–163.

Hautaluoma, J. E., & Brown, P. J. Attributes of the deer hunting experience: A cluster analytic study. *Journal of Leisure Research,* 1978, *10,* 271–287.

Hendee, J. C. A multiple-satisfaction approach to game management. *Wildlife Society Bulletin,* 1974, *2,* 104–113.

Hendee, J. C., & Harris, R. W. Foresters' perception of wilderness-users attitudes and preferences. *Journal of Forestry,* 1970, *68,* 759–762.

Hendee, J. C., & Schoenfeld, C. *Human dimensions in wildlife.* Washington, D.C.: Wildlife Management Institute, 1973.

Hendee, J. C., & Catton, W. R., Jr., Marlow, L. D., & Brockman, C. F. *Wilderness users in the Pacific Northwest—Their characteristics, values, and management preferences* (USDA Forest Service Research Paper PNW-61). Portland, Ore.: Pacific Northwest Forest Experiment Station, 1968.

James, G. A. Inventorying recreation use. *Recreation Symposium Proceedings,* USDA Forest Service. Upper Darby, Pa.: Northeastern Forest and Range Experiment Station, 1971, pp. 78–95.

Kellert, S. R. Attitudes and characteristics of hunters and antihunters. *Transactions of the Forty-third North American Wildlife and Natural Resources Conference.* Washington, D.C.: Wildlife Management Institute, 1978, pp. 412–423.

Kelly, J. R. Socialization toward leisure: A developmental approach. *Journal of Leisure Research,* 1974, *6,* 181–193.

King, D. A. *A market analysis of trout fishing on the Fort Apache Indian Reservation* (Report to Rocky Mountain Forest and Range Experiment Station, USDA Forest Service, Contract No. 16-736-GR). Tucson, Ariz.: School of Renewable Natural Resources, The University of Arizona, 1980.

Knopf, R. C., & Barnes, J. D. Determinants of satisfactions with a tourism resource: A case study of visitors to Gettysburg National Military Park. In D. E. Hawkins, E. L. Shafter, & J. M. Rovelstad (Eds.), *Tourism Marketing and Management Issues.* Washington, D.C.: George Washington University, 1980, pp. 217–237.

Knopp, T. B., Ballman, G., & Merriam, L. C., Jr. Toward a more direct measure of river user preferences. *Journal of Leisure Research,* 1979, *11,* 317–326.

Krumpe, E. E. *Redistributing backcountry use by a behaviorally based communication device.* Unpublished doctoral dissertation, Colorado State University, 1979.

Krutilla, J. V. Conservation reconsidered. *American Economic Review,* 1967, *57,* 777–786.

Krutilla, J. V. Evaluation of an aspect of environmental quality: Hells Canyon revisited. *Proceedings of the Social Statistics Section.* Washington, D.C.: American Statistical Society, 1970, pp. 198–207. (Also available as Reprint No. 93. Washington, D.C.: Resources for the Future, June 1971.)

LaPage, W. F., & M. I. Bevins. *Satisfaction monitoring for quality control in campground management* (USDA Forest Service Research Paper NE-484). Broomall, Pa.: Northeastern Forest Experiment Station, 1981.

LaPage, W. F., & Ragain, D. P. Family camping trends—An eight-year panel study. *Journal of Leisure Research,* 1974, *6,* 101–112.

Lime, D. W. *Factors influencing campground use in the Superior National Forest* (USDA Forest Service Research Paper NC-60). St. Paul, Minn.: North Central Forest Experiment Station, 1971.

Lime, D. W. Large groups in the Boundary Water Canoe Area—Their numbers, characteristics, and impact (USDA Forest Service Research Note NC-142). St. Paul, Minn.: North Central Forest Experiment Station, 1972.

Lime, D. W., & Stankey, G. H. Carrying capacity: Maintaining outdoor recreation quality. *Recreation Symposium Proceedings*. Upper Darby, Pa.: USDA Forest Service, 1971, pp. 174–184.

Litton, R. B., Jr. *Forest landscape description and inventories* (USDA Forest Service Research Paper PSW-49). Berkeley, Calif.: Pacific Southwest Forest and Range Experiment Station, 1968.

Lloyd, R. D., & Fischer, V. L. Dispersed versus concentrated recreation as forest policy. *Proceedings, Seventh World Forestry Congress*. Buenos Aires, Argentina, October 4–9, 1972.

Lucas, R. C. Wilderness perception and use: The example of the Boundary Waters Canoe Area. *Natural Resource Journal*, 1964, *3*, 394–411.

Lucas, R. C. *User evaluation of campgrounds on two Michigan National Forests* (USDA Forest Service Research Paper NC-44). St. Paul, Minn.: North Central Forest Experiment Station, 1970.

Lucas, R. C. *Use patterns and visitor characteristics, attitudes and preferences in nine wilderness and other roadless areas* (USDA Forest Service Research Paper INT-253). Ogden, Utah: Intermountain Forest and Range Experiment Station, 1980.

Lucas, R. C., & Shechter, M. A recreational visitor travel simulation model as an aid to management planning. *Simulations and Games*, 1977, *8*, 375–384.

Lucas, R. C., Schreuder, H. T., & James, G. A. *Wilderness use estimation: A pilot test of sampling procedures on the Mission Mountains Primitive Area* (USDA Forest Service Research Paper INT-109). Ogden, Utah: Intermountain Forest and Range Experiment Station, 1971.

Marcin, T. C., & Lime, D. W. Our changing population structure: What will it mean for future outdoor recreation use? In J. M. Hughes and R. D. Lloyd (Eds.), *Proceedings of a National Symposium, Outdoor Recreation Advances in Application of Economics* (USDA Forest Service General Technical Report. WO-2). Washington, D.C., 1977, pp. 42–53.

McKechnie, G. E. The psychological structure of leisure: Past behavior. *Journal of Leisure Research*, 1974, *6*, 27–45.

McQuaid-Cook, J. Effects of hikers and horses on mountain trails. *Journal of Environmental Management*, 1978, *6*, 209–212.

Miller, R. R., Prato, A. A., & Young, R. A. Congestion, success and the value of Colorado deer hunting experiences. *Transactions of the Forty-second North American Wildlife and Natural Resources Conference*. Washington, D.C.: Wildlife Management Institute, 1977, pp. 127–136.

More, T. A. Attitudes of Massachusetts hunters. In J. C. Hendee & C. Schoenfeld, *Human dimensions in wildlife*. Washington, D.C.: Wildlife Management Institute, 1973, pp. 72–76.

More, T. A., & Payne, B. Affective responses to natural areas near cities. *Journal of Leisure Research*, 1978, *10*, 7–12.

Moss, W. T., & Lamphear, S. C. Substitutibility of recreational activities in meeting slated needs and desires of the visitor. *Journal of Environmental Education*, 1970, *1*, 129–131.

National Academy of Sciences. *Assessing demand for outdoor recreation*. Washington, D.C.: 1975.

Outdoor Recreation Resources Review Commission (ORRRC). *National recreation survey* (Study Report 19). Washington, D.C.: U.S. Government Printing Office, 1962.

Owen, E. R. The growth of selected leisure industries. *Proceedings of the 1980 National Outdoor Recreation Trends Symposium* (USDA Forest Service General Tech. Rep. NE-57). Broomall, Pa.: Northeastern Forest Experiment Station, 1980, pp. 33–39.

Peterson, G. L. Evaluating the quality of the wilderness environment: Congruence between perceptions and aspirations. *Environment and Behavior*, 1974, *6*, 169–193.

Peterson, G. L., & Neumann, E. S. Modeling and predicting human responses to the visual environment. *Journal of Leisure Research*, 1969, *1*, 219–237.

Potter, D., Hendee, J. C., & Clark, R. Hunting satisfaction: Game, guns, or nature? *Human Dimensions in Wildlife Programs*. Washington, D.C.: Wildlife Management Institute, 1973, pp. 62–71.

Rajender, G. R., Harmston, F. K., & Blood, D. M. *A study of the resources, people, and economy of Teton County*. Laramie, Wyo.: Division of Business and Economic Research, University of Wyoming, 1967.

Randall, A. The economic value of atmosphere visibility. In D. G. Fox, R. J. Loomis, & T. C. Green (Technical Coordinators), *Proceedings of the Workshop in Visibility Values* (USDA Forest Service General Tech. Rep. WO-18). Washington, D.C.: USDA Forest Service, 1979, pp. 124–129.

Rosenthal, D. H., Driver, B. L., & Rauhauser, D. Skiing environments preferred by Colorado ski-tourers. *Proceedings, North American Symposium on Dispersed Winter Recreation*. St. Paul, Minn.: College of Forestry, University of Minnesota, 1980, pp. 57–63.

Schroeder, H., & Daniel, T. C. Progress in predicting the perceived scenic beauty of forest landscapes. *Forest Science*, 1981, *27*, 71–80.

Schreyer, R., & Nielson, M. L. *Westwater and desolation canyons: White water river recreation study*. Logan, Utah: College of Natural Resources, Utah State University, 1978.

Shafer, E. L., Jr., & Mietz, J. Aesthetic and emotional experiences rate high with northeast wilderness hikers. *Environment and Behavior*, 1969, *1*, 187–197.

Shafer, E. L., Jr., & Richards, T. A. *A comparison of viewer reactions to outdoor scenes and photographs of those scenes* (USDA Forest Service Research Paper NE-302). Broomhall, Pa.: Northeast Forest Experiment Station, 1974.

Shafer, E. L., Jr., Hamilton, J. F., & Schmidt, E. Natural landscape preferences: A prediction model. *Journal of Leisure Research*, 1969, *1*, 1–19.

Shaw, W., & Zube, E. *Wildlife values* (Institutional Series Report No. 1) Tucson, Ariz.: Center for Assessment of Noncommodity Natural Resource Values, School of Renewable Natural Resources, University of Arizona, 1981.

Shelby, B. B. Contrasting recreational experiences: Motors and oars in the Grand Canyon. *Journal of Soil and Water Conservation*, 1980, *35*, 129–131.

Soulé, M. E., & Wilcox, A., (Eds.). *Conservation biology: An evolutionary-ecological perspective* (Part II). Sunderland, Mass.: Sinauer Associates, 1980.

Stankey, G. H. Visitor perception of wilderness recreation carrying capacity (UDSA Forest Service Research Paper INT-142). Ogden, Utah: Intermountain Forest and Range Experiment Station, 1973.

Stankey, G. H., & Brown, P. J. A technique for recreation planning and management in tomorrow's forest. *Proceedings, Division 6, 17th World Congress*. Kyoto, Japan. International Union of Forestry Research Organizations, 1981, pp. 63–73.

Tombaugh, L. W. External benefits of natural environments. *Recreation Symposium Proceedings*. Upper Darby, Pa.: USDA Forest Service, Northeastern Forest Experiment Station, 1971, pp. 73–77.

Towler, W. L. Hikers' perception of wilderness. A study of the social carrying capacity of Grand Canyon. *Arizona Review*, 1977, *26*, 9–10.

Ulrich, R. S., & Addoms, D. L. Psychological and recreational benefits of a residential park. *Journal of Leisure Research*, 1981, *13*, 43–65.

USDA Forest Service. The visual management system. *National Forest Landscape Management* (Vol. 2). Washington, D.C.: U.S. Government Printing Office, 1974, (Chap. 1).

USDA Forest Service. *An assessment of the forest and range land situation in the United States.* Washington, D.C.: USDA Forest Service (FS-345), 1980, pp. 92–162.

USDI Bureau of Land Management. *Visual resource management program.* Washington, D.C.: Division of Recreation and Cultural Resources, 1980.

USDI Bureau of Outdoor Recreation. *Evaluation of public willingness to pay user charges for use of outdoor recreation areas and facilities.* Washington, D.C.: Prepared by Economics Research Associates, 1976.

U.S. Water Resources Council. Principles and standards for planning water and related land resources. *Federal Register*, 1973, *38*, 24778–24869.

U.S. Water Resources Council. Procedures for evaluation of national economic development (NED) benefits and costs in water resource planning. *Federal Register*, 1979, *44*, 72892–72976.

Wagar, J. A. The carrying capacity of wildlands for recreation. *Forest Science Monograph*, 1964, No. 7.

Wagar, J. A., & Thalheimer, J. F. *Trial results of net count procedures for estimating visitor use at developed recreation sites* (USDA Forest Service Research Note INT-105) Ogden, Utah. Intermountain Forest and Range Experiment Station, 1969.

Weaver, T., & Dale, D. Trampling effects of hikers, motorcycles, and horses in meadows and forests. *Journal of Applied Ecology*, 1978, *15*, 451–457.

Wellman, J. D., & Buhyoff, G. J. Effects of regional familiarity on landscape preferences. *Journal of Environmental Management*, 1980, *11*, 105–110.

Willis, C. E., Canavan, J. J., & Bond, R. S. Optimal short-run pricing policies for a public campground. *Journal of Leisure Research*, 1975, *7*, 108–113.

Witt, P. A., & Bishop, D. W. Situational antecedents to leisure behavior. *Journal of Leisure Research*, 1970, *2*, 64–77.

Wohlwill, J. F. What belongs where: Research on fittingness of man-made structures in natural settings. In T. C. Daniel, E. H. Zube, & B. L. Driver (Technical Coordinators), *Assessing amenity resource values* (USDA Forest Service General Tech. Rep. RM-68). Fort Collins, Col.: Rocky Mountain Forest and Range Experiment Station, 1979, 48–57.

Zube, E. H., Brush, R. O., & Fabos, J. G. *Landscape assessment, values, perceptions, and resources.* Stroudsburg, Pa.: Dowden, Hutchinson & Ross, 1975.

Index